PREFORMULATING THE NEWS

Pragmatics & Beyond
New Series

60

Geert Jacobs

Preformulating the News
An analysis of the metapragmatics of press releases

PREFORMULATING THE NEWS

AN ANALYSIS
OF THE METAPRAGMATICS
OF PRESS RELEASES

GEERT JACOBS
University of Antwerp

JOHN BENJAMINS PUBLISHING COMPANY
AMSTERDAM/PHILADELPHIA

 The paper used in this publication meets the minimum requirements of
American National Standard for Information Sciences — Permanence of
Paper for Printed Library Materials, ANSI Z39.48-1984.

Library of Congress Cataloging-in-Publication Data

Jacobs, Geert.
    Preformulating the news : an analysis of the metapragmatics of press releases / Geert
Jacobs.
      p.   cm. -- (Pragmatics & beyond, ISSN 0922-842X ; new ser. 60)
    Includes bibliographical references (p.) and index.
    1. Press releases. 2. Metalanguage. 3. Pragmatics. I. Title. II. Series.
HM1221.J33   1999
659.2--dc21   99-22395
ISBN 90 272 5074 X (Eur.) / 1 55619 823 X (US) (alk. paper)   CIP

John Benjamins Publishing Co. • P.O.Box 75577 • 1070 AN Amsterdam • The Netherlands
John Benjamins North America • P.O.Box 27519 • Philadelphia PA 19118-0519 • USA

Contents

Preface

Valdez and After

It was in the summer of 1992 that I first got interested in press releases. At that time, while I was working on a preliminary research project on the pragmatics of crisis, I happened to lay hands on a collection of some sixty press releases that had been issued by the American multinational Exxon in the wake of the widely publicized oil spill at Valdez, Alaska. This is the dramatic opening of the first press release in that corpus:

(Exxon, Houston, Texas: 27 March 1989)
LIGHTERING, OIL SPILL CLEANUP EFFORTS CONTINUE IN ALASKA
The Exxon Valdez, a 987-foot tanker carrying 1.3 million barrels of crude oil, ran aground on Bligh Reef about 25 miles south of the Trans Alaska Pipeline Terminal at Valdez about 12:30 a.m. Alaska time on Friday, March 24, while maneuvering to avoid ice. There were no personnel injuries. However, the vessel ruptured a number of cargo tanks, and an oil spill estimated at 240,000 barrels occurred in Prince William Sound.

I felt that I was very lucky with the data: while previous researchers had been forced to analyse the rhetoric of emergency response through various types of news reporting (cf. Rubin 1987 on the incident at the nuclear power station on Three Mile Island; Tyler 1992 on the Exxon Valdez oil spill; Triandafyllidou 1995 on the Chernobyl fall-out), here was a unique record of first-hand documents that had been specifically intended to antic-ipate such news reporting.[1] With the Valdez press releases I had gained direct access to the very sources of the *media*ting texts that others were using as their primary materials in examining what has come to be seen as a classic case study of 'miscommunication'.[2]

Soon I got carried away by the discursive intricacies of Exxon's 'news management' efforts and I decided to focus on the language of press releases as a subject worthy of research in its own right. I started working on a broader, more diverse corpus if only to fight down the dangerous urge to make 'the analysis live up to what is being analysed', the persistent assumption that 'something dramatic should get a monumental analysis, one proportional to the drama being addressed'.[3] It soon became clear to me that the Valdez press releases could by no means be considered a representative sample. To do so would lead to inordinate conclusions. Moore's analysis of the accident with the space shuttle Challenger is a case in point, resolving a complex engineering problem into a simple issue of inappropriate linguistic politeness (1992).[4] Similarly, Deborah Tannen (1995) provides a breathtaking, yet hardly plausible account of how misunderstanding between the pilot and co-pilot caused the 1982 Air Florida crash in the river Potomac in Washington.[5] With the oil business's 1,800-page contingency plan in South Alaska having been described as 'the biggest piece of American maritime fiction since *Moby Dick*' (Tyler 1992: 152), I realized that there was a distinct danger that, in focusing on the Valdez press releases only, I would be trying to match the sheer drama of what had happened. That is why I set out to exponentially increase my data, trying to get a better view of 'ordinary' press releases, which, in sharp contrast with those in the Valdez corpus, have been called 'dull', 'unimaginative' and 'simply brief recitations of some facts about an event' (Hess 1984: 77; 1989: 46).[6]

What, Why and How?

The present research report covers more than 500 press releases.[7] In particular, I shall explore the peculiar audience-directedness of press releases as a type of indirectly targeted, projected discourse and, drawing from corpus-based research, I shall argue that it can be traced in the various metapragmatic patterns that are characteristic of the data. In concentrating on the discourse of 'news management', I also set out to help document the asymmetrical relationships between some of the institutions involved in the news.

Crucially, as I hope to demonstrate, what makes press releases unique - and what constitutes the prime object of my investigation - is that their only *raison d'être* is to be retold: in particular, I shall provide evidence from the data that they are meant to be 'continued' as accurately as possible, preferably even verbatim, in news reporting.[8] Indeed, it could be argued that press releases just do not exist unless they are also, in some way or another, 'picked up' by journalists. Significantly, while most of the business organizations that I contacted were able to supply me with meticulously ordered files of press releases that had been issued by them even several years back, the journalists that agreed to collect press releases for this research project afterwards reported that they had had to constantly remind themselves of their promise to do so and, even then, dozens of the press releases I received from them showed obvious signs of crumpling: clearly, for press releases there is no middle course between a sad end in the waste-paper bin or the glory of coverage in the press.

The question could now be raised: if, for press releases, to be copied in the news is a question of life and death, what is the journalist's verdict determined by? From formulas for calculating newsworthiness over the impact of political or business interests down to sheer good luck, a wide range of factors have been shown to play a role in the media's 'gate-keeping'. In this book, I shall look at the frequently voiced claim that stories that are 'written and available' may well be retold ahead of stories that have to be researched from the ground up. In the words of Allan Bell, who is a linguist as well as a journalist, "the extent to which input materials can be reproduced rapidly and with little editing is a major factor in their being selected for publication" (1991: 59). I have to point out here that my interest lies not primarily in whether such 'prefabricated' stories are indeed selected. Instead, focusing on various metapragmatic patterns, I aim to find out what it really means to say that press releases are prefabricated.

All this has serious repercussions for the set-up of my research. From the very beginning, I decided to look at press releases only and not, for example, to compare them with the news reports they give rise to. For one thing, I believe that the complexity of the many factors determining journal-istic gatekeeping would render such a contrastive effort largely fruitless anyway.[9] In a way, the question of the effectiveness of press releases simply falls outside the scope of my study: whether a press release gets copied verbatim or not, does not change anything to the observation that it is prefabricated in the first place. Even more importantly, to concentrate on how journalists retell press releases would actually obscure how press releases are meant to be copied by them: starting from what journalists do with press releases, it might well be impossible to identify the prefabricated nature of a particular pattern if, for one or other reason, it proved ineffective.

This is, of course, not to say that the issue of uptake should be left out altogether. On the contrary, it plays a central role in my study since, I shall argue, it determines what press releases look like. Indeed, more broadly, the main target of this research is to contribute to the emerging view of a 'history of discourse' at the heart of the media business. By focusing on how the language of news reporting is anticipated - 'preformulated', I shall call it - in that of press releases, I aim at complementing previous work in the field, demonstrating that what we read in the papers and see on TV does not stand on its own, but is the product of an intertextual dynamics. In other words, I shall look at how the news is actually a diachronic phenomenon, one that consists of a chain of textualizations, right from 'news manage-ment' over 'newsmaking' to 'news consumption'.

Before I return to the set-up of my research, I would like to argue that the concept of 'genre' proves very useful for my purposes. From the dis-credited typological efforts of literary theory and critical practice, it may be assumed that genre cannot be illuminating with respect to the more down-to-earth linguistic processes we will be looking at. Certainly, no rigorously taxonomic generic classification is aimed at here, but rather a fine-grained empirical, core pragmatic analysis of selected features of language use within a well-targeted investigation of what might variously be called 'institutional', 'professional' or 'organizational' discourse.[10] What makes the concept of genre - and especially linguistic anthropologists' use of it - so interesting for my purposes, however, is that it draws attention to "the matrix of longer discourse" within which texts are distributed (Briggs and Bauman 1992: 138). In particular, I shall argue that, for my analysis of

press releases, genre does not only foreground the status of the utterance as
a 'recontextualization' of previous discourse, but also, and most prominently, as a 'precontextualization' of subsequent discourse.[11]

Furthermore, just as the fit between a particular, isolated text and its
generic model can never be perfect, the projection of news reports by press
releases that I hinted at above is bound to leave a 'gap' too. It is on how
this intertextual gap is manipulated that my research will concentrate, in
particular on the so-called strategies of 'entextualization' through which the
distance between press releases and news reports is minimized. In an earlier
paper, Bauman and Briggs (1990) introduced the term 'entextualization' for
this "process of rendering discourse extractable", of "[lifting a stretch of
linguistic production] out of its interactional setting" (73; cf. also Silverstein
and Urban 1996) and I would argue that it could serve as a particularly
suitable characterization of the way press releases can be almost imperceptibly transformed into news reports. Throughout this study I shall use the
term 'preformulation' to refer to the discursive resources of entextualization, i.e. those specific language features that make press releases look like
news reports and, in doing so, interactively accomplish the "prepared-for
detachability" that, I have suggested, is crucial to the genre (Bauman and
Briggs 1990: 74).

As for the set-up of my research, it is interesting to note that Briggs
and Bauman (1992) distinguish between synchronic and diachronic
perspectives on genre. Apart from the obvious relevance of a diachronic
perspective on genre, they also strongly believe in a synchronic perspective.
In a formula that seems to summarize my own approach, Briggs and
Bauman argue convincingly that, "[v]iewed synchronically, [genre provides]
powerful means of shaping discourse into ordered, unified, and bounded
texts"; it is this "generation of textuality" (147) in press releases, this entextualization that I set out to investigate in this book.

Finally, in doing so, I shall focus on the metapragmatics of press
releases. This means that my analysis is to be situated at that "metalevel at
which verbal communication is self-referential to various degrees"
(Verschueren 1995d: 367) and fits in with the research tradition represented
in John Lucy's (1993) collection of papers on *Reflexive Language*. My
interest in metapragmatics should not be surprising since, as Bauman and
Briggs (1990) point out, "[b]asic to the process of entextualization is the

reflexive capacity of discourse" (73). Significantly, apart from such marked metapragmatic features as third-person self-reference (chapter 3) and explicit semi-performatives (chapter 6), it is quotation, perhaps the intertextual device *par excellence*, that will occupy a central position in my analysis of preformulation in press releases (cf. chapters 4 and 5).

It should be clear by now that, in examining preformulation in press releases, I shall concentrate on the 'texts' that together make up my corpus, trying to relate the genre's peculiar audience-directedness to the specifics of the language use. This means that my analysis is an inductive one. Crucially, however, as I have suggested, the findings that follow from this 'closed' study will also have to be fully integrated in a wider theory of the news as an intertextual crossroads and, hence, an arena for power and ideology. After all, as Briggs and Bauman (1992) conclude, "generic intertextuality cannot be adequately understood in terms of formal and functional patterning alone - questions of ideology, political economy, and power must be addressed as well" (159).[12] From one point of view, then, the present study offers only a starting-point for further, ethnographic, research into the social practices by which power alignments are negotiated and distributed in the news:[13] comparing press releases with the news reports they give rise to - and drawing from the findings of the present study in doing so - is only one of the many challenging tasks that lie ahead.

Overview

In the first chapter, I shall explain in greater detail what this book is about. I hope to situate the questions my analysis sets out to answer with respect to some of the larger issues in the field as well as indicating relevant literature. Within a pragmatic perspective, the following three-step research method is proposed: first, to identify what press releases are supposed to do; next, to investigate how this goal can be traced in actual linguistic choices; and, finally, to describe some of the implications all this may have for the character of the overall interaction and its outcome. In particular, it is suggested that my research will focus on how the peculiar audience-directedness of press releases can be related to a number of metapragmatic features in the corpus and how this sheds light on the asymmetries of what can be termed the 'newsmaking' and 'news management' processes.

This peculiar audience-directedness of press releases is further explored in chapter 2. Drawing from corpus-based evidence, I shall decompose the concept of receiver into a number of minimal constituents. This will allow me to characterize press releases as indirectly targeted, i.c. 'projected', discourse, with the journalists serving as mediators and the journalists' own audiences as absent ultimate destinations. I shall argue that in view of such audience-directedness press releases need to be 'preformulated'.

The following four chapters present a data analysis of the metapragmatics of press releases.

In my effort to trace the peculiar audience-directedness of press releases, the first metapragmatic feature that I shall look at is the special brand of self-reference in my corpus (chapter 3). I shall argue that it is part of a point of view operation with the writers of press releases switching out of their own perspective towards that of the journalists. It is suggested that such self-reference plays a complex preformulating role. Evidence is provided from reflexive person, place and time deixis. While this data supports claims for a social-interactional view of the deictic field, it is suggested that self-reference in press releases may also serve less harmonious purposes.

The fourth chapter is the first of two to deal with what is probably the single most interesting feature of the metapragmatics of press releases, viz. self-quotation, including so-called 'pseudo-direct speech'. On the basis of evidence from the corpus, self-quotation in press releases is contrasted both with the more orthodox forms of non-reflexive quotation and with the reproductionist view of quotation. I shall suggest that while quoting normally serves as a *re*formulation of another's words, self-quotation in press releases may well play a *pre*formulating role, projecting how the writer's own words are to be retold in news reporting. In a final section, self-quotation in press releases is related to Bakhtin's notion of double-voicedness and to Voloshinov's distinction between the linear and pictorial styles.

In chapter 5 I shall argue that the typical brand of self-quotation in my corpus is part of a point of view operation: just like the special self-reference that I examined in chapter 3 it allows writers of press releases to

anticipate some of the concerns of journalists. A number of traditional functions of quotation in the news are identified and, for each of them, it is
demonstrated how self-quotation in press releases may serve a purpose of
preformulation. In particular, as far as the issue of objectivity is concerned,
ample corpus-based evidence is provided to show how self-quotation plays a
negotiating role, i.e. it seems to help reconcile the widely divergent
ambitions of those who issue press releases and those who receive (and
retell) them; on the other hand, it is argued that, even if self-quotation
makes press releases look more objective, no real objectivity is possible in
the news and, instead, a notion of 'objectively-voiced' text is proposed.

The final interesting feature of the metapragmatics of press releases that
I shall look at is the distribution of explicit semi-performatives in my corpus
(chapter 6). Drawing from various approaches to the concept of performativity, it is argued that, like self-reference and self-quotation, such explicit
semi-performatives can be shown to play a preformulating role in the data,
once again striking some kind of balance between the various parties'
conflicting requirements.

Chapter 7 presents a case study of the Valdez corpus. Zooming in on
the metapragmatics in this set of data, I shall try to bring together some of
the major points in my study of preformulation in press releases, documenting how Exxon managed the news over a longer period. The central purpose
is to confirm that what I have discussed in a number of separate chapters of
in-depth language analysis blends together into a holistic study addressing a
narrowly defined research question.

In the eighth and final chapter I shall first look back and present an
overview of the main issues in my study of preformulation in press releases.
Then, with a view to further efforts in the field, my research findings will
be related to the concept of commodification and it will be suggested that
they seem to support a hegemonic view of the news. At the end, I shall also
engage in a brief reflexive exercise, inquiring into the ideologies that have
informed my own analytical practice in this study. It will be argued that, in
Briggs and Bauman's terminology, this book is not just a description of how
press releases are precontextualized, but that very similar contextualization
processes are at work in my own description of press releases.

Scope and limitations

Clearly, from one point of view, this study is wide in scope. Apart from its obvious relevance to the analysis of media discourse, it bears a specific interest in the issue of 'hearers' and 'overhearers', in the metapragmatics of deixis, quotation and performativity, and in matters of ideology and hegemony. In addition, I shall draw attention to how some of the principles of interaction, which are traditionally restricted to the analysis of conversation, can be useful for investigating written data; in doing so, I have drawn inspiration from such apparently very different figures as Goffman and Bakhtin.

At the same time, though, as I hinted at above, throughout my research I have been driven by a narrowly defined research question, exploring preformulation in press releases, and the structure of the report strictly reflects the various steps of the method I have developed and used. This has resulted in a long series of limitations: for every problem that I am beginning to provide a solution for, at least two or three other problems remain unsolved. Surely, if few researchers of the media have focused on press releases, there are a lot of aspects of the news that I have not been able to incorporate in my own study and that deserve further research. For example, it is a central tenet of this study that the news is part of a history of discourse; as a result, in choosing to focus on press releases only, I have decided to present no more than a single phase of what is a long and complex process of telling and retelling. Even within the limited scope of press releases, my concern with metapragmatics serves to obscure a wide range of alternative text features that might carry at least equal weight (although, as I shall argue later on in this book, there is a sense in which metapragmatics play a pivotal role in media discourse). The present study should therefore be seen as a starting-point for more ventures into the domain.

Finally, it should be pointed out that, although this research started with an interest in the Valdez corpus and although the concept of genre is in some ways very relevant to my purposes, this book - strictly speaking - is not about press releases. It is about preformulation in press releases. That is why I have not avoided using such informal quantifications as 'exceptionally', 'usually' and even 'typically'. After all, they are only meant to provide background information, to answer the question if there are a lot of such preformulating metapragmatic features in press releases? Put simply, I am looking at self-quotation, for example, not because it is a frequently occurring phenomenon in my data - which it is - but because it is such an interesting phenomenon. In fact, self-quotation in press releases would not be any less interesting if it occurred only once.

Acknowledgements

I would first of all like to thank Jef Verschueren for his invaluable advice. In addition, I have appreciated the detailed feedback I received from Jan Blommaert, Jacob Mey, Stef Slembrouck, Srikant Sarangi, John Wilson and from anonymous referees of earlier versions of the manuscript. I am indebted to friends and colleagues at the University of Antwerp (UFSIA), in particular to Chris Braecke for supporting me throughout this project and to Luuk Van Waes for helping me out with countless matters of document design.

Finally, of course, my family. With all their enthusiasm and care, they have seen me through this.

Chapter 1
A Pragmatic Perspective on Press Releases

1. Introduction

What makes press releases so special is that they are *told only to be retold*. At least, that is what I argued in the introduction to this study. It is now the prime object of my investigation to document how, through what I shall call 'preformulation', press releases are indeed meant to be 'continued' as accurately as possible, preferably even verbatim, in news reporting.

In this first chapter, I shall explain in greater detail what this study is about and I shall also touch on some of the more general issues in the field. More particularly, apart from indicating the overall drift of my research, I hope to meet three goals: first, to situate my analysis of press releases with respect to some related research (section 2); next, to explain the research methodology (section 3) and, finally, in taking a first quick look at the various research questions, to highlight some of the themes that will come to dominate this study later on (sections 4, 5 and 6).

2. Institutional Discourse, Professional Discourse, Organizational Discourse

In this section, I would like to situate my analysis of press releases with respect to some related research. One rapidly expanding relevant domain, I shall argue, is that of institutional discourse. I set out to demonstrate that, even if there is no consensus on the boundaries of institutional and other, related types of discourse, there has recently been quite some interesting fieldwork as well as theory-making in the broader area, which provides the background to my own work.

Let me first, very briefly, illustrate the difficulties in defining institutional discourse. `

In a theoretical foreword to their collection of studies of language and social interaction called *Talk at Work*, Paul Drew and John Heritage characterize institutional discourse as "basically task-related" and they suggest that it "[involves] at least one participant who represents a formal organization of some kind" (1992: 3). In addition, they say, with institutional discourse there tend to exist specific constraints on what counts as an allowable contribution to the activity at hand (22). The book covers a wide range of specialized settings, including courts of law, newsrooms, businesses and health care centres, all of which, the editors point out, seem to support asymmetrical relationships.

If Drew and Heritage's informal definition and the research papers in *Talk at Work* are anything to go by, then press releases must be institutional discourse. For one thing, I shall demonstrate that they are positively task-related. Just as emergency phone calls to the police are focused on the request and dispatch of urgent assistance, with the participants sharing a stable understanding of the general task of their interaction, similarly press releases are used by formal organizations to pursue a well-defined goal and there can normally be no doubt among those involved about what is going on. In particular, as I hinted at above and as I shall argue in greater detail later on in this chapter, the bottom-line of press releases is that they do not just compete for journalists' attention *per se*, but that they are supposed to be 'continued' as accurately as possible, preferably even verbatim, in subsequent news reporting, in the papers, on the radio, on TV, etc.: press releases are meant to be retold and the various parties are normally aware of that. Apart from this task-relatedness of press releases, Drew and Heritage's two other characteristics of institutional discourse are also bound to feature prominently in my analysis: indeed, from one perspective it could be argued that it is a main objective of this study to investigate some of the (linguistic) constraints on press releases and that, in doing so, we will be able to help chart the balance of power between the parties involved with them.[1]

On closer scrutiny, however, it is clear that some - if not all - of the characteristics spelled out in the introduction to *Talk at Work* are not at all restricted to institutional discourse. Surely, - to give only one example - all communication, even the most phatic one, is in some or other way task-related. In the end, perhaps the only feature that survives is that in institutional discourse (one of) the participants represent(s) (a) social institution(s).

Of course, *Talk at Work* is by far not the only venture of its kind. In spite of its interest in ordinary, everyday interaction, the research perspective of Conversation Analysis (CA) as a whole has been in the vanguard of the study of institutional discourse ever since its origins in the 1960s, working on whatever naturally occurring data was available.[2] Far more importantly even, round the same time, from a broader point of view, the expansion of linguistics to incorporate pragmatics was moving institutional discourse into the centre of attention not just for CA, but for various other approaches to (both spoken and written) language and society. Since then, a rich and highly diverse research tradition has come to focus on the language of - most notably - politics and media,[3] covering a wide range of approaches, from discourse analysis and critical linguistics to rhetoric and argumentation studies. Here too, however, there seems to be little or no agreement on the family resemblances of institutional discourse, which looks like a haphazard category, putting together such very different types of discourse as electronic mail, talk-show programmes and classroom teaching.

It follows that the label 'institutional discourse' is a problematic one, glossing over categories of the public and private spheres. It might be suggested that, for my analysis of press releases, 'professional discourse' offers better perspectives (Bazerman and Paradis 1991, Gunnarsson, Linell and Nordberg 1997), but it has the disadvantage of being traditionally associated with particular vocations, such as medicine or law, as opposed to domain-related categories like social welfare or taxation, which are usually seen as part of institutional discourse. Another relevant label is that of 'organizational discourse', which has to do with the communication practices of social collectives and their members. One problem here is that, until recently, the focus was on communication-*within*-organizations (e.g. Mumby and Clair 1997 on sexual harassment in the workplace) and, while we have all grown used to hearing about what an organization 'claims' or 'announces' or 'has decided', this capacity to communicate *as* an organization - which, as we shall see, is so important in press releases - was strangely ignored. Indeed, for a long time, organizations were looked at as machines or as systems, and until today issues of discourse and pragmatics have remained largely underemphasized (Taylor and Cooren 1997).

In spite of this terminological confusion, a rich and highly stimulating research tradition has come into being. To give a very selective survey of the literature: some of Kenneth Burke's pioneering work on political language can be situated here as well as more recent contributions to the field by John Wilson and Teun van Dijk.[4] As far as critical approaches are concerned, a vast literature has emerged, from the early critical linguistic explorations in Fowler, Hodge, Kress and Trew (1979) to the critical discourse analysis in Caldas-Coulthard and Coulthard's state-of-the-art overview (1996); Sarangi and Slembrouck (1996) focus specifically on bureaucratic discourse. I have mentioned that Mumby and Clair (1997) and Taylor and Cooren (1997) present different views of organizational discourse while Bazerman and Paradis (1991) and, more recently, Gunnarsson, Linell and Nordberg (1997) bring together research on professional discourse. In addition, a number of scholars have drawn attention to issues of language planning and language politics (e.g. Heller 1994). An immense body of theory-making in this domain, finally, has come from such influential figures as Foucault, Bourdieu, Raymond Williams, Goffman, John B. Thompson and Pêcheux, drawing from the writings of Gramsci, Luckacs, Weber, Althusser, Giddens, Habermas and many others.[5]

It is within this fruitful, though by no means clearly unified, research perspective that the present study should be situated.

3. Towards a Research Method

3.1 A pragmatic perspective

What kind of task(s) are press releases meant to fulfil? And what are some of the obstacles on the way?

To answer such questions we shall have to take a pragmatic perspective on language and communication, with the specific context of use playing a crucial role. It is a perspective that takes into account the full complexity of the cognitive, social and cultural functioning of language and communication in the lives of human beings (Verschueren 1995c). Hence, complicated problems are raised that cannot possibly be tackled from a purely linguistic point of view only, and for the successful solution of which at least some interdisciplinary orientation will prove indispensable: understanding is framed understanding, it invariably involves knowledge about the nature of the activity in which the utterances play a role.[6]

Before focusing on what task(s) press releases are meant to fulfil, I shall now turn my attention to some of the signals of this 'unavoidable contextedness' in my data:[7] i.e. I shall try to find out why, in the specific case of analysing press releases, it is obvious that we have to step out of the text and describe how language use is embedded in human action.

3.2 Pragmatics as explicitness

Take the following exchange between the shopkeeper (referred to as S) and a customer (C) in a grocer's store:

C: (...) You've just got the one kind of lettuce?
S: Yes. Cos.
C: That's a nice one.
S: Yes. They are getting proper now, aren't they. Thirty six please.
(Levinson 1979: 372)

In this extract both interactants seem to use words rather sparingly and, as a result, it is just not possible to realize that C's "That's a nice one" counts as buying a lettuce without referring to the conventions of shopping in small stores. This is a clear case of what could be called 'implicitness': instead of "That's a nice one. I'll buy this lettuce", the customer simply says "That's a nice one". This brings the task-relatedness of the interaction to the foreground and, in doing so, it seems to render a fair degree of so-called 'membership knowledge'[8] indispensable both for the successful completion of the task and for our own post factum analysis. Significantly, Östman (1986) sees implicitness as a major object of pragmatic analysis.

At first sight, no such implicitness can be found in press releases. In fact, as the short press release shown in (1) demonstrates, exactly the opposite seems at work here.

(1)   (Bonduelle, Mechelen: 4 March 1994)
        De groep BONDUELLE Europa heeft André VRYDAGH aange-
        worven als Algemeen Direkteur voor BONDUELLE Belgium.
        Voordien had hij reeds belangrijke funkties bij MATERNE,
        nadien bij SPA.
        BONDUELLE Belgium kommercialiseert groentekonserven &
        diepvriesgroenten onder de merken MARIE THUMAS, BON-
        DUELLE, STAR & CASSEGRAIN.

        The BONDUELLE Europe group has hired André VRYDAGH
        as General Director of BONDUELLE Belgium. Previously he
        had important functions at MATERNE, later at SPA.
        BONDUELLE Belgium markets canned and frozen vegetables
        under the brands MARIE THUMAS, BONDUELLE, STAR &
        CASSEGRAIN.

Apparently, unlike the exchange at the grocer's store, the press release in
(1) is, so to speak, explicit. It is so complete that it looks as if no contextual
information is required at all. The press release as a whole seems to be a
self-sufficient, context-free document. With some exaggeration, even a
Martian with a decent knowledge of Dutch could be expected to understand
what is going on.

Let me give another example. In my corpus, all press releases issued
by the steel manufacturers Union Minière contain, in addition to the 'news
of the day', the following, rather lengthy, corporate profile:

(2)   (Union Minière, Brussels: 31 October 1995)
        Union Minière (UM), a Belgian-based, internationally active
        group, is a world leader in the non-ferrous metals sector.
        The UM Group is established in several countries in Europe
        (mainly Belgium and France), and also in the United States. It is
        organized into decentralized business units which cover the
        extraction, smelting, refining, primary transformation, recycling,
        engineering.
        UM produces and sells more than twenty non-ferrous metals for
        basic and advanced technology industries, the construction

sector, and research. Those metals are split into five main lines of development: zinc, copper, cobalt, germanium and the complex metallurgy of lead, precious metals and special metals.

The Group generated a turnover of BEF 123 billion in 1994 with a workforce close to 11,000. Owing to its sound financial structure the Group can absorb the cyclical swings of the sector in which it operates.

In its present form, Union Minière is a young company built on a long tradition: founded in the 19th century, it operated the copper mines of Katanga until their nationalization in 1967; thereafter, it essentially concentrated on refining and recycling. The Union Minière Group is the non-ferrous metals arm of Société Générale de Belgique. It was formed as the result of the merger, in 1989, between Acec-Union Minière, Metallurgie Hoboken-Overpelt, Vieille-Montagne and Mechim.

If the above extract looks stuffy and drawn-out to the analyst, it should not be difficult to imagine what impression it is bound to make on the hasty journalists who have to read this very same description in every press release they receive from Union Minière. Here again, like in (1), the question arises: why are press releases so complete? Clearly, if to be overinformative can be no strategic transgression of some simple overarching Co-operative Principle - simply because it has been shown that no co-operation should be taken for granted in interaction, anyway (e.g. Sarangi and Slembrouck 1992)[9] - it would be equally difficult to conclude that such apparent explicitness is merely a waste of time.

Here is one more example from my corpus of press releases:

(3) (Administratie der douane en accijnzen, Antwerp: 28 September 1994)
De Administratie der douane en accijnzen deelt mee dat haar Opsporingsinspectie te Antwerpen erin geslaagd is 32 kg zuivere cocaïne in beslag te nemen. De marktwaarde van de inbeslagge-nomen drug kan worden geraamd op 112 miljoen F.

> The Customs and Excise Administration announces that its investigation inspectorate in Antwerp has succeeded in confiscating 32 kg of pure cocaine. The market value of the confiscated drug can be estimated at 122 million F.

Again it looks as if the writer is making an unnecessary effort. He or she could simply have said:

> *De Opsporingsinspectie te Antwerpen van de Administratie der douane en accijnzen is erin geslaagd 32 kg zuivere cocaïne in beslag te nemen. De marktwaarde van de inbeslaggenomen drug kan worden geraamd op 112 miljoen F.*
>
> The Antwerp investigation inspectorate of the Customs and Excise Administration has succeeded in confiscating 32 kg of pure cocaine. The market value of the confiscated drug can be estimated at 122 million F.[10]

Interestingly, Levinson seems to point to a similar phenomenon when he singles out the use of questions in a rape trial to request details that are already known to the questioner:

> Q: (...) you have had sexual intercourse on a previous occasion haven't you?
> A: Yes.
> Q: On many previous occasions?
> A: Not many.
> Q: Several?
> A: Yes.
> Q: With several men?
> A: No.
> Q: just one.
> A: Two.
> Q: Two. And you are seventeen and a half?
> A: Yes. (1979: 380)

At the end of this extract the girl's age is asked, even though the basic facts of the case would be known to all parties.[11]

I shall argue later that this explicitness is strategically motivated, indeed that it is only a selective explicitness, which, in Östman's view, is merely an alternative form of implicitness.[12] For the time being, it should be noted that, almost paradoxically, just as implicitness serves as a signal of contextual dependence in the conversation between shopkeeper and customer, it is explicitness that calls for more information in press releases and trials.

3.3 The notion of context

Since context is bound to play a leading role in this study, then, what is really meant by it?

The debate about context has recently been dominated by two contrasting approaches: one is the text-intrinsic view of context proposed by Harold Garfinkel's ethnomethodology and largely adopted in CA (including Drew and Heritage's *Talk at Work* mentioned above), with consideration of background restricted to the specifics made relevant in the text; the other is the text-extrinsic view of context established in ethnography, which - put simply - includes reactions to and accounts of events as well as the events themselves. I shall now start by pointing out some of the motivations underlying the former, narrow, view of context, which CA is committed to, and then present my own approach, incorporating the analysis of press releases in a wider conception of the news as the product of societal influences, in particular as an intertextual crossroads and as an arena for the play of power.

Within the research perspective of CA, it is argued that if the notion of context is to be in any way operational, the analyst should start from what is made relevant in the data themselves and that, alternatively, if all details of the background could be used, serious research would just not be possible: any hypothesis about the functionality of specific linguistic features - including those of implicitness and explicitness - might be successfully defended.

Following the same argument, there is a second reason why the use of context should be limited in this way, viz. to overcome a distinct danger of

pre-interpreting the data: if anything qualifies as context, there is a real risk
that the research will be driven by contextual information and that certain
problems will be 'read into' the data rather than that these problems are
there in the first place and that selected contextual information is then used
to help solve them. The analysis should not be 'theoretically motivated'. In
Schegloff's words, the Conversation Analytic constraint on context "[serves]
as a buffer against the potential for academic and theoretical imperialism
which imposes intellectuals' preoccupations on a world without respect to
their indigenous resonance" (1997: 165). In his view it is the specific
responsibility of the analyst to show from the details of the discourse what
aspects of the context and what roles the various parties take into account.
Drew and Heritage (1992) talk about 'goal orientation' in this respect.

All this has far-reaching methodological repercussions: even if the
analyst thinks that he or she knows perfectly well what is going on, thanks
to membership knowledge or through some form of participant observation
for example, none of this information should be incorporated in the analysis
unless it is also in some or other way 'accomplished' in the discourse.
Schegloff (1993) says that context is "not separate and anterior; it inhabits
the talk" (114). As a result, a flexible and reflexive notion of context is
called for: flexible because context is not a static reality out there, it is
continually shaped and reshaped by the participants; reflexive because the
language is not just determined by the context, the context is equally
determined by the language. Context, then, has also been called an 'endogenous' construct (Heritage 1984): it is only achieved in the same interaction
which makes use of it.

I would now like to argue that this is a far too strict view of context and
that there is much to say in favour of relaxing it. Auer (1991, 1992, 1995),
Hinnenkamp (1992) and Meeuwis (1994), for example, have shown that
downplaying the role of so-called 'pretext' in favour of a narrow view of
context as locally constructed has left large provinces of (translocal)
knowledge inaccessible. Auer suggests that, for one thing, "notions of
person and personality in a given culture" should be included in the analysis
and he wonders if "a more comprehensive approach would not take us one
step further than [CA's] self-imposed restrictions" (1991: 185). He argues
that the endogenous character of context allows for degrees and that some

context is simply 'brought along' and not 'brought about' (cf. 1992: 26). As Hinnenkamp says about interaction in the health care sector, "doctor and patient already encounter each other as particular others, not as anybodies but as somebodies" (1992: 130). Auer concludes that Schegloff and the others start from a "very impoverished" notion of context (1995: 16).

As far as my own research of press releases is concerned, I shall argue that it is the very notion of pretext that sheds new light on media discourse, not just in the sense of the set of text-extrinsic conditions for the establishment of discourse, but also - and in particular - with reference to the notion of a 'history of discourse' that I developed in the introduction of this book. I have indicated that it is the main research target of this study to look at how press releases fit in a chain of textualizations and such a view of the news as the product of an intertextual dynamics is of course unthinkable if we stick to the microscopic notion of context advocated in CA. In addition, as for the second argument favouring the local construction of context, it should be clear that, no matter what methodological rigour is observed, pre-interpretation is unavoidable and a fair degree of background information will always be taken for granted. Certainly, to approach the question of power in the news by looking at press releases is a form of perspective-taking in itself. Finally, still another, related, reason for rejecting CA's objectivism - one that I shall develop in chapter 8 -, is that the data may have been pre-interpreted by the participants.

Crucially, all this is not to deny that, even if a lot of context is translocal, some aspects of the activity are oriented to - and indeed constructed - in the discourse. On the contrary, from one point of view, it could actually be argued that it is the very purpose of my research to explore how, in press releases, what is to be retold is actually negotiated in the very act of telling. As it is, my analysis presents what could be considered a 'combined' approach, blending text-extrinsic and text-intrinsic views of context, reconciling close attention to the details of the discourse with a consideration of some of the wider societal influences.

Within this framework, Duranti and Goodwin (1992) and Auer and di Luzio (1992) should be mentioned as seminal attempts to bring together research from Conversation Analysts and ethnographers, but so far, as Fitch and Philipsen (1995) argue, the endeavour to integrate the two has remained "more an intriguing challenge than a realized accomplishment" (269). Still, there is some common ground. For one thing, the idea of accomplishment through activity is not restricted to CA, but is also a major feature of ethnography. As Nelson (1994) puts it, "more than a fair number of ethnographers eschew theoretical motivation in gathering data of any sort and seek to understand culture from the native's point of view" (313).[13] From the other side, it has been argued that it is the very conversation analytic studies of interaction in institutional settings that I have been referring to, such as in *Talk at Work*, that mark a watershed in the development of ethnomethodology and that have finally led to "confrontation with questions regarding the desirability or acceptability of using ethnographic data conceived as information regarding contexts" (Nelson 1994: 312; 313, 324). Most noticeably, Drew and Heritage (1992) themselves seem to bring in extralinguistic context when they acknowledge that institutional discourse involves participants who represent formal organizations. In addition, they pay tribute to ethnography, and to the contribution of John Gumperz in particular, for "a reassessment of the dynamic nature of social contexts and the importance of linguistic details in evoking them" (1992: 8) and they claim to "[admit] the enriched sense of context in utterance that ethnographers have insistently advocated" (16).[14]

My own view of context - and of how it is reflexively linked up with text in a somewhat similar, but much more complex way than suggested in Conversation Analysis - is perhaps best summed up in these words of Jenny Cook-Gumperz:

> social knowledge frames linguistic interpretation, which in its turn provides essential coding of the social(-cognitive) information that establishes the guidelines for what can be expected in further social interaction. In other words, the relationship of language to social knowledge is both interactive and reactive. It is constitutive of social reality in the performance of the everyday activity of speaking (1992: 178).

3.4 Tentative research agenda

A tentative research agenda can now be formulated for my analysis of press releases.

I set out from the idea that, in Jef Verschueren's terms, "[t]alking, or using language expressively and/or communicatively in general, consists in the continuous making of linguistic choices, consciously or unconsciously, for linguistic or extra-linguistic reasons" (1995c: 2). This view seems to be widely accepted in pragmatic approaches to language. Gumperz, to give just one example, sees the language user as a manager, identifying available options, "strategically deploying variable choices in such a way as to be rhetorically effective in achieving particular communicative ends" (1992: 41).[15]

The first step in analysing language data then is to try and find out what those 'linguistic or extra-linguistic reasons', those 'particular communicative ends' could be. Verschueren talks about 'contextual objects of adaptation' in this respect. Next, the researcher will have to demonstrate what linguistic choices - at various so called 'structural layers of adaptation' - may be interadaptable with the objects of adaptation. Crucially, any pragmatic description must account for the 'dynamics of adaptation', i.e. how choices of production and interpretation are strategically negotiated.[16] A final notion, viz. 'the salience of adaptation processes', focuses on the question if choices are made consciously or not (Verschueren 1995c).

As for my own analysis, I have argued that press releases are meant to be retold, and this is what I shall first look at. In particular, I set out to investigate what it means to say that the bottom-line of press releases is that they do not just compete for journalists' attention *per se*, but that they are supposed to be 'continued' as accurately as possible, preferably even verbatim, in subsequent news reporting.

One way of doing so is to demonstrate in the details of the discourse what task(s) the parties orient to. As Levinson puts it, anticipating the second step in the research method described above: "[a] very good idea of the kind of language usage likely to be found within a given activity can (...) be predicted simply by knowing what the main function of the activity is seen to be by participants" (1979: 394). As Verschueren argues, however, - and as I suggested in the previous section - in trying to identify so-called 'objects of adaptation', we should not pay attention only to details on a micro-level of discourse organization (1995a). While Verschueren acknowledges that context is not manageable as long as it is seen as purely extralinguistic (1995a), he indicates that the objects of adaptation "potentially include all the ingredients of the communicative context" (1995c: 15).

Next comes the question how all this was implicated in the actual production of the discourse. As I hinted at above - and as I shall argue in greater detail below -, my analysis will focus on one specific 'layer of adaptation', viz. that of the metapragmatics in my data, and I shall investigate how such features as third-person self-reference, self-quotation and explicit semi-performatives are closely related to the peculiar ambition of press releases to be retold.

The final step in my research is to describe some of the repercussions that the above may have for the character of the interaction and its outcome, integrating my analysis of press releases in a wider view of power and ideology in the news. It should be noted that this need not lead up to a broad and open-ended view on the media. On the contrary, throughout this study, I hope to contribute to an emerging answer to the narrowly focused research question that started off my efforts in the first place: viz. how the language of press releases can be related to the history of discourse that makes up the news. Within this framework, the set of remarks made in the final chapter should best be seen as a starting-point for further research in the field.

So far, I have outlined a pragmatic method for my analysis of press releases. In the rest of this chapter I shall anticipate how this method can be applied to my corpus. The survey in this chapter is not meant as a summary of the whole investigation, but simply as a first exploration, highlighting some of the themes that will come to dominate this study later on.

4. The Activity of Issuing Press Releases

4.1 To be copied

In trying to identify the 'communicative ends' in my data, I would like to argue that the cover letters that accompany some of the press releases in my corpus serve as privileged sources of information, spelling out the specific task(s) that writers of press releases have in mind. Certainly, the following extract from a cover letter seems to leave no doubt about what the enclosed press release is meant to do:

(4)   (Bulo, Mechelen: 29 March 1994)
        Wij hopen (...) dat bijgaand communiqué ertoe mag bijdragen
        a) naamsverwarring te voorkomen. Bulo blijft in België markt-
        leider van het kwalitatief hoogstaand kantoormeubilair in hout en
        kunststoffen en is tevens specialist-kantoorinrichter.
        b) te onderstrepen dat bij de toekenning van een prestigieus
        order ook de bedrijfscultuur een doorslaggevende rol kan spelen.

        We hope (...) that the enclosed press release may help to
        a) avoid confusion of names. Bulo remains Belgium's market
        leader in high quality office furniture in wood and plastics and it
        is also a specialist in equipping offices.
        b) stress that in the allocation of a prestigious order also
        corporate culture can play a decisive role.

The writer of this press release must have had a very good idea of what he or she hoped to achieve with it. Still, the ambitions mentioned in this cover letter are in no way representative of the corpus since they miss out on what, according to most other cover letters, is the first task of press releases, viz. to make sure that journalists will use them in their own news reporting. Here are some typical extracts from cover letters:

(5)   (Tritec, Perwez: 28 March 1994)
        Hierbij vindt u hierover meer informatie.

U dankend bij voorbaat om dit aan uw lezers kenbaar te willen maken.

Enclosed you will find more information about this.
Thanking you in advance for informing your readers about it.

(6)   (Jadrimex, Elewijt: 30 March 1994)
Ingesloten vindt u een persbericht. Zoudt u zo vriendelijk willen zijn deze in Uw publikaties in te lassen. Deze informatie kan van nut zijn voor Uw lezers.

Enclosed you will find a press release. Would you be kind enough to insert it in your publications. This information may be of interest to your readers.

(7)   (Solvay, Antwerp: 7 September 1994)
Wij zouden het ten zeerste op prijs stellen, mocht u deze persme-dedeling laten verschijnen.

We would appreciate it very much if you could publish this press release.

(8)   (Pfizer, Brussels: 26 April 1994)
Ingesloten hebben wij het genoegen U een communiqué van onze Amerikaanse vennootschap te laten geworden.
Wij hopen dat U deze inlichtingen aan Uw lezers zult willen mededelen.

We have pleasure in enclosing a press release from our American partnership.
We hope you will communicate this information to your readers.

According to these cover letters, the enclosed press releases are meant to be copied by the journalists in their own news reporting. These data confirm what is in the literature on press releases, viz. that those who issue press releases count on, say, newspaper journalists "to in turn disseminate the information through published stories to that portion of the public that relies upon newspapers for information" (Vanslyke Turk 1986: 16). Similarly,

Rubin (1987) argues that it is the bottom line of the field of public relations to see one's own opinion prevail in the news: "[i]ndustry and public organizations spend vast amounts of money every year on PR, because it helps them to get the media to portray their views to the public" (19).

In some cover letters this goal orientation is phrased indirectly:

(9)   (Kamer van Koophandel en Nijverheid van Antwerpen, Antwerp: 14 October 1994)
       Ik dank u bij voorbaat voor de redactionele aandacht die u hieraan zult schenken.

       I thank you in advance for the editorial attention that you will pay to this.

Or, instead of in a cover letter, with a note at the end of the press release itself:

(10)   (Kredietbank, Brussels: 1 March 1995)
       Noot voor de redactie:
       Graag ontvangen wij kopie van uw redactionele bijdrage op het onderstaand adres.

       Note for the editor:
       We would like to receive a copy of your editorial contribution at the address below.

In other cover letters this goal orientation is formulated more directly as a request with special emphasis on one or other practical arrangement, including the time of publication

(11)   (Kamer van Koophandel en Nijverheid van Antwerpen, Antwerp: 9 September 1994)
       Wij vragen u vriendelijk dit bericht in uw eerstvolgende editie op te nemen.

       We kindly ask you to include this message in your next edition.

or the amount of money (not) to be paid for it

(12) (Antwerpse Waterwerken, Antwerp: 6 October 1994)
We zouden U ten zeerste dank weten zo U deze communiqué kosteloos kon opnemen in uw rubriek tentoonstellingen.

We would be extremely grateful should you be able to include this release in your section on exhibitions free of charge.

Note that for the following press release issued to an international press agency the role of mediators is recognized:

(13) (KIHA, Antwerp: 13 October 1994)
Gelieve in bijlage de persmededeling te vinden zoals ze kan verspreid worden door uw agentschap naar dag- en weekbladen.

Please find enclosed the press release as it can be distributed by your news agency to daily and weekly papers.

It is also clear from the corpus that press releases are not just meant to be retold in the written media. Very often coverage by radio and TV is aimed at too. How could the reference to pronunciation otherwise be explained in extract (14) from a press release?

(14) (Bulo, Mechelen: 29 March 1994)
Sportartikelenreus Nike (spreek uit: Naikie) heeft vanuit Amerika beslist: haar Europees verdeelcentrum langs de E313 in Laakdal-Meerhout zal worden uitgerust met kantoormeubilair van Bulo.

Sportswear giant Nike (pronounce: *Nikey*) has decided from America: its European distribution centre on the E313 at Laakdal-Meerhout will be equipped with Bulo office furniture.

The appeal to audio-visual media is even more explicit in the cover letter quoted in (15).

(15) (Grote Routepaden, Antwerp: s.d.)
Het bestuur van onze vereniging heeft de eer u te verzoeken onderstaand bericht te willen opnemen in uw publikaties of uitzending.

> *(...) Wij blijven steeds ter beschikking voor verdere informatie of medewerking aan uw programma.*

> The Board of our society is honoured to request you to include the message below in your publications or broadcast. (...) We always remain at your disposal for further information or co-operation in your programme.[17]

Some organizations seem to be rather strongly insistent. The following is from a cover letter to a press release which had been issued on a previous occasion, but which apparently had failed to be published. It is now issued again in the hope that it will not miss its target a second time.

(16)   (Noblesse, Londerzeel: 30 March 1994)

> *Vorige week zond ik onderstaand persbericht naar de redaktie "Ekonomie & Financiën". Het schijnt echter nog niet gepubliceerd te zijn. Mag ik op uw tussenkomst beroep doen?*

> Last week I sent the attached press release to the 'Economy and Finance' editors. It appears not to have been published yet. Could I ask you to intervene in this?

All these various extracts seem to provide conclusive evidence that press releases are meant to be copied and that writers indeed say so much, i.e. that they orient to this goal. But what about those other participants, the journalists, who receive press releases and who have to use them in their own news reporting? Beyond my corpus, there is ample evidence of how faithfully press releases are retold by the journalists who receive them.[18] Since I am working on a corpus of press releases only, not taking into account the journalists' reactions in their own reporting, such information about the readers' orientations to the goal of press releases falls outside the scope of this research. Still, it should be noted that some indication can be derived from the way writers of press releases anticipate the readers' reactions in their own writing, as in the following appeal for discretion:

(17)   (Aktiegroep rolstoelen en hulpmiddelen, Grimbergen: 26 September 1994)

> *Deze aktie werd niet aangekondigd op de kabinetten. Wij vragen u te mogen rekenen op uw diskretie.*

> This action has not been announced at the ministers' offices. We ask you if we can count on your discretion.

Here, this surprising request proves that the journalists' routine reaction to press releases is expected to be one of actually transmitting the news contained in them. This conforms to the intuition that if you want to keep something quiet, probably the last thing you should do is issue a press release about it. Similarly, the following warning in a cover letter can only be correctly understood if the different parties involved agree that press releases are meant to be copied.

(18)   (Bayer, Antwerp: 13 September 1994)
         LET OP: dit persbericht vervangt de versie van gisteren!

WATCH OUT: this press release replaces yesterday's version!

Apart from what is said in cover letters, there are many more indications that writers of press releases are preoccupied with the idea that their texts are to be copied. The routine use of the labels "press release" as a title, for example, and "end of press release" at the bottom of the handout serves to indicate the limits of the part to be copied by journalists, separating it from more private information for the journalists' use only.[19] It should also be noted that not all press releases have cover letters telling journalists what to do with them so that apparently it is sufficient to issue a statement labelled as a 'press release' in order to provoke the right reactions. Such a default assignment of roles, i.e. without any help from the 'contextualization cues' in cover letters listed above,[20] actually seems to confirm that not all context needs to be locally constructed (Auer 1992: 26-27). In addition, the so-called 'embargo' conventionally specifies the date and - often the time - before which the press release must not be copied. It could be argued that these regular features of press releases are part of what Goffman (1974) calls 'bracketing': i.e. they constitute ritual openings and closings, establishing and concluding certain kinds of participation. In particular, they serve to signal to the journalists that what follows or precedes is not really meant for them, but that it is supposed to be copied.

These data confirm that press releases are meant to be retold by journalists in their own news reporting. Apparently, press releases are supposed to be recycled, to actively encourage what in a lot of contexts would be denounced as plagiarism and I shall argue later that this peculiar audience-directedness is, as John B. Thompson (1995) argues, "partly constitutive of the action itself" (100). Still, it does not necessarily make press releases any different from, say, ordinary conversation. Indeed, it can be related to a characteristic of oral interaction that Harvey Sacks called 'tellability': just like gossip, for example, press releases are meant to be 'preserved' (1992a: 773), "their total currency turns on their being tellable" (776). The following account of ordinary conversation seems to be a surprisingly accurate description of the peculiarly institutional business of issuing press releases to journalists:

> people in interactions engage in attending what they do by reference to what it is that those others they're with might tell some others who might tell some others. And this is not merely a negative constraint. It can be the sort of thing one counts on. And indeed, one can select a co-participant whom one feels assured will have occasion to tell somebody, when one warrants something broadcast (779).[21]

In this extract from Sacks, the marked choice of the media term 'broadcast' in its more general meaning of 'told to a lot of people' proves a happy coincidence for my purposes. Clearly, what Sacks is saying about ordinary oral interaction, can equally be applied to that special sort of media discourse called press releases.

4.2 Multiple activity

If indeed press releases are meant to be copied in the news, then it remains to be explained why the cover letter quoted in (4) specifies a very different goal orientation.

(4)   (Bulo, Mechelen: 29 March 1994)
Wij hopen (...) dat bijgaand communiqué ertoe mag bijdragen
a) naamsverwarring te voorkomen. Bulo blijft in België markt-
leider van het kwalitatief hoogstaand kantoormeubilair in hout en
kunststoffen en is tevens specialist-kantoorinrichter.
b) te onderstrepen dat bij de toekenning van een prestigieus
order ook de bedrijfscultuur een doorslaggevende rol kan spelen.

We hope (...) that the enclosed press release may help to
a) avoid confusion of names. Bulo remains Belgium's market
leader in high quality office furniture in wood and plastics and it
is also a specialist in equipping offices.
b) stress that in the allocation of a prestigious order also corporate culture can play a decisive role.

To answer that question, I would now like to argue that from the data
shown above it is clear that press releases are not just aimed at the
journalists, who have to retell them, but, crucially, also at the journalists'
own newspaper readers, TV viewers, etc. In other words, press releases are
meant for different audiences and, naturally, they are also supposed to do
different things to them. While I have shown that most cover letters refer to
the journalists' task of retelling the news, (4) is rather unique in that it
spells out what, at least in the writer's view, this specific press release is
supposed to do to the general public when it is copied by journalists in their
own news reporting: viz. to put Bulo in the limelight as a successful
manufacturer of high-quality office furniture. More generally, even if most
cover letters focus on the journalists' retelling, throughout this study it
should be borne in mind that issuing press releases is not just a question of
getting media coverage; as extract (4) shows, media coverage itself is only a
means to serving more concrete interests.

   Apparently, issuing press releases should be characterized as a 'multiple activity' and, again, in this sense it does not seem to be very different
from ordinary talk, which, as Goodwin and Goodwin (1992) have shown,
often divides into several 'substreams': like participants in everyday
interaction, writers of press releases face the formidable task of co-
ordinating - within a single discourse - the different activities that they find

themselves engaged in, meshing separate objectives with each other, attending to distinct demands. In particular, they are performing the juggling act of providing the journalists with information to be retold and at the same time communicating, indirectly, with the journalists' own audiences.

In view of this peculiar audience-directedness, press releases could be labelled 'divided discourse'. In drawing attention to the dangers of increasingly intensive media coverage, Fill (1986) proposed the phrase to denote the predicament of politicians whose widely reported speeches have to please a great many different pressure groups (cf. also Gruber 1993a). Before him, Goffman (1974) had already drawn attention to the "controlled use of ambiguity" in political speeches, where "the speaker addresses special publics by means of second meanings that are not discernible (he hopes) to the larger audience" (515). More recently, Te Molder (1995) pointed to the complexity of such divided discourse in her analysis of the Dutch government's communication campaign on sexual harassment: how, for example, to formulate a message that will almost certainly be received by both the perpetrators and victims of the crime. As I suggested above, the notion of multiple activity is not restricted to highly specialized contexts. As early as 1969 Searle presented an invented example of a woman at a dinner party saying "It's really quite late" to the host, with her husband standing by: here, Searle argues, the utterance serves both as an objection addressed to the host and as a request to be taken home addressed to the husband.

Needless to say that so far I have only hinted at the peculiar audience-directedness[22] of press releases and I shall have to elaborate on it in chapter two. Before that, I shall continue my initial exploration and check how, as I suggested above, these 'communicative ends' are likely to be traced in the language use of press releases, in particular how the story's "candidacy as news" (Sacks 1992b: 12) is dealt with linguistically.

5.   The Language of Press Releases

5.1 Interactive writing

I have shown that issuing press releases can be characterized as a multiple activity. Following the research method spelled out above, the next step will be to try and find out how this is reflected in the language of press releases. As Fairclough (1991) points out about the divided discourse of political speeches, they "[tend] to have a complex distribution - perhaps an immediate audience of political supporters, but beyond that multiple audiences of political allies and opponents, multiple mass-media audiences, international audiences and so forth. Anticipation of the potential polyvalence of the texts that such complex distributions imply is a major factor in their design" (55). It is the anticipation of the 'polyvalence' of press releases and how it is a major factor in their design that I shall look at in this part of my research.

At this stage, before turning to the actual data, I would like to stress that, in directing my search and in interpreting what comes out of it, it will be crucial to bear in mind the peculiarly interactive nature of press releases. What I mean by 'interaction' can be made clear by reference to Bakhtin and his circle's stress on the "mediated or interdiscursive" - what Kristeva would later call 'intertextual' - relation between text and context (Gardiner 1992: 89).[23] In a late essay called "The problem of speech genres" Bakhtin provides his most explicit account. Basically, in Bakhtin's view, the speaker's seemingly unlimited choice from the wide range of linguistic possibilities is constrained by what was said before.

> Every utterance must be regarded primarily as a response to preceding utterances of the given sphere (we understand the word "response" here in the broadest sense). Each utterance refutes, affirms, supplements, and relies on the others, presupposes them to be known, and somehow takes them into account (1986: 91).

But interaction need not be exclusively retrospective: it is not just manifested in the relation with what came before, but also with what will come next. Using language is not just reacting to, it is also getting ready for:

> the utterance is related not only to preceding, but also to subsequent links in the chain of speech communion. (...) from the very beginning, the utterance is

constructed while taking into account possible responsive reactions, for whose sake in essence it is actually created. (...) The entire utterance is constructed, as it were, in anticipation of encountering this response (94).

It should be clear that the latter notion is of special interest to the analysis of press releases, which are meant to be copied in the news; 'addressivity' is Bakhtin's name for an utterance's quality of being addressed to someone, of actively trying to determine the addressee's 'actively responsive understanding' (95). It is a central aim of my research to investigate addressivity in the language of press releases or, in Bakhtin's words, "the addressee's influence on the construction of the utterance", i.e. how "[t]hese considerations also determine my choice of a genre for my utterance, my choice of compositional devices, and, finally, my choice of language vehicles, that is, the style of my utterance" (96).

Crucially, Bakhtin's notion of a mediated relation between text and context has serious repercussions for the analysis of concrete texts. In his view, naturally, we have to look at 'utterances', the boundaries of which are determined by a change of speaking subject and the classic form of speech communication is, what he calls, 'dialogue'. Here it should be noted that while dialogue and conversation are used as synonyms in everyday usage, it is clear that they are not the same for Bakhtin. Even if, prototypically, all rejoinders in a conversation are linked to each other in a dialogic way, dialogue is by no means restricted to direct oral interaction between two[24] or more interlocutors. Dialogue has to do with "the kind of relation that conversations manifest" (Holquist 1990: 40). It is, perhaps, at its most concrete in the turn-taking of conversation, but, strictly speaking, turn-taking is not dialogue *per se*; it is just one specific and manifest way of accomplishing dialogue. Just like in conversation, written discourse may "[react] intensely to someone else's word, answering it and anticipating it" (Bakhtin 1984: 197). Bakhtin's own research on Dostoevsky's novels shows that writing may be

> calculated for active perception, involving attentive reading and inner responsiveness, and for organized, printed reaction in the various forms devised by the particular sphere of verbal communication in question (book reviews, critical surveys, defining influence on subsequent works, and so on). Moreover, a verbal performance of this kind also inevitably orients itself with respect to previous performances in the same sphere, both those by the same

author and those by other authors. It inevitably takes its point of departure from some particular state of affairs involving a scientific problem or a literary style. Thus the printed verbal performance (...) responds to something, objects to something, affirms something, anticipates possible responses and objections, seeks support, and so on (1984: 95).[25]

Recently, the traditional view of writing as a non-involved, solitary activity has been dramatically challenged by the rise of computer technology, which allows for new modes of (electronically) written communication, including simultaneous terminal-to-terminal interaction (Ferrara, Brunner and Whittemore 1991). Similarly, based on extensive research about how people interpret such graphic features as typography and layout, document design theory has redefined writing as creating text for readers (Schriver 1997). From all this it follows that writing, even if it uses a very different set of mechanisms, must be as dialogic, as interactive, as conversation (cf. Linell 1995). As Voloshinov argues, "[a]ny utterance - *the finished, written utterance not excepted* - makes response to something and is calculated to be responded to in turn" (1973: 72 - my italics).[26]

Finally, since the concept of interaction takes such a prominent position, it should be noted that my research fits in not just with Bakhtin's ideas, but also with a more modern research perspective in which linguists have moved away from traditional, basically Gricean, paradigms assigning the locus of meaning to the individual intention, which is achieved by simply being recognized (cf. Duranti and Goodwin 1992, Auer and Di Luzio 1992, Hill and Irvine 1993). Press releases are, in John Gumperz's words, no matter of "unilateral action" but rather of "speaker-listener co-ordination", with the speaker (or, for my purposes, writer) tuning into the listener (or reader), negotiating a frame of interpretation (1982: 169). This means that, as far as the relation between text and context is concerned, I set out to demonstrate that press releases are both context-shaped and context-renewing: their task is to get journalists to retell them, but to fulfil this task I would suggest that they have to be specially adapted first. As Bakhtin puts it: "[w]hen constructing my utterance I try to actively determine [the reader's] response. Moreover, I try to act in accordance with the response I anticipate, so this anticipated response, in turn, exerts an active influence on my utterance" (1986: 95).

5.2 The metapragmatics of press releases

It is now time to turn to the question how this interaction is actually expressed in press releases.

Bakhtin stresses that any utterance, however monological, is bound to incorporate others' utterances through what may be called an 'internalized change of speech subjects'. Very often, "within the boundaries of his own utterance the speaker (or writer) raises questions, answers them himself, raises objections to his own ideas, responds to his own objections, and so on" (1986: 72). The relationship is "analogous (but, of course, not identical) to relations among rejoinders in dialogue" (92).

It follows that one promising level of analysis will be that of the 'metapragmatics' of press releases. In Verschueren's words, this has to with the "indicators of the language user's reflexive awareness in a usage event" (1995d: 367; cf. also 1985b, 1987). Following a wide-ranging research tradition that envelops - among many other approaches - George Herbert Mead's social psychology, Roman Jakobson's Prague School structuralism and Michael Silverstein's linguistic anthropology, it is on this metalevel at which verbal communication is self-referential that the present study will concentrate.[27]

Hoey (1994) provides a concrete example of metapragmatic awareness when he focuses on the problem-solution structure, in which there are clear signs that the reader's questions or comments have been incorporated by the writer. Here are some examples of such an internalized change of speech subjects from my corpus of press releases. In each case, the writer literally raises a question and then answers it himself':

(19)　(Kredietbank, Brussels: 2 November 1994)
　　　Op donderdag 3 november brengt de Kredietbank haar nieuwe Kasbon Plus uit. Dat betekent dat de KB-cliënt "zijn eigen kasbon op maat" kan creëren. Essentiële kenmerken van deze nieuwe beleggingsformule zijn flexibiliteit en onmiddellijke materiële leverbaarheid bij verkoop. Flexibel? De cliënt bepaalt zelf de looptijd, de dag van uitgifte, het belegde bedrag en het tijdstip waarop hij de rente wil innen. Bovendien wordt deze

kasbon op maat onmiddellijk in het kantoor gedrukt, zodat het
stuk op het ogenblik van de verkoop kan worden overhandigd.

On Thursday 3 November the Kredietbank will issue its new
Kasbon Plus. This means that the KB customer will be able to
create "his own made-to-measure bond". The essential features
of this new investment formula are flexibility and immediate
material suppliability when being sold. Flexible? The customer
himself decides on the term, the day of issue, the amount
invested, and the time when he wants to collect the interests. In
addition, this made-to-measure bond is immediately printed in
the office so that it can be handed over when it is sold.

(20)   (ASQ, Houthalen: 23 February 1994)
        Een Nederlands programma voor België, vraagt u zich af?
        "Wees gerust, zegt Paul Knippenberg, de typisch Belgische
        trekjes en zelfs de allerlaatste wijzigingen inzake BTW en
        boekhouding zitten er allemaal in".

        A Dutch programme for Belgium, you wonder? "Don't worry,
        says Paul Knippenberg, the typically Belgian features and even
        the very latest changes in VAT and accounting are all in it".)

(21)   (Bayer, Antwerp: 16 September 1994)
        De passagiers op het perron in Zürich keken verbaasd op: de
        Intercity naar Genève die net binnenliep, werd - zo leek het -
        voortgetrokken door een reusachtig grote Agfa-filmdoos. Ver-
        klaring? De Zwitserse spoorwegen gebruiken een aantal van hun
        locomotieven en wagons als rijdende reclamedragers.

        The passengers on the platform at Zürich looked up in amaze-
        ment: it appeared as if the Intercity to Geneva which was just
        coming in was towed by a gigantically big Agfa film box. Expla-
        nation? The Swiss railways are using a number of locomotives
        and wagons as rolling carriers of advertising.

One press release from the corpus even has such a question in its (second)
title:

(22)   (Kredietbank, Brussels: 29 November 1994)
        Waarom geeft de KB deze gids uit?

        Why does KB publish this guide?

These extracts all seem to provide traces of the interactive character of the discourse in that they anticipate the reader's questions and provide answers to them.

It is in the process of scanning my data at the various 'layers of linguistic adaptation'[28] that I have come across the special metapragmatic features of the language of press releases that are investigated here:

*   *self-reference* through person, time and place deixis, including - most prominently - third-person self-reference (chapter 3):

(23)   (Amdahl, Montreal/Quebec: 31 October 1995)
        AMDAHL GAINS MAJORITY CONTROL OF DMR GROUP
        AFTER RAISING BID TO £12.50 PER SHARE
        Amdahl Corporation announced today that Amdahl Canada
        Acquisition Inc., a wholly owned subsidiary of Amdahl Canada
        Ltd. has increased its bid for the DMR Group from $8.25 to
        $12.50 (Canadian) per share (...).
        In addition, the company announced it has entered into uncondi-
        tional and irrevocable deposit agreements with Oppenheimer &
        Co, Bear Stearns & Co., and Highbridge Capital Management
        (...).

*   *self-quotation* (chapters 4 and 5): here 'metapragmatics' includes the more specific, but perfectly compatible sense of "metapragmatic terms" or "linguistic action verbs" (Verschueren 1995d: 370)

(24)   (Nutricia, Zoetermeer: 18 November 1993)
        Directeur T.J.M. van Hedel is blij over de medewerking van de
        detailhandel. "Nutricia maakt een moeilijke tijd door. Dan is het
        prettig te merken dat je vrienden hebt. De handel biedt ons alle
        hulp om deze tegenslag te boven te komen. Nagenoeg alle win-

kels hebben, na de eerste oproep van Nutricia, de betreffende potjes zelf uit de schappen gehaald. "

Director T.J.M. van Hedel is happy with the retail trade's co-operation. "Nutricia is having hard times, and it's nice to see you have friends. The retail trade is offering all its help to overcome this setback. After Nutricia's first call, nearly all shops have taken the relevant pots from the shelves themselves".[29]

- *explicit semi-performatives* (chapter 6):

(25) (Kredietbank, Brussels: 16 January 1995)
De Kredietbank en haar dochterbank Crédit Général delen mee dat de IBOS-associatie, waarvan zij de vertegenwoordigende leden in België zijn, haar expansie in Europa voortzet met de toetreding van een Deense partner: UNIBANK.

The Kredietbank and its subsidiary Crédit Général announce that the IBOS association, whose representing members they are in Belgium, continues its expansion in Europe with the entry of a Danish partner: UNIBANK.

I shall demonstrate that these are closely related phenomena that reflect the peculiar audience-directedness of press releases.[30]

5.3 A note about press releases and mass media research

Since the news business has been traditionally associated with mass media, I would now briefly like to relate press releases to this - by no means uncontroversial - area of inquiry. In particular, I shall start from the notion of interactivity described above to point to a problem at the heart of mass media research.

Mass media are traditionally defined as "channels of communication which reach large and anonymous audiences". They are taken to include books, magazines, newspapers, manuals, directions for use, billboard advertising, street signs, icons at airports and railway stations, the Internet, paintings, architecture, CDs, dance, etc. (Jucker 1995: 1). Strictly speaking, press releases should not be in the list; they are part of so-called interpersonal communication since they are sent to a necessarily restricted audience of professional news media. However, I showed above that press releases are meant to be retold by journalists to their own large and anonymous audiences and so it could be argued that press releases are to be situated on the borderline between interpersonal communication and mass communication.

There is a further, more important point on which press releases can be compared with the traditional mass media, though. Looking at the distinction between mass communication and interpersonal communication, Heritage, Clayman and Zimmerman (1988) define mass communication as technologically mediated discourse. It is shaped by the technical constraints that are intrinsic to the print and electronic media, including lack of feedback and a corresponding separation of message production and message reception. As a result, research of mass communication, they say, has mostly been limited to thematic analyses: it has focused on systematic content patterns reflecting persistent stereotypes, biases and underlying presuppositions while the formal properties of mass media messages underlying this diversity of content have remained largely unexplored, e.g. how such mass media messages, whatever their content, are organized and assembled (77-78).

Recently, however, research articles on news interviews by Heritage (1985) and Clayman (1991, 1992, 1993) have started to investigate the mechanics of mass communication and seem to suggest that it is more interactive than is traditionally assumed. Jucker (1995), too, argues that a lot of mass media try to "modify, if not overcome, [this] unidirectionality". The term mass communication can therefore be considered a misnomer since it denies the interactivity at the heart of the news (Stevenson 1995: 13).[31] I would argue that my analysis of press releases seems to point in the same direction.

6.   Newsmaking and News Management

Following the tentative research method sketched above, the final step is to focus on how the peculiar audience-directedness of press releases and some of the linguistic choices that it is interadaptable with reflect on the distribution of power in the news. In this section, I set out to make a number of preliminary points to that extent.

6.1 Newsmaking

It has by now been generally accepted that any analysis of media discourse should start from the idea that the news is not out there waiting to be talked about by journalists,[32] but that, on the contrary, it is the journalists who have to *make* the news by talking about it. In other words, the news is not a set of events, it is the journalists' reactions to them. Particularly in the 1970s, a series of inside studies started to unravel the sociology of the news industry, leaving no doubt that the media play an active role transforming so-called 'reality' into what we read in the press and see on TV. Some of these studies have unmistakable titles, including Tuchman's *Making News: a study in the construction of reality* (1978) and Fishman's *Manufacturing the News* (1980).[33] It is interesting to note that the impact of journalists on the news seems to have gradually increased over the years. While newspapers are reported to have their origin in the early seventeenth century, for example, it was not until the 1860s that journalists began to actively make news by interviewing public figures (cf. Schudson 1978). Even more strikingly, in the early days of radio broadcasting, the BBC - with a total newsroom staff of only four - regularly announced that 'there was no news that night' (Bell 1991). Today this is unthinkable: there is always news unless a strike makes us do without.

   This notion of newsmaking occupies a central position in John B. Thompson's theory of 'mediazation'. In *Ideology and Modern Culture* (1990) and *The Media and Modernity* (1995) Thompson takes the break (or what he calls 'space-time distanciation') between sender and receiver to be one of the central defining features of today's news. He argues that the evolution of the technical and institutional apparatuses of the media has crucially extended the availability of news events beyond contexts of co-presence to a new range of absent recipients. The result is that many more events are now available to many more people.[34] In line with McLuhan's concept of implosion, humanity seems to have virtually collapsed in on itself, returning to the village-like state (cf. Stevenson 1995: 123). Clearly, the fact that most events are only available through the media lies at the basis of the journalists' newsmaking ability, their 'symbolic power' to actively create events. As Thompson puts it:

> For most people today, the knowledge we have of political leaders and their policies, for instance, is a knowledge derived largely from newspapers, radio and television, and the ways in which we participate in the institutionalized system of political power are deeply affected by the knowledge so derived. Similarly, our experience of events which take place in contexts that are spatially and temporally remote, from strikes and demonstrations to massacres and wars, is an experience largely mediated by the institutions of mass communication; indeed, our experience of these events as 'political', as constitutive of the domain of experience which is regarded as politics, is partly the outcome of a series of institutionalized practices which endow them with the status of news (1990: 216).

As I suggested above, it is this mediazation, these institutionalized 'news-making' practices that have come to be the focus of recent media research.

The notion of newsmaking can also be related to Erving Goffman's 'keying'. Dealing with the impact of on-the-spot TV news coverage, Goffman says that it "offers up the world", turning people into audiences "in connection with any and all events" (1974: 126). In his terminology, events are 'keyed' by the media. 'Keying' is of course a much broader concept than Thompson's 'mediazation'. Goffman uses the term to refer to a set of conventions by which "a given activity, one already meaningful in terms of some primary framework, is transformed into something patterned on this activity but seen by the participants to be something quite else" (1974: 43-44).[35] News reports, then, are 'keys' of the events they talk about: in particular, they are a special type of keys called 'documentations', i.e. replays "of a recording of a strip of actual activity for the purpose of establishing as fact, as having occurred, something that happened in the past" (68). Goffman recognizes that such documentations in general "are an important part of modern life yet have not been much discussed as something in their own right by students of society" (59). Crucially,

Goffman notes that the boundary between events and their documentations can be blurred. This is the so-called 'segregation problem', and it is directly relevant to the concept of newsmaking: since ordinary people usually have no direct access to events but only to the journalists' reactions to them, it is impossible for them to distinguish between the two and hence it is the journalists' reactions to events that make up the news.[36]

Surely, as critical linguistic and social semiotic approaches to mass communication have shown, if the news is not a set of events, but the journalists' reactions to them, it is certainly not a set of *random* reactions, if only because the journalists' professional activities are determined by a wide range of social structures and relations (Fowler and Kress 1979: 185, Fairclough 1989: 23; Hartley 1982). Media discourse has been amply shown to reflect economic pressures to win bigger audiences and advertising revenue, for example. At the same time, the news is not just influenced by the journalists' interpersonal context, it also serves as a social agent in its own right, shaping public opinion, setting people's agendas.[37] In Kress's terminology the media perform at least two functions (1983): an ideological function, viz. making sense of the world in accordance with the social structures that they are determined by, as well as a political function, viz. making sense of the world *for others* through creatively 'reproducing' these social structures.

6.2 News management

Crucially, Kress adds that the world may present itself in two ways to journalists: not just in the form of 'physical' events, which journalists can then classify in accordance with their own ideological positions, but also - and even much more frequently - in the form of events that have already been assimilated (by others) into an ideological schema. Events of the latter type belong to the domain of so-called news management and I would suggest that they include press releases:[38] since the news plays such an important political role, apparently a lot of parties and organizations have a stake in trying to furnish the media with their own news. News management allows them to play a pro-active role, i.e. to take the initiative with the news rather than to wait for the journalists' inquiries. The newsmakers' agenda-setting is anticipated by that of the news managers. The result is that journalists cannot simply reclassify the events; they are in some way forced to more or less literally present the classification that others have imposed on the events.[39]

The far-reaching impact of news management can be guessed at from the following sample of one day's international newspaper headlines (*The Times*, 29 November 1994):

> Norwegian PM warns of tough times ahead
> Balladur calls for a more flexible Union
> Yeltsin issues ultimatum to Chechnya
> China urged to deal with high inflation
> UN threatens to recall its forces from Bosnia
> "Major has issued death sentence"

These headlines seem to confirm Sigal's claim that "most news is not what has happened, but what someone says has happened" (1973: 69; 1986). This 'someone' clearly does not refer to the newsmaking journalist, but to the news managing politician, business organization, etc. As Allan Bell (1991) confirms: "[n]ews is what people say more than what people do. Much - maybe most - of what journalists report is talk not action: announcements, opinions, reactions, appeals, promises, criticisms" (53).

Again, John B. Thompson's theory proves useful here. In his investigation of the 'interactional impact' of today's news reporting, he argues that the deployment of the media described above "should not be seen as a mere supplement to pre-existing social relations; rather, we should see this deployment as serving to create new social relations, new ways of acting and interacting, new ways of presenting oneself and of responding to the self-presentation of others" (1990: 16). The media do not simply offer a unique, close-up and possibly distorted picture of the world, they actually serve to change the world. In particular, focusing on the impact of TV, Thompson draws attention to the fact that

> [t]he very existence of the medium of television gives rise to a category or categories of action which is carried out with the aim of being televisable, that is, capable of being regarded as worthy of transmission via television to a spatially distant and potentially vast audience. Today part of the purpose of

actions such as mass demonstrations and hijackings, summit meetings and state visits, is to generate televisable events which will enable individuals or groups to communicate with remote and extended audiences. The possibility of being televised is one of the conditions for carrying out the action itself, or for the staging and performance of a sequence of actions which may be viewed and heard by an indeterminate number of absent individuals (1990: 231).

Surely, issuing press releases belongs to this special category of actions that are carried out with the exclusive aim of being reportable, replicable even. Press releases are issued specifically to take advantage of what Thompson calls a process of 'discursive elaboration'. The term indicates that "media messages can be relayed beyond the initial context of reception and transformed through an ongoing process of *telling and retelling*, interpretation and reinterpretation, commentary, laughter and criticism" (1995: 42; my italics). Thompson used the term to point to a special feature of media messages, viz. that after primary consumption they tend to lead to a secondary - and very often a third or fourth - consumption, as when people at work talk about what they read in the morning papers or about what they saw on TV the night before. This is exactly what press releases are aimed at: as I showed above, they are not just meant to be read by journalists; they are meant to be retold by those journalists in their own reporting and to give rise to another reception process.

Actually, press releases belong to a special type of discursive elaboration which Thompson calls 'extended mediazation': it means that, rather frequently, one media message does not just lead to any kind of additional communication - a chat on the phone, a joke among friends - but to another media message; when the *New York Times* includes a particular news item on Monday, for example, it may well serve as the basis for an article in *Le Monde* on Tuesday.[40] We have a very similar situation with press releases, which are meant to be retold in much the same way. But there is one basic difference: if the newspaper that first carried the story is not acknowledged as the source of the news, appropriation by other newspapers is rather a disagreeable practice, which the first newspaper will, at best, put up with; for organizations that issue press releases, however, it is - I have shown - their central purpose to solicit, to actively facilitate, such appropriation and, preferably - as I shall argue later - at the same time to remain unacknowledged as a source.

Goffman too looks at the effect of news reporting on the nature of events and, like Thompson, argues that "[t]he reporting of an event and its documentation are not only seen as reductions or abstractions from the original, but are also understood to possibly influence later occurrences of the real thing" (1974: 79). This is the issue of 'reversibility': "the copy can come to affect the original" (48). Goffman gives the example of crime films that establish the language and style for actual criminals. Applied to media discourse, this means that news reporting may change the nature of subsequent (news) events. The course of events may be adapted (or 'prekeyed') to meet the media's requirements: the US bombing of Libya on 14 April 1986, for example, was timed for US 7PM prime-time TV news (Herman and Chomsky 1988: 341) and Taels and Vanheeswijck (1995) report the same for the start of the Gulf war on 28 February 1991. These are examples of what Schudson (1989) calls "the feedback loops in which generators of information for the press anticipate the criteria of the gatekeepers in their efforts to get through the gate, like teenagers trying to figure out how best to talk and look in order to get admitted to X-rated movies or establishments that serve liquor" (265-266). Conversely, in retrospect, it is now agreed that Churchill would not have bombed Dresden, if TV pictures had been available. Finally, and somewhat less conspicuously, the real race in the Tour de France only starts when the TV crews are getting ready for their live recording.[41]

Goffman even goes one step further. Events are not just adapted to meet the media's requirements; rather, just like Thompson, he argues that some events happen only because they will be reported. As Goffman says, "we sometimes act now with the sole intent to provide the hard evidence that can be called on later as documentary proof of our having (or not having) acted in the manner that comes to be questioned" (1974: 79). We can think of the historian Daniel Boorstin's 'pseudo-events' here, which are planned for the sake of media coverage only (1961).[42] Social happenings like charity balls, says Goffman, largely owe their existence to the media: they are organized to advertise a charity not through the balls themselves, but through the local newspapers and radio stations that cover them; similarly, often, when politicians make a speech, the transcription handed out to the press often is the reason for, and not the result of, the original performance.

Note that such a transcription of a political speech plays a special role: it can be considered a key of the political speech, this time not a documentation, but a 'demonstration', i.e. a performance of "a tasklike activity out of its usual functional context in order to allow someone who is not the performer to obtain a close picture of the doing of the activity" (66). Here again, we have a segregation problem: what is actually a key is frequently treated as the event itself; the press handout becomes more important than the speech, and starts to get coverage in its own right. When Churchill first talked about the 'Iron Curtain' in a speech in Fulton, Missouri, in March 1946, for example, most reporters that were on hand omitted the now famous phrase in their newspaper articles simply because it had not been included in the advance text that was given to them (Sigal 1973). Clearly, the confusion about what is a demonstration and what is the real thing may lead to, what Goffman calls, 'embarrassing ambiguities' (1974: 68).

It is not difficult to see where press releases come in. Just like charity balls and political speeches, they serve to invert the traditional causality of the news business. The world is being played backwards (Goffman 1974: 510): journalists are no longer looking for newsworthy events but would-be news managers are trying to actively encourage journalists to cover their self-created stories. In addition, like transcripts of political speeches, press releases do not just provide journalists with a topic to talk about, but also with the very words to do so. But we have to go one final step further: while transcripts of speeches simply serve as sources of information for journalists to use freely in their own reporting, I have shown that most press releases are not aimed at journalists *per se*, but they are actually meant to be retold by them, as accurately as possible, preferably even verbatim, in their own news reporting.[43] Clearly, press releases constitute a most radical form of 'prekeying', of creating news events merely by reporting them to the press.

6.3 A critical view of the news

In today's world of sound bites at carefully rehearsed press conferences and of photo opportunities led by omnipotent spin doctors, it may seem as if the journalists' newsmaking role is limited to selecting newsworthy stories from the mass of prefabrications that is offered to them. Apparently, the only thing journalists have to do is recycle, simply repeat what was talked about before. In other words, they are no more than 'gatekeepers' (Shoemaker 1991).[44] This observation has led Van Dijk, for example, to look at journalists' newsmaking as "source text management"; he claims that

> to a certain extent, the press will be a mouthpiece of the organizations that provide the necessary input texts. The assumed freedom of the press consists in the possibility to voice interests of conflicting organizations, to make rigorous selections in the mass of offered text data on the basis of news value criteria, to pay limited or biased interest to non-institutional events (e.g., protest demonstrations, squatters, strikes), and to transform the input data (1988: 129).

From one perspective Van Dijk's view is even too optimistic since it has been shown that the media fail to make these 'rigorous selections'. CNN's live reporting of the Gulf War was a case in point. At first sight it seemed to represent probably the closest we ever got to the ideal of objective reporting, i.e. the naive realism of 'showing history as it happens'. On closer scrutiny, though, the TV coverage of the Gulf War was the summit of news management: since they depended completely on the military, who provided them with information and who proofread journalists' news copy, the US media were giving a totally one-sided picture of what was happening (cf. Taels and Vanheeswijck 1995). Even more drastically, Van Ginneken (1996) reports that dozens of CIA agents have worked as journalists with all major US news organizations since World War II.

The impact of press releases, too, seems to leave very little room for optimism. By their very nature, they represent the views of the organizations that issued them. Hess (1989), for example, talking about U.S. government agencies, recognizes that press releases "are an agency's opportunity to order information in a manner that the agency considers most advantageous to its mission" (47). Unfortunately, instead of blowing the whistle, the media are very often guilty of 'whistle-*swallowing*'.[45] One reason is that most journalists simply do not have the time to check if the press release is correct. Even more so, Allan Bell, who, I have said, is a journalist as well as a linguist, reports that "[a] story which is marginal in news terms but written and available may be selected ahead of a much more newsworthy story which has to be researched and written from the ground up" (1991: 59). As early as 1924 Nelson Crawford, in *The Ethics of Journalism*, notes reporters' habits of giving most space to those who furnished them with "typed copies of speeches, ready-prepared interviews, and similar material" (quoted in Schudson 1978: 138). Apparently, news is first and foremost a "practical activity geared to deadlines" (Tuchman 1978: 82). As Gandy (1982) suggests, "[t]he absence of a satellite link in a foreign capital reduces the probability that news film from that nation will appear on the network news, just as budgetary limitations determine that a full crew will not be assigned to cover a demonstration at the local school board, especially if that meeting is scheduled to begin at 4 P.M." (57). Clearly, the use of press releases should also be viewed in economic terms as they form part of a time-saving as well as cost-reducing routinization of news production.

Herman and Chomsky (1988) go one step further: they provide what is probably one of the most elaborate accounts of how the media, far from manufacturing the news, actually 'manufacture consent',[46] i.e. they mobilize support for dominant special interest groups, simply because they depend on information provided by them. Instead of "enabling the public to assert meaningful control over the political process by providing them with the information needed for the intelligent discharge of political responsibilities", the effect of the media is "to inculcate and defend the economic, social, and political agenda of privileged groups that dominate the domestic society and the state" (298).[47] In Herman and Chomsky's so-called propaganda model the use of press releases is one of those 'filters' which - along with the size, ownership and profit orientation of the mass media - help dominant social forces to "fix the premises of discourse and interpretation, and the definition of what is newsworthy in the first place" (2).

Note that, in Goffman's theory, press releases could be seen as a special type of keying called 'fabrications', in which not all the participants have the same view of what is going on. As Hartley (1982) puts it, for people watching the TV news, for example, "[t]here is absolutely no way of telling in detail from the news broadcast itself how much of a newsreader's or reporter's script is written by the news organization and how much comes from press releases" (111). The general public is, in Goffman's terminology, "excolluded" and news reporting based on press releases is like a mode of "collusive communication" (1974: 84). This is one more segregation problem: it is difficult to distinguish between press releases and the news reports in which they are retold.

It is this dim view of the news that has recently come to dominate research into media discourse. Here we can situate Fairclough's critical linguistic effort to provide discursive evidence that the (British) media operate as a means for the expression of the power of dominant groups, as in the following extract from a newspaper article:

Quarry load-shedding problem

UNSHEETED lorries from Middlebarrow Quarry were still causing problems by shedding stones on their journey through Warton village, members of the parish council heard at their September meeting.
The council's observations have been sent to the quarry management and members are hoping to see an improvement. (1989: 50)

Here, according to Fairclough, the unspecified causality through passives and nominalization allows the journalist to avoid mentioning elites as the cause of the problem.

6.4 A different perspective

There can be no doubt that, in pointing to newsmaking and news management practices and denouncing the complicity of the press, critical researchers have drawn long overdue attention to a crucial influence in the social conditioning of the news. They rightly understand the news to be the product of bureaucratically functioning media, which in turn serve as mouthpieces of today's dominant social forces.

In an interesting review of critical theory, Peter Bruck, however, argues that critical researchers frequently fail to see that there may be at least some room for alternatives, i.e. that the media are not invariably, seamlessly reproducing the dominant ideology. He suggests that they show "discursive openings, inconsistencies, and contradictions" (1989: 113). To find these, Bruck continues, researchers should pay attention to how the media reprocess the discourses of others:

> we need to make the analytical separation between the discourses the media produce and the discourse they use as material to build on, process, and deliver. We need to be interested in the structures of transformation. We cannot ignore - as most content analysis does - the discursive components from which reports are constructed (117).

Of course, this is not to say that, so far, no research has focused on the media's reprocessing activities. On the contrary, Astroff and Nyberg (1992) confirm that the most useful studies within the critical literature are those that "have faced the need to untangle the relationship between various meaning-making institutions in society" (6). Norman Fairclough, for example, has drawn attention to how the British Labour Party leader Michael Foot cautiously criticized Ken Livingstone from the Greater London Council

> In general I do think that one factor that influenced the election was some of the affairs that have happened at the Greater London Council.

and how his words were then transformed into the fierce monosyllabic tabloid newspaper headline

> Foot blasts red Ken over poll trouncing (1992: 161)

Clearly, the idea that the media act as 'secondary definers', selecting and interpreting the information supplied by 'primary definers', is not new and, as I showed above, critical research actually played a major role in unravelling the newsmaking and news management processes. What Bruck seems to suggest, however, is that, if structures of transformations have been taken into account, then the analysis has been bent too much in one direction and that - in the words of Hall, Critcher and Jefferson (1978) - this may have obscured some of the 'strategies of negotiation' that are at the heart of the news.

Surely, too little research has so far focused on the language of news management as an object of analysis in its own right.[48] Dealing with the

U.S. media coverage of the U2 incident in 1960, Verschueren (1985a) looks at how political discourse is rendered in news reporting, but points to an interesting area for further research when he indicates that those who give a speech or issue a public statement are usually very much aware that journalists are listening and that therefore they will finetune their language with a view to future media coverage. Similarly, Fairclough too realizes that the statements of sources and press releases are not just reproduced by the media, but that sources also "design their statements and press releases to harmonize with discourses favoured by the media" (1995: 98). It is this question that my research aims to address: viz. how the language of press releases is designed - 'preformulated' I shall call it - for the media, and how this may shed light on the negotiated character of the news.

But what exactly, then, would be the 'room for alternatives' that Bruck has in mind? To answer that question, let's return to John B. Thompson's theory of the news once again. I argued that press releases are meant to actively encourage 'discursive elaboration'. If this is true, there can be no doubt that the news managers who issue them are exposed to uncertainty because they can never be sure what journalists are going to do with the press releases. This means that, ultimately, newsmakers and news managers are - to some extent - in the same position: just like journalists who make the news for a mass audience, news managers are 'acting blindly' (1995: 128); the journalists' reception of press releases - just like the general public's reception of news articles - really is an 'appropriation', it is an "active and potentially critical" effort to make "one's own something that is new, alien or strange" (1990: 319). As Thompson puts it,

> the uses that recipients make of symbolic materials may diverge considerably from the uses (if any) that the producers of these materials had in mind. Even if individuals may have relatively little control over the content of the symbolic materials made available to them, they can use these materials, rework and elaborate them in ways that are quite alien to the aims and intentions of the producers (1995: 39).

It follows that news managers are not always in the driving seat. They can tell newsmakers what to write in the papers or to broadcast on radio or TV, but often there is absolutely no guarantee that the latter will actually do so:

the ways in which media messages are received and understood, and the consequences which they may have for the maintenance or disruption of relations of power, will depend on a range of circumstances which lie beyond the production context and, to some extent, beyond the control of the producers. If the scope for the operation of ideology in modern societies has been greatly enhanced by the development of mass communication, the complexity and ambiguity of ideological phenomena have also increased, by virtue of the fact that symbolic forms now circulate in a multiplicity of contexts which are remote in space (and time), which are structured in differing ways and in which symbolic forms may be interpreted, assimilated, discussed or contested in ways that cannot be fully anticipated or controlled by the principal communicators (269).

To somewhat cope with this uncertainty, Thompson suggests, news managers have developed a variety of techniques. Just as newsmakers can do market research or keep an eye on their paper's subscriptions or their programme's ratings, news managers can hire clipping services to regularly monitor what newspapers do with their press releases. In addition, apart from closely observing patterns of reception, news managers can proactively manage their self-presentation. Gandy (1982) compares newsmakers and news managers on this point:

> Whereas the journalist selects from an array of sources and events on the basis of perceived utility in producing news that will meet organizational requirements, sources select from an even larger array of techniques on the basis of their perceived effectiveness in being covered, reported, and transmitted in the right form, at the right time, and in the right channel (14).

From the White House conventions of quoting US presidents (Sigal 1973: 107-114; Keane 1991: 102) to the use of embargoes, news managers can, to some extent at least, control how newsmakers retell the news. Reception may also be explicitly co-ordinated by some or other textual aspect of the message itself. Thompson refers to the use of prerecorded laughter sequences in comic TV shows, for example, and to the fact that as early as the 16th and 17th centuries books were composed with a view to being read aloud, i.e. they were produced with the aim of being re-embedded in contexts of face-to-face interaction. It is such design features that I shall look at in press releases. As Thompson puts it, "the study of ideology must take account of the new strategies of symbolic construction, and of the symbolic organization of self-presentation, which are constitutive features of the managed visibility of political leaders" (270).

Cook (1989) has an interesting example. Talking about American politics, he starts from the critical view that "the point of a press release is not accuracy so much as showing the representative in a good light". Next, however, he adds that "being aware of the needs of reporters can be crucial to getting as much coverage as possible on the most favorable terms possible". As an illustration, he tells the story of a press secretary to a five-term New England Democrat who moved the boss's name out of the headline and first paragraph of a press release and claims that this "demotion facilitated the verbatim publication of the release as if it were hard news" (76). It is such interactive decisions and the effect they have on the balance of power that I shall look at in this study.

One final remark. Since this study zooms in on press releases, it is crucial to keep in mind that they are only one tiny - if intriguing - component in the large and highly complex news business. Even to look at press releases as one homogeneous category serves to gloss over the many differences among the 500 or so items in my corpus: obviously, a press release issued to announce a major industrial crisis is not the same as one that is supposed to help launch a new product. As it is, terms like newsmaking and news management are only useful if we are constantly aware that they are radical simplifications.[19] Also, by focusing exclusively on discourse features, I do not want to suggest that the news is purely a language affair; as I suggested above, the media are of course determined by numerous extra-linguistic factors. It is within these important limitations that the present analysis of press releases provides a contribution to the study of the news.

Chapter 2
Projected Discourse[1]

1. Introduction

From some of the arguments presented in the first chapter it should now be clear that press releases do not normally compete for journalists' attention *per se* but that, on the contrary, they are primarily meant to be transmitted as accurately as possible, preferably even verbatim, in the media. Drawing from the cover letters accompanying the press releases in my corpus, I suggested that press releases seem to be aimed at two different audiences at the same time, viz. journalists as well as those journalists' own audiences of newspaper readers, TV viewers etc.: for the purposes of this chapter I shall refer to the journalists as h_1 and to those journalists' own audiences of newspaper readers, TV viewers etc., in short to the newspaper readers,[2] as h_2 respectively. In particular, the role of the journalists (h_1) seems to be the pivotal one of retelling press releases, of forwarding the news supplied to them.

It is this peculiar audience-directedness of what I called divided discourse that I shall further investigate in this chapter. I shall try to more accurately describe the two, rather different, receiver roles as they emerge from the data and, in doing so, to examine how the different tasks that press releases are supposed to fulfil towards h_1 and h_2 can be related to each other. I believe that this is a necessary start for the analysis of press releases. Only if first the discourse's typical participant constellations and its peculiarly institutional activities have been adequately specified, will it be possible to then set out to examine the language of press releases.

This means that the investigation of receiver roles in this chapter is not really an end in itself, but a precondition to a more detailed corpus-based research to follow. As Erving Goffman argued, language use can only be properly investigated in the context of the participation status of all parties relevant to the interaction (1981). Later, as we shall see, Stephen Levinson refined Goffman's ideas on the subject of studying roles and role assignments, especially in what he called 'institutional' discourse: "[a]lthough it would be foolish to pretend that such analyses take us far in the understanding of such complex events", he suggested, "they must surely be preliminary to any proper speech event analysis" (1988: 197-198). It is in this spirit that I shall look at receiver roles in the press releases in my corpus, confronting the data with a number of existing categorizations.

2. Models of Receiver Roles

2.1 Challenging the dyadic model

It is well-known that a lot of communication involves more than a (single) producer and a (single) receiver. For oral interaction in particular, it has been well documented that the primitive notions of speaker and hearer are inadequate. In an early contribution to the study of participant roles, Dell Hymes suggested that "[t]he common dyadic model of speaker-hearer specifies sometimes too many, sometimes too few, sometimes the wrong participants" (1974: 54). Still, the list of famous 'modern' scholars who gave preference to an archetypal dyadic model and who thus to some extent precluded theoretically interesting areas of research into non-dyadic communication modes is supposed to include Austin, Searle, Grice and Chomsky.[3] As far as the distribution of roles in writing is concerned, research has long been limited to literary studies (cf. Booth 1961, Iser 1974) and to composition theory (cf. Ong 1975, Ede and Lunsford 1984)[4] and it has only slowly become clear that much of what has been said about participants in speech can equally be applied to various kinds of writing.

The more recent effort in the field has focused on - both spoken and written - functionally specialized discourse. Goffman set the scene by looking at a wide range of social encounters, including university lectures, radio announcing and journalistic writing, to decompose, what he called, the "global folk categories of the two-person arrangement" into smaller, analytically coherent elements (1981: 124). Exploring Goffman's categorization, Levinson confirms that "much insight into the nature of participant roles may accrue from consideration of talk in specialized 'institutional' settings - law courts, seances, religious services, committee meetings and the like - where the gross roles of producer and receiver may be surgically dissected for institutional purposes, testing any analytical set of categories severely" (1988: 196-197).

From this perspective, analysing participant roles in press releases will not just provide a good basis for my own corpus-based research. It should also be a fruitful enterprise in its own right, especially since, as Bell (1984) argues, the complexity of receiver roles in particular is nowhere more evident than in mass communication, ranging from broadcast interviews and live sports commentary to newspaper columns and letters to the editor.[5] Before turning to the data, however, I shall now briefly highlight some of the classic contributions in the field of receiver roles.

2.2 Hymes

As I have already pointed out, Hymes is among the first to argue that "[e]ven if [the speaker-hearer scheme] is intended to be a model, for descriptive work it cannot be" and he calls for further "serious ethnographic work" to try and find out what other participant roles could be identified (1974: 54). Unfortunately, he does not propose a better scheme of his own.

In introducing his so-called 'components of speech', Hymes does make a number of interesting suggestions. For one thing, as far as receivers are concerned, he seems to realize that what is said may be meant for someone who is not even present, as when he discusses how the Wishram Chinook talk to the spirits of the surrounding environment. In addition, Hymes plays a pioneering role in calling attention to several cases where grammatical choice is determined by the specifics of the participant constellation. It will become clear later on in this chapter how both of these early observations are relevant to my analysis of receiver roles in press releases.

2.3 Goffman

Just like Hymes's, Goffman's writings are full of interesting comments on the roles of speaker and hearer in oral interaction. The article called

"Footing", first published in *Semiotica* in 1979, and then included in the 1981 collection *Forms of Talk*, provides the mature statement of Goffman's ideas on the topic and it is mainly from this article that I shall draw here. I shall come back to the general notion of 'footing' later in this chapter; for the time being I would like to focus on receiver roles.

While he never provides a list, Goffman seems to recognize the following set of receiver roles, or what he calls "participation framework"[6] (1981: 226):

---

1   participants:
1.a addressee
1.b unaddressed participant

2   bystanders:
2.a overhearer
2.b eavesdropper

In Goffman's terminology, participant receivers are set apart from non-participant receivers or 'bystanders'. Still, this concept of ratified participation, or 'participancy', is not clearly delineated. Participants are simply said to play a 'ratified' role in the interaction. Adding to the confusion, Goffman occasionally talks about 'ratified' or 'official' participant receivers; in that case bystanders, who are not normally participants, are referred to as 'adventitious' participant receivers. On the whole, it is not very clear what exactly accounts for the distinction between them.[7]

Within the category of participant receivers, Goffman distinguishes addressed from unaddressed ones, addressed ones normally being those that are expected to take over the speaking role. The bystanders include overhearers, who can easily follow the talk or, at least, catch bits and pieces of it, as well as eavesdroppers, who are secretly listening in.

Goffman's scheme has been very influential and most subsequent efforts in the field are based on it, but not always with great terminological precision. In discussing Goffman's scheme, Levinson (1988), for example, whose own contribution I shall look at in detail later on, suggests that 'bystanders' can be used as a synonym of 'overhearers'. This is clearly not what Goffman had in mind. Levinson's version of Goffman looks like this:

1   participants:
1.a addressee
1.b unaddressed participant

2   non-participants:
2.a overhearer or bystander[8]
2.b eavesdropper

To make things worse, Clark and Schaefer (1992), apart from adding a receiver category of self-monitoring and calling the unaddressed participant receivers 'side-participants', adopt Levinson's use of 'bystander' and turn 'overhearer' into the label of the superordinate class of non-participant receivers, which Goffman called 'bystanders':

1   monitor

2   participants:
2.a addressee
2.b side-participant

3   non-participants or overhearers:
3.a bystander
3.b eavesdropper

In spite of promoting terminological confusion, Goffman's framework of receiver roles has the undeniable merit of demonstrating that oral interaction is very often accessible to others than a single addressed hearer. In addition

- and this is something I shall have to come back to in greater detail for my analysis of press releases - he also shows that this accessibility can be 'managed'. One way of managing the accessibility of oral interaction is by relying on sight and sound: whispering can help to exclude eavesdroppers; on the other hand, to speak louder than is really necessary will actually involve overhearers. It has been pointed out that in the theatre, for example, the audience's peculiar form of overhearing is maximally facilitated by the actors on stage (Goffman 1974: 226). Alternatively, political speakers may be addressing "special publics by means of second meanings that are not discernible (...) to the larger audience" (515).

While Goffman's scheme was devised for oral, i.c. face-to-face, interaction, it does not require too much imagination to see how it may be applied to writing. Still, in trying to place the receiver roles for press releases in Goffman's scheme, the analyst would run into a number of serious problems. First of all, as I pointed out above, the question of participancy remains essentially unexplicated and so it is not clear, for example, if, for press releases, the newspaper readers (h_2) should be considered participant receivers or non-participant receivers. In addition, Goffman's framework, while being a major improvement on the traditional dyadic scheme, by far does not yet provide sufficient distinctions, and its distinctions are not fine-grained enough. As I shall point out later, even if it is possible to determine if newspaper readers (h_2) play a ratified receiver role in the reception of press releases or not, they would remain undesignated, anyway, since their impact cannot be reduced to that of any of Goffman's four categories. As for the journalists (h_1), they seem to be ratified and addressed receivers of press releases but I shall argue that their role is much more complicated than that of simple addressees.

2.4 Levinson

While amply drawing from Goffman's original categorization, Levinson (1988) tries to improve on it. In Levinson's words, "by sketch treatments of so many ecological niches of everyday life, [Goffman] inspired more detailed explorations of the collaborative effort beneath each smooth interactional surface" (224). Indeed, to explore some of the collaborative effort at the heart of the news in a more detailed way is also what my own corpus-based research on press releases is about.

Levinson's is a compositional analysis that is applicable to both spoken and written discourse, i.e. it breaks the traditional concepts of producer and receiver down into minimal constituents and reassembles them into new categories. To do so, Levinson uses a classification system borrowed from phonology.[9]

Levinson's four minimal constituents for receiver roles are the following:

- *address*: this category focuses on the question if a receiver is picked out by means of a feature of address, including, most prominently, second-person forms, vocatives, gesture and gaze. In addition, if no such explicit markers of address are available, "even just sheer singularity of possible recipients" (174) may qualify as evidence.

- *recipientship* (also referred to as 'recipiency'): it "is about who a message is *for*" (174), a feature of role defined by "the pertinence of the informational (or attitudinal) content" (178).

- *participancy*: in defining who is a participant, Levinson simply refers to Goffman's concept of 'ratified role'.

- *channel-linkage*: it comes down to the 'ability' to receive the message.

It should be clear straight away that Levinson's framework is hardly more definitive than Goffman's, with some of Goffman's unexplicated categories of receiver roles - most notably participant - simply replaced by equally unexplicated minimal constituents. Still, Levinson allows for many more distinctions - theoretically sixteen in all, as opposed to Goffman's four - and, what's more, as I shall demonstrate later on, he links up with Hymes in trying to provide empirical evidence from the language structure for the suggested interactional categories, i.e. he sets out to show how at least some of them are - what he calls - 'grammaticalized'.

2.5 Bell

It is finally to Bell's 1991 book on the language of the news that we have to turn for a systematic account of receiver roles in the media. Bell draws together various insights from existing categorizations and applies them to that specific brand of mass story-telling called news.

Crucially, Bell proposes the notion of 'embedding': news audiences are usually 'dual-layered', as when panel discussants talk both for the live audience in the TV studio and for the mass audience at home and, in his view, the task of 'teasing out' the details of these multiple receiver roles is important because "the linguistic form of many utterances can only be explained or decoded on the basis of [it]" (92).[10]

In line with Bell's analysis, I shall argue in this chapter that press releases, like most other news media, have a double audience and that this special audience-directedness can be traced in the language of press releases. At the same time, I shall introduce the notion of projected discourse, which renders the receiver roles in press releases so special and which has not been accounted for in Bell's or any of the other categorizations.

In order to identify the special receiver roles in press releases, I would now like to return to Levinson's framework. More particularly, I shall look at the details of the discourse to find out how the two sets of receivers of press releases specified above, viz. journalists (h_1) and newspaper readers (h_2), can each be broken down into the minimal constituents of address, recipientship, participancy and channel-linkage. Surely, this is not to say that Levinson's categorization is a perfect fit for the purpose of analysing press releases. On the contrary, as I suggested above, it is some of the very difficulties that I shall encounter with it that should help to clarify the peculiar audience-directedness of press releases.

3. Functional Analysis of Receiver Roles in Press Releases

3.1 Address

Drawing from the rather vague concept of 'sheer singularity of possible recipients' it looks as if it is the journalists (h_1) who serve as the addressees of press releases. Newspaper readers (h_2) cannot normally set their eyes on press releases. Instead, they only gain access to what the journalists made of them in their own reporting.[11] The term 'press release' is explicit enough in this respect: it means that the document is 'released to the press'. As far as address is concerned, my analysis of receiver roles in press releases can therefore be summarized as follows:

Fig. 1 Receiver roles in press releases: address

	address
h_1	+
h_2	−

Let's now turn to the actual data to see if this is confirmed. In doing so, I shall distinguish between the cover letters accompanying some of the press releases in my corpus and the press releases themselves.

As for the cover letters, there can be no doubt that they are addressed to journalists. While in oral interaction addressees are usually picked out by a vocative, the mail addresses and salutations in the cover letters constitute equally explicit addressing devices in my corpus. Equally, in terms of second-person forms, the cover letters seem to be addressed to h_1:

(1)   (Tritec, Perwez: 28 March 1994)
Geachte Heer Hoofdredakteur,
In een periode waar men het steeds heeft over bedrijven die in
moeilijkheden zitten, mogen wij er prat op gaan u het dynamisme
van het jong bedrijf TRITEC ADHESIVES aan te reiken. (...)

Hierbij vindt u hierover meer informatie.

Dear editor in chief,
At a time when one is always talking about companies that are in trouble, we are proud to present to you the dynamism of the young company TRITEC ADHESIVES. (...)
Enclosed you will find more information about this.

Conversely, unlike h_1, the newspaper readers (h_2) are never 'picked out' by means of any feature of address in the cover letters, which seems to confirm that they should be ruled out as addressees. They are almost exclusively referred to in the third person, as with "lezers" [readers] in extract (2) from a cover letter.

(2)   (De Beukelaer, Antwerp: 28 March 1994)
        Om u in staat te stellen uw lezers te informeren, sturen we u hierbij uitgebreide informatie over de nieuwe NIKON AF 210.

        Enclosed we send you comprehensive information about the new NIKON AF 210, so that you will be able to inform your readers.

Here the polite second-person forms "u" [you] and "uw" [your] refer to h_1.
    It is interesting to note, however, that when we move from the cover letters to the press releases themselves, there are hardly any second-person forms to refer to h_1. The journalists are only explicitly singled out in the notes that are traditionally at the end of press releases, as in:

(3)   (Allshare, Brussels: 11 May 1994)
        In bijlage vindt u het programma van dit evenement. Voor nadere informatie contacteer Nancy Laport - Allshare Belux - 02/725.16.44.

        Enclosed you will find the programme of the event. For further information contact Nancy Laport - Allshare Belux - 02/725.16.44.

So when we leave out the cover letters and the notes at the end of press releases, only very few second-person references to the journalists (h_1) can be found in the corpus. The following extract is an exception: it is taken from a press release issued by an organization of wheelchair users to announce that they will stage a public manifestation and, rather surprisingly, to request the press to keep quiet about it.

(4)   (Aktiegroep rolstoelen en hulpmiddelen, Grimbergen: 26 September 1994)
Deze aktie werd niet aangekondigd op de kabinetten. Wij vragen u te mogen rekenen op uw diskretie.

This action has not been announced at the ministers' offices. We ask you if we can count on your discretion.

Here, in the press release itself, the journalists (h_1) are referred to by means of a second-person form. On the whole, however, it is clear that those who, through 'sheer singularity of possible recipients', can safely be considered the addressees are almost never singled out by means of second-person deixis in press releases and, surely, this is something that my analysis will have to account for.[12]

As far as reference to the newspaper readers (h_2) in the press releases is concerned, the picture is more nuanced. In the following extract the Dutch brewer Heineken announces that fragments of broken glass have been found in some of their bottles of beer. Here in the press release itself, as in most cover letters, h_2 is referred to in the third person, viz. as "de consument" [the consumer]:

(5)   (Heineken, Amsterdam: 26 August 1993)
Heinekens Exportdirecteur Frans van der Minne:
We betreuren ten zeerste dat dit probleem zich heeft voorgedaan en we hebben elke mogelijke maatregel genomen om ervoor te zorgen dat de consument ons bier met vertrouwen kan blijven drinken.

Heineken's export director Frans van der Minne:
We deeply regret that this problem occurred and we have taken every possible measure to ensure that the consumer can continue drinking our beer with confidence.[13]

Comparable examples can be found in a lot of other press releases:

(6) (Kredietbank, Brussels: 26 October 1995)
Het publiek kan intekenen op 158.450 vastgoedcertificaten tegen BEF 10.000 (...).

The public can subscribe to 158,450 real estate certificates at BEF 10,000 (...).

(7) (Vlaams Blok, Antwerp: 28 September 1994)
Het Vlaams Blok is er niettemin van overtuigd dat ook deze bedenkelijke "verkiezingsstunt" het democratisch oordeel van de Antwerpse kiezers op geen enkel moment zal beïnvloeden.

The Vlaams Blok is nevertheless convinced that this dubious "election stunt" will not at any moment influence the democratic opinion of the Antwerp voters either.

(8) (BASF, Antwerp: 14 October 1994)
Wie belangstelling heeft voor het Milieurapport 1993 van BASF Antwerpen kan het aanvragen via een eenvoudige gele briefkaart (...).

Those who are interested in the Environment Report 1993 of BASF Antwerp can apply for it by way of a simple yellow postcard (...).

(9) (Electrabel, Brussels: 21 November 1994)
Een buitenkans voor de bezoekers is een blik in het hart van een stoomturbine en van een alternator. (...) Nieuwsgierigen kunnen ook een kijkje nemen in de ateliers en in het magazijn met een strategische stock van reserveonderdelen.

A unique opportunity for the visitors is a look in the heart of a steam turbine and of an alternator. (...)
Inquisitive persons can also take a look in the workshops and in the warehouse with a strategic stock of spare parts.

H_2 is sometimes also referred to even more indirectly, as in

(10)   (Gils & Gils, Antwerp: s.d.)
Platin laat zich goed combineren met Alba, Pergamon, Wit en Broadway.

Platin combines well with Alba, Pergamon, White and Broadway.

(11)   (Kredietbank, Brussels: 26 October 1995)
Inschrijven op de certificaten kan bij de Kredietbank (...).

Subscribing to the certificates is possible at the Kredietbank (...).

Still, and this is where the picture becomes more complicated, on the whole there are quite some press releases in which h_2 is referred to by means of second-person deixis:

(12)   (Allshare, Brussels: 11 May 1994)
Parallelle workshops, die U zullen toelaten Uw bestaande kennis uit te breiden, nieuwe functionaliteiten aan te leren, enz.

Parallel workshops, which will allow you to expand your current knowledge, to learn new functionalities, etc.

(13)   (Kredietbank, Brussels: 29 November 1994)
De gids zet uzelf ook aan het werk. U leert hoe u samen met de kinderen de veiligste weg naar school uitstippelt.

The guide makes you work too. You learn how to map out the safest way to school together with your children.

(14)   (IVEKA, Antwerp: 5 October 1994)
        ER ZIT ELEKTRICITEIT IN UW AFVAL

        THERE IS ELECTRICITY IN YOUR WASTE

Again, just like the question why the journalists are almost never picked out by second-person deixis in the press releases themselves, this is a significant finding that my analysis of receiver roles will have to explain: viz. why rather frequently the journalists' own audiences of newspaper readers (h_2), who - I first argued - are clearly not addressed by the press releases, are nevertheless referred to in the second person.

I shall argue that the two features can be related to what I have identified to be the central goal of press releases, viz. that they are meant to be retold by journalists. In fact there seem to be good reasons to assume that the cover letters are addressed to h_1, while the press releases themselves are - indirectly - addressed to h_2. Actually, the very existence of a cover letter directly addressed to journalists implies that the press release is not addressed identically, i.e. that it has a different readership. But first let me now turn to the next minimal constituent for receiver roles in Levinson's framework, viz. that of recipientship.

3.2 Recipientship

In Levinson's terminology, 'recipientship' comes down to the question who could be interested in the utterance's propositional content. In other words: who is it 'really meant for'? In the unmarked case that should be the addressee, in this case the journalists (h_1).[14] As the following extracts from cover letters in my corpus show, however, it appears to be the journalists' own audiences of newspaper readers (h_2) who are the true recipients of press releases.

(15)   (Puma, Herzogenaurach: 25 April 1994)
        Wij vermoeden dat deze informatie de lezers van Uw uitgave zeker zal interesseren en hopen dan ook dat U hen hiervan zal berichten.

We suspect this information is likely to be of interest to your publication's readers and therefore hope that you will be able to pass it on to them.

(16)   (Jadrimex, Elewijt: 30 March 1994)
Ingesloten vindt u een persbericht. Zoudt u zo vriendelijk willen zijn deze in Uw publikaties in te lassen. Deze informatie kan van nut zijn voor Uw lezers.

Please find enclosed a press release. Would you be kind enough to insert it in your publications. This information may be of interest to your readers.

(17)   (De Beukelaar, Antwerp: 28 March 1994)
Om u in staat te stellen uw lezers te informeren, sturen we u hierbij uitgebreide informatie over de nieuwe NIKON AF 210.
Mogen wij u vriendelijk verzoeken dit nieuw produkt in uw uitgaven aan te kondigen.

Enclosed we send you comprehensive information about the new NIKON AF 210, so that you will be able to inform your readers.
Could we please request you to announce this new product in your publications.

Clearly, the information in the press releases that these cover letters accompany is meant for h_2. This is not to say that the journalists (h_1) could not be interested in what press releases are about or that it does not matter if they are interested. On the contrary, if journalists are not interested in the information as news, they will simply throw the press release away. In addition, press releases may exceptionally be issued for the journalists only, as extract (4) shows:

(4)   (Aktiegroep rolstoelen en hulpmiddelen, Grimbergen: 26 September 1994)
Deze aktie werd niet aangekondigd op de kabinetten. Wij vragen u te mogen rekenen op uw diskretie.

This action has not been announced at the ministers' offices. We ask you if we can count on your discretion.

As I have pointed out, this is a marked case, though.[15] In general, press releases are primarily meant for the journalists' own audiences of newspaper readers (h_2) and not - or, at best, secondarily - for the journalists themselves (h_1). Whether the newspaper readers (h_2) are really interested is altogether another question of course, but it is clear that in most cover letters h_2's potential interest in the news is explicitly referred to as a convincing reason for the journalists to 'publish' it. They are encouraged to retell the news specifically because it is claimed to be interesting for their own readers. Exceptionally, business or political interests may be singled out, as in:

(18)   (APEC, Antwerp: 26 September 1994)
        Ik heb de eer U in bijlage een mededeling te laten geworden betreffende [het 14de APEC/UNCTAD Internationaal seminarie in "Container Terminal Management"] (...).
        Daar dit seminarie van belang is voor de overzeese betrekkingen van de haven, verzoek ik U hieraan de nodige ruchtbaarheid te willen geven.

        I have the pleasure of enclosing a press release concerning [the 14th APEC/UNCTAD International seminar on "Container Terminal Management"] (...).
        Since this seminar is of great importance for the overseas business of the port, I would be grateful if you could give it the publicity it deserves.

Here, it is not h_2's interest, but rather some vague commercial consideration that is picked out as a stimulus for retelling the press release. Similarly, in (19) it is political interests that are acknowledged to be the driving force. Here the authorities of the local airport of Antwerp are informing the journalists that the members of a government committee for public works will arrive in Antwerp from a trip to see the building of the Channel tunnel. Rather surprisingly, as an enclosure, a letter from the chairman of the committee is added, requesting the airport authorities to provide a shuttle service to the railway station as well as asking them to try and get the press interested in the event of the committee's arrival. This is an extract from the politicians' letter to the airport authorities:

(19)   (Vlaamse Luchttransportmaatschappij, Deurne: 19 May 1994)
Mogen wij u vragen dit door bemiddeling van uw diensten ter kennis te stellen aan de landelijke pers. (...)
Wij zouden het tevens op prijs stellen, mocht een transfert van onze delegatie naar het station van Berchem door een busje van de luchthavendiensten worden voorzien.
Wij danken u bij voorbaat voor uw medewerking.

Can we ask you, via your services, to inform the national press about this? (...)
We would also appreciate it if one of the airport authority buses could meet our delegation at Berchem station. We thank you in advance for your co-operation.

Apparently, the writer of the press release is now inviting the journalists to meet the committee members at their arrival and to spread the news of the trip, not because it might be interesting for the journalists' readers, but simply because politicians have asked for media coverage.

Even if, in the end, most press releases are, to some extent, motivated by commercial or political interests, such explicit acknowledgement of self-interest (in 18) or lobbying by third parties (in 19), is very unusual. Normally, receiver interests, i.e. the fact that the journalists' own newspaper readers will want to know about the news, are referred to. To see the politicians' letter added to the press release in (19) is rather embarrassing and, in Goffman's terms, can be compared to hearing the prompter talk to the actors on stage; it is a rare public display of what is normally considered back-region behaviour (1959: 100).

But let me return to the topic of this section, i.e. recipientship of press releases: I would like to conclude that whatever readers' real interests and whatever writers' real motivations, the journalists' own audiences of newspaper readers (h_2) are the recipients of press releases. At this stage the two receiver roles for press releases can therefore be represented as follows:[16]

Fig. 2 Receiver roles in press releases: recipientship

	address	recipient
h_1	+	−
h_2	−	+

3.3 Journalists as intermediaries

As far as the role of journalists (h_1) in receiving press releases is concerned, the table can now be completed by means of the following redundancy rules:

$$+ \text{ ADDRESS} \quad \rightarrow \quad + \text{ PARTICIPANCY}$$

$$+ \text{ PARTICIPANCY} \quad \rightarrow \quad + \text{ CHANNEL-LINK}$$

In Levinson's view, those who are addressed, by definition, have to be participants and since they are participants, they have to be channel-linked, i.e. they need to play a ratified role as well as being able to receive the message. This gives us the following:

Fig. 3 Receiver roles in press releases: h_1 as intermediary

	address	recipient	particip.	chann. link.
h_1	+	−	+	+
h_2	−	+		

Surely, at this stage it is already clear that Levinson's scheme allows us to make a much more accurate description of the journalists' role in receiving press releases than Goffman's scheme. In Goffman's scheme, the journalists would simply have been addressees. In Levinson's terminology, h_1 appears to serve as an 'intermediary', somewhat like a chairperson in formal meetings, where all interventions are addressed to the chairperson, even if they are really 'targeted' at somebody else.[17]

This mediating role of journalists is confirmed by an analysis of the turn-taking practices for press releases. As I pointed out above, addressees are normally expected to take over the speaking (or writing) role. It could now be argued that journalists who receive a press release take the floor in a rather special way, i.e. not by replying to the organization that issued it, but by transmitting the message to their own newspaper readers (h_2). In addition, when journalists retell the news more or less accurately this could be considered, in CA terminology, a sign of 'agreeing'. The silence of simply throwing the press release into the waste paper basket can be interpreted as a sign of disinterest or disagreement.[18] (20), from a cover letter, gives some idea of the standard response latency in this respect:

(20)   (Noblesse, Londerzeel: 30 March 1994)
        Vorige week zond ik onderstaand persbericht naar de redaktie "Ekonomie & Financiën". Het schijnt echter nog niet gepubliceerd te zijn. Mag ik op uw tussenkomst beroep doen?

        Last week I sent the attached press release to the 'Economy and Finance' editors. It appears not to have been published yet. Could I ask you to intervene in this?[19]

The above analysis of turn-taking in the news is not an isolated case. Focusing on the turn-taking procedures in the broadcast media, Heritage (1985) and later Heritage and Greatbatch (1991) note a very similar phenomenon. They suggest that the absence of news receipt tokens in interviews should be related to the fact that interviewees - like writers of press releases - produce their statements not (just) for the overtly ratified audience of journalists, who simply serve as go-betweens, but for various other, non-

addressed audiences, most prominently those watching TV at home.[20]
Here, just as in press releases, the traditional hierarchy of roles seems to
have been inverted (cf. Bell 1984: 177): the addressees, i.e. the journalists
(h_1), are only intermediaries while the real recipients, i.e. the newspaper
readers (h_2), are not even addressed.

3.4 Talk for an 'overhearing' audience

So far I have shown that journalists (h_1) are intermediary receivers of press
releases. It is now time to specify the role played by the journalists' own
audiences of newspaper readers (h_2). From fig. 2 it was already clear that
they serve as non-addressed recipients. Following Levinson's scheme, I still
have to discuss the questions of participancy and channel-linkage for h_2.

In view of the fact that Levinson's concept of participancy is largely
unexplicated, it is rather difficult to decide if h_2 is a participant or not. As
far as channel-linkage is concerned, however, I have pointed out before that
newspaper readers cannot normally set eyes on press releases. This means
that they are not channel-linked. The problem of participancy, finally, can
be solved by means of the corollary of one of Levinson's redundancy rules
specified above:

$$- \text{CHANNEL-LINK} \rightarrow \quad - \text{PARTICIPANCY}$$

I would like to add that this by no means settles the question of participancy
for h_2 and that in the next section I shall have to come back to it. For the
time being, though, the table can be completed as follows:

Fig. 4 Receiver roles in press releases: h_2 as ultimate destination

	address	recipient	particip.	chann. linkage
h_1	+	−	+	+
h_2	−	+	−	−

Fig. 4 shows the rather unorthodox situation that not just unaddressed receivers but indeed non-participants serve as recipients, confirming Clark and Schaefer's claim that, although speakers or writers primarily deal with participant receivers, they may also have goals toward non-participants (1992: 269). I would now like to suggest that writers of press releases, just like politicians who are interviewed on TV, even *primarily deal with* non-participants.[21] Goffman, referring to talk shows on TV and to a lawyer's examination of a witness in front of a jury, calls this type of discourse "a display for the encircling hearers" (1981: 133). Another example is Clark and Carlson's 'lateral talk', as in

> Mother, to three-month-old, in front of father: Don't you think your father should change your diapers? (1982: 337)

While the mother is addressing her baby child, she is of course really, though indirectly, targeting the father. Further on in the same article, Clark and Carlson introduce the notion of 'informatives': "[o]n many occasions, government officials, television newsmen, and others are ostensibly addressing certain hearers, but their primary aim is to inform the on-looking public of what they are saying to these hearers" (339).

Clark and Schaefer (1992), finally, highlight various uses of what they call 'audience design'. Significantly, the term echoes Sacks, Schegloff and Jefferson's (1974) recipient design, i.e. how the speaker variously takes the addressee(s) into account. Clark and Schaefer, however, draw attention to the fact that speakers often also take non-participants into account. While almost all theories of language use assume that the default attitude toward non-participants is indifference, i.e. the speaker does not mind if the other grasps what is said or not, Clark and Schaefer distinguish three more attitudes:

- *disclosure*: the utterance is designed so that non-participants can grasp it fully.

- *concealment*: the utterance is designed so that non-participants cannot grasp it and, at the same time, recognize that they cannot do so.

- *disguisement*: the utterance is designed so that non-participants cannot grasp it but, at the same time, fail to recognize that they cannot do so; in other words, the non-participants will be deceived into thinking that the utterance is something that it is not.[22]

I would like to suggest that the attitude of writers of press releases towards the journalists' audiences of newspaper readers (h_2) is basically one of disclosure: they have to design or 'engineer' their utterances not just for h_1, but also for h_2. In other words, the utterance must be interpretable for both of them. It is interesting to note in this respect that, in one of the few full-length studies of the language of press releases, Lebar (1985) refers to press releases as 'corporate *disclosure* documents'.[23]

But the question now is: how can such audience design be realized by writers of press releases and how can it be traced in the language by the analyst? According to Clark and Schaefer (1992) it cannot be accounted for without the notion of 'common ground', i.e. the information shared by the speaker or writer and the hearer or reader, "the sum of their mutual knowledge, mutual beliefs, and mutual assumptions" (248). Common ground plays an important role in ordinary recipient design since, in conversation for example, a speaker will not normally tell the addressee something that he or she already knows; on the other hand, the speaker will report the news in such a way that the addressee can make sense of it. For audience design, however, not just one, but two (groups of) receivers have to be thought of. In particular, writers of press releases will have to take into account both what the journalists (h_1) know and what the journalists' own audiences of newspaper readers (h_2) know.

There is still an extra difficulty. For purposes of recipient design, the speaker needs to have a rather good idea of what the addressee knows. This is especially difficult when the addressee is a 'stranger' or, worse, if the role of addressee can be taken by a multitude of strangers. In that case all the speaker can do is "make broad guesses" at what the receiver(s) know(s) and then "hope for the best" (264). This is clearly the case for press releases, where the writer will have to conjecture about the common ground that he or she shares with the journalists (h_1) as well as with the journalists' own audiences of newspaper readers (h_2). If his or her aim is really one of disclosure, the writer will have to try hard to avoid any discrepancies.[24]

I would now like to argue that the claim that press releases are very much 'engineered' in this way is confirmed by what, in the first chapter, I called their 'explicitness'. Unlike interlocutors in ordinary conversation, writers of press releases do not seem to presuppose the common ground that was almost certainly previously established with the addressed receivers, viz. the journalists (h_1). In Fairclough's words, the journalists are given no credit for what they already know (1991: 52). The reason, I would suggest, is that the information may be new to (some of) the other, non-participant, receivers, viz. to the newspaper readers (h_2). This also goes to explain why explicitness can, to a certain extent, be considered a more general feature of all mass media (Jucker 1995: 5). An interesting piece of evidence of such audience design can be found in the fact that a lot of organizations repeat the same corporate information in all of their press releases, as in the following standard company profiles, which are added to Motorola and Brook Hansen Belgium press releases (cf. chapter 1):

(21) (Motorola, Vilvoorde: 6 May 1994)
      Motorola is één van de leidinggevende leveranciers van draadloze communicatie en electronische uitrusting, systemen, onderdelen en diensten van wereldwijde markten.

      Motorola is one of the leading suppliers of wireless communication and electronic equipment, systems, components and services for worldwide markets.

(22) (Brook Hansen, Vilvoorde: 26 September 1994)
      Brook Hansen België, gevestigd te Vilvoorde, is de Belgische verkooporganisatie van de internationale Brook Hansen groep die een belangrijke produktie-eenheid voor tandwielkasten in Edegem heeft.

      Brook Hansen Belgium, located in Vilvoorde, is the Belgian sales organization for the international Brook Hansen group. Brook Hansen Belgium has an important gear-box plant in Edegem.

Extracts like (21) and (22) must be directed at the newspaper readers (h_2). Clearly, the writers of these press releases cannot just be talking to the journalists (h_1) since they would be telling them something they obviously already know, if only from previous press releases.[25]

Again, like with turn-taking, there is an interesting parallel between press releases and that other type of indirectly targeted media discourse, viz. news interviews. As Levinson indicates, interviews often have "a curious quality in that the interviewer states what the interviewee clearly already knows well (for example an interviewer addresses a newly elected mayor of humble origin with 'You were a very good milkman, you did a double round'), and in so doing reveals a depth of knowledge about the subject matter that makes his questions clearly only for the purpose of obtaining answers of benefit to overhearers" (1988: 221; cf. also Heritage and Roth 1995: 55).[26]

To conclude this section, I would like to illustrate a rather different, and somewhat more intriguing, use of explicitness in press releases. On 27 March 1989 the American multinational Exxon announced in a press release that

(23) (Exxon, Houston, Texas: 27 March 1989)
The Exxon Valdez, a 987-foot tanker carrying 1.3 million barrels of crude oil, ran aground on Bligh Reef about 25 miles south of the Trans Alaska Pipeline Terminal at Valdez about 12:30 a.m. Alaska time on Friday, March 24, while maneuvering to avoid ice. There were no personnel injuries. However, the vessel ruptured a number of cargo tanks, and an oil spill estimated at 240,000 barrels occurred in Prince William Sound.

In a subsequent press release, issued the next day, on 28 March, it is stressed that

(24) (Exxon, Houston, Texas: 28 March 1989)
Exxon Shipping Company continues to place a top priority on clean-up of the spilled oil resulting from the grounding of the tanker Exxon Valdez off southern Alaska last Friday.

Clearly, by the time this press release was issued, the much publicized oil spill and some of its specifications ought to have been 'common ground' - certainly between Exxon and the journalists, if only because they were firmly established in a press release issued the day before. Still, the place, time and cause of the accident are specified once again in (24). This seems to be a violation of the notion of common ground. Possibly, as I spelled out above, the writer was thinking that not all of the journalists' own newspaper readers (h_2) would know about the oil spill.

On March 29, it is further announced that

(25)   (Exxon, Darien, Conn.: 29 March 1989)
        An Exxon Chemical Company oil dispersant called Corexit is being used to help clean up crude oil spilled last Friday morning in a shipping accident in Alaska's Prince William Sound.

Note the reference to "crude oil" (rather than '*the* crude oil') and to "a shipping accident" (rather than '*the* shipping accident'). Here, the writer of the press release seems again to refuse to accept that everybody (not just the journalists, but the general public too) has come to know about the oil spill by now.[27] Clearly, it is hard to imagine that this explicitness should be related to the issue of audience design: even without it, all receivers - participants as well as non-participants - should be able to grasp the utterance. I would therefore like to suggest that treating the oil spill as news almost a week after it took place may serve to help downplay its impact on the public opinion. This could effectively be considered a form of disguisement.[28]

In this section I have suggested that press releases are directed at non-participants and that they are characterized by audience design. I shall now turn to the final one of Levinson's four minimal constituents of receiver roles, viz. channel-linkage.

3.5 Channel-linkage

So far I have assumed that press releases are identical in receiver constellation to other types of indirectly targeted discourse like broadcast interviews, cross-examinations in court or formal meetings with a chairperson. I shall now argue that what distinguishes press releases from such more orthodox (and far more widely investigated) talk for an overhearing audience is that, with press releases, there is no so-called channel-linkage between s and h_2, i.e. writers of press releases and newspaper readers are not normally within hearing, or - in this case more appropriately - 'reading', distance of each other. As I suggested before, the latter cannot normally get direct access to press releases.

That means that h_2 is no simple overhearer in Goffman's terminology. Goffman, by the way, only considers the "full physical arena in which persons present are in sight and sound of one another" (1981: 136) and his stress on oral interaction seems to have led to neglecting the possibility that discourse may involve (non-)participants who are further removed. This is not to say that absent interactants have not yet been taken into account, however. On the contrary, it is to what Levinson (1988) rather contemptuously calls 'earlier traditional schemes' that we have to turn for this. Shannon and Weaver (1949), for example, already distinguished between (present) 'receivers' and (absent) 'destinations'. Similarly, Roman Jakobson looks at whether interactants are present at or absent from the speech situation; in the latter case, like with press releases, the present addressee is merely a 'vehicle' or 'messenger' while the absent non-addressed party is the 'target' (cf. Levinson 1988). As I have pointed out, Hymes (1974) too was aware that what is said may be meant for someone who is not present. Bell (1984), finally, talks about 'referees' - they are "third persons not physically present at an interaction, but possessing such salience for a speaker that they influence speech even in their absence" (186).

By using the notion of channel-linkage, Levinson, too, takes absent receivers into account. Still, as I suggested above, Levinson's scheme of receiver roles is insufficient. To make this clear, let's look at the intermediary role of journalists (h_1) for press releases first. I mentioned above that Levinson's example of an intermediary is that of a chairperson in a formal meeting. But, surely, this chairperson does not play the same role as a journalist who receives a press release. While the chairperson is a passive intermediary, acting as a mere sounding board, the journalist has to play an active role: he or she can either throw the press release in the wastepaper basket and, in doing so, block any communication with h_2, or, alternatively, retell the news of the press release in his or her own news reporting.[29] A further distinction is therefore necessary here in the characterization of the journalist (h_1) as an intermediary: viz. if there is channel-linkage between the writers of the press releases and the journalist's own newspaper readers (h_2) or not. The role of h_1 as an intermediary fundamentally depends on whether h_2 is able to directly receive the message. Crucially, all this points to a power component that should be added to the existing categorizations of receiver roles: in Levinson's terminology, if h_2 is not channel-linked, h_1 has the choice to transmit the message or not; incumbency of the intermediary role - or at least the sender part of it - is negotiable.[30] As for the role of h_2 - or what Levinson calls the ultimate (non-channel-linked) destination - it is significant that the box for prototypical examples in Levinson's table has remained empty here. Levinson seems to indicate that such a receiver role is theoretically possible but he fails to come up with a fitting illustration. he fails to provide an example for this. I would now like to suggest that press releases could be mentioned here, viz. that the newspaper readers serve this role of ultimate destination when they read newspaper articles that are more or less faithfully based on press releases.

Note that, in spite of the limitations of his scheme, on two occasions Levinson does hint at receiver categories that seem to be close to those of press releases. First with an example from a New Guinean language in which he distinguishes between proximate sources (in the utterance event) and ultimate sources (in a subsequent utterance event), with a person A talking to B and, while doing so, simultaneously proposing that B will retell the utterance to C. Still, in this case, C is present to the original interaction between A and B and therefore channel-linked to A. As a result, B's power - unlike that of a journalist who receives a press release - is very limited because even if he or she decides not to transmit the message, C should have received it.

Levinson approaches the special receiver format of press releases even more closely when he refers to a "fuzzy area" of utterance events that project a succeeding utterance event and that he, rather hastily, decides to "gloss over" (1988: 174), for example in:

Harry to Sue: Tell Charles to empty the garbage.

where Sue can decide if she will tell Charles to empty the garbage or not - just as the journalists who receive a press release can control whether or not they will take on the receiver role for which they are being selected. Unlike for the example from New Guinea, h_2 - Charles - is not present and if h_1 - Sue - does not transmit the message, then h_2 - Charles - will never hear about it. Similarly, ordinary newspaper readers do not normally receive press releases and both the organizations that issue press releases and the newspaper readers fully depend on the journalists' willingness to transmit the message. This should be clear from the writer's use of flattery in the following extract from a cover letter.

(26) (Descon, Aartselaar: 17 May 1994)
Aangezien er in uw blad telkens weer een groot aanbod interessante artikels over bedrijven verschijnt, dachten wij dat wij met het volgende toch ook uw interesse konden wekken.

Since your paper always has a great number of interesting articles about companies, we thought you would also be interested in the following.

It can now be concluded that press releases are no ordinary divided discourse, represented as

$$s \rightarrow h_1$$
$$\rightarrow h_2$$

where one and the same utterance reaches different audiences, like a political speech addressed to various pressure groups (Fill 1986; cf. also my chapter 1). Although Bell seems to approve of the term for his analysis of embedding in the news media (1991: 98), there can be no doubt that it is inadequate for characterizing the special receiver format of press releases. What's more, I have shown that press releases are no regular indirectly targeted discourse either, as in

$$s \rightarrow h_1 \rightarrow h_2$$

Instead, I would like to characterize press releases as 'projected discourse', with one utterance projecting, i.e. giving rise to, another.[31] Projected discourse can be represented as follows:

$$s \rightarrow h_1$$
$$s' \rightarrow h_2$$

It now appears that what I have so far considered as one speech event (with the distribution of producer and receiver roles held constant) consists in fact of two separate utterance events, one leading to the other.[32] The question whether it should indeed be treated as one combined utterance event or, alternatively, as two separate ones lies at the heart of my analysis and will be dealt with in the next section.

4.   Projected Discourse

4.1   Preformulating the news

4.1.1   Preformulation as audience design

Based on the notion of projected discourse, it could now be argued that, in investigating press releases, it would be wiser to split up the speech event into its two constituent utterance events and to look at them separately. This would allow us to keep track of how producer and receiver roles shift, in particular how the journalist's initial receiver role (h_1) is, in the next utterance event, turned into a producer role (s'). In such an approach the journalists' power and their actual use of it could be further investigated.[33]

As I explained in the introduction to this study, I have opted to deal with the dynamic, diachronic speech event in its entirety, though, because it helps focus attention on the central question of audience design in press releases: viz. how a single utterance may be strategically exploited to try and assign categories of producer and receiver roles to other parties *across* the complete speech event, how it serves to establish, in Goffman's terminology, a well-defined participation framework in which the other parties will be guiding their deliveries. In particular, I have shown that journalists are supposed to retell press releases as accurately as possible, preferably verbatim, in their own news reporting. In Levinson's words, journalists are not meant to 'author', but simply to 'ghost'; there should be no interference with the original. It is my aim to demonstrate, *from the press releases themselves*, how the accessibility of press releases can be managed to that extent: i.e. how, through features of the language, the projected discourse of press releases is made maximally available so that it can simply be retold by journalists, thus indirectly realizing channel-linkage with the newspaper readers. I shall call this complex audience design 'preformulation'.

4.1.2   Preformulation$_i$ and preformulation$_{ii}$

Of course, as I suggested in the first chapter, there can be no doubt that other forms of divided discourse too should be carefully audience-designed. A politician being interviewed at a talk show, for example, will have to make sure that he or she produces appropriate replies to the interviewer's questions (h_1) as well as making a favourable impression on the public, both in the studio and at home (h_2). However, with the projected discourse of press releases there is a further task involved, though: just as the politician hopes to please the interviewer as well as the voters, the writer of a press release should try to meet both the journalists' (h_1) and the newspaper readers' (h_2) expectations; but this time, meeting the journalists' expectations actually implies that the press release can be copied by the journalists in their news reporting. It is this latter, radical, notion of audience design that I would like to call preformulation and that explains why press releases are sometimes mixed up with news reporting: Hess (1984), for example, says that press releases "almost substitute for objective wire service copy" (77) and that they are "written as ersatz news stories" (79).[34]

So this is what I mean by pre*formulation*: not just that, in some general sense, press releases meet the journalists' and the newspaper readers' requirements, but that the way press releases are formulated actually anticipates the way news reports are formulated. Through such preformulation, writers of press releases provide journalists with "written sources which are already prefabricated in an appropriate news style and therefore require the minimum of reworking" (Bell 1991: 58); they "go to great pains to make things easy for news organizations" by supplying them with "usable languages" (Herman and Chomsky 1988: 21-22). However, contrary to what the term might suggest, I would like to argue that preformulation is not restricted to issues of form. As Gandy (1982) shows in his political economic analysis of the news, not just "form" but "content" too may be "structured in such a way as to flow in sync with the media system's requirements" in order to have "a greater probability of gaining entry into the public-information environment" (57). In this study I shall refer to these two aspects of preformulation as preformulation$_i$ or preformulation$_{ii}$. Crucially, this is not to suggest that two separate preformulating processes are at work. On the contrary, preformulation$_i$ and preformulation$_{ii}$ are part of one and the same effort at audience design and the distinction here is simply meant as a heuristic device, i.e. I am using it for the purpose of analysis only.

4.1.3   Negotiation

There is another way in which the term '*pre*formulation' may be misleading: it could be taken to denote a one-way process, with writers of press releases telling journalists what to write; but this is certainly not what I mean. I have made it clear that journalists have the choice to take on the role for which they are being selected or not, and that certainly writers of press releases are in no position to unilaterally assign the receiver roles of intermediary and ultimate destination. It follows that preformulation is bound to involve negotiation: writers of press releases will have to reconcile what, ideally, they would like to get the journalists to say, on the one hand, with what, realistically, they know the journalists will want to say, on the other hand. Te Molder (1995) makes a similar comment on the divided discourse of government communicators: apart from saying what the politicians want them to say, they also find themselves actively orienting to the wishes of the press and the general public. So, according to Te Molder, in divided discourse, there is a need for "combined efforts" (70) and she concludes that "improving communication is primarily a matter of improving empathetic capacities" (71). I would like to suggest that, if this is true of the divided discourse of government communication campaigns, then it must be even more true of the projected discourse in press releases.

Throughout my analysis I shall take into account this notion of preformulation as a negotiating device: press releases preformulate the news, but equally the news preformulates press releases. Indeed, from one perspective, preformulation in press releases can be seen as a special form of what Allan Bell calls 'initiated' (rather than 'responsive') 'institutional accommodation' or 'convergence' (1984: 170, 185), with public-contact organizations trying hard to win the customers' approval: significantly, in Bell's view, such audience design reaches its high in mass communication[35] and it points to the enhanced salience of the readers as customers.

4.1.4   Optimal levels of preformulation

Crucially, it should be borne in mind that there are optimal levels of preformulation: as Bell points out, "speakers can converge too much, causing addressees to react unfavourably to what they may feel is patronizing or ingratiating behaviour" (1984: 162). It follows that the notion of the reader as a customer is ultimately inadequate. For my purposes, the information exchange between writers of press releases and journalists should not be approached, in the tradition of political economic studies of the news, as a pure commercial transaction.[36]

This means, practically, that preformulation in press releases can be no guarantee of success: even if a press release looks perfectly like a newspaper article, journalists may well, for one reason or another, prefer not retelling it or, at least, radically changing it. My analysis, in dealing with the dynamic, diachronic speech event of projected discourse in its entirety, therefore only sheds light on how press releases are preformulated; as I pointed out in the introduction to this study, it does not make any predictions about the possible success of the preformulations.

4.2 Tracing preformulation

In this chapter I have looked at the peculiar audience-directedness of press releases. My objective in starting this analysis was to check the common-sense intuition that press releases are not just meant for the explicitly ratified audience of journalists, but that they are aimed to be retold by those journalists in their news reporting. I have suggested that press releases are projected discourse.

I would now argue that all this is not just 'incidental but a constitutive feature' (cf. Jucker 1995: 11 on the mass media in general): just as the conversation on a phone-in program is different from a private chat, it would be wrong to look at press releases without taking into consideration that they are meant to be retold by journalists. More particularly, I have suggested that projected discourse must be characterized by preformulation. In the next few chapters I shall look for traces of such preformulation, i.e. I shall try to find out from the corpus how the interactional categories of non-prototypical receiver roles specified above may be grammaticalized.[37]

Levinson (1988) offers a nice example of what kind of constructions we should be looking for. Take the following utterance:

A to B: Johnny is to come in now.

Without providing much of empirical evidence to support his claim, Levinson argues that this utterance is usable just in case the addressee (B) is not the recipient: a doctor (A) may say this to his secretary (B), thus instructing the latter to call in the patient called Johnny. Alternatively, the utterance may also be used if the speaker (A) is not the source, like when the secretary (A) calls in Johnny (B), after having been instructed by the doctor to do so.[38] Levinson says that it is the use of the infinitive construction that, in both cases, turns the secretary into an intermediary. He concludes that this 'minor sentence type' is only one of a great many grammaticalizations of non-prototypical producer and receiver roles and that it "is of interest because it suggests that many minor sentence types of this sort have escaped the grammarians' notice, and not only in unfamiliar languages" (189). It is some of these other minor sentence types that I shall be looking for in my analysis of preformulation in press releases.

Of course, preformulation in press releases may take a variety of forms. Lebar (1985), for example, looks at headlines in press releases and says that they are prefabricated to meet the requirements of newspaper reporting. She indicates that, very much like for newspaper articles, the headlines of press releases are designed to attract attention (cf. also Bernaers, Jacobs and Van Waes 1996). In addition, Lebar notes that the most important information is presented in the first few sentences and paragraphs of the text while the least important text is left for last so that the journalists can easily edit if not enough space is available for the complete story (1985: 115).

As I suggested in the previous chapter, in this research I shall look at the preformulating role played by the metapragmatics of press releases. In particular, I shall focus on self-reference (chapter 3), self-quotation (chapters 4 and 5) and explicit semi-performatives (chapter 6) in my data. Note that some - if not all - of these are standard features of press releases and their preformulating roles can easily go unnoticed in a cursory reading. In Allan Bell's words, they have become "predictable, a norm, even a cliché", "institutionalized, responsive rather than initiative. We may hazard that it is through just such a process that certain topics become associated with certain styles" (185, 186).

Crucially, I would like to stress that it is no coincidence that a simple search for candidate phenonema in my corpus has directed my analysis of preformulation in press releases to such metapragmatics: indeed, I pointed out in the introduction to this study that in Bauman and Briggs's (1990) terminology as well as in that of Silverstein and Urban (1996) they serve as devices of 'entextualization'. As Goffman would have put it in frame analytical terms, the metapragmatics in press releases can be seen as boundary markers, which "like the wooden frame of a picture, are presumably neither part of the content of activity proper nor part of the world outside the activity but rather both inside and outside" (1974: 252). For my purposes, it could be argued that the metapragmatics I shall investigate are part of press releases and of the news reports they anticipate. They are 'framing' devices, which allow writers of press releases to gracefully manage the divergent tasks of projected discourse specified above. They can be situated in the border zone where

> discourse is at once anchored in literal experience yet not restricted by it. Identifying the outer frame of an activity, the point at which it is most firmly linked to the literal world, is only a starting point in exploring what is going on. More revealing of the nature of an activity, often, is the way in which participation frameworks (...) are layered and mixed (Hoyle 1993: 142).

In particular, since in this study I set out to investigate how the specific receiver roles of press releases may be cast by the ways in which writers refer to themselves or to the organizations they represent, Goffman's popular, but largely undefined concept of footing is of course vital here: it is the alignment that speakers or writers take up not just to the hearers or readers but also to themselves as a way of constraining the subsequent reception of utterances (1981: 128). Crucially, according to Goffman it is linguistics that "provides us with the cues and markers through which (...) footings become manifest" (157). Some of his numerous and wide-ranging examples of footing include President Nixon's switch from the political rhetoric of a press conference to personal remarks about a journalist's dress, the use of prescripted text combined with spontaneous self-commentary in a university lecture and a radio announcer's change in voice consequent on a change of subject matter.[39]

The fact that self-reference has an effect on the reception of utterances is explicitly stated by Goffman:

> In (...) introducing the name or capacity in which he speaks, the speaker goes some distance in establishing a corresponding reciprocal basis of identification for those to whom this stand-taking is addressed. To a degree, then, to select the capacity in which we are to be active is to select (or to attempt to select) the capacity in which the recipients of our action are present (...). All of this work is consolidated by naming practices and, in many languages, through choice among available second-person pronouns. (Goffman 1981: 145; cf. also Goffman 1959 on identity management processes).

Since I have shown that writers of press releases orient to a rather intricate reception, according to Goffman's claim, self-reference should in some way be special too. Benveniste makes a more specific claim that is particularly applicable to what we previously observed for press releases:

> *Je n'emploie je qu'en m'adressant à quelqu'un, qui sera dans mon allocution un tu.* (1966: 260)
> I only use 'I' in addressing somebody who I shall use 'you' for.

I have demonstrated that writers of press releases do not normally refer to the addressees (h_1) as 'you', so in Benveniste's view there must be something special about the self-reference too; certainly no simple 'I' is to be expected, he suggests.

Goffman's claim about the relation between self-reference and reader-orientedness goes back to Weinstein and Deutschberger's (1963) famous essay on 'altercasting'. They say that speakers can of course make explicit the identity they wish the receiver to assume, as in

Now Joe, as a good friend of mine, I know you would ...

However, they argue that another, much more subtle and implicit way of 'altercasting' is that of self-presentation: 'coming on strong', for example, may point out to the other restrictions on the identities he or she can assume while maintaining a working consensus (cf. Malone 1995).

4.3 Participancy revisited

Let's finally come back to the question of participancy for the journalists' own audiences of newspaper readers (h_2).

I have shown that there can normally be no channel-linkage between writers of press releases and newspaper readers (h_2). However, from one perspective it could be argued that the very point of preformulation in press releases is to accomplish indirect channel-linkage between them. This would open the whole debate of participancy again: if, in the case of success, the writer of a press release and the newspaper readers become - indirectly - channel-linked after all, then there are no redundancy rules or corollaries to show that the newspaper readers are no participants. On the contrary, as I suggested above, the patterns of second-person reference in press releases seem to suggest that newspaper readers (h_2) can in some way even be considered addressees, which would imply that they are participants after all.

There is a third argument to support that newspaper readers may be participants. I have shown that, through disclosure, press releases are designed in such a way that even newspaper readers can easily recognize what is being said. Since, in Clark and Schaefer's (1992) theory, it is only participants who can recognize what speakers or writers mean, while non-participants have to conjecture about it, this actually means that disclosure aims at turning what are basically non-participants into participants. In this sense, it could be argued that press releases aim at turning the newspaper readers from non-channel-linked non-participants into (indirectly) channel-linked participants.

It is interesting to note in this respect that, in trying to define what participancy really means, Clark and Schaefer distinguish 3 types of responsibilities:

- *collaborative responsibilities*: viz. asking if the other party understood or spontaneously indicating one's own understanding
  [towards addressees only]

- *conversational responsibilities*: viz. keeping track of "an accumulating body of information called the discourse record" and enabling the other parties to keep track of it too (251)
  [towards participants only]

- *politeness responsibilities*
  [towards all]

First of all, it is clear that writers of press releases feel no collaborative responsibilities towards newspaper readers (h_2) so this settles the question of address. It can now be concluded that newspaper readers are no (direct) addressees of press releases. In practice it is the opportunity for collaboration which makes the difference between addressees and all other receivers, i.e. the possibility to interactively check on what the other means. No such opportunity is available either for writers of press releases or for the newspaper readers (h_2).

On the other hand, writers of press releases seem to feel conversational responsibilities (as well as politeness responsibilities of course) towards newspaper readers (h_2). I have shown that press releases are phrased in such a way, e.g. through explicitness, that the general public can relatively easily keep track of what is being said. Since in Clark and Schaefer's theory, non-participants do not normally benefit from such conversational responsibilities, h_2 should be considered participants.

Still, there seems to be a contradiction at the heart of Clark and Schaefer's reasoning: one attitude towards non-participants is disclosure (i.e. making sure that the other understands); at the same time, it is suggested that such disclosure turns all hearers or readers, including non-participant ones, into participants. Clark and Schaefer address this point directly: "[d]isclosing to an overhearer may look at first sight just like informing a side participant, but it isn't" (265). In their view the basic difference is this: when treating a hearer or reader like a side-participant you intend him in true Gricean style to infer what you mean by recognizing that very intention; the hearer or reader is supposed to realize that the utterance was prefabricated for him or her. With disclosure, however, you do not intend the non-participants to realize that the utterance was specifically adapted for them. Clark and Carlson (1982) make the same point when they claim that speakers' intentions toward non-participants are different from those toward participants in that non-participants "are not intended to be recognized as intended to be recognized"; in other words, non-participants "are generally not meant to realize how utterances have been designed for them." (334).

This means that the above question of participancy can now be rephrased for press releases as follows:

are newspaper readers (h_2) supposed to realize that what writers of press releases (s) say is engineered at them?

or, since there is no channel-linkage between s and h_2:

are newspaper readers supposed to realize that what journalists say in their news reporting is based on press releases?

The answer is clear: no. While occasionally, in the act of retelling, journalists acknowledge that their information came from a press release[40] such acknowledgment is certainly not the explicit aim of writers of press releases. On the contrary, this research will show that, through preformulation, press releases are so engineered that, in Goffman's terms, the frame of press releases almost imperceptibly disappears and melts with that of news reporting; in Bakhtin's theory of voicing, through preformulation writers of press releases 'ventriloquate' journalists' news reporting (1981: 299; cf. also Wortham and Locher 1996).[41]

Chapter 3
Self-Reference in Press Releases[1]

1. The Institutional Voice

1.1 Introduction

In the previous chapter I showed from the details of the discourse what it means to say that press releases are not just aimed at journalists *per se*, but that they are meant to be retold by them in their own news reporting. At the end, it was suggested that this peculiar audience-directedness might well be reflected in some of the metapragmatics of press releases.

In this chapter I shall make a start with the analysis by looking at simple self-referencing, viz. how writers of press releases and/or the organizations they represent are referred to. After all, in Pamela Downing's words, such referential choices constitute an interesting domain for linguistic pragmatic analysis in that they are far from self-evident and often prove to be intricately constrained by "the demands of the larger social agendas" (1996: 95). To give just one example: Paul Drew (1994) says that the caller's self-reference through 'we' in the following extract from a telephone conversation reveals the institutional character of the exchange.

    Desk: Mid-city emergency (...) Hello? What's thuh problem?
    Caller: We have an unconscious, uh diabetic.

It should be noted, however, that such metapragmatics are not just determined by the context. As I pointed out previously, any suggestion of a unidirectional relationship between context and language should be strongly resisted. On the contrary, it will prove crucial for my purposes to keep in mind that context determines, say, referential choices, but also that, in turn, referential choices determine context. As Ford and Fox (1996) suggest, they "are made not only to fit into, but also to manage and to transform conversational activities and participation structures" (162; cf. Gumperz 1982). In particular, I hope to demonstrate that the metapragmatics of press releases are fully 'interadaptable' with the peculiar audience-directedness described in the previous chapter: they do not just reflect, but actively help fulfil the ambition to influence news reporting, i.e. they play an active role in encouraging journalists to copy press releases (instead of, for example, ignoring them or drastically rewriting them).

1.2 Third-person self-reference

The first rather general observation from the corpus is that there are hardly any first-person pronouns to be found. This is unexpected, to say the least, since press releases by their very nature can be considered egocentric:[2] organizations normally issue them because they want to say something about themselves. Still, hardly any traditional semantic mappings of the writers of the press releases onto 'I' or 'we' could be found in my corpus; instead, it is a characteristic feature of the production format of press releases that self-referencing is almost exclusively realized in the third person, in particular through the use of the organization's proper name. Here are some examples, all taken from headlines of press releases:

(1)   (Alcatel Bell, Antwerp: 28 February 1994)
        ALCATEL BELL LEVERT INTELLIGENTE NETWERKEN AAN ZUID-KOREA

        ALCATEL BELL SUPPLIES INTELLIGENT NETWORKS TO SOUTH KOREA

(2)   (Boelwerf Vlaanderen, Temse: 24 February 1994)
        BOELWERF VLAANDEREN DOOPT 2 KOELSCHEPEN

        BOELWERF VLAANDEREN CHRISTENS TWO COOLING SHIPS

(3)   (Europay, Waterloo: 5 May 1994)
       EUROPAY DOET HET GOED IN TURKIJE

       EUROPAY PERFORMS WELL IN TURKEY

(4)   (GB, Brussels: 13 April 1995)
       GB start samenwerking met QUELLE - Postorderverkoop

       GB starts co-operation with QUELLE - Mail order sale

(5)   (Exxon, Valdez, Alaska: 27 April 1989)
       EXXON BUILDING OTTER CENTER IN SEWARD

1.3 Institutional voice

Clearly, what happens in these examples is that the individual writer's personal identity is deleted, or at least disguised, in favour of that of the organization that issues the press release. For Lerman (1983, 1985) such third-person self-reference is a typical feature of institutional discourse, which she defines as "that broad category of language use in which the speaker is a representative of an institution, speaking not as 'I', the personal ego, but as a public identity or role" (1983: 77). Focusing on Nixon's presidential Watergate speeches and on the media coverage of them, she introduces the term 'institutional voice' to denote the dual role played by a sender who necessarily speaks or writes as an individual, but at the same time speaks or writes as (i.e. personifies) or for (i.e. represents) an institution. Here is Nixon talking about his own role in the Watergate affair:

Many people assume that the tapes must incriminate the President, or that otherwise he would not insist on their privacy (83).

As far as writing is concerned, it is reported that Nixon used his initials "RN" to refer to himself in memos to his aides (cf. also Brown and Levinson 1987 on reference terms as 'I' avoidance in the English of kings and presidents, 204). Similarly, in business, so-called 'spokespersons' invariably represent corporations. Rogers and Swales (1990) and Swales and Rogers (1995), for example, look at ethical codes and mission statements, and observe a pattern of third-person self-reference through proper names that looks similar to that of press releases, as in:

> Honeywell manages its business in ways that are sensitive to the environment and that conserve natural resources (1995: 235).

Thompson and Thetela (1995), finally, provide comparable data from advertising:

> And that's exactly why Lufthansa will never abandon its uncompromising commitment to the very highest standards of quality and service (117).

Before turning to a more detailed, corpus-based survey of third-person self-reference in press releases later on in this chapter, I shall now - just as for receiver roles - first try to situate my preliminary findings with respect to existing categorizations.

1.4 Hymes

As I argued in the previous chapter, Hymes is among the first to challenge the dyadic model. In his view, there is an addressor (who speaks) and a sender (who initiates the words spoken by the addressor), like when - among the Wishram Chinook - a spokesperson repeats a source's words in front of an audience. Hymes adds that the source whose words are repeated may not be present to the ceremony.

1.	addressor
2.	sender

1.5 Goffman

Goffman (1974, 1981) distinguishes three producer roles:

1.	animator
2.	author
3.	principal[3]

The animator is Hymes's 'addressor'. Dealing primarily with oral interaction, Goffman defines the animator (originally also referred to as 'emitter') as "the current, actual sounding box from which the transmission of articulated sounds comes" (1974: 517). He or she is "the talking machine, a body engaged in acoustic activity, or, if you will, an individual active in the role of utterance production" (1981: 144). As I said, Goffman seems to have formulated his definitions for oral interaction. Still, they are equally applicable to writing, where the animator would be the person who actually puts pen to paper or who types on the computer. For obvious reasons, it is normally not possible and, at least for my purposes, not relevant to know who 'animated' (or, in Hymes's terms, 'addressed' a press release.[4] Surely, the animator is never explicitly referred to in the corpus and I shall leave this category out of the discussion, confirming Lerman's view of a 'dual role'.

As for Hymes's 'sender' role, Goffman splits it into two: the author and the principal. The author, then, "has selected the sentiments that are being expressed and the words in which they are encoded" (1981: 144). It is "the agent who puts together, composes, or scripts the lines that are uttered" (1981: 226). For my analysis of press releases, it would be the press officer or any other member of the organization or contractor who served as author. Just as for the animator, the author of a press release seems mostly absent from the data.

Goffman's third category is that of the principal, i.e. the individual or party "who is held responsible for having wilfully taken up the position to which the meaning of the utterance attests" (1974: 517). The principal is "someone whose position is established by the words that are spoken, someone whose beliefs have been told, someone who is committed to what the words say" (1981: 144). Even though the repetition of the word 'someone' seems to stress that the principal should be a human being, Goffman is aware "that one deals in this case not so much with a body or mind as with a person active in some particular social identity or role, some special capacity as a member of a group, office category, relationship, association, or whatever, some socially based source of self-identification" (1981: 145), "an identity which may lead him to speak inclusively for an entity of which he is only a part" (226). In the case of press releases the principal usually is the organization that issued them. Clearly, the 'principal' is Goffman's equivalent of the institutional voice and, on the basis of the preliminary observations described above, it can be concluded that it is this category that, through third-person self-reference, writers of press releases orient to most frequently, with the author and animator hiding beneath it.

1.6 Levinson

Just as in the case of receiver roles, Levinson turns Goffman's set of basic distinctions into a more refined scheme, employing the following minimal constituents:

- *transmission* (or emission): "the property that utterers or actual transmitters have"; this seems identical to Goffman's concept of animation

- *source - motive*: the "desire to communicate some particular message"

- *source - form*: devising the form or format of the message

- *participancy*: playing a ratified role (1988: 171).

In the following table, the organization's principal role is represented as s_1, that of the individual who actually authored the text but who is in no way visible in it is represented as s_2.

Fig. 1 Producer roles in press releases

	transm.	motive	form	particip.
s_1	−	+	−	−
s_2	−	+/−	+	+

While motive (what exactly is the 'desire' to communicate?), like participancy, remains largely unexplicated, Levinson's scheme draws attention to the fact that there are at least two possible author roles, depending on whether he or she has the desire to communicate or not. It might be argued that if press releases are written by a hired professional from an outside agency, no such direct motive is involved.[5] In Levinson's terminology, s_2 then serves the role of a 'ghostor'. Note that Goffman, well before the golden age of consultancy, already seemed to be aware of this possibility when he talked about the role of the so-called 'strategist', who is responsible for "assessing the situation and diagnosing what ought to be done in the circumstances" (1974: 523). Levinson (1988) agrees that in many cultures there are professionals who specialize in some or other specific participant role (198). Surely, the role of the PR professional writing press releases could be situated here.

In spite of various shortcomings, some of which I hinted at above, Levinson's - as well as Goffman's - classification is a major improvement on the traditional view. Still too little has been done with it in the field of functionally specialized writing, though. Scollon and Wong Scollon (1995), for example, in one of the rare, but cursory, analyses of the participation framework of press releases, say that there are two kinds of reader-writer relations to be considered: "the relationship between the actual writer and the actual reader on the one hand, and the relationship between the implied writer and the implied reader on the other hand" (90). I would like to argue that Scollon and Wong Scollon's characterization, while stuck in the terminology of literary analyses, seems to hint at what I would suggest is the specific nature of the participation framework for press releases, viz.

that the peculiar audience-directedness described in the previous chapter finds its counterpart in the self-reference of press releases.

1.7 Bell

There are at least two ways in which Bell (1991) has made a contribution to the study of producer roles in the media. First, he has demonstrated how in the newsroom news copy is passed on from one newsworker to the next along what he calls a news 'assembly line', which includes journalists, editors, typesetters, proofreaders and printers. A somewhat similar division of labour is to be expected for the writing of press releases, but I have already argued that this is not of direct interest to the present research project.

Another - more important - reason why the production of the news deserves close inspection is that hardly any journalists write their own texts (Bell 1991: 52). It is this what Bell means when he says that the news is 'embedded talk' and I have already argued that press releases play a major role here. Crucially, while Bell is aware that input texts may have been prefabricated, his is basically a study of how they are then modified by journalists and other newsworkers into what we read in the papers and see on TV. In this chapter I shall turn to those very input texts for a more detailed analysis of the various forms of self-reference in them and of how they can be related to this special feature of news production.

2. Data Analysis

2.1 Other forms of third-person self-reference

As I pointed out above, third-person self-reference is the norm in press releases, with the overwhelming dominance of the organization's proper name occasionally varied with definite description[6] or what Maes (1991) calls nominal anaphor. (6), (7) and (8) are characteristic extracts combining initial self-reference through a proper name with subsequent definite description:

(6)   (R.J. Reynolds, Brussels: 23 February 1994)
       Per 1 maart 1994 zal R.J. Reynolds Tobacco International haar
       sales- en marketingactiviteiten in België, Nederland en Luxem-
       burg integreren in een nieuwe Benelux-organisatie. De onderne-
       ming wil hiermee onder andere een hechte samenwerking
       bereiken tussen de commerciële functies in Nederland (Hilver-
       sum) en België (Brussel).

       On 1 March 1994 R.J. Reynolds Tobacco International will
       integrate its sales and marketing activities in Belgium, the
       Netherlands and Luxembourg in a new Benelux organization.
       This way the company hopes to achieve, among other things,
       close co-operation between its commercial outlets in the Nether-
       lands (Hilversum) and Belgium (Brussels).

(7)   (Vertongen, Puurs: s.d.)
       VERTONGEN N.V. TERUG FAMILIEBEDRIJF
       (...) Het bedrijf stelt zich de verdere ontwikkeling van de eigen
       produkten alsook de organisatie van een dealernet binnen
       Europa als één van de prioriteiten.

       VERTONGEN N.V. AGAIN A FAMILY BUSINESS
       (...) The company considers the further development of its own
       products as well as the organization of a dealer network within
       Europe as one of the priorities.

(8)   (BASF, Brussels: 17 March 1994)
       BASF: geen voorjaarsmoeheid
       De onderneming zet haar structurele aanpassingen onverminderd
       voort

       BASF: no spring fatigue
       The company continues its structural adjustments without
       abatement

In addition, self-reference is of course also realized through third-person
pro-forms (see also (6), (7) and (8) above):

(9)   (Bekaert, Kortrijk: 25 March 1994)
        N.V. BEKAERT S.A. BEEINDIGT ZIJN SAMENWERKINGSAK-
        KOORD MET BRIDGESTONE CORPORATION

        N.V. BEKAERT S.A. TERMINATES ITS CO-OPERATION
        AGREEMENT WITH BRIDGESTONE CORPORATION

(10)   (ATAB, Antwerp: 30 March 1994)
        Als eerste in zijn sektor en gelijktijdig voor zijn drie operationele
        afdelingen behaalde ATAB driemaal ISO 9002 (...).

        As the first in its sector and simultaneously for its three opera-
        tional divisions ATAB obtained ISO 9002 three times (...).[7]

Here, not surprisingly, like in newspapers (Jucker 1996), the more explicit
reference forms, especially proper names, precede the less explicit ones,
including pro-forms.

Another interesting feature of self-reference in press releases is the use
of impersonal 'one':

(11)   (ASQ, Houthalen: 23 February 1994)
        Het softwarehuis ASQ maakt het zichzelf eerlijk gezegd niet
        gemakkelijk in zijn streven naar topkwaliteit. Heel wat energie
        gaat naar het selekteren van de beste produkten en de betrouw-
        baarste partners, zodat men de klanten een optimale service kan
        garanderen.

        Honestly, the software house ASQ is not making things easy for
        itself in its striving for top quality. A lot of energy is geared
        towards selecting the best products and the most reliable
        partners, so that one can guarantee an optimal service to the
        customers.

(12)   (Stork, Sint-Niklaas: 28 March 1994)
        Het nettoresultaat van het Stork-concern over het boekjaar 1993
        bedraagt 1,024 miljard BEF, dit betekent een stijging van 103
        miljoen BEF of 11% ten overstaan van 1992. (...)

Gedurende 1993 kende men een stijging van de orderontvangsten
met 4,8 miljard BEF (=7,5%) ten opzichte van 1992 (...).

The net result of the Stork concern over the financial year 1993
amounts to 1.024 billion BEF, which means a rise of 103
million BEF or 11% compared with 1992. (...)
During 1993 one knew a rise of the receipt of orders of 4.8
billion BEF (=7.5%) compared with 1992 (...).[8]

Alternatively, there is the use of passive or passive-like constructions,
rendering any explicit self-reference altogether unnecessary.

(13)   (CMB: 6 February 1995)
        De geconsolideerde winst over het boekjaar 1994 wordt geraamd
        op 1050 miljoen BEF, tegenover 571 miljoen BEF in 1993.

        The consolidated profit for the financial year 1994 is estimated
        at 1,050 million BEF, compared with 571 million BEF in 1993.

(14)   (Kredietbank, Brussels: 15 November 1994)
        De voorkeur van de Kredietbank voor Taiwan als vestigings-
        plaats voor een nieuwe branch is vooral het resultaat van de
        positieve ervaring die in zeer korte tijd werd opgedaan met (...).

        The preference of the Kredietbank for Taiwan as the location for
        a new branch is mainly the result of the positive experience that
        was gained in a very short time with (...).

(15)   (Electrabel, Brussels: 15 December 1994)
        Noodplanoefening in Kerncentrale Doel is gestart

        Emergency exercise at Nuclear Power Station Doel has started

(16)   (Citibank, Brussels: April 1994)
        Famibank-agenten worden geïntegreerd in Citibank-netwerk
        Citibank Belgium: van 58 tot 316 verkooppunten

        Famibank agents are integrated into Citibank network Citibank
        Belgium: from 58 to 316 points of sale

(17)   (Exxon, Houston, Texas: 30 March 1989)
       The clean-up continued as two more airborne sprays of
       COREXIT dispersant were conducted, with other aerial sprays
       planned for Wednesday. Poor weather had prevented the
       application of dispersants on Monday.

(18)   (BBL, Brussels: 27 April 1995)
       BBL TRAVEL: 1995 kondigt zich veelbelovend aan.

       BBL TRAVEL: 1995 looks very promising.

Also note the following nominalizations:

(19)   (Recticel, Brussels: 11 March 1994)
       TERUGKEER NAAR WINST IN EEN MOEILIJKE ECONO-
       MISCHE CONTEXT

       RETURN TO PROFIT IN A DIFFICULT ECONOMIC
       CONTEXT

(20)   (Electrabel, Brussels: 7 December 1994)
       AANKONDIGING NOODPLANOEFENING DOEL 1994

       ANNOUNCEMENT EMERGENCY EXERCISE DOEL 1994

(21)   (ibens, Antwerp: 21 March 1994)
       Oprichting dochterbedrijven in Hongarije en Polen
       JUBILERENDE AANNEMINGEN J&E iBENS OP DE OOSTEU-
       ROPESE MARKT

       Foundation of subsidiaries in Hungary and Poland
       JUBILEE CONTRACTORS J&E iBENS ON THE EASTERN
       EUROPEAN MARKET

(22)   (Kredietbank, Brussels: 31 January 1995)
       De afsluiting van dit kaderakkoord speelt in op de internationali-
       sering van de Zuidafrikaanse economie en draagt tevens bij tot
       de bevordering van de Belgische export naar Zuid-Afrika.

The conclusion of the frame agreement anticipates the internationalization of the South African economy and also contributes to the promotion of the Belgian export to South Africa.

A final and even more drastic way of avoiding self-reference is to formulate the news in such a way that the autobiographical nature of the press release remains as much hidden from view as possible: in a number of press releases from the corpus the German chemical multinational Bayer, for example, is parading its new products; but instead of emphasizing the company's central role as a manufacturer and supplier, as most press releases do (e.g. extracts (1) to (5) in this chapter), it is the customer's use of the product that is put in the limelight. This is the first paragraph from Bayer's press release about its new Bayblend® T 85 MN product:

(23)   (Bayer, Antwerp: 29 September 1994)
       Mobiele telefoons zijn in: deze minitelefoons zijn nauwelijks groter dan een briletui, maar je kan ermee bellen naar om het even waar in Europa. Een van de nieuwste ontwikkelingen op de innovatieve markt is de "Teleport 9020" van AEG Mobile Communication GmbH in Ulm (Duitsland). Om aan de eisen van de gebruikers m.b.t. de stevigheid van de toestelletjes te voldoen, bestaan beide behuizingshelften van het nieuwe produkt uit Bayblend® 85 MN, een PC+ABS-blend van Bayer AG.

       Mobile telephones are in: these mini telephones are hardly bigger than a spectacle case, but you can use them to call anywhere in Europe. One of the latest developments on the innovative market is the "Teleport 9020" from AEG Mobile Communication GmbH in Ulm (Germany). To meet the users' demands about the firmness of the devices, both outer halves of the new product are made of Bayblend® T 85 MN, a PC+ABS blend from Bayer AG.

From this paragraph, it looks as if the press release is about mobile phones, and in particular about one of another company's, viz. AEG's, new models. Unsuspecting readers might even be led to assume that the press release was issued by AEG. Only at the end of this paragraph does it become clear that the press release is meant to focus on one of Bayer's products that goes into mobile phones. The next paragraph provides a short description of the Bayer product. The third and final paragraph, however, is again completely devoted to AEG's mobile phones:

(24)   (Bayer, Antwerp: 29 September 1994)
       De handige telefoon met een vermogen van 2 Watt meet 166 bij 57 bij 20 mm en functioneert met de "grote" standaardtelefoonkaart (SIM). Het toestel weegt slechts 140 g en de batterij afhankelijk van het type weegt ± 110 g: dat is goed voor 20 uur standby en 1 uur spreektijd.

       The handy telephone with a power of 2 Watt measures 166 by 57 by 20 mm and operates with the "big" standard telephone card (SIM). The device weighs only 140 g and the battery weighs ± 110 g, depending on the type: this guarantees 20 hours of standby and 1 hour of speaking time.

The following is the start of a similar three-paragraph press release issued by the same organization:

(25)   (Bayer, Antwerp: 16 September 1994)
       De passagiers op het perron van Zürich keken verbaasd op: de Intercity naar Genève die net binnenliep, werd - zo leek het - voortgetrokken door een reusachtig grote Agfa-filmdoos. Verklaring? De Zwitserse spoorwegen gebruiken een aantal van hun locomotieven en wagons als rijdende reclamedragers. Zo werd ook de 8300 PK sterke Intercity-locomotief "Dübendorf II" met een 2K-PUR-waterlaksysteem omgetoverd in een hoogglanzende filmverpakking met Agfa-logo.

       The passengers on the platform at Zürich looked up in amazement: it appeared as if the Intercity to Geneva which was just coming in was towed by a gigantically big Agfa film box. Explanation? The Swiss railways are using a number of locomotives and wagons as rolling carriers of advertising. That's why the 8300-HP-strong Intercity locomotive "Dübendorf II" was turned into a high gloss film package with an AGFA logo by means of a 2K-PUR water dye system.

Just like with the previous example, Bayer's product is absent from most of this first paragraph and it is only in the second paragraph that the reader gets the product information that the press release is meant to publicize in the first place. Typically, the press release concludes:

(26)   (Bayer, Antwerp: 16 September 1994)
De locomotief zal rijden op de belangrijkste Intercity-lijn in Zwitserland: van St.-Gallen over Zürich naar Genève. Fervente treinreizigers foto-amateurs zullen dus volop de gelegenheid krijgen om hem te fotograferen.

The locomotive will ride on the main Intercity line in Switzerland: from St Gallen over Zürich to Geneva. So passionate train passengers amateur photographers will get ample opportunity to take pictures of it.

(27), finally, is from another organization:

(27)   (Brook Hansen, Vilvoorde: 26 September 1994)
De watermolen van Rotselaar is sinds de 13e eeuw de spil van een woon- en werkomgeving. Toen reeds lieten de dorpelingen in de molen hun graan malen. (...)
De molen werd later als monument geklasseerd en in 1985 aangekocht door een vzw die, naast het restaureren van de molen en het creëren van vier woningen, er ook zal voor zorgen dat de maalderij terug in werking wordt gesteld en de turbine voor de nodige electriciteit zal zorgen.
Voor dit renovatieproject leverde Brook Hansen België onlangs een tandwielkast van de nieuwe generatie "Hansen P4".

The water mill of Rotselaar has been the centre of a living and working environment since the 13th century. Then already the villagers had their grain milled at the mill. (...)

The mill was later classified as a monument and in 1985 it was
bought by a non-profit organization which, apart from restoring
the mill and creating four houses, will also make sure that the
milling house is operated again and that the turbine will provide
the necessary electricity. For this renovation project Brook
Hansen Belgium recently supplied a gear cupboard from the new
generation "Hansen P4".

In all these cases, self-reference is significantly delayed and substantially
restricted. While these last few examples, strictly speaking, fall outside the
scope of my analysis of producer roles, I think that they deserve to be
mentioned here because they constitute the most radical departure from standard self-reference and I shall have to come back to them later when I try to
account for the special patterns of self-reference typical of the press releases
in my corpus.

2.2 *Referential switch*

Taken together, the wide range of examples quoted above shows that writers
of press releases make every effort to avoid self-reference through the first
person. The few first-person pronouns that I have found in my corpus are
marked forms.[9] Almost all occurrences are of the plural 'we', which has
been shown to be popular as a solidarity-builder in other types of institutional writing (e.g. Rogers and Swales 1990, Sacks 1992b: 391, Lerner
1993, Swales and Rogers 1995, Schegloff 1996). In my corpus compare one
bank's announcement of a rise in interest rates:

(28)   (Argenta, Antwerp: 22 September 1994)
        *De marktsituatie is voor ons aanleiding tot het aanpassen van
        onze hypotheektarieven.*

        The market situation is an occasion for us to adjust our mortgage
        rates.

with the announcements of two other banks:

(29)   (BBL, Brussels: 6 April 1995)
De BBL zal vanaf vandaag de kasbonrente op 3 en 5 jaar even-
als de achtergestelde BBL-certificaten op 6 en 8 jaar aanpassen.

From today the BBL will adjust the bond interest rate for 3 and
5 years as well as the subordinated BBL certificates for 6 and 8
years.

(30)   (Generale Bank, Brussels: 13 September 1994)
Wegens de evolutie van de rente op de obligatiemarkten, past de
Generale Bank haar rentetarieven voor kasbons aan vanaf
vrijdag 16 september 1994.

Due to the evolution of the interest on the share market, the
Generale Bank will adjust its interest rates for bonds starting 16
September 1994.

In a small number of cases first-person and third-person self-reference have
- rather awkwardly - been combined:

(31)   (Christelijke Vakbond van Communicatiemiddelen en Cultuur/
ACOD, Brussels: 8 March 1994)
Indien dat werkelijk het geval is, zal het GEMEENSCHAPPE-
LIJK VAKBONDSFRONT uiteraard onmiddellijk reageren. We
zullen ons verzetten tegen maatregelen die verder zouden gaan
dan wat in het ONDERNEMINGSPLAN voorzien is, en 2000 tot
3000 banen zouden kosten.

If this is really the case, the JOINT TRADE UNION FRONT
will of course react immediately. We will oppose measures that
would go further than what is anticipated in the BUSINESS
PLAN, and would cost 2,000 to 3,000 jobs.

In two consecutive sentences the organization that issued the press release is
first referred to in the third person and then in the first person. Here are
two more examples of such a frame break or, what Thompson and Thetela
(1995) call, a 'referential switch':

(32) (Ter Beke, Waarschoot: 28 March 1994)
Aansluitend op dit kwaliteitsbeleid besliste Ter Beke haar ganse
operationele organisatie verder te systematiseren (...).
Ter Beke beschouwt het ISO-certifikaat niet als een finaliteit
maar als de start van een vernieuwde kwaliteitsaanpak met een
blijvende en aanhoudende uitdaging steeds weer aan deze strenge
eisen te voldoen met als doel, door onze klanten beschouwd te
worden als een leidende en betrouwbare kwaliteitsleverancier.

In line with this quality policy Ter Beke has decided to further
systematize its complete operational organization (...).
Ter Beke considers the ISO certificate not as a finality but as the
start for an innovating quality approach with a permanent and
continuing challenge to always meet these stringent demands
with the aim of being considered by our customers as a leading
and reliable quality supplier.

(33) (GB, Brussels: 26 April 1995)
GB RAADPLEEGT VERSCHILLENDE AGENTSCHAPPEN
VOOR DE COMMUNICATIE VAN DE GB PRODUKTEN
GB heeft beslist 3 agentschappen te raadplegen (Gabarsky
EURO RSCG, TWBA, LHHS) omtrent de communicatie van de
produkten eigen merk GB. (...)
Gabarsky Euro RSCG is en zal ons adviserend agentschap
blijven en blijft als dusdanig ons vertrouwen behouden.

GB CONSULTS SEVERAL AGENCIES FOR THE COM-
MUNICATION OF THE GB PRODUCTS
GB has decided to consult 3 agencies (Gabarsky EURO RSCG,
TWBA, LHHS) about the communication of the products of its
own brand GB. (...)
Gabarsky Euro RSCG is and will remain our advisory agency
and continues to have our confidence.

It is not easy to decide if such referential switches result from a mere slip-
up or if they should be considered a strategic device. John Wilson has a fine
example from one of Margaret Thatcher's pre-scripted speeches, in which

three different forms of self-reference - none of which is the standard first person singular (!) - are combined in a single sentence:

> Indeed if one wants enough resources to do everything we wish to do you have to be resolute about other matters too (1990: 64).

Wilson argues that if this is from a prescripted speech, it is extremely doubtful that it is a production error and he therefore concludes that Thatcher is consciously performing a juggling trick here. Similarly, Thompson and Thetela (1995) provide an example from advertising, another type of discourse which - like press releases - tends to be cautiously formulated:

> You see Bosch believe not just in building a better machine technically speaking, we insist it's easy on the eye too (118).

Lerman, on the other hand, draws attention to cases of shifting self-reference in Richard Nixon's Watergate rhetoric and argues that "[i]n a time of crisis, when a system is disordered, the constitutive rules of the language game are more apparent":

> I want there to be no question remaining about the fact that the President has nothing to hide in this matter (1983: 83).

She seems to suggest that the President's repeated referential switches were the result of slip-ups caused by the stress of the situation. Hence, Lerman argues, a closer look at them should illuminate the use of third-person self-reference in more controlled contexts.

It is not clear whether the referential switches in my corpus constitute production errors or not.[10] Certainly, it can be concluded at this stage that the third-person forms are to be taken as having first-person reference.

2.3 More data

I have shown that there is a wide variety of options for self-reference in press releases. I would now like to show that, combined with some of the special forms of reference to the readers h_1 and h_2 described in the previous chapter, this may lead to rather disorienting discourse, as in:

(34) (Ericsson, Brussels: 16 March 1994)

De nieuwe generatie mobiele telefoons van ERICSSON heeft een nieuwe gebruikersinterface met een toetsenbord dat er anders uitziet dan de telefoons waaraan we gewend zijn.

De ontwikkelde techniek is bedoeld om de telefoon gebruiksvriendelijker te maken. Met pijltjestoetsen kiest men via een menu de gewenste functie. Op die manier komt men tegemoet aan de wensen van een nieuwe gebruikersgroep en is de telefoon ook geschikt voor datacommunicatie.

Met bijvoorbeeld een laptop computer en printer zal men kunnen communiceren met andere computers of faxapparaten.

ERICSSON's new generation of mobile telephones has a new user interface with a keyboard that looks different from that of the telephones we are used to. The developed technique is meant to make the telephone more user-friendly. With arrow buttons one chooses the desired function via a menu. That way one meets the requirements of a new group of users and the telephone is also suitable for data communication. With, for example, a laptop computer and a printer one will be able to communicate with other printers and fax machines.

The organization that issued the press release is first identified as Ericsson. In the same sentence 'we' does not refer to Ericsson, but to the general public, or at least those readers and potential customers (h_2) who are familiar with mobile phones. Subsequently, a passive is used, rendering any form of explicit self-reference unnecessary, followed by a double use of the impersonal pronoun: first to refer to the readers and potential customers that were previously referred to as 'we' (h_2); then to refer to Ericsson, the organization that issued the press release. In the next sentence, the impersonal pronoun again refers to h_2. Further on in the same press release, the same h_2 is, rather awkwardly, referred to by means of a passive:

(35)   (Ericsson, Brussels: 16 March 1994)
Met de GH 337 zal voor het eerst van naderbij kennis kunnen worden gemaakt op de vakbeurs CEBIT van 16 tot 23 maart.

The GH 337 will be launched on the CEBIT trade fair from 16 to 23 March.

It should by now be clear that self-reference in press releases - just like reference to the receivers - is worth close attention. I would argue that the various forms of third-person self-reference can even be seen as a generic, a constitutive feature of press releases: indeed, any alternative patterns, including the presence of a first-person pronoun, may lead the journalist as well as the analyst to conclude that here is no press release, but another type of related discourse.[11] The following two extracts, for example, are taken from press releases which serve to advertise a new range of heaters:

(36)   (Jaga: November 1994)
Terloops wil ik toch even vermelden dat alle radiatoren milieu-vriendelijk worden gelakt, zonder gebruik van solventen.

Incidentally, I would like to mention that all radiators are dyed in an environment-friendly way, without use of solvents.

(37)   (Jaga: December 1994)
Rest mij nog te vertellen dat de kourante modellen altijd in voorraad leverbaar zijn.

It only remains for me to say that the current models can always be supplied from stock.

In terms of self-reference these extracts are very different from the examples quoted earlier on in this chapter and I would say that they look more like extracts from sales letters or even like transcripts of commercials on radio or TV.

Similarly, the following extract from a (signed) press release issued by a local politician has more in common with a personal letter, or, since it was sent to the media, with a 'letter to the editor' of a newspaper:

(38)   (Patsy Sörensen, Antwerp: 18 September 1994)
Ik wens met klem te protesteren tegen de manier waarop mijn naam misbruikt werd.

I would like to strongly protest against the way in which my name was abused.[12]

2.4 Research question

The question now is: why such complex self-reference? Why, basically, such 'slippage', in which the grammatical category of person (viz. the third-person form) does not match the interactional participant role (viz. that of writer of the press release)? And also: why this use of a proper name ('Exxon' or 'Ericsson') and of definite description ('het bedrijf', [the company]), which clashes with the pre-emptive nature of a pure deictic word like 'we'; after all, as Levinson argues, "it takes special conventions to make it appropriate for a speaker to refer to himself by name" (1983: 75).

In asking some of these questions, I am not the first to draw attention to the interest of deictic reference to the analysis of functionally specialized discourse. Levinson (1988) suggests that "the potential vagueness of the participant role associated with the institutional role is of course an exploitable resource" (203). Similarly, Thomas (1989) distinguishes between social roles (in this case PR officer for an organization, for example, vs. journalist) and discourse roles (writer vs. reader) and concludes that the crossroads of the two is "an area of pragmatic indeterminacy which interactants exploit in discourse" (330). Zupnik (1994) looks at what she calls the speaker's or writer's "ability to shift in and out of various roles" (342) and sees it as a resource for persuasion (cf. also De Fina 1995).

Most research so far has focused on the strategic use of personal pronouns: Brown and Gilman (1960) is a classic work in this respect; subsequent research has dealt, among other topics, with the use of 'he' as the unmarked form (Cameron 1985) and with solidarity-building 'we' (Rounds 1987 on teaching settings; Myers 1989 on scientific articles; Fairclough 1989, Wilson 1990, Zupnik 1994 on political language, Rogers and Swales 1990, Swales and Rogers 1995 on business language). Goffman (1974), Lerman (1983, 1985) and Wilson (1990), to name only some ventures into the domain, have looked at third-person self-reference. In the next section I would like to briefly argue that, even earlier, the French scholar Emile Benveniste, dealing with the narrative style of history textbooks, touched on the research question at the heart of my analysis of third-person self-reference in press releases.

2.5 Benveniste's "discours indirect"

Here is Benveniste's definition of 'histoire' from his *Problèmes de Linguistique Générale*:

> *Nous définirons le récit historique comme le mode d'énonciation qui exclut toute forme linguistique "autobiographique". L'historien ne dira jamais je ni tu, ni ici, ni maintenant (...). On ne constatera donc dans le récit historique strictement poursuivi que des formes de "3e personne"* (1966: 239).
>
> We shall define the historic narrative as a mode of utterance that excludes all "autobiographical" linguistic forms. The historian will never say I, you, here or now (...). One will therefore only find "third-person" forms in a strict historic narrative.

Benveniste's 'histoire' can be considered equivalent to Halliday's 'co-textually anchored' discourse (cf. Brown and Yule 1983), in which there is no reference whatsoever to the speaker and which can be found, for example, in fairy tales. Here is an illustration from Adamson (1995):

> Once upon a time, in a far distant country, there lived a king and the king had a daughter, who was famed for her beauty. One day, while she was walking in the garden in front of her father's palace, she met an old woman whom she had never seen there before ...

As far as press releases are concerned, I have shown that first-person pronouns prove very rare in my corpus and I shall demonstrate later in this chapter that the same is true of words like 'here' and 'now'. As a result, press releases look very much like 'histoire'.

At the same time, though, there can be no doubt that the third-person forms of press releases have first-person reference and it follows that, even if they share some of the reference forms of history textbooks and fairy tales, press releases really are a type of autobiographical discourse, which seems to be closer to Benveniste's notion of 'discours', viz.:

> *toute énonciation supposant un locuteur et un auditeur, et chez le premier l'intention d'influencer l'autre en quelque manière* (242).
> each utterance that presupposes a sender and a receiver and with the former the intention to influence the other in some way or another.

Benveniste's 'discours' can be considered equivalent to Halliday's 'contextually anchored' discourse. Here is a typical example from a nature film, with words like 'we', 'here' and 'now' putting the speaker in the centre of attention:

> We're walking towards the head of the glen and we should soon catch our first glimpse of the eagle's nest. Yes, there it is, up in front ... One of the parent birds has already arrived ... and here's the other one coming in now. Oops! they've seen us ... (Adamson 1995)

Again this is no perfect fit, though. Clearly, I have shown that, in terms of reference, press releases are very different from the example quoted above[13] and it now seems as if they can be situated midway between Benveniste's 'histoire' and 'discours'.[14] Although they look like 'histoire', they share the egocentric perspective of 'discours'; in a way, they are 'discours' disguised as 'histoire'. Interestingly, and this is the reason why I turned to *Problèmes de Linguistique Générale* in the first place, Benveniste seems to take the possibility of such a mixture into account when he introduces a third type called 'discours indirect':

> *Indiquons par parenthèse que l'énonciation historique et celle de discours peuvent à l'occasion se conjoindre en un troisième type d'énonciation, où le discours est rapporté en termes d'événement et transposé sur le plan historique; c'est ce qui est communément appelé 'discours indirect'* (242).
> Let's indicate incidentally that the historic utterance and the discursive one may combine in a third type of utterance, in which the discourse is reported in terms of an event and transposed to the historic level; this is what is commonly called 'indirect discourse'.

Unfortunately, 'discours indirect' is no more than a footnote in Benveniste's theory and he does not add a single word on the topic.

2.6 Point of view operations

Returning to my research question, I would now like to suggest that - in line with Levinson's (1988) and Thomas's (1989) remarks quoted earlier about the strategic use of deixis - the various forms of third-person self-reference in my corpus can only be correctly interpreted if the peculiar audience-directedness of press releases is taken into account. In particular, I shall argue that they help to 'take the other fellow's point of view' (Fillmore 1975: 44), i.e. through third-person self-reference writers of press releases switch out of their own perspective and move some way to that of the journalists, who are expected to retell the press release in their own news reporting. In other words, third-person self-reference is part of what Brown and Levinson (1987) call a 'point of view operation'. Here is a simple example of a point of view operation from everyday oral interaction:

> Mother talking to father, in the presence of little Billie: Can Billie have an ice-cream, Daddy? (Levinson 1983: 82)

In this extract the speaker addresses her husband as 'daddy' and, in doing so, she seems to adopt the language of the overhearing child.

I shall now argue that point of view operations play a double 'preformulating' role in my corpus. First of all, by anticipating the journalists' typical reference forms, they help writers of press releases meet the formal requirements of news reporting. This is what I called preformulation$_i$ in the previous chapter. Next, I shall demonstrate that preformulation is not just a question of meeting the formal requirements of news reporting. As I argued before, it was Gandy (1982) who suggested that "content" too may be structured in such a way as to flow in sync with the media system's requirements" in order to have "a greater probability of gaining entry into the public-information environment" (57). Hence, there is a second way in which third-person self-reference may serve a preformulating purpose, viz. by making press releases look more objective. This is preformulation$_{ii}$.

3. Meeting the Formal Requirements of News Reporting (Preformulation$_i$)

3.1 Person deixis

That third-person self-reference allows a speaker or writer to switch out of his or her own perspective was already noted by Goffman (1974), who suggests that first-person pronouns usually refer to the speaker or writer from his or her own point of view, while third-person self-reference seems to suggest hearer- or reader-directedness. The following are Goffman's examples of a departure from the normal, unmarked deictic centre in the speaker or writer:

> This unworthy barbarian would like three gallons of gas.
> The author ...
> Your reporter ... (519)

The same reader-directedness can be found in press releases, but this time in its most concrete form since it allows the reader, i.c. the journalist, to simply copy the press releases. In this chapter I have already provided ample corpus-based evidence from person deixis. Therefore let's now briefly examine if references to time and place in my data work in the same direction.

3.2 Time deixis

Time first of all. (39) is a typical example:

> (39) (Union Minière, Brussels: 23 February 1995)
> *De Raad van bestuur van Union Minière heeft op donderdag 23 februari het geconsolideerd Groepsresultaat onderzocht op basis van de beschikbare elementen.*
>
> On Thursday 23 February the Board of Directors of Union Minière examined the consolidated Group result on the basis of the elements available.

Clearly, the press release is not just deictically neutral as far as self-reference to Union Minière is concerned, but also in terms of time. The normal form would have been "Today the Board of Directors examined ..." Just like the use of the proper name ('Union Minière' instead of 'we'), the use of the date (Thursday 23 February instead of 'today') clashes with the pre-emptive nature of pure deictic words. As Levinson says, "it would be strange to say *Do it at 10.36* instead of *Do it now*, when now is 10.36" (1983: 75). Still this is what actually happens in (39) and in most other press releases in my corpus.

It should be noted that there are a number of exceptions, where no point of view operations have taken place, like the mixed forms in:

> (40)   (GB, Evere: 20 September 1994)
> *Vandaag dinsdag 20 september om 20.00 uur wordt de nieuwe Maxi GB van Kortrijk-Kuurne ingehuldigd.*
>
> Today Tuesday 20 September at 20.00 h, the new Maxi GB at Kortrijk-Kuurne will be inaugurated.

> (41)   (Kredietbank, Brussels: 22 November 1994)
> *Vorige zaterdag, 19 november 1994, had in Brussel de officiële ondertekening plaats van een kaderakkoord tussen de Kredietbank en de State Export-Import Bank of the Republic of Kazakhstan.*
>
> Last Saturday, 19 November 1994, the official signing of a frame agreement between the Kredietbank and the State Export-Import Bank of the Republic of Kazakhstan took place in Brussels.

Or even:

> (42)   (Union Minière, Brussels: 27 October 1995)
> *De Directie van Union Minière heeft deze vrijdag aan de ondernemingsraden van de Groep haar nieuw industrieel plan toegelicht.*

This Friday the Direction of Union Minière explained its new industrial plan to the Group's works councils.

(43)   (BBL, Brussels: 30 March 1995)
Vanmorgen omstreeks 8.30 uur hebben twee gemaskerde en gewapende overvallers zich toegang verschaft tot het BBL-kantoor in de Kerkstraat 7 te Londerzeel.

This morning around 8.30 hours two masked and armed attackers gained access to the BBL office in the Kerkstraat 7 in Londerzeel.

(44)   (Exxon, New York: 30 June 1989)
EXXON NOW HAS 10,000 WORKERS AT OIL SPILL AS CLEANUP COSTS EXCEED $ 200 MILLION
(…) To date, Exxon has paid claims totalling more than $ 19 million (…).

I would argue that one reason why the point of view operation is overruled in these cases, i.e. why 'today' and 'now' are used instead of 'on 30 March 1995' etc., may have to do with what Sacks (1992b: 171-172) analyzes as the preference for "today" rather than "Thursday", or "January 12 1962" (Sacks's example!) in telling the news. He suggests that situating an event 'today' is not simply "naming some day on which the reported event happened; it's doing a bunch of other things. For one, 'today' is not equivalent to the series of other days in the sense of being just some day. 'Today' in part constitutes the warrant for the report, i.e., to say it happened 'today' is to claim it as potential '*news*'" (172) . This would mean that in some of the above examples from the corpus point of view operations are subordinated to the requirements of newsworthiness.

3.3 Place deixis

Finally, press releases also tend to be deictically neutral as far as reference to place is concerned. Here are two typical examples:

(45)   (Puma, Herzogenaurach: 25 April 1994)
        Aanvankelijk werd voor 1994 een consolidatie vooropgesteld,
        maar gezien de positieve resultaten tijdens het eerste kwartaal
        verwacht men in Herzogenaurach dit jaar al met winst te kunnen
        afsluiten.

        Initially a consolidation was foreseen for 1994, but in view of
        the positive results during the first quarter in Herzogenaurach
        one expects to be able to close this year with a profit.

(41)   (Kredietbank, Brussels: 22 November 1994)
        Vorige zaterdag, 19 november 1994, had in Brussel de officiële
        ondertekening plaats van een kaderakkoord tussen de Krediet-
        bank en de State Export-Import Bank of the Republic of
        Kazakhstan.

        Last Saturday, 19 November 1994, the official signing of a
        frame agreement between the Kredietbank and the State Export-
        Import Bank of the Republic of Kazakhstan took place in
        Brussels.

Words like 'here' and 'there' are very rare indeed in my corpus of press
releases. The following references (to the location of the Alaska oil spill)
are notable exceptions:

(46)   (Exxon, Valdez, Alaska: 13 April 1989)
        Exxon has opened an expanded facility for sea mammal rescue
        operations here.

(47)   (Exxon, Valdez Alaska: 29 May 1996)
        With more than 8,500 people now involved in the cleanup here,
        Exxon reported 64 miles of shoreline treated thus far in its
        continuing operations in Prince William Sound.

3.4 Preformulation*ᵢ*

It is not difficult to see how such point of view operations serve a preformulating$_i$ purpose: they help writers of press releases meet the formal requirements of news reporting. Items like 'I', 'you', 'here' and 'now' are 'shifters' (cf. Jakobson 1971, Silverstein 1976): i.e. they constantly change in reference, depending on who is speaking or writing. The use of 'I' or 'we' in a press release, for example, would refer to the organization that issued it; if it was copied in a newspaper article, its reference would automatically shift to the journalist.[15] Alternatively, third-person self-reference helps keep the reference constant: the proper name 'Exxon' refers to that organization, whoever it is used by; in the act of retelling it is only the writer who shifts, and not the reference. It follows that, through third-person self-reference, writers of press releases seem to anticipate the typical reference forms of news reporting and that, in doing so, they allow journalists to simply copy the press releases.[16]

That third-person self-reference plays such a preformulating$_i$ role seems to be indirectly confirmed by the following extract, in which self-reference is, uncharacteristically, realized in the first person:

(48)   (Electrabel, Brussels: 15 December 1994)
        Zoals aangekondigd in ons eerste persbericht melden we nu dat de noodplanoefening in Kerncentrale Doel beëindigd is.

        As pointed out in our first press release we now announce that the emergency exercise at the Nuclear Power Station Doel has been terminated.

Here, from the nature of the information contained in the extract, it can be safely derived that the press release was not meant to be retold in the media. Therefore, no preformulation through third-person self-reference was required.

It is now also clear why in (49), for example, the proper name 'Exxon' is repeated several times where normally we could have expected other forms of (third-person) self-reference, including pro-forms or definite description.

(49)   (Exxon, Valdez, Alaska: 9 June 1989)
EXXON FUNDS EAGLE RESCUE TEAMS
Exxon, in conjunction with the United States Fish & Wildlife
service (USFWS), has established an eagle capture program
designed to locate and retrieve bald eagles and other raptors
(birds of prey) affected by the oil spill.
Under guidelines set forth by the USFWS, the Exxon-funded
program places two teams of trained raptor specialists in the
field for active search and rescue operations. Six experienced
raptor experts were selected by the USFWS and hired by Exxon.

I would argue that, apart from making sure that the reader cannot lose sight
of the identity of the institutional sender (cf. Thompson and Thetela 1995:
118, 126 on advertising),[17] this repeated use of the proper name - or what
Wales (1996) calls 'over-topicalization' (33) - plays a preformulating role.
At first sight, such explicitness, like the use of corporate profiles discussed
in chapter 1, appears to involve redundancy, flouting Grice's quantity
maxim stipulating economy of expression. In view of the peculiar audience-
directedness of press releases, however, it is clear that the repetition of
'Exxon' in (49) serves a purpose of enhanced accessibility: i.e. it contributes to the ease with which journalists may retell extracts from the larger
press release; in fact, they can pick any sentence and use it verbatim in their
own reporting.[18] Interestingly, Sanford, Moar and Garrod (1988) show that
proper names increase referential availability: i.e. they play a major role in
focus control since it means that the person or party under discussion is
more likely to be used in continuations. As Downing argues about oral
interaction, proper names "[guarantee] that current non-speakers will have
maximum access to the implications of the current speaker's talk, and thus
the maximum warrant to participate when it is their turn"; in particular,
they provide a preferred source for future reference (1996: 109, 110).

3.5 Empathetic discourse

Surely, if writers of press releases really wanted to make things easy for
journalists, they would normally be expected to go all the way and not just
switch out of their own perspective but actively encode that of the journal-

ists. This can be related to what John Lyons calls 'empathetic discourse' (1977: 677), where the deictic anchorage is relocated in the reader or hearer.[19] In this section I shall demonstrate that this actually happens in press releases, but that it is much more exceptional than the first kind of point of view operations.

3.5.1 Asserting common ground

The simplest, and at the same time the most common, form of empathetic discourse in the corpus is when the writer uses 'we' to refer to people in general (including the organization he or she represents as well as the readers h_1 and h_2) rather than for purposes of self-reference:

(50) (Solvay, Antwerp: 7 September 1994)

Dit is het bewijs dat "de Passie voor de Vooruitgang" voor Solvay een dagelijkse realiteit is, die men terugvindt in de bekommernis elke dag nog beter te doen ter voldoening van de klant, zodoende bijdragend tot de verbetering van de kwaliteit van het leven van ieder van ons.

This is evidence that "the Passion for Progress" for Solvay is a daily reality, which one sees in the concern to do still better for the customer every day, in this way contributing to an improvement of the quality of the life of each of us.

By using "ieder van ons" [each of us] the writer of the press release seems to stress his solidarity with the reader. Here are some more similar examples:

(51) (Group Van Hecke, St-Genesius-Rode: s.d.)

In minder dan vijf jaar groeide dit bedrijf in ons land door tot de top drie in de branche en bevestigde zich tevens als grootste Belgisch informatiekantoor.

In less than five years this company grew into one of the top three in this sector in our country and confirmed as the biggest Belgian information office.

(52)   (Bedevaart naar de Graven aan de IJzer, Diksmuide: 30 September 1994)
Het IJzerbedevaartkomitee verheugt zich over het voornemen van de Vlaamse regering de motor te zijn van een nieuw gesprek van volk tot volk m.b.t. onze staatshervorming.

The IJzerbedevaartkomitee is happy with the intention of the Flemish government to be the motor of a new dialogue from people to people about our state reform.

As far as time deixis is concerned, note the related use of "vandaag" [today] to refer to 'nowadays' in (53):

(53)   (Oerlikon: s.d.)
Vandaag biedt Oerlikon een extra troef (...).

Today Oerlikon offers an extra trump (...).

Finally, the Belgian Kredietbank frequently refers to itself as "de bank van hier" [the bank from here], where "hier" [here], obviously, does not only refer to the writer's specific location but also to the home country of all readers (h_1 and h_2).

I should add that, strictly speaking, the above examples are no point of view operations since it could be argued that the writer of the press release is not really switching out of his or her own perspective: writer and readers simply happen to share some categorization of identity, time or location and the writer is happy to assert this common ground.

3.5.2   Edwina Currie's talk show performance

Let me illustrate what real empathetic discourse in press releases would be. Take extract (39) again.

(39)   (Union Minière, Brussels: 23 February 1995)
De Raad van bestuur van Union Minière heeft op donderdag 23 februari het geconsolideerd Groepsresultaat onderzocht op basis van de beschikbare elementen.

> On Thursday 23 February the Board of Directors of Union
> Minière examined the consolidated Group result on the basis of
> the elements available.

I have shown that the reference to today as 'Thursday 23 February' is a
point of view operation of the first type. But since, most probably, this
news is ready to be included in the newspaper of the day after, i.e. on 24
February, the question could be raised why, instead of saying that the
decision was taken 'on 23 February', the press release does not say that the
decision was taken 'yesterday'. After all, that is what journalists would have
to write in the newspaper of 24 February anyway. Why does the writer of
the press release not go for a radical preformulation and fully encode the
journalist's perspective?

It is probably not surprising to hear that such extreme reader-
directedness proves very rare in my corpus of press releases. One simple
reason of course is that there are limits to preformulation: journalists who
get this press release faxed on 23 February and who read 'yesterday' might
actually be led to think that the decision was taken on 22 February.

Still, there are exceptions, where true empathetic discourse is at work
in press releases:

(54)   (London Weekend Television, London: 19 June 1987)
         Outspoken Junior Health Minister Edwina Currie has suggested
         that Margaret and Dennis Thatcher's courtship might have taken
         place on the floor of her Oxford University room ...
         Speaking on LWT's *The Late Clive James* show tonight (Satur-
         day, 20 June 1987) at 10.30 pm, Mrs Currie - who went to
         Oxford after the Prime Minister - says that when she and Mrs
         Thatcher were at Oxford, few other women studied there, and
         house rules were very strict.[20]

This press release was issued on 19 June. The TV show that it talks about
was probably recorded some time before that. Still, 'tonight' does not refer
to that moment of recording or to 19 June. As is spelled out between
brackets, it refers to the day of broadcasting, viz. 20 June. So what, from
the point of view of the writer, is 'tomorrow night' is actually referred to as

'tonight'. I would suggest that here is a point of view operation of the second type: the writer of the press release takes the perspective of the journalists, who will write about Edwina Currie's TV performance in the newspapers of the day of the broadcasting, i.e. 20 June. Note that this is actually a mixed form since, to avoid the kind of confusion I referred to above, 'tonight' is further identified as '20 June'.

Significantly, this special time reference is not the only example of empathetic discourse in (54). The press release opens with a typically tabloid newspaper reference to "outspoken Junior Health minister Edwina Currie".[21] This proved a very effective preformulation because both the *Daily Mail* and *Daily Mirror* reports of 20 June included those very same words. I shall briefly come back to this type of stylistic preformulation later on in this chapter.

3.5.3   Bekaert's embargo

Another, related, example of preformulation, in my corpus of press releases can be found in the following brand of financial reporting:

(55)   (Bekaert, Kortrijk: 16 March 1995; embargo until 16.45 h.)
RECORDWINST IN 1994 VOOR BEKAERT
De Bekaertgroep maakte vandaag op een persconferentie te Brussel haar resultaten bekend voor het boekjaar 1994.
(...)
Bij de voorstelling van de resultaten op de persconferentie gaf Baron Velge, Voorzitter van de Raad van Bestuur, volgende commentaren. (...)

RECORD PROFIT IN 1994 FOR BEKAERT
The Bekaert group announced its results for the financial year 1994 at a press conference in Brussels today. (...)
At the presentation of the results at the press conference Baron Velge, Chairman of the Board of Directors, gave the following comments. (...)

Here the embargo, requesting the media not to publicize the news before 16.45 h. on the same day, indicates that the press release was almost certainly issued to journalists before the start of the press conference that is referred to in the press release. Hence we could have expected

Bekaert will announce this afternoon ...

and

Baron Velge will give the following comments ...

Instead, (55) has a reference to the past, which, I would suggest, serves to anticipate the point of view of the journalist who will use the press release in writing up an article some time after the press conference.

This case provides counterevidence to the traditional assumption that the assignment of tense, as Robin Lakoff puts it, simply depends on "the time at which the act described occurred or is expected to occur, relative to the time of utterance" (1970: 838). Lakoff is aware that there may be one or two exceptions to this rule. She draws attention to the use of the historical present and of the epistolary past tense in Latin, as in Cicero's

Neque tamen, haec cum scribebam, eram nescius quantis oneribus premere

But she suggests that a literal translation in English

Nor while I wrote this was I ignorant under what burdens you are weighed down

would be "ludicrous" and that only in Latin may the point of view of the writer be ignored in favour of that of the reader (847).

Fillmore (1975), however, is less stringent on this point and seems to imply that the reader's point of view may be taken into account in the choice of tense in English too. This is his common-sense argument: suppose I write you a letter before you go on holiday and I know that you will receive the letter after you return. Fillmore suggests that I have two options basically. I could write

I hope you'll have a good holiday

in which the writing time is central. As far as the choice of tense is concerned, this utterance is appropriate from the writer's point of view, but not from that of the reader who will only read the letter after he has returned from holiday. The alternative, according to Fillmore, is:

I hope you had a good holiday (84)

in which the reading time is central. This utterance is appropriate from the reader's point of view, but it requires a point of view operation on the part of the writer.

Levinson (1983) makes a similar point when he notes that in face-to-face interaction 'receiving time' can be assumed to be identical to 'coding time'; this is the assumption of deictic simultaneity and Levinson claims that it is the canonical speech situation. On the other hand, in letter-writing or in pre-recorded TV or radio programmes, Levinson argues, a decision has to be made whether the deictic centre will remain with (the writer's or speaker's) coding time, as in

This programme is being recorded today, Wednesday April 1st, to be relayed next Thursday.

or whether it will be projected onto (the reader's, viewer's or hearer's) receiving time, as in

This programme was recorded last Wednesday, April 1st, to be relayed today (74).

Clearly, in the extract from the Bekaert press release (55), the second option was chosen for. The centre is not the time when the message is being encoded by the writer but rather the time when the message is being decoded by the reader.[22]

Note that, since there are at least two sets of reader roles in press releases, the question could be raised whose decoding activity is anticipated, viz. that of the journalists (h_1) or that of the journalists' own audiences of newspaper readers (h_2)? I would like to suggest that both options are possible. In the Bekaert press release (55) the reference to 'vandaag' [today] implies that the writer of the press release is taking the position of the journalist writing up an article on the same day and not that of the newspaper readers browsing through the financial pages on the next day. For London Weekend Television's press release about Edwina Currie (54), however, it could be argued that the central time is not really that of the journalists, who will have to write the article on 19 June (i.e. the day before the TV broadcast) at the latest, but that of the newspaper readers, who will read it on 20 June (i.e. the day of the broadcast). Otherwise how can we account for the reference to 20 June as 'tonight'? I would like to suggest that what we have here is a double point of view operation, where the writer of the press release anticipates not just the journalists' (h_1) stand, but also that of the journalists' own readers (h_2). The reason is of course that the journalists, in their capacity as s', would in turn anticipate their own readers' (h_2) stand anyway.[23]

One final remark about this type of empathetic discourse. It should be noted that in my corpus, especially in headlines, there are relatively few examples of such past tense reference to an event that will take place after the press release is issued and before the journalists report about it. I would suggest that the picture is distorted, though. In (2), for example, the simple present is used to announce the naming of two ships:

(2)   (Boelwerf Vlaanderen, Temse: 24 February 1994)
       BOELWERF VLAANDEREN DOOPT 2 KOELSCHEPEN

       BOELWERF VLAANDEREN CHRISTENS TWO COOLING SHIPS[24]

It could be argued that the writer of this press release fails to switch into the point of view of those journalists who will have to write an article to be published after the naming ceremony. For such a preformulation, a past tense would have been in order, just like in (55). However, I would suggest that the present tense used by the writer of the press release does anticipate the journalists' stand: after all, newspaper headlines frequently use the simple present to refer to the past (cf. Vandenbergen 1981).

All in all, press releases seem to belong to one of those domains where there are, as Allerton (1996: 624) puts it, conventions requiring that one party's, in this case the reader h_1's, point of view should be adopted. This preliminary finding appears to be in sharp contrast with Clark and Wilkes-Gibbs's (1986) claim that, in oral interaction, speakers often bring hearers into the referential process by the very design of their utterance, but that this is very different from writing, where reference is assumed to be controlled by the writer only.[25] My analysis of third-person self-reference in press releases suggests that, as far as reference is concerned, writers and speakers are equally concerned about their readers and hearers. Indeed, since writers, unlike speakers, cannot rely on immediate feedback to check on the others' acceptance of the reference, I would suggest that, to some extent at least, writers even have to put in a bigger effort than speakers.

4.   Content 'in Sync' (Preformulation$_{ii}$)

I have shown so far that third-person self-reference helps writers of press releases meet the formal requirements of news reporting (preformulation$_i$). As I have explained, there may, however, be another way in which it plays a preformulating role: as Gandy (1982) argues, not just "form" but also "content" may be "structured in such a way as to flow in sync with the media system's requirements" in order to have "a greater probability of gaining entry into the public-information environment" (57) (preformulation$_{ii}$). I shall now explain what is meant by this second type of preformulation and then demonstrate how third-person self-reference fits in.

I have argued that press releases are egocentric documents. In Hartley's words they "present the case of whatever organization issues them" (1982: 111). As any short visit to a newsroom will confirm, journalists usually distrust this "suspect subjectivity" (Vanslyke Turk 1986: 23). In turn, writers of press releases are themselves "indoctrinated to expect that attitude of distrust from journalists" (26-27) and they can be expected to try hard to prove their credibility. In particular, as Gandy (1982) argues, since information from interested sources tends to be seen as less credible than that from disinterested sources, writers of press releases may "have an incentive to hide or disguise their relationship to the information they provide" (61). I would suggest that this is where third-person self-reference comes in: it serves a preformulating$_{ii}$ role in that it makes press releases look disinterested and neutral rather than self-interested, promotional. Brown and Levinson talk about 'point of view distancing' in this respect (1987: 204). In contrast, the use of first-person 'we' to refer to a business organization has been called an advertising device (Fairclough 1989 on 'synthetic personalization', 1994: 225). Compare the apparent matter-of-factness of extract (9) from a press release

(9). (Bekaert, Kortrijk: 25 March 1989)
N.V. BEKAERT S.A. BEEINDIGT ZIJN SAMENWERKINGSAK-
KOORD MET BRIDGESTONE CORPORATION

N.V. BEKAERT S.A. TERMINATES ITS CO-OPERATION AGREEMENT WITH BRIDGESTONE CORPORATION

with the 'axe to grind' feel in

We beëindigen ons samenwerkingsakkoord met Bridgestone Corporation

We terminate our agreement with Bridgestone Corporation

Similarly, the use of the passive makes the estimate in (13) more authoritative.

(13) (CMB: 6 February 1995)
De geconsolideerde winst over het boekjaar 1994 wordt geraamd op 1050 miljoen BEF, tegenover 571 miljoen BEF in 1993.

The consolidated profit for the financial year 1994 is estimated at 1,050 million BEF, compared with 571 million BEF in 1993.

And the announcement in (19) looks more objective because of the nominalization:

(19)   (Recticel, Brussels: 11 March 1994)
        TERUGKEER NAAR WINST IN EEN MOEILIJKE ECONO-
        MISCHE CONTEXT

        RETURN TO PROFIT IN A DIFFICULT ECONOMIC
        CONTEXT

That writers of press releases indeed want to 'hide their relationship to the information they provide' is probably even clearest in the extracts from Bayer press releases quoted above, where the organization's own products are backgrounded by AEG mobile phones and intercity trains with Agfa advertising.[26]

Note that in the following extract from a press release it seems to be the style of news reporting that is anticipated:

(56)   (ASQ, Houthalen: 23 February 1994)
        ASQ: maatgesneden efficiëntie
        Wil hoogste kwaliteit in informatiseringsprojekten
        Het softwarehuis ASQ maakt het zichzelf eerlijk gezegd niet
        gemakkelijk in zijn streven naar topkwaliteit.

        ASQ: tailor-made efficiency
        Strives for the highest quality in computerization projects
        Honestly, the software house ASQ is not making things easy for
        itself in its striving for top quality.

The use of an 'overline' preceding the headline is of course a typical feature of newspaper reporting. In addition, the self-reference through the proper name in the overline and headline and, more explicitly, with definite description in the lead equally conforms to the conventions of newspaper reporting (cf. Jucker 1996). There can be no doubt that this press release meets the formal requirements of newspaper reporting (preformulation$_i$). More subtly, the use of the disjunct 'honestly' implies that the writer's perspective is that of a disinterested reporter, typically a journalist (preformulation$_{ii}$). Another feature of journalistic style in the same press release is the direct question:

(57)   (ASQ, Houthalen: 23 February 1994)
        Een Nederlands programma voor België, vraagt u zich af?

A Dutch programme for Belgium, you wonder?

Surely, such stylistic empathy is hardly ever found for hard-core news items. One reason perhaps is, as I suggested in the previous chapter, that too much preformulation may very well be counter-productive in that, instead of enhancing, it actually reduces the organization's credibility as a disinterested news source.

Of course, I have only provided a sketchy treatment of preformulation$_{ii}$ and the issue of objectivity here and I shall have to come back to it in greater detail later on (cf. chapter 5).

5. Displaced Discourse

Third-person self-reference has been shown to play two distinct preformulating roles: one is to try and meet the formal requirements of news reporting, by anticipating the journalists' typical reference forms (preformulation$_i$), the other is to get 'the content flow in sync', by making press releases look more objective (preformulation$_{ii}$).

Interestingly, Maes (1991) seems to agree with my suggestion to link the referential choices discussed above to the audience-directedness of press releases when he looks at self-reference through definite description in civil court decisions and says that it requires "explanations in terms of non-identificational (i.e., semantic and pragmatic) functions and that these should be related to the peculiarly institutional nature of the discourse" (217). On closer scrutiny, Maes also arrives at very similar conclusions. First, he argues that the prototypically mixed form "wij, de rechtbank" [we, the court of law] serves to disambiguate the self-reference in case it gets read by others; this is closely related to the preformulating$_i$ role of third-person self-reference in press releases. At the same time, Maes says, the use of definite description in court is aimed at 'disindividualizing', creating "a mise en scène in which the interaction between conflicting parties is objectified" (240); this is almost exactly the same as preformulation$_{ii}$ in my data.

Auer (1988), finally, introduces the notion of 'displacedness', as opposed to 'situatedness', in order to distinguish this same 'I'-less discourse that, like press releases, proves widely accessible and looks more objective.[27] He even seems to suggest that such displaced discourse is a prototypical type of language use when he quotes ... Benveniste:

> Le caractère du langage est de procurer un substitut de l'expérience apte à être transmis sans fin dans le temps et l'espace, ce qui est le propre de notre symbolisme et le fondement de la tradition linguistique (1966: 61).
> The nature of language is to furnish a substitute for experience fit to be transmitted without end in time and space, which is specific to our symbolism and the foundation of the linguistic tradition.

Indeed, I would argue that press releases provide a perfect illustration of Auer's claim that it is "possible to construe relatively self-contained and relatively de-contextualized texts on which the situational aspects of context are neutralized" (1995: 15).[28]

6. Co-operation and Beyond

6.1 Against egocentric deixis

Some of the point of view operations described above clearly shed new light on the traditional conceptualization of deixis.

Typically, deixis is supposed to be organized in an egocentric way, with the unmarked anchorage point zero invariably located in the writer or speaker; Russell, for example, talks about deictic terms as 'egocentric particulars' (cf. Levinson 1983: 57). Lyons (1977: 579), like Fillmore, mentions the possibility of what he calls 'deictic projection' but fails to give more information about it, and Levinson (1983) admits that there may be 'derivative usages' that do not fit into the egocentric paradigm, but hastens to add that it is beyond the scope of his textbook. Moreover, the terminology used by both Lyons and Levinson serves to maintain the primacy of writer- or speaker-centred deixis.

Recently, Peter Jones radically criticized this standard account of deixis for its "a-social, one-sided focus", the first casualty of which is the reader or hearer, who is simply missing from the co-ordinate system (1995: 31). Instead of the egocentric system, Jones stresses the social-interactional nature of the deictic field. His is a co-operative - and, for that matter, highly romanticized - view of interaction as a "joint, goal-directed activity (...) mediated by language" (41-42). Jones believes that the default situation is a harmonious order of orientation and that reader- or hearer-centred as well as egocentric, i.e. writer- or speaker-centred, deixis are departures from it. It is interesting to note that, in Jones's view, such departures are conventionally required under certain circumstances, "determined by the concrete nature of the social activity (...) and by conventionally established, and activity-related, discourse norms" (43).[29] The following account of oral interaction could equally well be applied to press releases:

> what the speaker says is "addressee-centred", the viewpoint and expected response of the addressee is already, as it were, built into the utterance itself. The utterance consequently realizes a complex social dialectic in which the traditional categories of speaker and hearer, though indispensable as coarse empirical notions, do not capture the essence of the intersubjective communicative dynamic at work in any event of verbal communication (47).

Crucially, through the point of view operations described above, in press releases this 'intersubjective communicative dynamic' seems to be in the opposite direction of what is commonly assumed: it is not (just) the readers who adapt to the writers,[30] but writers (too) go out of their way to take readers into account.

6.2 Leaps and shortcuts

While some of the examples quoted above seem to serve as evidence for Jones's somewhat naively co-operative account, surely a thorough analysis of my corpus of press releases does not support Brown and Levinson's (1987) claim that such "taking the perspective of others is indeed the heart of the Gricean account" (9). Instead, as I suggested in the previous chapter, the type of preformulation described above should be seen as negotiation, not as co-operation. Third-person self-reference is a double-edged sword: writers of press releases adapt to the standard set by news reporting, but, in doing so, they are setting a standard for news reporting to adapt to. It may look innocent to 'take the other fellow's point of view', but there may always be some self-interest, as when telephone salespeople introduce themselves by "This is ..." instead of "My name is ..." in order to create the false impression of familiarity (Fillmore 1975). I shall now give a couple of examples from the data to support this claim. Before that, I shall distinguish between the referential and attributive functions of third-person self-reference.

6.2.1 Referential function

Here is Wilson's illustration of less-than-co-operative third-person self-reference in political discourse:

> It was not the Chancellor of the Duchy of Lancaster who made the complaint but the Chairman of the Conservative Party (1990: 78).

This is Norman Tebbit speaking to journalists back in 1986 about his attack on the BBC's coverage of the U.S. bombing of Libya. At the time Tebbit happened to be the Chairman of the British Conservative Party as well as being the Chancellor of the Duchy of Lancaster. Here the third-person self-reference serves a double purpose: in Donnellan's (1971) terminology, it has a referential function, viz. to pick out one individual (Norman Tebbit), and an attributive function, viz. to describe one or other particular feature of that individual (Norman Tebbit as Chancellor of the Duchy of Lancaster, Norman Tebbit as Chairman of the Conservative Party). Maes (1991) talks about the 'identificational' and 'qualificational' roles in this respect. As far as the attributive function is concerned, it is clear that Tebbit's elevated self-references help to invest him with authority. Wilson calls this 'role identification'. I shall come back to this attributive function in some of the following sections.

As for the referential function, surely it would have been much clearer for the speaker to refer to himself as "I" or "me" or as "Norman Tebbit". Instead, Wilson argues, the two definite descriptions seem to have the effect of drawing the hearer's attention away from Norman Tebbit as an individual towards some more generic role. He argues that speakers should normally only use definite descriptions when they can rely on their audience to retrieve the reference. Here this is not the case and the link between subject and speaker seems to be deliberately obscured as "a ploy to deflect, or delimit (...) 'existential involvement'" (79). Note that Lerman (1983, 1985) makes the same suggestion when she associates such third-person self-reference with 'dominant' discourse.

Let me now give a somewhat similar example from my corpus of press releases:

(58)   (Union Minière, Brussels: 27 October 1995)
        Union Minière gelooft in de toekomst van haar raffinage-
        activiteiten in België. Het programma dat deze aanwezigheid wil
        versterken via investeringen en een reorganisatie van de Groep,
        is daarvan het beste bewijs. Het kan echter niet uitgevoerd
        worden zonder gevolgen voor het huidige tewerkstellingspeil.
        De uitvoering van het industrieel plan zal globaal over een
        periode van twee jaar een vermindering meebrengen van 1.681
        arbeidsplaatsen in België en 212 arbeidsplaatsen in Frankrijk.
        (...) Voor werknemers die niet in aanmerking komen voor
        pensionering of brugpensioen zal er naar herklasseringsmogelijk-
        heden gezocht worden.

        (Union Minière, Brussels: 27 October 1995)
        Union Minière firmly believes that its refining operations in Belgium have a future, as is demonstrated by the investment and reorganization programme designed to consolidate its presence on this market. However, it will not be possible to do this without affecting present staffing levels.
        Overall, the implementation of the Industrial Plan will result in 1,681 job losses in Belgium and 212 in France over a period of two years.

(...) Alternative employment will be considered for those members of staff who do not qualify for retirement or early retirement.[31]

Here, apparently, Union Minière has some bad news to announce and it could be argued that the use of the passive and of nominalized constructions serves not just to make the information appear more objective (preformulation$_{ii}$), but also to obscure who is responsible.

In the first few sentences of extract (58), relatively good news is communicated and, strikingly, at this stage of the press release the organization's proper name features prominently in subject position. Later, when it comes to the bad news, passives and passive-like utterances are used: through the passive voice nothing is changed to the propositional content, but clearly a different degree of personal commitment on the part of the organization is expressed.[32] Here are some more examples:

(59)   (R.J. Reynolds, Brussels: 23 February 1994)
        Deze integratie zal leiden tot een verlies van 7 arbeidsplaatsen.

        This integration will lead to a loss of 7 jobs.

(60)   (Wagons-Lits, Brussels: 25 March 1994)
        Wagons-Lits: Vermindering van 97,5 arbeidsplaatsen ingevolge het verlies van de spoorrestauratie

        Wagons-Lits: Decrease of 97.5 jobs due to loss of railway catering

Of course, this is not to say that all third-person self-reference serves to obscure who is responsible. On the contrary, as I have shown before, in quite a number of cases the use of proper names, which is so typical of press releases, actually exposes the identity of the organization. Take, for example, (9) again.

(9)   (Bekaert, Kortrijk: 25 March 1989)
        N.V. BEKAERT S.A. BEEINDIGT ZIJN SAMENWERKINGSAK-KOORD MET BRIDGESTONE CORPORATION

N.V. BEKAERT S.A. TERMINATES ITS CO-OPERATION AGREEMENT WITH BRIDGESTONE CORPORATION

If here third-person self-reference makes the press release look more neutral, it also leaves no doubt about who the news is about.

6.2.2 Attributive function

As I suggested above, self-reference through definite description does not just have a referential function. At the same time, it may serve to attribute some qualities. This may be relatively innocent as in

(61) (HBK, Antwerp: s.d.)
HBK-Spaarbank reikt voor de derde maal een prijs uit ter stimulering van de wetenschappelijke studie omtrent werknemersparticipatie in ondernemingen. Op die manier wil deze Belgische spaarbank het onderzoek naar de participatie van werknemers in hun onderneming steunen.

For the third time HBK-Spaarbank is awarding a prize to stimulate the scientific research into employee participation in companies. In that way this Belgian savings bank aims to support the research into participation of employees in their companies.

The reference to HBK-Spaarbank as a 'Belgian savings bank' is perfectly acceptable, even for the most sceptic of journalists. In the following example, the reference to BTR plc as an 'international group' may be said to attribute more outspokenly positive qualities to the organization:

(62) (BTR: 8 September 1994)
Met ingang van 7 september 1994 werd Paul Buysse benoemd tot Executive Director van BTR plc.
Deze internationale groep stelt meer dan 125.000 mensen te werk en realiseerde vorig jaar een omzet van 528 miljard BEF met een winst voor belastingen van 69 miljard frank.

> Starting 7 September 1994 Paul Buysse has been appointed
> Executive Director of BTR plc.
> This international group employs more than 125,000 people and
> last year realized a turnover of 528 billion BEF with a profit
> before taxes of 69 billion francs.

Since the reader can only make sense of the extract by inferring that "this
international group" is BTR plc, he or she is led to unquestioningly accept
BTR's status as an international group. Donnellan (1971) calls such use of
definite description 'parasitic' (105-106). The following case is even
clearer:

(63)   (Europay, Waterloo: 5 May 1994)
        EUROPAY DOET HET GOED IN TURKIJE
        Grootste geldautomatennet van Turkije wordt voor het toeristi-
        sche zomerseizoen uitgebreid

        EUROPAY PERFORMS WELL IN TURKEY
        Biggest cash dispenser net in Turkey is expanded for the tourist
        summer season.

Maes (1991) says that definite descriptions must be relevant to what he,
rather awkwardly, calls 'the intention of the text'. For example, it makes
little sense to refer to President Clinton as the "saxophone enthusiast" in a
text on U.S. government legislation (cf. also de Fornel 1987). As far as
press releases are concerned, the question arises what text's intention is
taken into account: that of the press release or that of the subsequent
newspaper article? In (63) it was part of Europay's 'intention' to portray
itself as the biggest in the trade, but we might wonder if that intention is
shared by journalists.

No doubt, journalists are aware that the 'intentions' in press releases
may be different from their own. Here is an extract from a press release
issued by General Motors:

(64)   (General Motors, Antwerp: 8 March 1994)
        *"Zowel de produktievestigingen als de administratieve centra van
        het bedrijf zullen zo geassocieerd worden met de naam waarin
        miljoenen automobilisten en potentiële klanten hun vertrouwen
        stellen" [, zei voorzitter Louis Hughes van GM-Europa].*

        "Both the production sites and the administrative centres of the
        company will thus be associated with the name in which millions
        of drivers and potential customers have confidence [, said
        chairman Louis Hughes of GM Europe].

In (64) GM is referred to as "de naam waarin miljoenen automobilisten en
potentiële klanten hun vertrouwen stellen" [the name in which millions of
car drivers and potential customers have confidence]. Significantly, in a
subsequent article in the Flemish quality newspaper *De Standaard* the next
day, the euphoric definite description of the press release is substantially
toned down:

> *"Wij willen dat zowel de produktievestigingen als de verkoop- en
> administratieve centra in Europa geassocieerd worden met de
> merknaam van de auto die we produceren", zei voorzitter Louis Hughes
> van GM-Europa.*

> "We would like both the production sites and the sales and administra-
> tive centres in Europe to be associated with the brand name of the car
> that we produce", said chairman Louis Hughes of GM Europe.

I would like to add that there may be a similar problem with indefinite
description, as in the following extract from an Exxon press release about
the Valdez oil spill.

(65)   (Exxon, Anchorage, Alaska: 3 October 1989)
        For a company that has always placed great emphasis on safety
        and reliability in its operations, the spill is "like a bad dream,"
        Stevens said.

Here Exxon identifies itself as "a company that has always placed great emphasis on safety and reliability in its operations". In the context of the tragic events in South Alaska, this is of course no uncontroversial identification. Still, the attribution is just slipped into the text as a presupposition.

The following extract, from a press release issued by Flanders' extreme right-wing party Vlaams Blok, presents an even more subtle case:

> (66)   (Vlaams Blok, Antwerp: 28 September 1994)
>
> *Het Vlaams Blok vraagt zich af of het de taak is van universiteitsrectoren (...) om zich enkele dagen voor de gemeenteraadsverkiezingen met dergelijke demagogische en laag bij de grondse propaganda te keren tegen een bepaalde politieke partij.*
>
> *Het Vlaams Blok klaagt het feit aan dat alhoewel het gebruik van alle affichage groter dan 4m² voor alle partijpolitieke verkiezingspropaganda verboden is, anti-propaganda tegen een partij blijkbaar wel kan.*
>
> The Vlaams Blok wonders if it is the task of university Presidents (...) to turn themselves against a particular political party with such demagogic and vulgar propaganda a couple of days before the municipal elections. The Vlaams Blok condemns the fact that, although the use of all posters larger than 4m² has been banned for all party-political election propaganda, anti-propaganda against a party proves to be allowed.

The extract only makes sense of course if

> *Het Vlaams Blok klaagt het feit aan dat anti-propaganda tegen een partij blijkbaar wel kan.*
>
> The Vlaams Blok condemns the fact that anti-propaganda against a party proves to be allowed.

is taken to mean

> *Het Vlaams Blok klaagt het feit aan dat anti-propaganda tegen het Vlaams Blok blijkbaar wel kan.*

The Vlaams Blok condemns the fact that anti-propaganda against the
Vlaams Blok proves to be allowed.

The fact that the Vlaams Blok calls itself a political party, just like any
other, is not as innocent as it may seem. It has been frequently suggested
that they are rather more of an extremist group that tries to implement some
of its undemocratic policies through our parliamentary institutions. Clearly,
self-reference through indefinite description is a powerful mechanism: even
if we do not believe that the Blok is just a party like any other, the
reference works; the question if the reference matches the object designated
within the world is simply evaded.

That the Vlaams Blok is preoccupied with its status of political party is
also clear from other press releases:

(67)   (Vlaams Blok, Antwerp: 14 September 1994)
        Het Vlaams Blok drukt, ondanks de pogingen tot polarisatie van
        het AFF en co., de hoop dat alle partijen de kans zullen krijgen
        om op een eerlijke en open manier hun programma uit te dragen.

        In spite of the attempts at polarization from the AFF and co, the
        Vlaams Blok hopes that all parties will get the chance to spread
        their programmes in an honest and open way.

Here again the extract only works if 'all parties' includes the Vlaams Blok.
And clearly, if 'parties' may mean 'sides in an argument' here, the sense of
'regular and respectable political organization that you can vote for in
democratic elections' is never far away. In another press release (16
September 1994) "de meeste partijen" [most parties] and "zowat alle partijen" [almost all parties] are also meant to include the Vlaams Blok.[33]

Note, finally, in the following extract from a press release issued by
the radically left-wing PVDA that it is not only the Vlaams Blok that is
preoccupied with its status as a party:

(68)   (PVDA, Antwerp: 29 September 1994)
        Volgens de PVDA is het echter komplete juridische nonsens en
        een uiterst gevaarlijk precedent dat een persoon verantwoordelijk

wordt gesteld voor al het plakwerk "van zijn partij" (...). [De PVDA] wijst er op dat op deze manier "in naam van bezorgdheid voor het milieu" het Vlaams Blok wel in alle rust zijn racistisch ideeëngoed mag spuien, maar dat een konsekwente anti-racistische partij uit het straatbeeld verwijderd wordt.

However, according to the PVDA it is complete juridical nonsense and an extremely dangerous precedent that a person is made responsible for all the pasting "of his party" (...). [The PVDA] points out that in this way, "in the name of concern for the environment", the Vlaams Blok is allowed in all peace to spread its racist ideology, but that a consistently anti-racist party is removed from the street scene.

6.2.3   Presupposition manipulations

The discussion started above opens up a whole domain of what Brown and Levinson (1987) call 'presupposition manipulations',[34] most of which is beyond the scope of this study. In this section I shall provide two examples that are not exclusively related to self-reference.

The following extract is the headline of a press release in which, shortly before Belgium's 1994 municipal elections, a petition in favour of legalizing euthanasia is announced. The way the headline is formulated, however, seems to anticipate on the results of the petition; any explicit self-reference is carefully avoided and a successful completion of the petition seems to be taken for granted:

(69)   (Recht op waardig sterven, Antwerp: 21 October 1994)
        Kiezer eist recht op vrijwillige milde dood

        Voter demands right to voluntary mild death

The following is also a less than innocent headline:

(70)   (Exxon, Houston, Texas: 27 March 1989)
        LIGHTERING, OIL SPILL CLEANUP EFFORTS CONTINUE
        IN ALASKA

This is from the first of the Exxon press releases in my corpus. In the body of the press release, Exxon announces that one of its mammoth tankers, the Exxon Valdez, has had an accident in South Alaska and that 240,000 barrels of crude oil have been spilt into the sea. Somewhat suspiciously, Exxon is very much absent from the headline. But there is more going on: the title treats the oil spill - and even the start of the clean-up operations - as old news and directs the media's attention to the organization's continued efforts to deal with the contingency. In other words, the title is not a summary of the bad news that the press release is meant to report. Instead, it focuses on the positive aspects of the story. Most headlines abstract the main event of the story, but some deal with a secondary event or a detail; as Bell (1991) notes, "[t]hese are particularly revealing cases" (188-189).

Clearly, this is not just a point of view operation; it is close to what Brown and Levinson call a 'presupposition manipulation': "something is not really mutually assumed to be the case, but S speaks as if it were mutually assumed" (1987: 122). Stalnaker (1974) makes a very interesting comment on it:

> If one is talking for some other purpose than to exchange information, or if one must be polite, discreet, diplomatic, kind, or entertaining as well as informative, then one may have reason to act as if the common background were different than one in fact knows it to be. (...) a speaker may act as if certain propositions are part of the common background when he knows that they are not. (...) In such a case, a speaker tells his auditor something in part by pretending that his auditor already knows it (201-202; cf. also Soames 1982).

This is not to say, however, that, as Brown and Levinson's use of the term 'manipulation' suggests, such communicative behaviour is always unethical. Stalnaker (1974) emphasizes that the "pretense need not be an attempt at deception. (...) In some cases it is just that it would be indiscreet, or insulting, or tedious, or unnecessarily blunt, or rhetorically less effective to openly assert a proposition that one wants to communicate" (202). Karttunen (1974) provides a fine example of the polite use of what he calls such 'leaps and shortcuts':

We regret that children cannot accompany their parents to commencement exercises.

Here, strictly speaking, 'that children cannot accompany their parents to
commencement exercises' is considered presupposed knowledge. Still, the
whole point of this utterance is to let parents know that they should not
bring their kids along.[35] In (70) quoted above the question of ethics is
more pertinent of course. I would argue that what happens here is that the
readers are being manoeuvered into a position in which they have to accept
the presuppositions held forward by the writer of the press release.
Significantly, however, similar strategies are used not just to cover up bad
news, but also to announce good news. This is the title of a press release in
which Alcatel Bell announces a new contract:

(71)   (Alcatel Bell, Antwerp: 15 November 1994)
        *Multimedia-contract van Alcatel Bell in de UK is van strategisch
        belang*

        Multimedia contract of Alcatel Bell in the UK is of strategic
        impact

Here we could have expected an even more flattering headline like

*Bell sleept strategisch belangrijk Multimedia-contract in the UK in de
wacht*

Bell carries off strategically important Multimedia contract in the UK

In general, there can be no doubt that the preformulating efforts shown
above are not always fully co-operative.[36] It is interesting to note that
preformulations are not very different from what Brookes (1995) calls
"naturalized *re*formulations, where one word is invariably substituted for
another, rendering certain aspects of an event invisible while foregrounding
others and setting up contextual relations of synonymy (...) that blur
previous boundaries of meaning and create new ones which become
embedded within a particular discourse" (471; my italics).

7.   Conclusions

In this chapter I have provided corpus-based evidence to show how self-reference in press releases may serve a double preformulating purpose: through a point of view operation the special forms of reflexive person, time and place deixis I have analysed help 'structure both form and content' of press releases to meet the journalists' requirements. I have also suggested that such preformulation may serve less harmonious purposes.

At the end of the Santa Cruz lectures on deixis, Fillmore (1975) suggests that one of the other topics he would have liked to cover was the relation between direct discourse and indirect discourse - or quotation -, as it also depends on matters of deictic anchoring. Recently, Wortham (1996) confirmed that, in studying interactional patterns, analysis of deictics is not enough and he too singled out quotation as a fruitful and highly complementary field of analysis (344).

At several points in this chapter, I have already hinted at the link between issues of self-reference and quotation. In the next two chapters I shall investigate patterns of quotation in my corpus of press releases in greater detail and I shall demonstrate that they too serve a purpose of preformulation.

Chapter 4
Self-Quotation in Press Releases

1. Quotations in Press Releases

1.1 Introduction

In the previous chapter I provided corpus-based evidence to demonstrate that the various forms of self-reference in press releases play a complex preformulating role. At the end I suggested that it might well be worthwhile to also have a look at the quotation practices in my data to see if they too could in any way be related to the peculiar audience-directedness of press releases. This is what I set out to do in this chapter.

A quick glance at the corpus shows that quotations are indeed an interesting feature of press releases. Here are some typical examples:

(1)　(Exxon, Valdez, Alaska: 16 August 1989)
In an effort to aid Alaska fishermen in the wake of the Exxon Valdez oil spill, Exxon has developed a nine-point program and paid more than $38 million in fishermen claims. (...) Otto Harrison, general manager of Exxon's Valdez operations, said: "We are committed to treating fairly those who have been indirectly impacted by this accident. We view our work with the fishermen as a very important part of this effort."

(2)　(Nutricia, Zoetermeer: 18 November 1993)
Directeur T.J.M. van Hedel is blij over de medewerking van de detailhandel. "Nutricia maakt een moeilijke tijd door. Dan is het prettig te merken dat je vrienden hebt. De handel biedt ons alle hulp om deze tegenslag te boven te komen. Nagenoeg alle

winkels hebben, na de eerste oproep van Nutricia, de betreffende potjes zelf uit de schappen gehaald. "

Director T.J.M. van Hedel is happy with the retail trade's co-operation. "Nutricia is having hard times. Then it's nice to see you have friends. The retail trade is offering all its help to overcome this setback. After Nutricia's first call, nearly all shops have taken the relevant pots from the shelves themselves.

(3)   (EMC, Brussels: 20 April 1994)
EMC Corporation deelt mee dat de omzet in het eerste kwartaal van dit jaar 267.058.000 dollar beloopt (...). "De manier waarop wij onze groei aanpakken, werkt goed", zegt Michael C. Ruettgers, voorzitter en chief executive officer van EMC. "Wij breiden ons huidig klantenbestand verder uit door gerichte marketingacties in welbepaalde regio's en sectoren en investeren tegelijk heel wat in R&D om onze toonaangevende marktpositie te behouden".

EMC Corporation announces that the turnover in the first quarter of this year amounts to 267,058,000 dollars (...). "The way we approach our growth works well", says Michael C. Ruettgers, EMC's chairman and chief executive officer. "We are making new customers by means of targeted marketing operations in specific areas and sectors, and at the same time we are making substantial investments in R&D to preserve our leading market position".

Apparently, in Goffman's terminology of the production format, press releases seem to be characterized not just by the marked presence of a principal (or 'institutional voice') described in chapter 3, but also, since they frequently incorporate the words of others, by the use of so-called 'cited figures' (1974: 529-530).

1.2 Pseudo-direct speech

But what does it really mean to say that press releases incorporate the words of others? Significantly, more than the frequency, the overwhelming numbers, I shall suggest that it is the nature of quotations in press releases that constitutes the prime reason for looking at the phenomenon here. In particular I shall focus on two crucial questions:

* who are these 'figures', these others that are 'cited' in press releases? whose words do press releases really incorporate?

* what kind of words are they, i.e. how were they originally verbalized by the quoted sources and, linked to that, how are they now incorporated in the press releases? In particular, are the quotations in press releases an accurate rendering of those others' words?

To clarify what I mean by these two questions - and indeed why I have come to think of asking them in the first place -, let's now look at the following extract from a press release that was issued by the Belgian Kredietbank to announce that it had obtained a licence from the Tunisian authorities to open an office in Tunis.

> (4)   (Kredietbank, Brussels: 21 November 1995)
> *De Kredietbank nu ook vertegenwoordigd in Tunesië*
> *De Kredietbank heeft onlangs van de Tunesische autoriteiten een vergunning verkregen voor het openen van een vertegenwoordigingskantoor in Tunis. Met dit nieuwe kantoor, dat zal worden geleid door de heer Mustapha Mosreane, zal de Kredietbank zich nu ook verder profileren in de Maghreb-landen.*
> *De nieuwe vertegenwoordiging in Tunis past in de internationale strategie van de Kredietbank, die er onder meer op gericht is haar rol en aandeel in de internationale handel te verstevigen. Frequentere contacten met lokale autoriteiten, financiële instellingen en bedrijven zullen de kwaliteit van de cliëntenservice en - begeleiding ten goede komen. Het nieuwe vertegenwoordigings-*

kantoor in Tunis zal ook de cliënten van de Kredietbank bijstaan bij hun transacties met Tunesische handelspartners.

The Kredietbank now also represented in Tunisia
The Kredietbank has recently obtained a licence from the Tunisian authorities to open a representation office in Tunis. With this new office, which will be headed by Mr Mustapha Mosreane, the Kredietbank will continue its expansion in the Maghreb countries.
The new representation in Tunis is part of the Kredietbank's international strategy, which, among other objectives, is aimed at strengthening its role and share in international trade. More frequent contacts with local authorities, financial institutions and businesses will contribute to the quality of customer service and assistance. The new representation in Tunis will also assist customers of the Kredietbank in their transactions with Tunisian trade partners.

A couple of months later another press release is issued by the Kredietbank about the bank's representation in Tunisia, this time to report on the official opening of the bank's Tunis office:

(5) (Kredietbank, Brussels: 31 January 1996)
Kredietbank-vertegenwoordiging in Tunis officieel geopend.
Vorige week vond in Tunis de officiële opening plaats van de Kredietbank-vertegenwoordiging. De openingsreceptie werd onder meer door tal van prominenten uit de Tunesische politieke, financiële en zakenwereld bijgewoond en vond heel wat weerklank in de Tunesische pers.
"Deze vertegenwoordiging ligt in het verlengde van de recent ondertekende associatie-akkoorden tussen de Europese Unie en respectievelijk Tunesië en Marokko", aldus de heer M. Cockaerts, voorzitter van het Directiecomité van de Kredietbank.
"De vertegenwoordiging in Tunis past in de internationale strategie van de Kredietbank, die er onder, meer op gericht is haar rol en aandeel in de internationale handel te verstevigen.

Frequentere contacten met lokale autoriteiten, financiële instel-
lingen en bedrijven zullen de kwaliteit van de cliëntenservice en -
begeleiding ten goede komen. Het nieuwe vertegenwoordigings-
kantoor in Tunis zal ook de cliënten van de Kredietbank bijstaan
bij hun transacties met Tunesische handelspartners".

Kredietbank representation in Tunis officially opened
Last week the official opening took place of the Kredietbank
representation in Tunis. The opening reception was attended by,
among others, lots of important people from the Tunisian
political, financial and business worlds and was widely covered
in the Tunisian press.
"This representation follows naturally from the recently signed
association agreements between the European Union and
respectively Tunisia and Morocco", according to Mr. M.
Cockaerts, chairman of the Kredietbank's direction committee.
"The representation in Tunis is part of the Kredietbank's
international strategy, which, among other objectives, is aimed
at strengthening its role and share in international trade. More
frequent contacts with local authorities, financial institutions and
businesses will contribute to the quality of customer service and
assistance. The new representation in Tunis will also assist
customers of the Kredietbank in their transactions with Tunisian
trade partners".

I would like to draw attention to the quotation in this extract (5). Here the
chairman of the bank's direction committee, Mr. M. Cockaerts, is directly
reported to have made a statement about the impact of the new Tunis office.
It is implied, though not explicitly stated, that the words were spoken at the
reception described in the first paragraph of the extract.

I would like to make two remarks here. First, it should be clear that
the quoted source is no real 'other' since it is a top figure of the same
organization that issued the press release. What is even more interesting,
though, is that the quoted words are identical to the text of the press release
rendered in extract (4). I would suggest that this observation casts at least
some doubt on the status of the quotation in the press release (5) as a literal

rendering of words that were actually spoken by Mr. Cockaerts at the reception in Tunis. Surely, it provides no conclusive evidence that the words attributed to Mr Cockaerts in (5) were not spoken by him, or even that they were not spoken by him in exactly that way; it may for example well be that he was reading from a pre-scripted speech that was based on the press release issued some months earlier and quoted in (4). Still, the above remarks seem to indicate that here we could be looking at a case of 'pseudo-direct speech', where the words, according to Allan Bell (1991) "were almost certainly not verbalized by the named source[, but] written by a press officer and merely approved by the source (sometimes not even that)" (60). Cook (1989), focusing on the PR practices of US politicians, seems to point to the same phenomenon when he suggests that Congressmen who want to make it into the newspapers frequently 'interview themselves' (20) and issue press releases in which they are 'ostensibly being quoted' (94).

Before I turn to a more systematic analysis of quotations in press releases, let's look at another, even more interesting case. (6) is from a press release in which the same Kredietbank announces the entry of the Danish Unibank into the international IBOS banking association.

(6)   (Kredietbank, Brussels: 16 January 1995)
        Bij de verwelkoming van Unibank als nieuw lid van de associatie verklaarde Charles de Croisset, voorzitter van de IBOS-associatie: "Het kantorennet van Unibank op de Deense markt maakt haar tot een uiterst geschikte partner voor de associatie. We zijn verheugd dat Unibank lid wordt van onze groep. Het is duidelijk dat door de toetreding van gerenommeerde bankinstellingen zoals Unibank, de internationale mogelijkheden van elk lid op het vlak van commercieel bankieren zullen toenemen. Aldus zullen we beter kunnen voorzien in de groeiende behoeften van onze kliënten."

        On welcoming Unibank as a new member of the association, Charles de Croisset, chairman of the IBOS association, declared: "Unibank's office network on the Danish market makes it into an extremely suitable partner for the association. We are happy that Unibank becomes a member of our group. It is clear that through the entry of renowned bank institutions like Unibank, the international possibilities of each member at the level of commercial banking will increase. That way we will be able to better meet the growing needs of our customers."

Interestingly, some time later, in a subsequent press release, the same Mr Charles de Croisset is reported to have spoken exactly the same words on a similar occasion, this time welcoming a new, Italian member to the IBOS association. Only the name of the bank and the reference to the bank's country of origin have - naturally - been replaced:

(7)   (Kredietbank, Brussels: 27 June 1995)
Bij de verwelkoming van Istituto Bancario San Paolo di Torino als nieuw lid van de associatie verklaarde Charles de Croisset, voorzitter van de IBOS-associatie: "Het kantorennet van San Paolo op de Italiaanse markt en de kwaliteit van zijn financiële dienstverlening maken hem tot een uiterst geschikte partner voor de associatie. We zijn verheugd dat San Paolo lid wordt van onze groep. Het is duidelijk dat door de toetreding van gerenommeerde bankinstellingen zoals San Paolo, de internationale mogelijkheden van elk lid op het vlak van commercieel bankieren zullen toenemen. Aldus zullen we beter kunnen voorzien in de groeiende behoeften van onze cliënten."

On welcoming Istituto Bancario San Paolo di Torino as a new member of the association, Charles de Croisset, chairman of the IBOS association, declared: "Istituto Bancario San Paolo di Torino's office network on the Italian market and the quality of its financial service make it into an extremely suitable partner for the association. We are happy that San Paolo becomes a member of our group. It is clear that through the entry of renowned bank institutions like San Paolo, the international possibilities of each member at the level of commercial banking will increase. That way we will be able to better meet the growing needs of our customers."

And again, on the entry of the Dutch ING Bank three months after:

(8)   (Kredietbank, Brussels: 25 September 1995)

Bij de verwelkoming van ING Bank als nieuw lid van de associatie verklaarde Charles de Croisset, voorzitter van de IBOS-associatie dat "het kantorennet van ING Bank op de Nederlandse markt en de kwaliteit van haar financiële dienstverlening, de bank maken tot een uiterst geschikte partner voor de associatie. We zijn verheugd dat ING Bank lid wordt van onze groep. Het is duidelijk dat door de toetreding van gerenommeerde bankinstellingen zoals ING Bank, de internationale mogelijkheden van elk lid op het vlak van commercieel bankieren zullen toenemen. Aldus zullen we beter kunnen voorzien in de groeiende behoeften van onze cliënten."

On welcoming ING Bank as a new member of the association, Charles de Croisset, chairman of the IBOS association, declared that "ING Bank's office network on the Dutch market and the quality of its financial service make the bank into an extremely suitable partner for the association. We are happy that ING Bank becomes a member of our group. It is clear that through the entry of renowned bank institutions like ING Bank, the international possibilities of each member at the level of commercial banking will increase. That way we will be able to better meet the growing needs of our customers."

Just like for the words attributed to Mr Cockaerts in (5), I do not want to claim that it is not possible that Mr de Croisset repeated the same words on each of the three occasions and that the quotes in the various press releases are, after all, a literal rendering of what the chairman of the IBOS banking association said. However, this is highly unlikely. More probably, whoever authored these press releases has been simply drawing from a number of standard expressions that he or she could simply attribute to the quoted source, leaving out altogether any consideration of what that source may really have said or if that source really said anything at all on the occa-

sion.[1] This again would support Bell's view of quotations in press releases
as pseudo-direct speech.

1.3 Research questions

Based on the notion of pseudo-direct speech, I shall now direct my attention
to investigating the claim that quotations in press releases do not conform to
what could normally be expected from them in two respects:

1. quotation is normally taken to provide a faithful reproduction of the
    original; but the examples quoted above show that some quotations in
    press releases may be no literal rendering of the quoted source's words
    at all. In fact, as I suggested above, the quoted words may well have
    been completely invented. I shall use the term 'constructed quotation'
    here (cf. Tannen 1989).

2. quotations normally point to heterogeneous text (Kress 1983), they
    present a portrait of the other (Buttny 1995); in (5), like in so many
    other press releases in the corpus, however, the writer of the press
    release and the quoted source (chairman of the Kredietbank's direction
    committee, Mr M. Cockaerts), represent one and the same institution.
    In other words, the quotations are of a self-referential, reflexive nature.
    They are really self-quotations (cf. Maynard 1996).

Interestingly, the same two points are singled out by Oswald Ducrot in *Le
Dire et le Dit* when he complains that direct speech has too often been
viewed on its own. This has led, he says, to the mistaken beliefs that
quotation is based on a real previous utterance ("un discours effectivement
tenu") - let alone that it provides an accurate rendering of that utterance -
and that the quoted words belong to a speaker who is different from the
reporter ("un locuteur différent de celui qui fait le rapport") (1984: 198).

In this chapter I shall look at these two peculiarities in some detail before
trying to relate them to the peculiar audience-directedness of press releases
in the next chapter.

2. Self-Quotation

2.1 Forms of self-quotation

I shall first deal with the claim that for quotations in press releases the writer and the quoted source frequently represent one and the same institution. This is certainly the case in the above extracts (1), (2) and (3) where the quoted sources most probably were not the writers of the press releases, but are nevertheless clearly contributing to the co-ordinated communicative efforts of the organization that issued the press releases. In the extract from an Exxon press release (1) it is the general manager of Exxon's Valdez operations who is quoted. In the Nutricia press release (2) it is Nutricia's director who is quoted. In EMC's press release (3), finally, it is EMC's Chief Executive Officer who is quoted. The following examples are even clearer:

(9) (Ericsson, Brussels: 16 May 1994)

In vergelijking tot andere mobiele telefoons doet de Ericsson GH 337 het op praktisch alle punten aanzienlijk beter, aldus het bedrijf.

In comparison to other mobile telephones the Ericsson GH 337 performs considerably better in practically all areas, according to the company.

(10) (Exxon, Washington, D.C.: 17 April 1989)

Valdez oil spill is not the reason for gasoline price hikes, says Exxon.

Here it can be safely assumed that the organization that issued the press release is - literally - quoting itself. There can be no doubt that the principal writer and the quoted source are identical.

Clearly, in all these cases the situation is very different from the standard quoting practices, in which, say, a newspaper journalist writes an article and includes a number of quotations of people - eyewitnesses for example - that he or she interviewed.

2.2 Non-reflexive quotation

This is not to say that the conventional, i.e. non-reflexive, type of quotation, in which 'external' sources, i.e. Goffman's real others, are quoted is altogether absent from press releases. I would like to stress that such more orthodox quotations also occur in the corpus. (11), which we looked at in some detail for different purposes in the previous chapter, is from a press release issued by London Weekend Television, announcing one of its programmes featuring an interview with a politician.

(11)   (London Weekend Television, London: 19 June 1987)
        Outspoken Junior Health Minister Edwina Currie has suggested that Margaret and Dennis Thatcher's courtship might have taken place on the floor of her Oxford University room ...
        Speaking on LWT's *The Late Clive James* show tonight (Saturday, 20 June 1987) at 10.30 pm, Mrs Currie - who went to Oxford after the Prime Minister - says that when she and Mrs Thatcher were at Oxford, few other women studied there, and house rules were very strict.
        She says: "There was a rule that you couldn't have more than two men in your room at any one time - why two men was alright I don't know. One of the other rules was that we had to put beds in the corridor during the day. It was alright to invite a man for tea, but the bed had to come out into the corridor."
        At this point, Clive James asks what might have happened when Dennis came to call on Mrs Thatcher, to which Mrs Currie replies: "... she could do it on the floor ..."

(12) is from a press release issued by the Kredietbank, quoting an independent agency's evaluation of the bank's performance.

(12)   (Kredietbank, Brussels: 2 October 1995)
        Deze 'dubbel A' rating is volgens Thomson BankWatch gebaseerd op de continu hoge rendabiliteit van de Kredietbank en het lage risicokarakter van de balans, de uitstekende kwaliteit van de activa en de sterke solvabiliteit. (...) Thomson Bankwatch

verwijst eveneens naar de halfjaarresultaten die de bank onlangs bekendmaakte.

According to Thomson Bankwatch this 'double A' rating is based on the constantly high profitability of the Kredietbank and the low risk character of the balance, the outstanding quality of the assets and the strong solvency. (...) Thomson Bankwatch also refers to the half-year results that the bank recently announced.

Interestingly, in the corpus there are even some quotes drawn from press releases of other organizations:

(13)   (GB, Brussels: 2 December 1994)
        Fedis schrijft in haar Persbericht van 17 oktober het volgende: "Dit KB heeft zich uiteindelijk beperkt tot de bevestiging dat de maaltijdcheques voor voedingswaren bestemd zijn."

        Fedis writes the following in its Press release of 17 October: "This Royal Decree has eventually been restricted to the confirmation that the meal cheques are meant for food products".

(14)   (Exxon, Valdez, Alaska, 8 August 1989)
        In a news release, the Alaska Department of Environmental Conservation said the testing will determine the effectiveness of the reformulated product. "Exxon Company, U.S.A. has sought use of the compound in the hope of speeding the oil removal," the department said. "State and federal agencies also wish to expedite the removal but have been cautious in granting permission for area-wide use because this is a new chemical which has not been used before."

Following a framework proposed by Verschueren (1985), the different communicative layers involved in such non-reflexive quotations, e.g. in (11), can be visualized as follows :

Fig. 1 Non-reflexive quotation

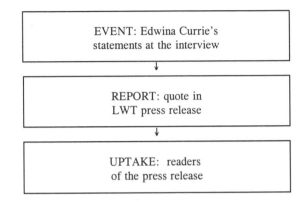

It should be added, though, that this orthodox type of non-reflexive quotation proves relatively rare in my corpus of press releases. Apparently, news managers prefer quoting themselves to quoting others. The predominance of self-quotation in the corpus confirms the view of press releases as self-centred documents: here the separate communicative layers represented in fig. 1 have got intertwined, because those participating in the event also turn out to be responsible for reporting about it in a press release.[2] The quote in (1) can be visualized more or less as follows:

Fig. 2 Reflexive quotation

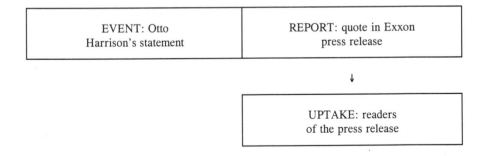

2.3 Mixed forms

Finally, it should be noted that it is not always possible - and indeed, as I shall argue below, not necessary - to make clear-cut distinctions between reflexive and non-reflexive quotations. (15), for example, is taken from an Exxon press release, reporting on an agreement the company made with the National Steel and Shipbuilding Company (NASSCO) to repair the damaged tanker Exxon Valdez. (16) is from a statement by Europay on the company's co-operation with big Turkish banks such as the Akbank.

(15)   (Exxon, San Diego, California: 12 June 1989)
         NASSCO President Richard Vortmann said, "NASSCO original-
         ly built the Exxon Valdez and welcomes the opportunity to
         return the ship to its original condition."

(16)   (Europay, Waterloo: 5 May 1994)
         "De opening van het Europay-kantoor in Istanbul is meer dan
         symbolisch. Na een jaar begint de expansie, vooral in de
         betaalsector, tastbare voordelen op te leveren voor mijn bank,
         onze klanten en reizigers die Turkije aandoen," aldus Akin
         Kozanoglu, Assistant General Manager van de Akbank.

         "The opening of the Europay office in Istanbul is more than
         symbolic. After one year, the expansion, especially in the
         payment sector, is starting to pay off for my bank, our cus-
         tomers and travellers in Turkey," according to Akin Kozanoglu,
         Akbank's Assistant General Manager.

Strictly speaking, these quotations are non-reflexive: Exxon quotes a NASSCO official, the Akbank Assistant General Manager is quoted by Europay. However, as both press releases deal with some form of business co-operation among several companies, they come close to joint declarations and the (external) quoted sources may be considered internalized. As a result, the words between quotation marks sound very much reflexive.[3]

3.　Constructed Quotations

3.1　Introduction

I have demonstrated that writers of press releases and the 'cited figures' usually represent one institution. The next step now is to investigate Bell's claim that quotes in press releases are no literal rendering of the quoted source's words and that in fact most quoted words have been completely invented. In this sense quotes in press releases again do not accord with the standard view of quotation. In particular, I showed above that while quotations normally present a portrait of the other, in press releases they present a picture of the self; now I shall demonstrate that they do not accord with what Clark and Gerrig (1990) call "the verbatim assumption" (795), i.e. the idea that the words between quotation marks are an accurate reproduction of some previous speech.

The reproductionist view has dominated the study of quotations for a long time, ranging, as Slembrouck (1992a) notes, from the Chomskyan transformational-derivational paradigm (with the belief that direct speech could be simply transformed into indirect speech on the basis of syntactic criteria, cf Partee 1971, Banfield 1982[4]) to the presentationalist taxonomy (with focus on the quote's semantic status qua representational mimesis, cf. McHale 1978). The latter is clearly at work in Leech and Short's cline of apparent narrator interference, where direct speech is taken to indicate a minimum of narrator control (1981; cf. also Roeh and Nir 1990, Sanders 1994). I shall now briefly explain this traditional view, because it seems to highlight the fundamental misunderstanding at the heart of what may be called the 'reproductionist fallacy': the mistaken assumption that the quoted words are an accurate reproduction of words previously spoken by others.

At the same time, though, as I shall demonstrate in the next chapter, it is crucial to bear in mind that it is this very same traditional view of quotation as accurate reproduction that determines the actual functioning of quotations, including the quotations in press releases: even if they can be no accurate reproductions, part of their force derives from the fact that they do *look like* accurate reproductions and that readers therefore tend to treat them as if they are.

3.2 The reproductionist view of quotation

Let me now illustrate the reproductionist view. Sanders (1994: 46) argues that quotations are characterized by low accessibility. She means that the reporter cannot normally 'reach' the words that are between quotation marks.[5] Drawing from Fauconnier's mental space theory, she suggests that the reality of the reporter is the basic mental space (B) while what she calls a "linguistic instruction" like

Jan says: "..."

serves to set up a new, embedded subspace (M). In her view the distance between the base space (B) and the subspace (M) is reflected in the possibility of interpreting references to entities in (M) indirectly from (B), in addition to the default interpretation directly from (M). In the case of (direct) quotation, the distance between (B) and (M) seems to be considerable and access to the referents between quotation marks is provided only directly in the subspace (M), which has become a new, embedded base space (B') bound to the quoted source.

Crucially, as is clear from Sanders's thesis, the reproductionist approach relies on the idea that quotation is supposed to entail a single point of view, viz. that of the quoted source. This is the so-called 'oratio recta': it invites a 'de dicto' interpretation because it adopts the frame of orientation of the reproduced speech event and claims to convey it as it actually occurred. Since it is indexically anchored to the reproduced event and bears no necessary formal relationship to the reporting event, it foregrounds form (cf. Lucy 1993).[6] This is what Quine (1960) calls 'referential opacity', viz. that the quoted words are referentially impenetrable and that any interference with the form affects their truth status.

3.3 Against the reproductionist view of quotation

It is this claim, viz. that the words between quotation marks are inaccessible to the reporter and entail a single point of view, that has recently come under fire. More specifically, various researchers have set out to actually compare the original utterance with the subsequent quoted version to see if the quoted words are indeed so inaccessible to the reporter.

It is not surprising then that the interest in the non-reproductionist view of quotation coincides with a move to look beyond the traditional object of analysis, viz. literary discourse. Leech and Short (1981: 160), for example, argue that in novels "language is used to simulate, rather than simply to report what goes on in the fictional world" so "there is no specific speech event against which the report can be measured as a more or less accurate record". McHale, in review of the transformationalist-derivationalist paradigm, seems to confirm this:

> In the everyday production and use of represented/reported speech, it is theoretically always possible to recover the 'original' direct utterance, or at least to think of it as being recoverable, (...). This is obviously not so in fiction, in which there is no 'direct original' prior to or behind an instance of ID [indirect discourse] or FID [free indirect discourse]; the supposedly 'derived' utterances are not versions of anything, but themselves the 'original' in that they give as much as the reader will ever learn of 'what was really said' (1978: 256).[7]

That is the main reason why Slembrouck (1992a, b) prefers looking at specific quoting practices in non-literary contexts, especially in the media: viz. because here there is an extra-textual antecedent correlate for the quotation to be compared with. He wants to bring the relationship with the original words as they really occurred to the forefront. Too long, Slembrouck claims, the relationship between what he calls the 'reported speech' and the 'reporting context' has been neglected. Similarly, Baynham (1996) argues for an approach to quotation that goes beyond the canonical narrative discourse context and investigates reporting in a wider range of uses (79-80).

My research of quotations in press releases is clearly part of this renewed effort to look at non-literary contexts. Still, if it is true that the quotes in press releases are indeed pseudo-direct speech, then press releases are an example of non-literary discourse where, contrary to what could be expected, no recorded evidence of the originals is available to systematically compare, simply because the quotes have no such originals. So, ironically, the study of quotation in such a decidedly non-literary context as press releases would bring us back to the old, literary situation that this new type of research was meant to get away from in the first place, viz. one in which the inaccessibility of the quoted words could not be tested simply because there was no antecedent to compare with.

It is exactly for this reason, though, that I turned to quotations in press releases. I turned to non-literary discourse for the opposite reason than Slembrouck, viz. not because there was an original to compare with, but because it struck me that there might be no original. Of course I am not the first to draw attention to such constructed quotations outside fiction. Even Sanders (1994), despite her focus on the inaccessibility of the quoted words, is aware that quotations may be hypothetical or counterfactual.[8] Slembrouck himself notes the phenomenon of 'simulated quotations' in non-fiction genres; in particular he mentions advertising (1992a: 48). I have hinted that constructed quotations even crop up in newspaper reporting, as Caldas-Coulthard (1994) suggests when she interviews a newspaper crime journalist:

> When I needed quotes, I used to make them up, as did some of the others (...) for we knew what the 'bereaved mother' and the 'mourning father' should have said (...) (300).

3.4 Methodological remarks

Let's now try to find out if there is any hard evidence to confirm that quotations in press releases are indeed pseudo-direct speech.

Of course, it has been argued that a faithful rendering of previously spoken words is usually just not practically possible: Sternberg (1982a) and Lehrer (1989), among others, note that our understanding of the power of memory indicates that the alleged quoted words cannot conceivably have been spoken exactly that way by the person to whom they are attributed. As the Greek historian Thucydides put it:

> I have found it difficult to remember the precise words used in the speeches which I listened to myself and my various informants have experienced the same difficulty; so my method has been, while keeping as closely as possible to the general sense of the words that were

actually used, to make the speakers say what, in my opinion, was called for by each situation (quoted in Sternberg 1982a: 86).[9]

I believe that this in itself is not sufficient evidence to reject the reproductionist view, though. Similarly, I do not think that the absence of what Leech and Short (1981) call features of normal non-fluency like hesitation pauses, false starts and syntactic anomalies (161) may serve as evidence that a written quote is not a literal rendering of previously spoken words, nor if what can be shown to be part of a longer exchange is represented by just one move. Indeed, Caldas-Coulthard (1994) says that, even with today's sophisticated recording equipment, a report of interaction is always "a simplification and a reduction of the organizational characteristics of real interaction" (297).[10] In Waugh's (1995: 156) terminology spoken language is 'stylized' into written quotation. This probably explains why very few instances of vocatives, colloquialisms, emotive lexis, syntax of spoken language, interjections (Slembrouck 1992a) can normally be found in written quotation of spoken discourse.

While, no doubt, all this seems to call the words between quotation marks into question, I would suggest that, as far as my analysis of press releases is concerned, there is a far more compelling reason for rejecting the reproductionist view. I think that the reproductionist ideas should be rejected here not because most quotes are not a 100% accurate rendering of the original, but rather because often no accuracy was aimed at in the first place. Even more so I shall suggest later on that even if a quotation was formally 100% accurate, there could be no faithful reproduction since the very act of quoting serves to drastically change the original words.

Keeping this in mind, let's now return to the formal properties of the text. As I suggested above, the simplest way to find out the status of a quotation is of course what Sternberg calls 'the juxtaposing method' (1982a, 1982b): try to recover the original and compare it with what the reporter made of it. The problem with this procedure for my purposes is that it does not only presuppose access to the original, it also presumes that there *is* an original altogether, which, in this case, I intend to show there is not.

In Sternberg's view, what remains then is the 'conjectural' or 'reconstitutive' method, i.e. trying to recover the original *from the reported version* - or, in my case, trying to prove that there cannot have been any original using the linguistic information in what is presented as a 'copy'. Slembrouck calls it the "assignment of a semantic status to strings of discourse representation on the basis of properties of the reporter's text" and adds that, to confirm the results of such textual analysis, informant testing may be useful (1992a: 129, 132).

I would like to argue that this 'conjectural' method has two advantages for my purposes. First of all, it accords with my focus on press releases only. Secondly, it reflects the psychological reality of the addressees of press releases, viz. the journalists (h$_1$), who normally have no access to any original either: journalists who receive press releases, if they wanted to, normally do not have the time nor the means to check if the offered quotes are an exact rendering of some previous statement. It is for this reason that, even if the original were available, the juxtaposing method may be misleading since, as Slembrouck rightly notes, there tends to be a big difference between, in this case, the analyst's detailed *post hoc* juxtaposition of the anterior discourse and the representation of it in a press release on the one hand and the journalist's transient, routine experience of - if not complete disregard for - the relationship between them on the other hand (1992: 133).

Even though the conjectural method looks very promising, the results prove disappointing for my data. While informant testing massively confirms that reflexive quotations in press releases have been 'made up', close to no linguistic data can be found in the corpus to support this view. That is remarkable as recent work by Sternberg (1982a, 1982b) on the direct speech fallacy in fiction, as well as by Tannen (1986, 1989), Mayes (1990) and Fludernik (1993) on 'constructed dialogue' in conversational narrative, indicates that strong textual, internal and/or contextual, situational evidence is usually available to cast doubt on the status of a quotation as reproduction. I shall now first provide a selected survey of the various types of evidence that have been presented to show that a quote is not a literal rendering and then demonstrate what (scant) evidence is available for my corpus of press releases.

3.5 *Evidence against the reproductionist view in press releases*

First, there may be various types of textual evidence inside the quote: for
example, when the quoted words include vague referents "that would have
made no sense had they actually been uttered" (Tannen: 1986: 314), as in

> "Come in, come in," he said cheerfully, as if he had been expecting
> me.
> "My name is *so-and-so*," I said. (Nabokov quoted in Sternberg 1982a:
> 98, my italics)[11]

Secondly, there may be textual evidence in the attributing clause, e.g.

> and so she'd then married Bobby to have a roof over her head *is what*
> *she practically said in those words* (*Survey of English Usage* quoted in
> Fludernik 1993: 419, my italics)

Or, as when the commentator on an England/Wales rugby match tries to
guess what the referee has just been saying to the players on the pitch:

> keep behind the player who's kicking the ball he's saying *or at least*
> *that's what I think he's saying* (quoted in Baynham 1996: 66, my
> italics)

Thirdly, and finally, there may be contextual information to render
quotations 'impossible', as when the words are attributed to an animal or a
thing, when the words of a speaker of a foreign language are translated or
as in the following line of dialogue, suggesting a chorus-like verbalization:

> And then all the Americans said "Oh in that case, go ahead." (Tannen
> 1986: 314)

As for the present corpus of press releases, the simultaneous deliveries in
(17) and (18) are among the rare indications to the effect that the quotations
in press releases are not a literal rendering.

(17)   (Bulo, Mechelen: 29 March 1994)
        "De uiteindelijk keuze voor Nike heeft veel te maken met bedrijfskultuur. Die is voor Nike even belangrijk als kwaliteit en design. De creatie van een aangename en motiverende werkomgeving stond bij Nike voorop," zeggen Dirk en Luk Busschop, gedelegeerd bestuurders van Bulo.
        "Ook de uitzonderlijke flexibiliteit van onze wandsystemen en het nieuwe concept Bulorondo (...), plus de ergonomische en logistieke troeven die wij konden bieden, speelden zeker een rol bij de toekenning van het order," aldus beide broers.

        "The final choice for Nike has a lot to do with corporate culture. That is as important for Nike as quality and design. The creation of a pleasant and stimulating working environment was a priority for Nike", say Dirk and Luk Busschop, Bulo's managing directors.
        "Our wall units' exceptional flexibility and the new Bulorondo concept (...), combined with the ergonomic and logistic advantages we offered also played a clear role in the allocation of the order", according to the two brothers.

(18)   (Group Van Hecke, Sint-Genesius-Rode: s.d.)
        De gebroeders Van Hecke: "Onze familienaam staat reeds 38 jaar borg voor kwaliteit en wij wensen deze reputatie eer aan te doen."

        The Van Hecke brothers: "Our family name has been a symbol of quality for 38 years and we wish to honour that reputation".[12]

Equally unlikely attributions are to be found in (9) and (10):

(9)   (Ericsson, Brussels: 16 May 1994)
        In vergelijking tot andere mobiele telefoons doet de Ericsson GH 337 het op praktisch alle punten aanzienlijk beter, aldus het bedrijf.

In comparison to other mobile telephones the Ericsson GH 337 performs considerably better in practically all areas, according to the company.

(10)   (Exxon, Washington, D.C.: 17 April 1989)
Valdez oil spill is not the reason for gasoline price hikes, says Exxon.[13]

In the following extract, finally, the speaker's original English words have been translated in Dutch:

(19)   (ITT Sheraton, Liège: March 1994)
ITT Sheraton is volgens haar nieuwe President en Afgevaardigd Bestuurder, Daniël P. Weadock (33 jaar en één van de directeurs van ITT), "het best bewaarde geheim van de hotelindustrie".

According to its new President and Managing Director, Daniël P. Weadock (33 years and one of the directors of ITT), ITT Sheraton is "the hotel industry's best kept secret".

It should be noted, however, that, even if such examples indicate that the quotations in press releases are not wholly reliable, they come no way close to a method for 'linguistic fingerprinting' (Coulthard 1994) providing conclusive evidence that the quotation was never verbalized by the named source. The reason for this is of course that it is one thing to demonstrate that there are differences between a quotation and the anterior speech event it draws from, yet quite another to definitely prove no such speech event ever took place.

At the same time, the fact that no internal lexical or syntactic evidence, and only very few data from the wider discourse situation, could be found to show that the quotation was not a literal rendering seems a measure of how effectively the quotations in the corpus are paraded as verbatim reports. Apparently, while quotations in press releases are almost invariably known to have been invented, they are at the same time successfully made to appear genuine. This is certainly something that will have to be accounted for later on.

3.6 'Reproductionist' self-quotation in press releases

I may by now have given the impression that all self-quotations in the corpus are pseudo-direct speech. That would be wrong. In the following extracts the references to explicitly ratified audiences seem to confirm that the quotations report on real past speech events:

(20)   (Exxon, Parsippany, New Jersey: 18 May 1989)

Exxon's effort to clean up the Alaskan oil spill now involves almost 7,000 people, more than 700 vessels, 56 aircraft and over 90 miles of boom, L.G. Rawl, chairman of the Exxon Corporation, told the company's shareholders at the company's annual meeting.

Mr Rawl declared, "The Board and all of our employees are profoundly sorry about the impact this major accident has had on the natural environment and the people who live and work in the region."

(21)   (General Motors, Antwerp: 8 March 1994)

De nieuwe Omega werd op het 64ste Internationale Autosalon van Genève in première aan het publiek voorgesteld door GM Europe-voorzitter, Louis R. Hughes.

"Hoewel de autoverkoop het voorbije jaar een dramatische terugval kende, steeg het aandeel van Opel/Vauxhall op de West-Europese markt met 0,7%. Dat is het sterkste groeiritme van alle Europese autoproducenten", zo zei Hughes in Genève.

The new Omega was first introduced to the public by GM Europe chairman Louis R. Hughes at the 64th Geneva International Car Show. "In spite of a dramatic fall in car sales during the last year, Opel/Vauxhall's share of the West European market rose by 0.7%. That is the strongest growth rate of all European car producers", said Hughes in Geneva.

Even here the question remains of course whether the words between quotation marks constitute an accurate report of what was said. The following quotes refer to written sources and can therefore be assumed not just to simply have an original, but also to be a relatively faithful rendering of it:

(22)   (Exxon, Houston, Texas: 7 July 1989)
        Exxon Company, U.S.A. has released a letter from its associate general counsel to the attorney general of Alaska. The following text is an excerpt:
        "In response to your comments reported in the press, I want to note that Exxon's attorneys first discussed the loss of computer backup tapes with your office late Monday, July 3."

(23)   (BASF, Antwerp: 14 October 1994)
        BASF Antwerpen heeft haar eerste Milieurapport aan de pers voorgesteld. (...) Daarin zegt BASF Antwerpen "een open dialoog te willen voeren met publiek en overheid en zich bewust te zijn van haar maatschappelijke rol en haar verantwoordelijkheid voor veiligheid, gezondheid en leefmilieu."

        BASF Antwerp has presented its first environment report to the press. (...) In it BASF Antwerp says that "it wants to hold an open dialogue with the public and the authorities and that it is aware of its social role and its responsibility for safety, health and environment."

In the next example the reporter's use of brackets (...) serves as a typographical indication of minute quoting practices, marking where some of the original words were left out and therefore making rather ambitious claims as far as the accuracy of the reproduction is concerned:

(24)   (Charta 91, Berchem: 12 September 1994)
        Om dit alles betaalbaar te maken vinden de auteurs van de tekst dat er een "ingrijpend politiek initiatief nodig is, (...) bijvoorbeeld (...) een moratorium en/of een herschikking" van de stadsschuld, naast andere, meer klassieke oplossingen.

> To make all this affordable the text's authors feel that "a far-reaching political initiative is needed, (...) for example (...) a moratorium and/or a readjustment" of the state debt, in addition to other, more classic solutions.[14]

Here, because I happened to have a copy of the original, the juxtaposing method could be applied and the reporter's claim to accuracy proved justified. This was in the original:

> *Om van de verstikkende schuldenlast af te geraken is er een ingrijpend politiek initiatief nodig, dat bijvoorbeeld aanstuurt op een moratorium en/of een herschikking.*

> To get rid of the suffocating debt burden a far-reaching political initiative is needed, which is for example directed at a moratorium and/or a readjustment.[15]

On the other hand, comparing extract (25) from a press release with the transcript of the speech it reports about confirms that even these 'real' self-quotations may incorporate quite some authorial editing.

> (25) (Hilaire van de Haeghe, Harsewinkel: s.d.)
> *Het tekort van het boekjaar bedraagt 20,9 miljoen DM. Helmut Claas: "Een nauwkeurige analyse toont aan dat dit cijfer te wijten is aan voorzorgsmaatregelen naar de toekomst toe."*
>
> The fiscal year's deficit amounts to 20.9 million DM. Helmut Claas: "Detailed scrutiny proves that this figure is due to precautions for the future.

This is from the transcript of the speech as it was distributed to the press along with the press release:

> *Het tekort van ons boekjaar beloopt 20,9 miljoen DM, tegenover een jaaroverschot van 16,9 miljoen DM het jaar voordien.*

Op het eerste gezicht lijkt dit cijfer zorgwekkend. Bij een grondige analyse wordt het echter duidelijk dat dit cijfer het resultaat is van voorzorgsmaatregelen naar de toekomst toe.

Our fiscal year's deficit amounts to 20.9 million DM, as opposed to a surplus of 16.9 million DM the year before.
At first sight this figure looks alarming. On closer scrutiny, though, it becomes clear that this figure is the result of precautions for the future.

Still, in spite of the undeniable evidence of 'doctoring' presented above, it is clear that, far from having been invented, the quotations in these final few extracts seem to provide a more or less accurate reproduction of previous speech events. In contrast with pseudo-direct speech, they are 'real' - though reflexive - quotations, restoring, to some extent at least, the notion of reproduction.[16]

At the end of this section, however, it is important to remember that such real self-quotations are rather exceptional and that, on the whole, most quotations in my corpus of press releases seem to have been invented, indeed coming close to what could be called 'direct writing'.[17]

4. (P)reformulation

4.1 Research question

The question now is: why such reflexive and constructed quotations in press releases or, in Bell's terminology, why such pseudo-direct speech? Why do writers of press releases go to such lengths to fabricate all these self-quotations instead of just saying what they have to say? Surely, it must play some or other role? After all, it is pre-emptive for an organization to say simply

In vergelijking tot andere mobiele telefoons doet de Ericsson GH 337 het op praktisch alle punten aanzienlijk beter.

In comparison to other mobile telephones the Ericsson GH 337 performs considerably better in practically all areas.

rather than

(9)   (Ericsson, Brussels: 16 May 1994)
        In vergelijking tot andere mobiele telefoons doet de Ericsson GH 337 het op praktisch alle punten aanzienlijk beter, aldus het bedrijf.

        In comparison to other mobile telephones the Ericsson GH 337 performs considerably better in practically all areas, according to the company.

As Mayes (1990) suggests, the fact that "many direct quotes are invented supports the hypothesis that their purpose is to perform discourse functions" (337).

I would like to suggest that, just like for the special self-reference described in the previous chapter, the use of pseudo-direct speech plays a preformulating role in press releases. I argued above that press releases are peculiarly audience-directed and that this is reflected in - as well as reinforced by - the way writers of press releases anticipate the requirements of the target medium, for example by realizing self-reference in the third person. I would like to suggest that the constructed self-quotes in press releases can be linked to the target medium, too. For one thing, since media discourse tends to be "very heavily dependent on direct and indirect speech reporting of the actual words of politicians, judges, and people in the news" (Toolan 1988: 119-120), the use of quotations described above helps press releases meet this major stylistic requirement of news reporting. So this would mean that self-quotation in press releases is also part of a point of view operation and that it plays the same preformulating$_i$ role as third-person self-reference. In addition, just like third-person self-reference, self-quotation does not only help 'structure the form but also the content of press releases to flow in sync with' news reporting (preformulation$_{ii}$). Before I start to investigate this complex question in the next chapter, let me first situate it in a broader discussion.

It is useful to explain at this stage why I prefer to talk about (self-)quotation rather than reported speech. I would argue that for my purposes the term 'reported speech' should be discarded because, as Fairclough argues, writing as well as speech may be quoted (1988: 125). The reason why, at first sight, I would not adopt the term 'discourse representation' is that in most cases, as I showed above, there is no previous discourse to be represented and the relation between the original words and the subsequent reporting of them cannot be further examined simply because there is no extra-textual correlate to be recovered.

Or is there? What if we consider, in line with the concepts of preformulation and projected discourse introduced above, not just *previous*, but also *subsequent* discourse? What if we do justice to our own claim in the first chapter that context should not be taken as a static reality out there, but rather as a flexible notion, an emergent construct, something which - to some extent at least - is achieved in the same interaction which makes use of it (Auer 1992; Goodwin and Duranti 1992)? Turning things upside down, could it be that the 'original' words are being created in the very process of reporting? While most quotes are a more or less accurate *re*formulation of some previous utterance, I would like to suggest that self-quotation in press releases, like third-person self-reference, serves as a *pre*formulation of some projected, 'to-be-reported' utterance: in other words, it spells out a preferred reading, one that the journalists are warmly recommended to adopt in their own reporting.[18] I shall now first explore the notion of quotation as reformulation and then turn to preformulation in press releases.

4.2 Reformulation and preformulation

In Slembrouck's view, reformulation is about "to what extent the referential forms of the anterior discourse are retained, modified or complemented within a particular reporting context" (1992a: 62). He suggests that the original words of an interviewee or of any quoted source are reformulated in quotations in newspapers in order to meet the requirements of newspaper reporting. The quoted version is "attuned to considerations about addressees" (74), it will have to "conform *qua* formulation to the stylistic matrix of the genre in which it occurs" (75). Voloshinov talks about the teleology of the reporting context in this respect (1973: 122). Fillmore

(1975) provides a nice example of an astronaut who has just landed on the moon and addresses a fellow member of the landing crew

My wife said I'd never get here

where it would be understood that the astronaut's wife had said

You will never get on the moon.

Thomas (1989) has an extract from a police series on British TV called *Bergerac*. The scene is that of shooting a film at the top of a cliff with a famous actor (A) talking to floor manager Timothy (F), who in turn is communicating over a walkie-talkie with director Carlton (D), who is at the foot of the cliff.

A: What's the hold up now, Timothy?
F: We're nearly there, Sir. Now, on 'action' if you just move to cliff edge, that'll be fine. then we cut and bring in Greg.
A: The double is unnecessary. I always do my own stunts.
F: Ah right? *Tim to Carlton. Tim to Carlton. He says he'll do it himself.*
D: *For god's sake, Tim, tell the bloody eejit he can't.*
F: Carlton says he appreciates the offer, Sir but
A: tell him to roll or I leave. Come on, man, let's get on with it.
F: *Carlton, he insists.*
D: *With luck we'll have a fall and kill the hun, but we couldn't afford a death clause.*
F: Carlton's just a tiny bit worried about your insurance, Sir (141).

Clearly, the notion of a literal rendering is far removed from this extract.

As it is, most hearers and readers simply do not expect a literal rendering from reporters. In terms of relevance theory, it has been argued that the 'optimally relevant' interpretation of a quote, i.e. the one that entitles the hearer to expect adequate contextual effects for the minimum necessary processing effort, is that the quotation provides a summary rather than a literal rendering (Blakemore 1993: 105): for example a student who is asked by one of his colleagues what was said in a lecture would not satisfy the principle of relevance if he or she read out the content word for word. The hearer would obtain adequate contextual effects for much less processing effort from a summary.

All this means that some of the features of quotation, including its non-reproductionist quality, are imposed by the constraints of maxims. Short (1988), for example, argues that the 'maxim of strikingness' appears to be more important in news reporting than Grice's quality maxim (69), and confirms that quotes in newspapers are often mere 'speech summaries': i.e. they provide eyecatching versions of what was originally said; what counts is the gist rather than precise wordings or so-called phraseological faithfulness (75). Short assumes that readers' canonical expectations related to quotation, viz. that it provides a literal rendering, are not just suspended in novels, but also in newspaper reporting.

Clearly, then, quotation necessarily has a dual perspective. Sternberg (1982a: 69) suggests that the reported message forms an inset surrounded by and incorporated into a frame. Slembrouck (1992a) talks about contextual embedding and 'perspectival montage' (26) in this respect: the quoted words are taken out of their original context (decontextualization) and they need to fit into a new one (recontextualization) (27).[19] Sternberg introduces the term communicative subordination (1982b: 109).

I would now like to suggest that while quotations in, say, newspapers typically reformulate previous discourse in accordance with the requirements of newspaper reporting, self-quotations in press releases serve to *preformulate subsequent discourse* in accordance with the requirements of ... newspaper reporting, i.e. they are meant to anticipate media discourse and will conform qua formulation to the stylistic matrix of that target. There is no original utterance to be first decontextualized and then recontextualized. Rather, the utterance is contextualized, pre-contextualized that is. Slembrouck's claim that "quotations are inevitably affected by the style of the reporting context" (1992a: 75) acquires a new meaning here.

4.3 *The notion of a balancing act*

Let's be clear about the possibilities and limits of preformulation, though: it should be kept in mind that just as, in quoting an eyewitness for example, a newspaper journalist cannot normally completely reformulate the original words to exclusively meet the requirements of the reporting context and has, to some extent, to take into account the source as well, the writer of a press release has to find a compromise between his or her goals (what he or she would like the journalist to write) and the target medium's requirements (what the journalist would be willing to write). As Slembrouck says about the assimilation between reported speech and reporting context: "the process of discourse representation can be seen as involving some sort of 'balancing act' between accomplishing a sense of conformity to the anterior discourse and meeting the (possibly contradictory) discursive requirements of the reporting. discourse" (1992a: 141). Practically, this means that in the act of reformulating the reporter will have to trade off the normative principle of 'exact words used' against the concerns of the reporting context. Sternberg (1982a) makes an interesting point when he says that a quotation is the "product of a tug-of-war between representational fidelity and communicative demand" (69). Bakhtin stresses that while there is no "mechanical bond" between the original reported speech and the subsequent reporting context, they are certainly not completely independent either; instead, he talks about a "chemical union" (1981: 340).

All this seems to suggest that there is much more to self-quotation in press releases than offering journalists a nice quote. If writers of press releases have to balance their own organization's PR ambitions with the requirements of newspaper reporting, as I suggested above, then surely a lot more is going on. In the next chapter I shall examine how the special type of quotation described above operates both in press releases and in newspaper articles; I shall have a closer look at how actual instances of self-quotation in press releases allow the writer to strike a delicate balance between his or her own intentions and the journalists' wishes.

4.4 Further remarks

It is necessary to point out at this stage that while my interest in quotations in press releases has certainly grown out of its special pseudo-direct speech nature, the central research question formulated above is not exclusively related to such constructed self-quotations. I would like to argue that if the difference between pseudo-direct speech and real reflexive quotations is not always easy to pinpoint in my corpus, it is not essential for my purposes either. In fact I follow Mayes (1990) when she proposes a continuum from quotes which could be authentic renditions to those which are undoubtedly invented. As Tannen (1989) concludes from her research on constructed dialogue in everyday oral interaction:

> My claim would not be undermined even by a tape recording "proving" that the words were spoken as reported. Neither am I claiming that when the reported words were not actually uttered, the reporter is lying or intentionally misrepresenting what was said. Rather, the point is that the spirit of the utterance is fundamentally transformed (109).

Similarly, my analysis of what I take to be pseudo-direct speech in (1) as a preformulation would not be undermined if somebody came up with a videotape of Otto Harrison on the Alaskan beach, saying exactly those words that are quoted in the Exxon press release.

(1)   (Exxon, Valdez, Alaska: 16 August 1989)
        In an effort to aid Alaska fishermen in the wake of the Exxon Valdez oil spill, Exxon has developed a nine-point program and paid more than $38 million in fishermen claims. (...) Otto Harrison, general manager of Exxon's Valdez operations, said: "We are committed to treating fairly those who have been indirectly impacted by this accident. We view our work with the fishermen as a very important part of this effort."

Rather, the point is, as I suggested above, that through the very act of self-quotation, whether it is actually pseudo-direct speech or not, the spirit of the original utterance is fundamentally transformed. The question now is: in what way?

As Fludernik (1993) argues,

> reported discourse constitutes a fiction that language fabricates in accordance
> with discourse strategic requirements, whether these are brevity, poignancy,
> pithiness, verisimilitude, exaggeration, ironic over-characterization or, simply,
> truthful representation. Representation inherently includes fictionalization, and
> fictionalization, like all rhetoric, has its own interests, its strategies, its
> tendencies. One traditional way of saying this has been to consider all
> discourse representation as either mediated or 'framed', but mediation and
> framing are formal concepts and they need to be complemented with more
> specific stylistic, rhetorical and historical analyses of the precise functions of
> quotation, of the different purposes of typicality or pretended reproductiveness
> in represented speech and thought (22).

What, then, are these 'precise functions' of self-quotation in press releases?
This is what I shall explore in the next chapter.

5.   The View from Bakhtin

5.1 Quotation and dialogue

Before I turn to the functions of self-quotation in press releases, I would
like to shed light on the theories of Bakhtin and Voloshinov, who have
repeatedly drawn attention to the role played by quotations in the interactive
way I suggested above. Indeed the idea of quotation as preformulation,
rather than just reformulation, is in some way already present in their work.
More generally, Bakhtin's and Voloshinov's writings have been very
influential in this field, and it is therefore necessary as well as enlightening
to situate what I have said about pseudo-direct speech in press releases with
respect to their theories. In doing so, I shall resume some of the points
made earlier in this chapter and prepare for the functional analysis in the
next one.

In the first chapter I showed that Bakhtin and Co claim that "the real unit of
language that is implemented in speech (...) is not the individual, isolated
monologic utterance, but the interaction of at least two utterances" (1973:
117) and that such dialogue is not restricted to conversation, but can also be

extended to writing. It is Voloshinov, the linguist of the Bakhtin circle, who actually talks about the role of quotation in this respect. In particular, just as a turn at talking shows the current speaker's strategic accommodation to what was said before, written quotation provides objective documentation of how the quoted words were actually received by the reporter (1973: 117). The fact that in most press releases we are not looking at real quotation but rather at self-quotation, i.e. that in the case of pseudo-direct speech no two distinct voices are in play, makes no real difference. Bakhtin (1984: 184) himself provides the answer: "dialogic relationships are also possible toward one's own utterance as a whole, toward its separate parts and toward an individual word within it".

It is not surprising in this respect that Bakhtin and his circle devote most of their attention to the relationship with what was said before (cf. 1981: 337-340). Still, their views have all the ingredients to venture one step further: as I have shown, they also stress the relationship between a text and what comes next. So it is not too eccentric to argue that, just as a turn at talking is not only geared to what was said before, but also to what will be said afterwards, so the very point of self-quotation in press releases may be to anticipate how the writer hopes his or her own words will be received and, possibly, retold. This would mean that an analysis of self-quotation in press releases constitutes an important methodological resource for making otherwise elusive speaker aims available for empirical scrutiny. In addition, since for Bakhtin this process of discursive assimilation is at the origin of the variety of functionally specialized types of discourse, this type of quotation can be directly linked to the institutional character of press releases. As Bakhtin says, in a powerful claim that seems to underpin one of the central tenets throughout my research of press releases: "[e]ach speech genre in each area of speech communication has its own typical conception of the addressee, and this defines it as a genre" (1986: 95).

Let's now look in greater detail at what Bakhtin and Voloshinov further have to say about this role of quotation in a dialogic relationship. Two directions are suggested: Bakhtin (1984) on double-voiced discourse; and Voloshinov (1973) on linear and pictorial styles.[20]

5.2 Double-voiced discourse

It is important to note first of all that not all quotation is equally dialogic. Looking at discourse from the viewpoint of its relation to someone else's utterance, Bakhtin (1984), in his typically abstract and wordy style, seems to distinguish three discourse types:

a. direct, unmediated, object-oriented discourse
b. objectified discourse
c. double-voiced discourse

Direct, unmediated discourse serves to express the speaker's ultimate semantic authority and, at best, merely includes some influence from other people's words, which serves as 'scaffolding': i.e. the others' words are never explicitly incorporated into the 'architectural whole' (187).

In objectified discourse, the words of others play a much more important role. They are typically rendered between quotation marks. It is called objectified because a clear distance appears to be preserved between the original words and the report. In scientific research articles, for example, previous literature on the same topic is traditionally quoted either for refutation or confirmation; there is no genuine interaction, but rather an "objectified (plotted) clash" of two independent positions. Interestingly, one of them is "subordinated wholly to the higher, ultimate authority" of the other, so Bakhtin seems to confirm that even here, in spite of the distance, the quotation is not entirely inaccessible to the reporter since "it is treated as an object of authorial understanding, and not from the point of view of its own referential intention" (186-188).[21]

With double-voiced discourse, finally, the reporter penetrates inside the other's words, "works with [the other's] point of view", "uses [the other's] discourse for [his or her, i.e. the reporter's] own purposes, by inserting a new semantic intention into a discourse which already has, and which retains, an intention of its own" (189). Bakhtin's set of examples includes parody and the use of a narrator as a compositional substitute for the author's words in fiction.

I would like to argue that the pseudo-direct speech described above can be characterized as double-voiced too. While the egocentric discourse of press releases should be expected to be very much *object-oriented*, I have shown in this chapter that there are, maybe quite unexpectedly, a lot of quotations in my data, which seem to *objectify* the press releases. Since most of the quotes are instances of pseudo-direct speech, however, it can be concluded that press releases are in fact *double-voiced*: the reporter can simply penetrate inside the other's words because they happen to be his or her own. Just as an author of fiction puts his own words in the mouth of a narrator, writers of press releases make up quotes that were never verbalized by the named source. Even more so, in line with the notion of preformulation, it could actually be argued that here it looks as if the reporter is using someone else's discourse for his or her own purposes, but that, on closer scrutiny, he or she is using his or her own words for someone else's, i.e. the journalist's, purposes. I shall suggest later that what happens through such self-quotation is that, as Bakhtin says about double-voiced discourse, a "slight shadow of objectification is cast over [the reporter's own words]" (190); they are 'cooled down' by 'refraction' (201). Further in Bakhtinian terms, the double-voiced discourse of press releases can be called 'conditional' (189) in that the success of self-quotation as a preformulating device depends on the journalists' reactions to it.

5.3 Incorporation and dissemination

Another perspective on the dynamic interrelationship between quoted words and their reporting is offered by Voloshinov's distinction between the linear and pictorial styles.

The linear style of writing is marked by a clear-cut distinction between the quoted words and the report. As a result, it serves to maintain the authenticity of the quoted words, to "forge hard and fast boundaries" for them, "screen [them] from penetration by the author's intonations", "to condense and enhance [their] individual linguistic characteristics" (1973: 119). The linear style is typical of rhetoric with its "acute awareness of property rights to words" and its "fastidiousness in matters of authenticity" (122), as in the languages of the law and of politics, and in matters of hierarchy.

Next we have, what Voloshinov calls, the pictorial style, where the quoted words and the report typically interact: this means that the 'boundaries between them are obliterated' (120). There are two directions in which the quoted words and the report may interact: either the source's words may start to change those of the reporter or the reporter may penetrate the source's words.

In the former case, with the source's words dominating the report, Fairclough (1988), who looks at what he calls 'boundary maintenance strategies' between the reporter's primary discourse and the quoted source's secondary discourse, talks about 'dissemination', e.g. the use of the newspaper headline

Mrs Thatcher will not stand for any backsliding

to refer to Thatcher's statement

I will not stand for any backsliding (128).

Here, the original words are retained and presented as if they were the journalist's own language, and not a more or less literal quote of what the politician said. So, Thatcher's language has infiltrated that of the newspaper.

Alternatively, when the quoted words get infiltrated with comments from the reporter, Fairclough talks about 'incorporation': i.e. the quotation is not a literal rendering of what the quoted source said, as it includes features that unmistakably derive from the reporter's language, as in the tabloid headline

Maggie must get out, says Kinnock

which serves to represent the former Labour leader's statement

Margaret Thatcher must resign (128).

Fairclough comments that "of course" Kinnock did not say that 'Maggie' had to 'get out'. Here the politician's statement is rendered in the popular newspaper jargon and it is not possible to determine to what extent the quoted source is responsible for the quoted words. Hartley (1982) calls this

the "colonization of commonsense language", with newspapers translating
the sayings of the elites into a familiar idiom (179; cf. also Hardt-Mautner
1995 on the media's *media*ting role).

It should be clear from the above that while the quoting style of press
releases looks very 'linear', there is quite some interaction between the
quoted words and the report. So this means that press releases are actually
pictorial in style. Especially, the notion of pseudo-direct speech implies
incorporation, since what is actually the author's discourse is attributed to a
quoted source: remember the words in the Kredietbank press release in (4),
which were subsequently attributed to the chairman of the Kredietbank's
direction committee in (5).

But there is also dissemination. Let's give an example. (26) presents
the beginning of a press release:

(26)   (BASF, Brussels: 17 March 1994)
        BASF: geen voorjaarsmoeheid
        De onderneming zet haar structurele aanpassingen onverminderd
        voort
        Ter gelegenheid van de persconferentie, waar Dr. Jürgen Strube,
        Voorzitter van de Raad van Bestuur, enkele toelichtingen gaf bij
        de balans van de BASF-Groep, gaf hij eveneens zijn kijk op de
        actuele situatie in het volgend beeld weer: "Wij hebben een
        goede start genomen en een uitstekende tijd gelopen over de
        eerste meters van de wedstrijd. Maar wij zijn er ons eveneens
        heel goed van bewust dat wij niet alleen een sprint lopen. Wij
        moeten een beroep doen op al onze krachten om de hele weg, die
        nog voor ons ligt, af te leggen. Wij beschikken niettemin over de
        nodige reserves om de eindstreep te halen.

        BASF: no spring fatigue
        The company continues its structural adjustments without
        abatement
        At a press conference, where Dr. Jürgen Strube, chairman of the
        Board, provided some comments on the BASF Group balance,
        he also offered his views on the current situation by means of
        the following image: "We have taken a good start and run an

excellent time over the first metres of the race. But we are also very much aware that we are not only running a sprint. We have to use all our resources to complete all the way in front of us. Nevertheless, we have the necessary reserves to make it to the finish line."

The press release starts with a double headline, followed by a real, more or less plausible self-quotation. What is interesting, though, is that direct speech soon starts giving way to indirect speech and, further on, to even more narrative portions with Dr Strube's views getting increasingly filtered by the author of the press release. In (27), for example, the responsibility for the propositional content still lies with the quoted source, but the deictic centre (who is 'I', where is 'here', when is 'now'?) has moved to the writer of the press release:

(27)   (BASF, Brussels: 17 March 1994)
        Volgens Dr. Jürgen Strube is de samenwerking met de Russische partner Gazprom veelbetekenend en exemplarisch te noemen.

        According to Dr. Jürgen Strube the co-operation with the Russian partner Gazprom can be called significant and exemplary.

Further on, in (28), not even the propositional content is left with Dr. Strube:

(28)   (BASF, Brussels: 17 March 1994)
        Dr. Jürgen Strube sprak over een lichte heropleving tijdens de eerste twee maanden van 1994.

        Dr. Jürgen Strube talked about a slight rise during the first two months of 1994.

The interesting thing about this smooth transition towards ever less direct modes of quotation - and indeed the reason why I decided to have a close look at this press release   is that, towards the end, authorial narrative and quoted statement are merged, almost imperceptibly, in:

(29)   (BASF, Brussels: 17 March 1994)

In het algemeen kunnen we de gang van zaken in 1993 als ontgoochelend bestempelen.

In general we can call the course of events in 1993 disappointing.

Here, what is most probably an extract from Dr Strube's speech is rendered directly, without quotation marks: this is clear dissemination. (29) presents what Fairclough (1988) calls the 'UNSIG(nalled) mode': what should have been presented between quotation marks and attributed to the quoted source - like in (26) -, is adopted by the reporter as his or her own language. The embedded statement takes over. As Bakhtin (1984: 190) says, the reporter's enthusiasm for the quoted source's words destroys the distance between them and goes to weaken the deliberate sense of a separate voice. In Goffman's writing, this type of merger is referred to as 'downkeying' or 'delamination' (1974).

This case is also a good example of what Voloshinov, talking about literature, calls 'substituted direct discourse' in which the author says what the hero might or should have said. Interestingly, he adds that

> [this talking in another's stead] presupposes a parallelism of intonations, the intonations of the author's speech and the substituted speech of the hero (what he might or should have said), both running in the same direction. When a complete solidarity in values and intonations exists between the author and his hero within the framework of a rhetorically constructed context, the author's rhetoric and that of the hero begin to overlap: their voices merge (138).

Such parallelism of intonations is, of course, not surprising between the chairman of a corporation's Board of Directors and the writer of a press release for that same corporation.

The above example of dissemination, along with the 'incorporating' pseudo-direct speech, illustrates how thin the line between the quoted words and the report in press releases really is. Still, I would like to stress again that it does not *look* thin at all. I have shown that for most cases of incorporation in my corpus of press releases, for example, no conclusive textual evidence could be found to show that they were not a literal rendering; alternatively, the BASF press release presents what is only a very rare case of dissemination. In other words, most double-voiced discourse in the corpus is effectively paraded as verbatim, single-voiced reporting. In Thompson and Yiyun's (1991) terminology, we are looking at writer acts (words on the part of whoever, as Goffman would put it, 'authored' the press release) carefully disguised as author acts (words attributed to a quoted source).

6.   Conclusions

At this stage, the original research question presented earlier in this chapter, viz. 'why go to such lengths to quote oneself instead of just saying what one has to say?', can be reformulated as 'why resort to such carefully disguised double-voiced discourse?' Surely, it should be clear by now that, as Marjorie Goodwin (1990/91) suggests, reports should not be accepted as instances of the events they describe - rather the process of reporting itself should be investigated as a situated conversational activity (276).

One more remark. All the time I have been focusing on direct quotations, and I have only rarely referred to indirect modes of quoting. I would now argue that it is not so much the difference between direct and indirect speech that counts (and how the various ways of reporting relate to the events they describe) as the difference between embedded and non-embedded statements. Indeed a theory which says that direct quotes are not inaccessible and have a dual perspective actually serves to reduce the difference between direct and indirect ways of quoting.[22] It is not the difference between

(30)   (Exxon, Darien, Conn.: 29 March 1989)
        "Aerial spraying of Corexit 9527 began late Sunday or early Monday and has continued through the week as weather conditions permit", said Al Bilderback, Energy Chemicals marketing manager for the Gulf Coast region in Houston.

and

(31)   (Exxon, Darien, Conn.: 29 March 1989)
        Bilderback said that dispersants such as Corexit are most
        effective at the outset of a spill when oil is most concentrated.

that counts as that between

(30)   (Exxon, Darien, Conn.: 29 March 1989)
        "Aerial spraying of Corexit 9527 began late Sunday or early
        Monday and has continued through the week as weather condi-
        tions permit", said Al Bilderback, Energy Chemicals marketing
        manager for the Gulf Coast region in Houston.

and

Aerial spraying of Corexit 9527 began late Sunday or early Monday
and has continued through the week as weather conditions permit.

as well as that between

(31)   (Exxon, Darien, Conn.: 29 March 1989)
        Bilderback said that dispersants such as Corexit are most
        effective at the outset of a spill when oil is most concentrated.

and

Dispersants such as Corexit are most effective at the outset of a spill
when oil is most concentrated.

Chapter 5
The Functions of Self-Quotation in Press Releases

1. Point of View Operation

Take the self-quote in the following extract from a press release:

(1)   (Exxon, Valdez, Alaska: 16 August 1989)
        In an effort to aid Alaska fishermen in the wake of the Exxon
        Valdez oil spill, Exxon has developed a nine-point program and
        paid more than $38 million in fishermen claims. (...) Otto
        Harrison, general manager of Exxon's Valdez operations, said:
        "We are committed to treating fairly those who have been
        indirectly impacted by this accident. We view our work with the
        fishermen as a very important part of this effort."

Here the writer of this Exxon press release has attributed what, I have
shown, may well be his or her own words to the general manager of
Exxon's Valdez operations Otto Harrison. I would now argue that this is
part of the same point of view operation as third-person self-reference: it
appears as if the writer of the press release is switching out of his or her
own perspective and takes that of the journalists, who are expected to retell
the press release in their own news reporting. As I have argued, news
reporting typically includes quite a lot of quotations and self-quotation
therefore seems to anticipate the typical reference forms of news reporting.
Hence self-quotation serves a preformulating$_i$ role.

    The question could now be raised why news reporting is so dependent
on quotation in the first place. I shall argue that, broadly speaking, two
traditional, inter-related functions can be distinguished:

- the use of quotation makes news reporting more lively (dramatic function)

- the use of quotation makes news reporting more objective (distancing function)

As for objectivity, I shall further suggest that two issues have dominated the analysis of quoting in the news, viz.

- if the quotation provides an accurate rendering of the original words (reliability function)

- what the reporter thinks about the views expressed in the quotation (attitude function)

For each of these functions I shall look at how it operates in my corpus of press releases and at what happens to it if the self-quote gets copied in news reporting (which, I have argued, seems to be the rationale behind press releases).[1] I shall conclude that if self-quoting 'helps structure the form of press releases to flow in sync with news reporting', 'content-wise' too it serves to anticipate the media's expectations (preformulation$_{ii}$). In particular, I shall argue that self-quotation in press releases helps reconcile the - sometimes - widely divergent ambitions of those who manage the news and those who make it.

Note, finally, that there has of course been an overwhelming amount of previous research on quotation and the various functions it may have, especially in media discourse. It is certainly not my intention to present any kind of survey of the literature in this place. Rather, I shall draw on selected relevant sources as I go along, just as I did in the previous chapter.

2.   The Dramatic Function

There can be no doubt that self-quotations makes press releases appear a great deal more lively and that for journalists to copy those self-quotations has a similar effect on news reporting. Hence, it can be concluded that self-quotation plays a preformulating$_{ii}$ role. In this section I shall present a selection of data-based evidence to support this claim.

2.1 Retaining first-person deictics

Take the following utterance:

> *Onze tests van verschillende veelgebruikte 100 Megabit netwerk-adapters tonen aan dat onze nieuwe Smart 100 AT Ringnode-adapters verreweg de snelste DDI-client-kaarten zijn die voor ISA-bus-systemen verkrijgbaar zijn.*

> Our tests of several frequently used 100 Megabit network adaptors show that our new Smart 100 AT Ringnode adaptors are by far the fastest DDI client cards available for ISA bus systems.

In chapter 3 I provided corpus-based evidence that the references to "onze nieuwe Smart 100 AT Ringnode-adapters" [our new Smart 100 AT Ringnode adaptors] and to "onze tests" [our tests] are unlikely in a press release. Instead, third-person self-reference would normally be preferred because it serves as a more appropriate preformulation$_i$, as in:

> *De tests door Madge van verschillende veelgebruikte 100 Megabit netwerk-adapters tonen aan dat de nieuwe Smart 100 AT Ringnode-adapters van Madge verreweg de snelste DDI-client-kaarten zijn die voor ISA-bus-systemen verkrijgbaar zijn.*

> Madge's tests of several frequently used 100 Megabit network adaptors show that Madge's new Smart 100 AT Ringnode adaptors are by far the fastest DDI client cards available for ISA bus systems.

Still, the author of this Madge press release apparently preferred

(2)   (Madge, Hoofddorp: 26 April 1994)
       B. McGiffert, General Manager van LANQuest, zegt: "Onze tests van verschillende veelgebruikte 100 Megabit netwerk-adapters

tonen aan dat de nieuwe Smart 100 AT Ringnode-adapters van Madge verreweg de snelste DDI-client-kaarten zijn die voor ISA-bus-systemen verkrijgbaar zijn".

[B. McGiffert, LANQuest's General Manager, says: "Our tests of several frequently used 100 Megabit network adaptors show that Madge's new Smart 100 AT Ringnode adaptors are by far the fastest DDI client cards available for ISA bus systems".]

In (2), through pseudo-direct speech, the reference to "onze tests" [our tests] is part of a quotation and since here the deictic centre lies with the quoted source and not with the reporter, the first-person pronoun should not keep journalists from copying the extract in their own news reporting. This means that embedding allows the writer to retain first-person deictics and still produce a perfectly preformulated$_i$ press release. Even more so, I would argue that while the typical third-person self-reference may seem to render press releases rather dull and lifeless, quotation has the advantage of keeping at least some of the drama of self-centred discourse[2] and that, unlike third-person self-reference, this may not just allow, but actively encourage journalists to retell press releases. So this is one reason why (2) would be a more attractive preformulation$_{ii}$ than its non-embedded deictically neutral counterpart.

2.2 Temporal shifts

Note that in (2) a sense of liveliness is further conveyed by the use of the present tense "zegt" [says]. If we look at the wider context of the quote, it is clear that the simple past and present perfect could normally have been expected: in the first sentence of (3) it is announced that tests 'were recently executed' and that they 'have proved' the adaptors' capacity to offer uninterrupted network capacity of 3500 Kbyte p.s.

(3)   (Madge, Hoofddorp: 26 April 1994)
        Uit tests die onlangs zijn uitgevoerd door het in San José, Californië, gevestigde LANQuest Labs is gebleken dat de Smart 100 AT ringnode-adapters van Madge goed zijn voor een

ononderbroken netwerkverkeer van bijna 3500 Kbyte/sec. B. McGiffert, General Manager van LANQuest, zegt: "Onze test van verschillende veelgebruikte 100 Megabit netwerk-adapters tonen aan dat de nieuwe Smart 100 AT Ringnode-adapters van Madge verreweg de snelste DDI-client-kaarten zijn die voor ISA-bus-systemen verkrijgbaar zijn".

[Tests that were recently executed at LANQuest Labs based in San José, California, have proved that Madge's Smart 100 AT Ringnode adaptors offer uninterrupted network interaction of almost 3500 Kbyte p.s. B. McGiffert, LANQuest's General Manager, says: "Our tests of several frequently used 100 Megabit network adaptors show that Madge's new Smart 100 AT Ringnode adaptors are by far the fastest DDI client cards available for ISA bus systems".]

With the quotation in the next sentence, however, the writer switches to the simple present. As Declerck (1993) has shown, such a shift of temporal perspective from past to present is typical with verbs of saying and hearing. Here are some of his examples:

I hear you have been promoted.
They tell me she is pregnant again.
I gather/understand there's been trouble again.
The 9 o'clock news says that oil prices are going to rise again (cf. also Goffman 1974: 508-509; Brown and Levinson 1987: 106-107).

According to Declerck, this use of the simple present serves to heighten the relevance of the past situation and I would argue that this is a second way in which self-quotation in press releases plays a preformulating$_{ii}$ role.[3]
     That such tense shifts are meant to appeal to the reader is also clear from the fact that they frequently occur in the headlines of press releases, with past tenses for the rest:

(4)   (Exxon, Washington, D.C.: 17 April 1989)

Valdez oil spill is not the reason for gasoline price hikes, says Exxon

Claims that recent increases in crude oil and petroleum prices in the United States are largely the result of the oil spill in Valdez, Alaska, are incorrect, J.T. McMillan, senior vice president of Exxon Company, U.S.A., said today.

Schiffrin (1981) as well as Johnstone (1987) see such tense variation as an evaluative device to underscore that the event in question is the story's main point.[4]

2.3 Personification

Apart from allowing first-person self-reference and promoting the use of the simple present, representing one's own words between quotation marks also makes explicit reference to a quoted source necessary. As Van Leeuwen (1996a) argues, such "[r]epresentations include or exclude social actors to suit [the writers'] interests and purposes in relation to the readers for whom they are intended" (38). I would argue that here, through pseudo-direct speech, writers of press releases seem to make a specific effort at 'inclusion' and that this again can be related to the peculiar audience-directedness of press releases. In (2), strictly speaking, the reference to Mr B. McGiffert, LANQuest's General Manager, is not really necessary. It is only through the use of self-quotation that, in Van Leeuwen's terms, 'assimilation' with the collective and impersonal Madge has been replaced by 'specification' and 'individualization'.

Simply put, this means that pseudo-direct speech allows for personification, and I suggest that this can be linked to questions of newsworthiness. As far as newsworthiness is concerned, Galtung and Ruge (1973: 67-68), for example, argue convincingly that news about a person is more attractive. Pseudo-direct speech, then, allows the writer to present the organization as antropomorhic, i.e. one with a human face, and this further enhances the press release's chances of being retold by the journalists in their own news reporting.

Also, in (2) McGiffert is in subject position: this means that, thanks to self-quotation, the organization he represents can be shown as an active, dynamic force, taking the initiative rather than simply undergoing the activity. Extract (4), for example, is taken from a press release that was issued by Exxon in the wake of the Valdez oil spill and the 'activation' in it helps the company present a positive image of itself in the middle of a serious public relations crisis. It should be added that it is not just the news managers who have a stake in this way of putting things but that, as Galtung and Ruge have argued, the newsmakers too may be very happy to keep the quoted source in subject position. After all, journalists have been shown to favour the western cultural ideal that 'man is master of his own destiny' (67). This is yet another way in which self-quotation serves a preformulating$_{ii}$ role.

To wrap up my analysis of the dramatic function, it can be concluded that the use of self-quotations makes press releases more lively in various ways. This enhances the press releases' chances of being retold.

3.   The Distancing Function

3.1 Self-quotation as distancing

Let's return to (1):

(1)   (Exxon, Valdez, Alaska: 16 August 1989)
        In an effort to aid Alaska fishermen in the wake of the Exxon Valdez oil spill, Exxon has developed a nine-point program and paid more than $38 million in fishermen claims. (...) Otto Harrison, general manager of Exxon's Valdez operations, said: "We are committed to treating fairly those who have been indirectly impacted by this accident. We view our work with the fishermen as a very important part of this effort."

I would argue that self-quotation does not just make the press release more lively and hence more attractive for journalists to retell. More importantly, what seems to happen is that the writer of the press release is taking a distance from what are after all his or her own words. In Bakhtin's terminology, those words, since they appear between quotation marks, are endowed with a sense of "purity and otherness"; they acquire "an enhanced reality", "the incontestable truth of the overheard" (Tannen 1989: 105). Self-quotation, then, is a simple, but powerful trick that helps turn 'internally persuasive' discourse into 'authoritative' discourse through the use of 'speaking persons' (Bakhtin 1981: 339, 348). Erving Goffman seems to provide a perfect description of the metapragmatics of press releases when he argues that "[i]nstead of stating a view outright, the individual tends to attribute it to a character who happens to be himself, but one he has been careful to withdraw from in one regard or another" (1974: 551).

As a result, press releases look disinterested and neutral rather than self-interested, promotional. Since I have argued that journalists consider information from disinterested sources more credible than that from interested sources, it can be concluded that self-quotation in press releases also serves a preformulating$_{ii}$ role as far as the question of credibility is concerned. Actually, journalists themselves use quotation to be objective and hence more credible. As Gaye Tuchman (1972) suggests "[b]y interjecting someone else's opinion, [newsmen] believe they are removing themselves from participation in the story, and they are letting the 'facts' speak" (668). So self-quotation serves to objectify press releases, just as quotation serves to objectify news reporting.

Of course, we are talking about *self*-quotations and it could be objected that no journalists will normally be fooled into thinking that the words attributed to Harrison in (1) are any 'purer or *other*' than those in the rest of the press release; in the end, their truth proves no more incontestable. Still, I would join Teun van Dijk in arguing that it is "not so much the real truth as the illusion of truth that is at stake in the rhetoric of news" (1988: 86). After all, in the mouths of the journalists the original self-quotations are turned into quotations and they seem to function as *real* distancing devices. Take (5) for example:

(5)   (Exxon, Houston, Texas, 30 March 1989)
        Exxon Shipping Company announced it has terminated the
        employment of Captain Joseph J. Hazelwood. The termination

followed the announcement by government investigators that this employee had failed the blood alcohol tests administered on the Exxon Valdez last Friday morning.

Frank Iarossi, president of Exxon Shipping Company, said that the decision to terminate the employee was made because he violatcd company policy concerning alcohol.

"We are all extremely disappointed and outraged that an officer in such a critical position would have jeopardized his ship, crew and the environment through such actions. Our policies in this area are very clear," Iarossi explained.

The facts of Hazelwood's dismissal can simply be retold by the journalists and they are presented more or less directly in the press release. On the other hand, Exxon's feelings of 'extreme disappointment' and 'outrage' about the Captain's conduct and the company's assertion of 'very clear' safety policies have to be channelled between quotation marks before journalists can safely copy them. In my corpus of press releases, such so-called 'extreme case formulations' (Pomerantz 1986) or 'maximizing devices' (Vandenbergen 1996) are invariably attributed to a quoted source, as in the following extract, where Ericsson's proud claim that its new mobile phone is the smallest and lightest, with the longest speaking time, is apparently presented with a fair degree of scepticism:

(6)   (Ericsson, Brussels: 16 May 1994)

In de steeds hardere strijd om mobiele-telefoonklanten doen de fabrikanten hun uiterste best om de spreektijden zo lang mogelijk te maken. Tegelijkertijd neemt de vraag naar kleinere en lichtere telefoons toe. Van de nieuwe GSM telefoon van Ericsson wordt nu beweerd dat hij 's werelds kleinste en lichtste is, met de langste spreektijd.

In the ever harder struggle for mobile telephone customers the manufacturers are doing their utmost best to make the speaking times as long as possible. At the same time, the demand for smaller and lighter telephones is increasing. Of Ericsson's new

GSM telephone it is now claimed that it is the smallest and lightest in the world, with the longest speaking time.

Alternatively, it is striking that in one of the last press releases of the Valdez corpus extreme-case formulations like "closing in on the finish line", "mounting all-out efforts" and "not a single bag of waste" for once do not appear between quotation marks, and I would suggest that this is a slip-up, reflecting Exxon's frustration with the unfortunate end of the clean-up effort and illustrating Lerman's claim that "[i]n a time of crisis, when a system is disordered, the constitutive rules of the language game are more apparent" (1983: 83).

(7)   (Exxon, Valdez, Alaska: 18 September 1989)
        Exxon's 1989 shoreline cleanup operations personnel in Prince William Sound are closing in on the finish line. Over 1,088 miles have been treated, and less than one mile remains.
        Three task forces are mounting all-out efforts (...). (...)
        After enduring nearly four months of bureaucratic run-around that resulted in not a single bag of waste being burned, Exxon is releasing the incinerator barge at Kodiak Island. More than $5 million was spent to have it sit idle while the state of Alaska stalled the permitting process for the waste disposal system they once called the "preferred method".

Similarly, from the Belgian extreme right party Vlaams Blok, after another of their political rallies had been disrupted by a bomb alarm:

(8)   (Vlaams Blok, Antwerp: 28 September 1994)
        De schrik voor een Vlaams Blok verkiezingsoverwinning zit er diep in. Blijkbaar zijn alle middelen, ook de meest laag-bij-de-grondse, goed om het Vlaams Blok electoraal de nek om te wringen.

        The fear for a Vlaams Blok election victory is strong. Apparently all means, even the most down-to-earth, are good to strangle the Vlaams Blok electorally.

On the whole, however, these are exceptions and 'extreme case formulations' are usually expressed between quotation marks in press releases.

3.2 Other examples of distancing through quotation

Interestingly, it should be noted that the same 'distancing' use of self-quotation has been observed in other forms of media discourse. Hill and Irvine (1993), for example, look at news interviews and say that interviewees may want to be cautious to avoid offending co-interactants or to say or do something that they are not entirely convinced of. To mitigate such sensitive action they can "[give] a view which is portrayed as credible but not authored as their own" (623) (cf. also Jucker 1986: 147).

Focusing on Oliver North's self-presentation practices in his testimony before the Iran-Contra committee, Kline and Kuper (1994) point to the same strategy. Here is an example of how the US Marines Lieutenant Colonel and National Security Council staff member made up quotes to try and construct a positive identity for himself in court:

> People give me a lot of credit. I - if someone wants to say, "it was a speech by Ollie North that made me want to give money to help the Nicaraguan resistance", I appreciate that (30).

Kline and Kuper distinguish sixteen such instances of what they call "double-staging" and conclude that "[e]ven though North was the author of these dialogues, the grammatical shifts from first to third person make it sound like another person was reporting on North's actions, which enabled us to alter our view of North from a testifier to a character in an unfolding story" (30). Crucially, Kline and Kuper add that here is a radical type of altercasting, which, because it enables North to be positive about himself without appearing too arrogant or self-interested, allows journalists to copy his words in their own reporting.

Clayman (1992) points to a similar phenomenon for interviewers and singles out what he calls 'footing shifts' as a method of "interactional caution" when talking about "assessable matters" (163). In the following extract, a journalist is interviewing Robert Dole, then U.S. Senate majority leader for the republican party.

Senator, President Reagan's elected thirteen months ago: an enormous landslide. It is said that his programs are in trouble, though he seems to be terribly popular with the American people. It is said by some people at the White House we could get those programs through if only we had perhaps more effective leadership   (...). What do you think the problem is really?

Here quotation serves a strategic purpose of allowing the interviewer to make a particular point without going on record as endorsing it (cf. also Chafe 1986; Heritage and Roth 1995).

More generally, it should be pointed out here that this use of quotation apparently is not just typical of media discourse. Brown and Levinson, for example, show that quotation may be "a specific way of doing a speech act via a messenger" in everyday interaction, as in

John says do you want to come too? (1987: 121)

Recanati has a nice example of self-quotation when he says that in the following utterance the report functions as an order and that it does so no matter if the speaker really told Du Barry or not.

Madame du Barry is arriving at the station in an hour and I told her that you would be there to pick her up (1987: 91).

A lot of research has focused on children's quoting practices. Hill and Irvine (1993): "As we attain psycho-social maturity through reflection and social interaction, we can learn to 'experimentally objectify' the coercive discourse of the other and adopt those alien words which are most in concert with our values and experiences" (40). This seems to be in line with Goffman (1981), who argues that the child learns "to embed the statements and mannerisms of a zoo-full of beings in its own verbal behavior": he stresses that, in spite of simple syntax and lexicon, children's language is characterized by complex laminative features (151). Marjorie Goodwin (1990) looks at so-called "he-said-she-said-accusations", i.e. gossip dispute in black girls' peer groups, and notices that instead of bald, direct charges like boys'

    William: Boy you broke my skateboard!

or

    Vincent: You messin' up my paper.

girls' offense is phrased typically in terms of a report of what some intermediary said, as in

    Bea: That girl say you have ugly sneaks on (1990/91: 264)

where Bea is disclaiming personal responsibility for the accusation; its potentially troublesome communicative load is deflected on to the quoted source.[5]

In all these cases I would suggest (self-)quoting is part of a point of view operation: the words between quotation marks seem to belong to "a voice slightly different from the one the speaker had been using, one which presumably allows the speaker and his listeners to align themselves over against the figure to whom the remarks are to be attributed" (Goffman 1974: 531). In press releases, in particular, self-quotation serves to anticipate the typical objectivity requirements of news reporting and, hence, it plays a preformulating$_{ii}$ role. I shall now look at objectivity in greater detail and focus on two aspects of it that are traditionally considered important in the media: one is that journalists are expected to provide an accurate rendering of the quoted source's words - I shall call this the 'reliability function' -, the other is what attitude the journalists take towards the quoted words (the 'attitude function'). Surely, for journalists to be objective, it is not enough to simply include a couple of quotes. What counts is that they represent the words the way they were actually spoken and that they remain neutral to them. The question is now raised how all that can be preformulated in the self-quotes of press releases.[6]

4.   The Reliability Function

4.1 Reporter's reliability

As I explained in the previous chapter, quotation marks are traditionally assumed to signal verbatim reporting. I would now argue that, as a result, they lend an air of reliability to the report. This is probably what Zelizer (1989) means when she says that quotes are "the credit cards of contemporary public discourse" (369). Here is Weizman's example from a newspaper called *The Globe and Mail*:

> Federal and Canadian National Railways investigators, looking into a crash that sent 70 persons to hospital yesterday, are trying to determine how two trains travelling in opposite directions ended up on the same track near Ingersoll.
> Both trains were assigned tracks by the same dispatcher in London, Ontario, John Reoch, general superintendent of transportation for CNR, said in an interview at the crash site, 20 kilometers east of London.
> 'We're trying to find out if there was a breakdown in the process of issuing the order, in its interpretation or in the way it was carried out', Mr Reoch said (1984: 41).

Let's be clear about this straight away: the reliability function at best may serve to make the journalist of *The Globe and Mail* a reliable reporter in the readers' minds. It does not *per se* render Mr Reoch an authoritative source. Weizman, in discussing the reliability function, even contributes to this confusion by pointing out that Reoch's name is accompanied by his official and rather impressive title "general superintendent of transportation for CNR" and that this serves to characterize him as a person of authority and prestige. This, however, strictly speaking, has nothing to do with the reliability function. Above I quoted Van Leeuwen's claim that "[r]epresentations include or exclude social actors to suit their interests and purposes in relation to the readers for whom they are intended" (1996a: 38) and I suggested that self-quotes make press releases more lively. I would now like to argue that the reference to a specifically named source - John Reoch and not just '*a* railway spokesperson' - also makes the report more reliable; as

Locher and Wortham (1994) point out, "[u]sing specific names gives the report a realism that is central to the inhabitance of an objective voice" (526).[7] Clearly, reference to any specifically named source would do. The elevated reference to Reoch as CNR's general superintendent of transportation is irrelevant to the report's reliability. Even if Reoch were a very unqualified spokesperson, the fact that *The Globe and Mail* quote him (i.e. purport to have made the effort to go for an interview at 'the crash site, 20 kilometers east of London',[8] and to report accurately what he said) would still provide evidence of the paper's reliability. Van Dijk (1988), for example, shows that while the eyewitnesses quoted may be wrong in their testimonies, the reporter's reliability remains unaffected. Of course, the description of Reoch as an elite source does matter, as I shall demonstrate below: the reliability of the reporter and the authority of the source are inextricably linked, if only since reporters prefer to quote authoritative sources; this, I shall argue, is part of the attitude function, though.

So what the reliability function does seem to suggest is that the words were actually spoken as they are quoted and that the reporter can therefore be relied on. The simple act of quoting somebody else turns you into a reliable reporter. In other words, if you take the trouble to render another's words the way they were actually spoken - or at least if you manage to give that impression - , then people will just more easily believe you. The question that I am now interested in is if this reliability function is also at work in the pseudo-direct speech of press releases. Is the writer of the Exxon press release in (1) more reliable for the journalists who read it simply because he or she includes a quotation of what one of the organization's top managers, Mr Harrison, is supposed to have said?

(1)   (Exxon, Valdez, Alaska: 16 August 1989)
         In an effort to aid Alaska fishermen in the wake of the Exxon Valdez oil spill, Exxon has developed a nine-point program and paid more than $38 million in fishermen claims. (...) Otto Harrison, general manager of Exxon's Valdez operations, said: "We are committed to treating fairly those who have been indirectly impacted by this accident. We view our work with the fishermen as a very important part of this effort."

The preliminary answer has to be 'no'. I have shown that self-quotations in press releases do not render the quoted words the way they were actually spoken simply because most of them have been invented. Journalists of course know that. In fact, I have argued that there is quite some reason to assume that no quotation can ever be considered a literal, verbatim reproduction. Does this mean, then, that no reliability function can be at work with pseudo-direct speech in press releases - in fact that no reliability function can be at work in any quotation? To try and answer this question, let's take a closer look at the reliability function. Crucially, as I suggested in the previous chapter, I shall have to distinguish between the facts of quotation and the interactants' perception of it.

4.2 The reality effect

The reliability function of quotation is linked up with the reproductionist view, which - as I have argued - has dominated the study of quotation for a long time and which has been fiercely criticized of late. The result is that, as far as the facts of quotation are concerned, there are no real grounds for the reliability function.

Still, if it is common knowledge that quotes can never be literal, why is it that there still seems to be some kind of reliability function at work, in people's perception of them anyway? I would like to suggest that, just like for the truth of the quoted words, it is the illusion of the reporter's faithful reproduction of the quoted statement that counts rather than the real faithfulness of the reporting: what matters is that the reporter *looks* reliable more than that he *is* reliable. It has been shown, for example, that most members of court juries realize that some of the 'facts' that lawyers render in quotes are seriously misrepresented, but that they still give more credit to those lawyers' overall reports (Philips 1986). Similarly, focusing on media discourse, John Hartley (1982) says that interviews on the TV news, including quotes of the so-called vox pop, "provide [the narrative] with authenticity, the *reality effect*", even though, when asked about it, the viewers are usually well aware that none of the interviewees "simply speaks" and that they "are all subordinate to the overall structure of a story as presented by the professional broadcasters" (109-110).

This explains why the reliability function continues to feature prominently in any analysis of quoting practices, and it also leaves some room for
self-quotes in press releases to play a reliability role. Even if journalists
realize that the quoted words have simply been written up by a press officer
and then later, perhaps, approved by the quoted 'source', they may well
suspend their disbelief and be willing to continue this illusion.[9] What would
happen is that, in the act of borrowing the quotation from the press release,
a (false) sense of reliability is extended from the writer of the press release
to the journalist and it will seem to the eventual newspaper reader as if the
journalist worked hard to get his or her information straight from the
horse's mouth. After all, as I already indicated at the end of chapter 2, the
general public is in no position to check if the quote was not nicely
preformulated in a press release.

It could of course be argued that such preformulation$_{ii}$ is - to use a
rather loaded word - manipulative: viz. that in the end newspaper readers
are furnished with all sorts of quotes of words that were actually never
spoken at all. But to claim so would be to ignore what I shall later call the
'performative nature' of these self-quotes in press releases   (cf. the next
chapter). They are not so unreliable after all, because it could be argued
that they are self-realizing and therefore ultimately verbatim: it may be true
that, before the press release got issued, the quoted words *were* not spoken,
but, from another perspective, there is no doubt that, in the very process of
issuing the press release, they ι.. ˀ actually *being* spoken. When, in an
Exxon press release, one of the organization's top managers is quoted as
saying that the victims of the Valdez oil spill will be fully compensated as
in (1), then there can be no doubt that this manager actually says so - and,
indeed, that Exxon promises to fully compensate the victims, the press
release being an authentic Exxon document. This means that the distinction
between real self-quotes and pseudo-direct speech - the question whether the
statement was first made through issuing the press release or else whether it
had already been made previously on location in Alaska or at a press
conference - is not so important after all. In Sinclair's (1986) terminology,
pseudo-direct speech is no simple fiction, viz. a set of utterances which are
'averred' by a speaker without regard for their correspondence with facts
and where this curious relationship is recognized by other participants (here
journalists), who expect the correspondence to be irrelevant. Instead, since

in the act of self-quotation the quoted words get spoken, press releases actually parade a rare one-to-one correspondence between the facts and what is averred about them. Clearly, if quotes are like credit cards, neither journalists (h_1) nor the journalists' own audiences (h_2) should have any fears about the solvency of press releases.[10]

5. The Attitude Function

5.1 From 'careful reservation to ironic rejection'

"Quotations are terribly interesting things", Harvey Sacks says, "and if you start to ask why do people do quotations, then it isn't at all an issue of, for example, they do quotations to be more accurate" (1992b: 310). Sacks does not believe that quotations make the reporter more reliable. Instead, he seems to stress that they may serve an attitude function, i.e. to express a variety of attitudes of the reporter towards the quoted statement, ranging - in Weizman's view - from "careful reservation to ironic rejection" (1984: 41).[11] The object of these attitudes can be the propositional content or the style or both. Here is Weizman's example from the *Toronto Star*:

> The Beirut-based Armenian Secret Army for the Liberation of Armenia (ASALA), the most prominent of several Armenian guerrilla groups, claimed responsibility for the attack. (...)
> ASALA said it chose the airport as a target because "the mercenaries of the North Atlantic alliance" were using it as a bridge to Nato bases in what is called "occupied Armenia" (42).

Clearly, while the journalist who wrote this piece saw no bones in calling the ASALA an Armenian 'guerrilla' group, he or she nevertheless wanted to make sure that the readers understood that it was the ASALA, and not the newspaper, that talked about NATO 'mercenaries' and about 'occupied Armenia'. The journalist's attitude to these selected labels is - at least - one of 'careful reservation': through distancing, the quoted words are exposed as representing a marginal point of view, which the writer is eager to reject. Lakoff (1982) seems to point to the same attitude function when he says that quotation indicates "the writer's abdication of responsibility for the locution so enclosed, a sort of ironic lift of the eyebrow in print: 'I represent it like this, but do not fully take responsibility for the sentiments thus expressed'" (245-246).

Here is an example of a non-reflexive quote from my corpus of press releases. In (9) the writer clearly rejects the quoted words:

(9)   (Exxon, Valdez, Alaska: 18 September 1989)
        After enduring nearly four months of bureaucratic run-around that resulted in not a single bag of waste being burned, Exxon is releasing the incinerator barge at Kodiak Island. More than $5 million was spent to have it sit idle while the state of Alaska stalled the permitting process for the waste disposal system they once called the "preferred method".

In this extract the negative connotations of lexical items like "bureaucratic run-around", "not a single bag" and "have it sit idle" set the scene for Exxon's 'ironic rejection' of the state of Alaska's words.

It is significant that both in the extract from the press release (9) and in Weizman's example from newspaper reporting, the utterance quoted is incomplete. It has been argued that whenever the quoted words constitute a discourse unit smaller than the sentence, some critical detachment normally takes place (Weizman 1984: 43). Geis (1987) draws attention to the subsentential units in so-called snigger quotes (89); similarly, Sanders claims that partial quotation is particularly useful in expressing the reporter's negative attitude towards the quoted information (1994; cf. also Van Ginneken 1996: 91).

Not all partial quotation seems to express a negative attitude, though, as is suggested by the following self-quotes from my corpus:

(10)   (Exxon, Houston, Texas: 17 July 1989)
        The U.S. Coast Guard has announced test results showing that a large slick widely reported to be from the Exxon Valdez off the coast of California contains no oil. Exxon said it was "gratified" with the announcement.

(11)   (Exxon, Juneau, Alaska: 13 September 1989)
        Exxon has conducted cleanup work on nearly 1,100 miles of
        shoreline impacted by the Exxon Valdez spill, Exxon Corpora-
        tion Chairman Lawrence G. Rawl said. Rawl said he had flown
        over many cleanup areas earlier this week and walked on some
        of the shorelines in order to have first-hand knowledge of the
        "impressive" cleanup results before reviewing detailed winter
        plans.[12]

(12)   (Exxon, Anchorage, Alaska: 3 October 1989)
        [President of Exxon USA W. D.] Stevens extended his "heartfelt
        thanks" to the more than 11,000 people, most of them Alaskans,
        who took part in the clean-up effort and again stated that "Exxon
        regrets, deeply, what happened".

Here, in each case, it would be most odd to conclude that the writer of the
Exxon press release is lifting his or her eyebrows ironically at what a
spokesperson of that same organization - in (12) even the organization's top
executive - is supposed to have said. Clearly, there must be more to the
attitude function than the 'careful reservation' and 'ironic rejection'
Weizman is talking about.

5.2 A broader range of attitudes

The negative attitude function of quotation illustrated above is certainly
common in scientific research papers, where often previous work on the
topic is quoted for refutation. However, just as partial quotes need not
always imply 'careful reservation' or 'ironic rejection', quotation in
academic papers is not necessarily refutation. On the contrary, previous
research may be quoted for purposes of confirmation: Thomas and Hawes
(1994), for example, claim that what they call 'citation' frequently acts as a
co-operative rather than a competitive rhetorical device of persuasion, viz.
to obtain support for the arguments that the writer is putting forward.[13]
Swales (1990) looks at quotes in the introduction sections of research
articles and takes an in-between position by claiming - cautiously - that they
are meant to 'lead up' to the writer's own research purpose.

What this seems to suggest is that the attitude function of quotation works in two directions: the other's words may not just be exposed as an individual's point of view, which the writer is eager to reject (negative attitude); on the contrary, through the very act of quotation, they may also get endowed with enhanced authority and thus effectively serve as support for the writer's point of view (positive attitude). Crucially, both the positive and negative attitude functions are derived from a distancing effect, i.e. the quoted words are not the writer's own.

All this would mean that Weizman's original concept of attitude should be formulated more broadly, ranging from rejection over neutrality right to agreement. In addition, the attitude function does not simply mean that quotation allows the reporter to express what he or she thinks about the quoted words; it also enables the reporter to reinforce his or her own words. As a quick look at scientific research papers confirms, to quote what somebody else has said may be a very effective way of defending your own views (cf. also Pomerantz 1984, Lucy 1993).

Of course, this positive attitude function is not restricted to academic discourse. Here is a politician trying to reassure the public about the health hazard posed by the mad cow disease and appealing to the views of an authoritative international committee to strengthen his case:

> The EEC standing veterinary committee has very firmly agreed with Britain that there is no danger to human health through BSE (Vandenbergen 1996: 396).

The following illustration of a positive attitude function is from my corpus of press releases:

(13)   (Royal Life, Brussels: 20 April 1994)
       Starheid kenmerkt tot op vandaag heel wat verzekeringsproduk-
       ten. De markt daarentegen is continu onderhevig aan verande-
       ringen op fiscaal, sociaal en financieel vlak. Bijgevolg is de
       onzekerheid groot. (...) Wat bij ziekte of tijdelijke werkonge-
       schiktheid? Wat met het rendement van mijn pensioenvoorzie-
       ning? Neem ik genoegen met 4,75%?

Zoals consumentenmiddens reeds aanhaalden: "de consument wil maatwerk, flexibiliteit en indien mogelijk actief deelnemen aan de besteding van zijn investeringen".

Until today rigidity is a feature of a lot of insurance companies. In contrast, the market is in constant change, fiscally, socially and financially. As a result, the uncertainty is big. (...) What in case of illness or temporary inability to work? What about the return of my pension provision? Am I satisfied with 4.75%?
As consumer organizations have already pointed out: "the consumer wants made-to-measure work, flexibility and if possible active participation in the expenditure of his investment".

Here, the use of "zoals" [as] serves to explicitly mark the quoted words as an argument in support of what came before. In addition, the quoted source seems to be of more than average authority: consumer organizations are usually very critical so if you can show that they agree with what you think, then there can be no doubt left that you are right. So, clearly, the quotation in (13) serves a positive attitude function.

The quote in (13) is of course a non-reflexive one. I shall now concentrate on the attitude function played by the typical self-quotes of my corpus like those in (10), (11) and (12). While I have argued that there can be no negative attitude function at work here, I shall demonstrate that the case for a positive attitude function is less than obvious.

5.3 Data analysis

Take another example of pseudo-direct speech:

(14)   (Nutricia, Zoetermeer: 18 November 1993)
      Directeur T.J.M. van Hedel is blij over de medewerking van de detailhandel. "Nutricia maakt een moeilijke tijd door. Dan is het prettig te merken dat je vrienden hebt. De handel biedt ons alle hulp om deze tegenslag te boven te komen. Nagenoeg alle winkels hebben, na de eerste oproep van Nutricia, de betreffende potjes zelf uit de schappen gehaald."

> Director T.J.M. van Hedel is happy with the retail trade's co-operation. "Nutricia is having hard times. Then it's nice to see you have friends. The retail trade is offering all its help to overcome this setback. After Nutricia's first call, nearly all shops have taken the relevant pots from the shelves themselves".

Here, like in (10), (11) and (12), there can be no doubt that the reporter agrees with what the quoted source says. The alternative, as suggested above, would be that the writer of the press release is lifting his or her eyebrows ironically at the words of a top representative of the same organization that issued the press release. This is just not possible. There must be a positive attitude function. In Spooren and Jaspers's (1990) terminology, the views expressed between quotation marks 'percolate' (upward) to the overall perspective. After all, as I showed in the previous chapter, through self-quotes it is the writer's (or the organization's) own views that were brought down to the level of a supposedly quoted source in the first place. But what textual evidence is there to confirm that the quoted views are shared by the reporter?[14]

It is interesting to add in this respect that according to Spooren and Jaspers percolation will take place as soon as there are no indications 'to the opposite'. Take a simple exchange:

> Mike: What do you expect from tonight's game?
> Sue: John says that the Rangers are going to win.

Spooren and Jaspers argue that, normally, a short dialogue like this can only make sense if John's opinion is treated as authoritative and therefore shared by Sue. Drawing from Ducrot's theory of polyphony (i.e. that any utterance implies a dialogue between two or more implicit voices), Cornelis (1995) agrees that in a case of embedding like

> *Hij veronderstelt dat het heeft geregend.*

> He presumes that it has rained.

the embedded information will be shared by the speaker, unless there is special marking to the opposite.

It is not difficult to see why this view cannot be successfully defended. Clearly, in "John says that the Rangers are going to win", percolation is possible, but not necessary. Sue may well be treating John as a complete ignoramus as far as football is concerned and therefore, in quoting his views, suggest that the Rangers have no chances at all. In a more recent publication, Cornelis (1997) states that the relationship between quoting and percolation remains unclear. While the use of a passive main clause may be expected to qualify as an indication 'to the opposite', she finds that no definite conclusions can be drawn. There may, for example, well be percolation in

> *In het profiel wordt geconcludeerd dat het verminderde kerkbezoek niet een uitsluitend Limburgs fenomeen is.*

> In the profile it is concluded that the diminished church visit is not exclusively a Limburg phenomenon.

since "terecht" [rightly] can be added, as in

> *In het profiel wordt terecht geconcludeerd dat het verminderde kerkbezoek niet een uitsluitend Limburgs fenomeen is.*

> In the profile it is rightly concluded that the diminished church visit is not exclusively a Limburg phenomenon.

So if it is true that the information in the self-quotes in my data are bound to be shared by the writers of the press releases, the question now is what sort of textual evidence can be found to explicitly mark such percolation.

To try and answer this question I shall take a closer look at how the self-quotations in my corpus of press releases are introduced[15] and at what really are the words between quotation marks. In particular, the following points will come up for discussion:

• *what linking words are used to explicate the relation between the quoted words and the writer's own views in the rest of the press release* e.g. the use of "zoals" [as] in (13)

(13)   (Royal Life, Brussels: 20 April 1994)
        Starheid kenmerkt tot op vandaag heel wat verzekeringsproduk-ten. De markt daarentegen is continu onderhevig aan verande-ringen op fiscaal, sociaal en financieel vlak. Bijgevolg is de onzekerheid groot. (...) Wat bij ziekte of tijdelijke werkonge-schiktheid? Wat met het rendement van mijn pensioenvoorzie-ning? Neem ik genoegen met 4,75%?
        Zoals consumentenmiddens reeds aanhaalden: "de consument wil maatwerk, flexibiliteit en indien mogelijk actief deelnemen aan de besteding van zijn investeringen".

        Until today rigidity is a feature of a lot of insurance companies. In contrast, the market is in constant change, fiscally, socially and financially. As a result, the uncertainty is big. (...) What in case of illness or temporary inability to work? What about the return of my pension provision? Am I satisfied with 4.75%?
        As consumer organizations have already pointed out: "the consumer wants made-to-measure work, flexibility and if possible active participation in the expenditure of his invest-ment".

• *how the quoted sources are identified*
  e.g. the reference to "consumentenmiddens" [consumer organizations] in (13) and to Otto Harrison as "general manager of Exxon's Valdez operations" in (1)

(1)   (Exxon, Valdez, Alaska: 16 August 1989)
       In an effort to aid Alaska fishermen in the wake of the Exxon Valdez oil spill, Exxon has developed a nine-point program and paid more than $38 million in fishermen claims. (...) Otto Harrison, general manager of Exxon's Valdez operations, said: "We are committed to treating fairly those who have been

indirectly impacted by this accident. We view our work with the fishermen as a very important part of this effort. "

- *how the contexts of delivery are identified*
  e.g. in (15) the reference to the fact that the quoted words were spoken "in testimony to the Senate Energy Regulation and Conservation Subcommittee"

  (15)   (Exxon, Washington, D.C.: 17 April 1989)
         In testimony to the Senate Energy Regulation and Conservation Subcommittee, McMillan said, "Petroleum prices in the United States are impacted by a number of factors, including events well beyond the border of the country. "

- *what linguistic action verbs are used*
  e.g. the use of "said" in (15)

- *what the words between quotation marks are and how they can be related to what's in the rest of the press release*
  e.g. the close correspondence between the quoted words and the reporter's own headline in (16)

  (16)   (Exxon, Valdez, Alaska: 1 April 1989)
         EXXON WAS READY FOR FULL-SCALE APPLICATION MARCH 25
         Exxon Shipping Company Frank Iarossi today said that Exxon was ready to begin full-scale application of aerial dispersants to the Exxon Valdez oil spill on Saturday, March 25.

5.3.1   Linking words

The most straightforward evidence that the quoted words serve to support what the reporter says is in the use of linking words. As I showed above, the use of 'zoals' [as] leaves no doubt about the positive attitude function in (13):

(13)   (Royal Life, Brussels: 20 April 1994)

Starheid kenmerkt tot op vandaag heel wat verzekeringsproduk-
ten. De markt daarentegen is continu onderhevig aan verande-
ringen op fiscaal, sociaal en financieel vlak. Bijgevolg is de
onzekerheid groot. (...) Wat bij ziekte of tijdelijke werkonge-
schiktheid? Wat met het rendement van mijn pensioenvoorzie-
ning? Neem ik genoegen met 4,75%?
Zoals consumentenmiddens reeds aanhaalden: "de consument wil
maatwerk, flexibiliteit en indien mogelijk actief deelnemen aan
de besteding van zijn investeringen".

Until today rigidity is a feature of a lot of insurance companies.
In contrast, the market is in constant change, fiscally, socially
and financially. As a result, the uncertainty is big. (...) What in
case of illness or temporary inability to work? What about the
return of my pension provision? Am I satisfied with 4.75%?
As consumer organizations have already pointed out: "the
consumer wants made-to-measure work, flexibility and if
possible active participation in the expenditure of his investment".

In the following extracts, there are also subtle, but unambiguous cues
indicating that the writer of the press release and the quoted source are in
agreement:

(17)   (BASF, Brussels: 17 March 1994)

"Wij moeten de oorzaak van verliezen wegnemen en ons volledig
toeleggen op renderende activiteiten", verklaart Dr. Jürgen
Strube nog. Zo heeft BASF tijdens de laatste jaren bewust
geopteerd om twee miljard minder omzet te realiseren en de
verliezen die hiermee gepaard zouden gaan ook te vermijden.

"We have to take away the cause of our losses and fully concentrate on cost-effective activities", added Dr. Jürgen Strube. For
example, for the last two years, BASF have deliberately chosen
to realize two billion less in turnover and to also avoid the losses
that would result from this.

(18)   (General Motors, Antwerp: 8 March 1994)
"Deze maatregel is een gevolg van de beslissing van General Motors om het merk Opel meer internationale bekendheid te geven", verklaarde de voorzitter van GM Europe, Louis R. Hughes, op het Autosalon van Genève. "Zowel de produktie-vestigingen als de administratieve centra van het bedrijf zullen zo geassocieerd worden met de naam waarin miljoenen automobi-listen en potentiële klanten hun vertrouwen stellen". De autodivi-sies van GM in de Verenigde Staten (Buick, Cadillac, Chevrolet, Oldsmobile, Pontiac, Saturn) werken overigens al jaren onder hun eigen merknaam, zonder een direkte en zichtbare verwijzing naar de moedermaatschappij.

"This measure results from General Motors' decision to give more international fame to the Opel brand", stated GM Europe's chairman, Louis R. Hughes, at the Geneva car show. "Both the company's production plants and administrative centres will thus be associated with the name that millions of drivers and potential customers have faith in". For that matter, GM's US car divi-sions (Buick, Cadillac, Chevrolet, Oldsmobile, Pontiac, Saturn) have already been working under their own brand names for years, without any direct and visible reference to the parent company.

(19)   (AB Computers, Brussels: 18 April 1994)
Volgens Doubi Ajami, directeur van AB Computers, is de benoeming van een Value Added Distributor, zoals AB Compu-ters, van vitaal belang voor de verdeling van nieuwe serverver-sies van Lotus Notes op UNIX en Novell.
Inderdaad, AB Computers heeft een erkende reputatie op het vlak van systeemintegratie en een bewezen kennis van UNIX- en Novell-omgevingen.

According to Doubi Ajami, director of AB Computers, the appointment of a Value Added Distributor, like AB Computers, is of vital importance for the distribution of new server versions of Lotus Notes on UNIX and Novell.

Indeed, AB Computers has an acknowledged reputation for system integration and a proven knowledge of UNIX and Novell environments.

Far from implying that the quoted words represent Dr Strube's, Mr Hughes's and Mr Ajami's private opinions only, the authors' uses of transition signals like "zo" [for example], "overigens" [for that matter] and "inderdaad" [indeed] have the effect of transporting the embedded information to the overall perspectives. These are clear indicators of (upward) percolation.

I would like to stress, however, that throughout the corpus there are relatively few such explicit links. (20) is a far more typical example, with the quoted words simply juxtaposed to those of the writer of the press release:

(20)   (Citibank, Brussels: April 1994)

De naam Famibank verdwijnt door deze integratie niet. "De naam Famibank is belangrijk", zegt J.-P. Votron. "Het is een merknaam met grote bekendheid die veel betekent voor de klanten."

The name Famibank does not disappear through this integration. "The name Famibank is important", says J.-P. Votron. "It is a brand name with great renown that means a lot to the customers".

So in spite of the exceptions in (13), (17), (18) and (19), the overall impression, as far as linking words are concerned, is that, while there is no special marking to prevent the quoted views from percolating, press releases contain hardly any explicit transition signals to promote the words between quotation marks as evidence for the reporter's own views.

5.3.2   Quoted sources

Functionalization. Above I suggested that self-quotation, through specific nominated reference to the quoted source, makes press releases more lively as well as more reliable. I would now argue that the way the sources of self-quotation are typically introduced in my corpus of press releases also contributes to a positive attitude function: in particular, it confirms that the quoted words may serve as evidence for what is in the rest of the press release. Compare the reference to the general manager of Exxon's Valdez operations Otto Harrison in the self-quote in (1) with that to the State of Alaska in the non-reflexive quote in (9):

> (1)   (Exxon, Valdez, Alaska: 16 August 1989)
>   In an effort to aid Alaska fishermen in the wake of the Exxon Valdez oil spill, Exxon has developed a nine-point program and paid more than $38 million in fishermen claims. (...) Otto Harrison, general manager of Exxon's Valdez operations, said: "We are committed to treating fairly those who have been indirectly impacted by this accident. We view our work with the fishermen as a very important part of this effort."

> (9)   (Exxon, Valdez, Alaska: 18 September 1989)
>   After enduring nearly four months of bureaucratic run-around that resulted in not a single bag of waste being burned, Exxon is releasing the incinerator barge at Kodiak Island. More than $5 million was spent to have it sit idle while the state of Alaska stalled the permitting process for the waste disposal system they once called the "preferred method".

Note that in (1) the quoted source is not just specifically identified as Otto Harrison vs. the vague attribution to the collective and impersonal state of Alaska bureaucracy in (9); Harrison is further introduced as 'the general manager of Exxon's Valdez operations'. This is what Van Leeuwen calls 'functionalization' and I would suggest that, far more than simple nomination, it contributes to Harrison's authority. Gruber (1993b), for example, notes that the use of full names and titles gives quotation more "gravity" (478-479).[16] The corpus of course abounds with the rhetoric of impressive job titles and no further examples need to be given here. The quoted sources are invariably introduced as corporate spokespersons, i.e. they are distinguished representatives of a well-defined group rather than relatively powerless individuals. In contrast, it is significant that for the non-reflexive quote in the following extract no description of the source's former job is given:

(21)   (Exxon, Houston, Texas: 24 July 1989)
        Allegations in the press that Exxon destroyed documents related to the Alaskan oil spill were conclusively disproved by sworn affidavits filed by the company with the Superior Court in Anchorage, Alaska. The entire computer tape saga is a nonissue, the company said.
        The controversy began in July when a recently fired Exxon employee contacted the media, saying that he had accidentally erased duplicate computer tapes containing data regarding the spill.

Elsewhere, in another of Exxon's press releases on the issue, the same person is even referred to as a "disgruntled former Exxon employee" (24 July 1989). In (4) there is an interesting contrast: the source of the 'claims' that Exxon is responsible for a rise of the oil price is bluntly excluded while the source of the Exxon reply is elaborately identified as 'J.T. McMillan, senior vice president of Exxon Company, U.S.A.'

(4)   (Exxon, Washington, D.C.: 17 April 1989)
        Valdez oil spill is not the reason for gasoline price hikes, says Exxon
        Claims that recent increases in crude oil and petroleum prices in the United States are largely the result of the oil spill in Valdez, Alaska, are incorrect, J.T. McMillan, senior vice president of Exxon Company, U.S.A. said today.

Interestingly, in the following two extracts the quoted sources' job titles are combined with references to their educational backgrounds; no doubt, they make the quoted words even more authoritative and further promote percolation:

(22)   (Exxon, Valdez, Alaska: 2 May 1989)
Sea otter and bird rescue centers at Valdez, Alaska, have been
buried under a mountain of towels donated by concerned
residents of the United States and Canada.
"The interest in our work at the otter and bird rescue centers has
been overwhelming," says Randall Davis, PhD, director of the
Otter Rescue Center. "We are very grateful for the outpouring
of concern and support expressed by people who donated
thousands of towels. Fortunately, though, we do not need any
more towels at either center."

(23)   (Hilaire Van de Haeghe, Harsewinkel: s.d.)
Ir. Helmut Claas, beherend vennoot van het huis CLAAS
verklaart de oorzaak van de algemene malaise in de landbouw-
machine-industrie als volgt: "Het tekort wordt gedeeltelijk door
de algemene recessie veroorzaakt."

Engineer Helmut Claas, general manager of the CLAAS house
explains the reason for the general malaise in the agricultural
machinery industry like this: "The deficit is partly caused by the
general recession."

Among Van Leeuwen's other methods of identification, age, gender, race,
as well as relational and physical identification are mentioned but they prove
rather unimportant in this corpus. As far as gender is concerned, Caldas-
Coulthard (1994) says that women are usually unaccessed voices. This is
confirmed in my corpus of press releases, partly of course because business
and politics, two of the major domains from which my press releases were
drawn, are traditionally male-dominated. It is significant that one of the
only women quoted in the corpus is Edwina Currie, who is referred to
specifically for her inappropriate outspokenness (cf. previous chapter).
Exceptionally, in (24) the source's (surprisingly young?) age is foreground-
ed.

(24)   (ITT Sheraton, Liège: March 1994)

ITT Sheraton is volgens haar nieuwe President en Afgevaardigd Bestuurder, Daniel P. Weadock (33 jaar oud en één van de directeurs van ITT), "het best bewaarde geheim van de hotelindustrie".

According to its new President and General Manager, Daniel P. Weadock (33 years old and one of ITT's directors), ITT Sheraton is "the hotel industry's best kept secret".

In general, it can be concluded so far that the specific way of referring to the sources of self-quotation in press releases points to a positive attitude: by describing them as authoritative speakers, writers pave the way for the quoted words to serve as evidence for what the rest of the press release is about. It should be noted, however, that none of the identifications referred to above makes percolation strictly necessary. This seems to be in line with my observation that there are only few linking words to explicitly mark a positive attitude function.

Authoritative by familiarity. In examining how the quoted sources are identified, I have so far assumed that the weight of the quoted words depends on the source. Things can also be turned upside down, though. As Van Dijk (1988) suggests, continued exposure as a news source will also contribute to the speaker's authority. In other words, if you get quoted frequently, people will more easily believe you. Let's take a look at the long extract (25) in this respect:

(25)   (Exxon, Valdez, Alaska: 23 August 1989)

The man who is heading Exxon's cleanup of the Exxon Valdez oil spill today called on Alaska Governor Steve Cowper to "stop playing politics and start working constructively to serve the best interest of Alaska."

In response to Governor Cowper's claim that Exxon failed to address concerns raised by the state, Otto Harrison, general manager of Exxon's Valdez operations, said: "This is truly amazing. I have to question the governor's motives because once again he has prepared his press statement before thoughtfully considering a very comprehensive plan which clearly addresses concerns previously raised by the state." (...)

Harrison said most of the activities which Governor Cowper claims were omitted from the Exxon plan "are there in black and white", and "raise the question of whether the governor had even taken the time to read it."

"The key suggestion from Governor Cowper which is not included in Exxon's plan," Harrison said, "could jeopardize the safety of workers on the shorelines. We have no intention of playing Russian roulette with work crews by following the governor's suggestion that we try to operate an additional six weeks after winter winds and waves make it unsafe to be there."

Harrison said: "Following this morning's briefing, Commissioner Kelso asked a few clarifying questions. But despite the quote attributed to Kelso in the governor's press release, he made no reference to 'a blizzard of numbers' and, to the contrary, gave no indication that Exxon's winter program was not reasonable."

Harrison said (...).

Interestingly, at the start of this extract (which coincides with the start of the press release), the identification of the quoted source is delayed: the speaker is first described in true tabloid fashion as "the man who is heading Exxon's cleanup of the Exxon Valdez oil spill" and only later identified as "Otto Harrison, general manager of Exxon's Valdez operations". This means that Harrison is initially referred to as somebody that is supposed to be well-known to the reader or, at least, whose mere responsibility as head of the clean-up in Alaska makes him newsworthy. The effect is that the speaker's identity looks more important and that his authority is therefore enhanced.[17]

All other quotations are attributed to "Harrison". Two things deserve our attention here. First, it is a simple reference to "Harrison" and not to "Mr Otto Harrison" or so; this again seems to increase familiarity and thus - in Van Dijk's view - authority. Second, the repeated use of the proper name is of course highly redundant. As Toole (1996) has shown, proper names are 'low accessibility markers' and they are normally used for entities that are not salient. This is clearly not the case here. A pronoun would have done the job too. In Downing's words, such a "deliberate choice of a proper name where a pronoun would be understood" must have "important strategic consequences" (1996: 119). I would argue that, apart from enhancing extractability (see chapter 3),[18] the sheer repetition of Harrison's name - not just in this extract, but in several, successive Exxon press releases on the Valdez crisis - once again serves to render Exxon's spokesperson more familiar and thus more authoritative. In Downing's words, proper names are indicators of protagonism (1996: 115), endowing the referent with topicality (135).

Co-opting the experts. There is a final interesting feature of the identification of quoted sources in press releases, one that can be situated on the border between self-quotes and non-reflexive quotes: viz. when organizations ask independent specialists to do specific research for them and announce the results in their press releases by quoting the specialists directly. This is what Herman and Chomsky (1988) call 'co-opting the experts'. Clearly, the words of such specialists have a lot of authority. As Herman and Chomsky report, "[t]he corporate funding and clear ideological purpose in the overall effort [have] no discernible effect on the credibility of the intellectuals so mobilized" (24). Fairclough (1996) too draws attention to the emergence of expert discourse technologists whose interventions carry the aura of truth because they have privileged access to (scientific) information or because of their relationship to institutions (73).[19]

Let me give an example from the corpus. On 13 April 1989, only two weeks after the Valdez oil spill, Exxon reports that it has hired Dr. Randall Davis of the Seaworld Research Institute as director of its facility for sea mammal rescue operations in South Alaska and Alice Berkner, director of the International Bird Rescue and Research Center in Berkeley, California, as manager of its bird rescue operations. The two are abundantly quoted in their praise for Exxon's clean-up effort:

(26)   (Exxon, Valdez, Alaska: 13 April 1989)
        "Although we were faced with significant problems in mounting
        a successful rescue effort, we were fortunate enough to have the

complete backing of Exxon in mobilizing our forces," Dr. Davis says. "Exxon has given us total commitment and complete cooperation. We appreciate Exxon's fast response in meeting our needs for a new mammal center. They have been terrific in their support." Alice Berkner, manager of the bird rescue operations, also offered high marks for Exxon's support of the rescue activities. "(...) The support we're receiving from Exxon in this process has been absolutely tremendous".

A few days later Exxon also announces that it has assembled "an outside group of renowned oil spill and wildlife experts" to gather data on the scene (17 April) and these promptly report the good news that "some 70 percent of the oil which was spilled into Prince William Sound on March 24 has evaporated, dispersed or been collected" (24 April). Subsequently, Exxon announces that it has retained the Alaska Heritage Group to develop a cultural resources program for the region (27 April). Its chairman is "Alaska anthropologist Dr. Charles M. Mobley, (...) on leave from Sheldon Jackson College in Sitka, where he is professor of anthropology and Alaska native political science".

In summary, I have pointed to various aspects of the identification of the sources of self-quotation in press releases, which together seem to be geared at enhancing the authority of the quoted words. However, as I suggested above, the question of percolation remains unanswered since none of them actually explicates the relationship of the views between quotation marks to those of the writer of the press release.

5.3.3   Context of delivery

Let's now focus on the context of delivery in self-quotes. For the authority of the quoted words, it matters a great deal how they get contextualized.[20] Geis (1987: 104), for example, draws attention to the question whether something was said at an official public meeting or in private. Note, however, that the problem of such contextualizations can only be relevant for what I previously referred to as *real* self-quotations. For the constructed self-quotations (or pseudo-direct speech), there was of course no previous verbalization and no context of delivery can therefore normally be identified.

As far as real self-quotes are concerned, the following are typical examples:

(15)   (Exxon, Washington, D.C.: 17 April 1989)
       In testimony to the Senate Energy Regulation and Conservation Subcommittee, McMillan said, "Petroleum prices in the United States are impacted by a number of factors, including events well beyond the border of the country."

(27)   (Exxon, New York City: 7 November 1989)
       The oil spill in Alaska has reaffirmed the need for a more workable response procedure among federal, state and local authorities as well as private industry, W.D. Stevens, president of Exxon USA, said.
       Stevens spoke at the Second International Conference on Industrial and Organizational Management hosted by New York University.

Here the fact that the words were spoken in testimony to the U.S. Senate Energy Regulation and Conservation Subcommittee and at an international management conference hosted by New York University does not seem to do their authoritativeness any harm. On the contrary, it makes them a great deal more influential than if they had been spoken in private and, in doing so, it promotes percolation. Here are a number of other examples from the corpus:

(28)   (Exxon, Parsippany, New Jersey: 18 May 1989)
       Exxon's effort to clean up the Alaskan oil spill now involves almost 7,000 people, more than 700 vessels, 56 aircraft and over 90 miles of boom, L.G. Rawl, chairman of the Exxon Corporation, told the company's shareholders at the company's annual meeting.

(29)   (Service Station, Kortrijk: 24 April 1994)
       Op zondag 24 april werd door de heer De Graeve, voorzitter van de Belgische Petroleumfederatie, de 2de editie van Service Station officieel geopend. (...)
       Deze opening genoot heel wat belangstelling. Alle exposanten en een groot aantal parlementairen uit de streek waren aanwezig.

       On Sunday 24 April the 2nd edition of Service Station was officially opened by Mr De Graeve, chairman of the Belgian Petroleum federation. (...)
       This opening received a lot of attention. All participants and a large number of local members of parliament were present.

(30)   (Exxon, Juneau, Alaska: 3 April 1989)
       William D. Stevens, president of Exxon Company, U.S.A., met last Friday with Alaska Governor Steve Cowper, the leaders of the Alaska House and Senate, and legislative representatives from the Valdez, Cordova and Prince William Sound areas to discuss action which should be taken to assure effective organization and coordination of the ongoing oil spill cleanup effort. (...)
       On behalf of the men and women of Exxon," Stevens told the Alaskans, "I wanted personally to express our deep regret over the tanker accident."

(31)   (Bayer, Antwerp: 10 November 1994)
       Enkele weken geleden werd de nieuwe produktie-installatie officieel ingehuldigd in het bijzijn van talrijke eregenodigden uit de politieke en economische wereld en de eigen medewerkers.
       In zijn toespraak (...) verklaarde [Dr. Pol Bamelis, lid van de Bayer-"Vorstand"]: "Wij gaan ervan uit dat het Natrena-bedrijf in Mijdrecht een essentiële bijdrage zal leveren tot een versterkte merkenaanwezigheid in Europa."

       A couple of weeks ago the new production installation was officially inaugurated in the presence of numerous guests of honour from the political and economic worlds and Bayer's own employees.

In his speech (...) [Dr. Pol Bamelis, member of the Bayer-"Vorstand"] declared: "We assume that the Natrena company in Mijdrecht will make an essential contribution to an enhanced brand presence in Europe."

(32)   (Groepering der havenbelangen van Antwerpen, Antwerp: 4 October 1994)

Tijdens een druk bijgewoonde bijeenkomst in de Londense Café Royal werden de mogelijkheden van de haven van Antwerpen als distributiecentrum voor Engelse goederen toegelicht.

During a widely attended meeting in the London Café Royal the opportunities for the port of Antwerp as distribution centre for English goods were explained.

In contrast, the words in the non-reflexive quote in (9) are only vaguely contextualized by reference to 'once' and, together with the identification of the quoted source, this seems to be in line with the reporter's negative attitude.

(9)   (Exxon, Valdez, Alaska: 18 September 1989)

After enduring nearly four months of bureaucratic run-around that resulted in not a single bag of waste being burned, Exxon is releasing the incinerator barge at Kodiak Island. More than $5 million was spent to have it sit idle while the state of Alaska stalled the permitting process for the waste disposal system they once called the "preferred method".

In (33) it is, among other indications, the vague reference to the audience as 'the media', instead of the *New York Times*, that seems to cast doubt on the authority of the words in the non-reflexive quote.

(33)   (Exxon, Houston, Texas: 11 September 1989)
The controversy began in July when a recently fired Exxon employee contacted the media, saying that he had accidentally erased duplicate computer tapes containing data regarding the spill.

It can be concluded that, like the identification of the quoted source, the description of the context of delivery of self-quotes generally allows for percolation. It should be borne in mind, however, that, once again, in none of the data shown above is it strictly necessary that the quoted views are shared by the reporter.

5.3.4   Report verbs

What report verbs are used? As illustrated in the table below, the vast majority of self-quotes in the corpus is introduced by forms of 'say' as well as by equally neutral *verba dicendi* (or what Verschueren (1985) calls linguistic action verbs) like 'continue' and 'state', and non-finite expressions like 'according to'.

Fig. 1   Report verbs in press releases[21]

TOTAL	156	100%
Say	96	61%
According to	14	9%
Continue	11	7%
Explain, Ø [22]	7	4%
Declare, state	5	3%
Add	4	2%
Point out	3	2%
Tell, note	2	1%

As far as the verbs' evaluative potential is concerned, the reporter's stance towards the validity of the reported information is consistently neutral.[23] In their analysis of reporting verbs in academic writing, Thompson and Yiyun (1991) call this non-interpretation.[24] So at first sight not much seems to come out of our analysis of report verbs for the question if the quoted words are encouraged to percolate to the overall perspective or not.

Interestingly, however, Caldas-Coulthard (1994) argues that when a reporter uses 'say' he or she is "*apparently* neutral in relation to the *supposed* saying" (295, my italics). For my purposes I believe that this is a more accurate way of putting things for two reasons: I have already suggested that, at least for pseudo-direct speech, the saying is only supposed; in the next few sections I shall investigate if embedding through 'say' is really neutral.

Caldas-Coulthard distinguishes four types of verbs in this respect (305-306):

- neutral, structuring glossing verbs (no explicit evaluation):
  e.g. 'say'

- illocutionary glossing verbs (reporter interprets):
  e.g. 'grumble', 'urge'

- descriptive verbs (describe the 'represented interaction'):
  e.g. 'yell', 'whisper'

- discourse-signalling verbs (mark the relationship of one part of a quote to another part):
  e.g. 'repeat', 'add', 'continue'

Most self-quotes in my corpus of press releases are introduced either by neutral, structuring glossing verbs (most prominently 'say') or by discourse-signalling verbs (including 'continue', 'add'). The absence of descriptive glossing verbs is somewhat predictable from the fact that most self-quotes are pseudo-direct speech, so there is no previous interaction to be described. However, it still has to be accounted for why what Caldas-Coulthard calls illocutionary glossing verbs are exceptional in the corpus as far as self-quotes are concerned. Interestingly, in the following extracts, 'contend' and 'charge', which are traditionally used to shed some doubt on the truth of the embedded statement, seem to express no such negative attitude and should rather be taken to express a neutral stance:

(34)　(Exxon, Houston, Texas: 11 September 1989)
Exxon had contended from the beginning that the incident was a non-issue and that the tapes in question were backups, never designed, intended or used for permanently retaining documents.

(35)　(Exxon, Anchorage, Alaska: 26 October 1989)
In the counterclaim filed in the Superior Court, Exxon charged that the Alyeska Oil Spill Contingency Plan approved by the state made clear that immediate use of dispersants was a central feature for dealing with a large spill.

Similarly, the following use of 'confirm' has the relatively neutral meaning of 'say with emphasis' rather than the positive 'say that something is definitely true, esp. by providing more proof':

(36)　(Bekaert, Kortrijk: 15 May 1996)
In response to news reports that Bekaert is considering the sale of its Bridgestone-Metalpha Corporation (BMA) stake, Bekaert confirms that there is no immediate plan to sell shares it holds in BMA.

Clearly, in almost all of the self-quotes in my corpus, the reporter remains obsessively uncommitted to the truth of the quoted information.

In contrast, with the non-reflexive quotes there is a much wider range of linguistic action verbs, from relatively neutral ones like "stellen" [state]

(37)　(Kredietbank, Brussels: 31 October 1995)
In een mededeling stelt Standard & Poor's dat deze ratingverhoging een weerspiegeling is van de positie van de Kredietbank als leidinggevende financiële instelling in België.

> In an announcement Standard & Poor's states that this rating increase reflects the Kredietbank's position as leading financial institution in Belgium.[25]

to radically evaluative ones, most of which express negative distancing, like 'claim':

(38)   (Exxon, Valdez, Alaska: 23 August 1989)
       In response to Governor Cowper's claim that Exxon failed to address concerns raised by the state, Otto Harrison, general manager of Exxon's Valdez operations, said: "This is truly amazing. I have to question the governor's motives because once again he has prepared his press statement before thoughtfully considering a very comprehensive plan which clearly addresses concerns previously raised by the state." (...)
       Harrison said most of the activities which Governor Cowper claims were omitted from the Exxon plan "are there in black and white", and "raise the question of whether the governor had even taken the time to read it."

(4)   (Exxon, Washington, D.C.: 17 April 1989)
       Valdez oil spill is not the reason for gasoline price hikes, says Exxon
       Claims that recent increases in crude oil and petroleum prices in the United States are largely the result of the oil spill in Valdez, Alaska, are incorrect, J.T. McMillan, senior vice president of Exxon Company, U.S.A. said today.

Note that in the last two examples there is also a sharp contrast with the way the pseudo-direct speech attributed to Harrison and McMillan is introduced. Finally, in both extracts, Governor Cowper's words are embedded in a nominal group, which, according to Vandenbergen (1996: 403) lends a quality of thingness to the quotation and thus further serves to shed doubt on it.

Note that in the following example the neutral 'tell' is qualified by 'apparently':

(39)   (Exxon, Houston, Texas: 24 July 1989)
        The controversy arose early this month after a disgruntled
        former Exxon employee, Kenneth Davis, apparently told the
        New York Times (...).[26]

Often, ironically, the very kind of media reports that press releases are
directed at are treated as less than authoritative sources in those press
releases:

(40)   (Vlaams Blok, Antwerp: 4 October 1994)
        *Vandaag maken verschillende kranten melding van de afgelasting
        van de manifestatie van het Antwerps Beraad, dat vandaag had
        moeten doorgaan in het Antwerpse Bosuilstadion. De organisato-
        ren zouden doodsbedreigingen hebben ontvangen.*
        *Geïnsinueerd wordt dat deze doodsbedreigingen het gevolg
        zouden zijn van de campagne die het Antwerps Beraad momen-
        teel tegen het Vlaams Blok voert.*

        Today several newspapers announce the cancellation of the
        manifestation of the Antwerps Beraad, which should have taken
        place today in the Antwerp Bosuil stadium. The organizers
        would have received death threats.
        It is insinuated that these death threats would be the result of the
        campaign that the Antwerps Beraad is currently holding against
        the Vlaams Blok.

Note that in (40) the use of "zouden hebben ontvangen" [would have
received] illustrates an alternative way of reporting another's words and
expressing a negative attitude towards them. Also:

(41)   (Bekaert, Kortrijk: 23 November 1994)
        *Via de media heeft N.V. Bekaert S.A. vernomen dat een gerech-
        telijke procedure aanhangig is gemaakt betreffende handel met
        voorkennis in Bekaertaandelen. De feiten zouden teruggaan tot
        december 1992.*

> Through the media N.V. Bekaert S.A. has learnt that a legal procedure has been started about insider trading in Bekaert shares. The facts would date back to December 1992.

In (42) below the lack of authority of the press ('allegations') is contrasted with the organization's own authority ('conclusively disproved', 'sworn affidavits with the Superior Court'):

(42) (Exxon, Houston, Texas: 24 July 1989)
      Allegations in the press that Exxon destroyed documents related to the Alaskan oil spill were conclusively disproved by sworn affidavits filed by the company with the Superior Court in Anchorage, Alaska.

As I pointed out at the beginning, the pattern for self-quotes is what I am interested in, though, and clearly it is in sharp contrast not just with the non-reflexive quotes in my corpus, but more generally, with, for example, quotation in oral narrative[27] as well as with that in the newspapers.[28] On the whole, it can be concluded that the distribution of linguistic action verbs in press releases has the same effect as the use of linking words, the identification of quoted sources and the description of the contexts of delivery: there is no evaluative distance between the reporter's and the quoted source's positions, but they are not explicitly reconciled either.

There can, of course, be no doubt that it is only apparent neutrality. As I pointed out above, the views in self-quotes, by their very nature, are bound to percolate to the overall perspective. The question arises then why, if press releases are so egocentric, no self-quotes are introduced by positive linguistic action verbs.

Tense. I shall now focus on the use of tense since this may also affect percolation. In particular, Kress (1983) argues that the use of the present tense in reporting, apart from adding liveliness (cf. above), normally also confers validity on statements.[29] Interestingly, as far as the self-quotes in my corpus of press releases are concerned, quite a lot of reporting verbs are in the present:

(22)   (Exxon, Valdez, Alaska: 2 May 1989)
Sea otter and bird rescue centers at Valdez, Alaska, have been buried under a mountain of towels donated by concerned residents of the United States and Canada.
"The interest in our work at the otter and bird rescue centers has been overwhelming," says Randall Davis, PhD, director of the Otter Rescue Center. "We are very grateful for the outpouring of concern and support expressed by people who donated thousands of towels. Fortunately, though, we do not need any more towels at either center."

(3)   (Madge, Hoofddorp: 26 April 1994)
Uit tests die onlangs zijn uitgevoerd door het in San José, Californië, gevestigde LANQuest Labs is gebleken dat de Smart 100 AT ringnode-adapters van Madge goed zijn voor een ononderbroken netwerkverkeer van bijna 3500 Kbyte/sec. B. McGiffert, General Manager van LANQuest, zegt: "Onze test van verschillende veelgebruikte 100 Megabit netwerk-adapters tonen aan dat de nieuwe Smart 100 AT Ringnode-adapters van Madge verreweg de snelste DDI-client-kaarten zijn die voor ISA-bus-systemen verkrijgbaar zijn".

Tests that were recently executed at LANQuest Labs based in San José, California, have proved that Madge's Smart 100 AT Ringnode adaptors offer uninterrupted network interaction of almost 3500 Kbyte p.s. B. McGiffert, LANQuest's General Manager, says: "Our tests of several frequently used 100 Megabit network adaptors show that Madge's new Smart 100 AT Ringnode adaptors are by far the fastest DDI client cards available for ISA bus systems".

On closer scrutiny, this use of the present is certainly not surprising for the above examples of pseudo-direct speech: since there is no previous utterance to be referred to, there is no real reason for using the past tense anyway.[30]

Even more noticeably, in the course of the following extract with a real self-quote, deictic time gets recentred. The shift helps to suggest strongly that the writer of the press release, rather than being neutral, shares Mr Hughes's embedded perspective.

(43)   (General Motors, Antwerp: 8 March 1994)
       Louis R. Hughes verwees ook naar de strategische beslissing van GM Europe om de naam en produkten van Opel verder te internationaliseren en over de hele wereld te verspreiden. "Het Opel Technical Development Center is toonaangevend in design en ontwikkeling van wagens voor onze internationale operaties buiten Noord-Amerika, " zo zegt hij.

       Louis R. Hughes also referred to GM Europe's strategic decision to further internationalize and globally distribute Opel's name and products. "The Opel Technical Development Center is the leader in car design and development for our international operations outside North America," he says.[31]

Note also the use of the present tense in the embedded words, between quotation marks, as in (3), which I referred to in my discussion of the dramatic function above, as well as - even more clearly - with indirectly quoted words, including those introduced by a verb in the past, as in

(44)   (Exxon, Valdez, Alaska: 8 August 1989)
       [Harrison] said work crews are collecting about 8,000 bags of debris per day and have collected about 12,000 tons. The bulk is being barged to an Oregon landfill because of the lack of permit approvals by the state, Harrison said.

As Declerck and Tanaka (1995) have shown, such present tense choice with past reported speech implies that the reporter subscribes to the situation referred to in the complement clause. In other words, it seems to point to percolation.

5.3.5 Between quotation marks

One final way of checking if the quoted words and the press release as a whole are in agreement is to simply compare their propositional contents. In the next extract there is no doubt about percolation since the information between quotation marks in the first paragraph is taken up by the author of the press release as his or her own in the headline.

(16)   (Exxon, Valdez, Alaska: 1 April 1989)
EXXON WAS READY FOR FULL-SCALE APPLICATION MARCH 25
Exxon Shipping Company Frank Iarossi today said that Exxon was ready to begin full-scale application of aerial dispersants to the Exxon valdez oil spill on Saturday, March 25.

This seems a common pattern in the Exxon press releases:

(45)   (Houston, Texas: 19 April 1989)
ALASKA RESIDENTS EXPECTED TO FILL VALDEZ CLEANUP HIRING NEEDS
Alaska residents will fill most available jobs in connection with the cleanup of Prince William Sound, Exxon said Tuesday.

(46)   (Valdez, Alaska: 24 April 1989)
EXXON AHEAD OF SCHEDULE ON ALASKA SHORELINE CLEANUP
Exxon is ahead of schedule on the shoreline cleanup in Prince William Sound (…), the company announced today.

(47)   (Houston, Texas: 2 May 1989)
ALASKA SHORELINE CLEANUP MOBILIZATION NEAR-ING PEAK
Mobilization of people, material, and equipment in Alaska to meet the schedule set in Exxon's cleanup plan for 305 miles of shoreline in Prince William Sound is nearing its peak, W.D. Stevens, president of Exxon Company, U.S.A., affirmed today.

Remember also the extracts from a BASF press release discussed in the previous chapter where Dr Strube's words are first rendered in various forms of quotation, as in:

(48)   (BASF, Brussels: 17 March 1994)
        Ter gelegenheid van de persconferentie, waar Dr. Jürgen Strube,
        Voorzitter van de Raad van Bestuur, enkele toelichtingen gaf bij
        de balans van de BASF-Groep, gaf hij eveneens zijn kijk op de
        actuele situatie in het volgend beeld weer: "Wij hebben een
        goede start genomen en een uitstekende tijd gelopen over de
        eerste meters van de wedstrijd. Maar wij zijn er ons eveneens
        heel goed van bewust dat wij niet alleen een sprint lopen. Wij
        moeten een beroep doen op al onze krachten om de hele weg, die
        nog voor ons ligt, af te leggen. Wij beschikken niettemin over de
        nodige reserves om de eindstreep te halen".

        At a press conference, where Dr. Jürgen Strube, chairman of the Board, provided some comments on the BASF Group balance, he also offered his views on the current situation by means of the following image: "We have taken a good start and run an excellent time over the first metres of the race. But we arc also very much aware that we are not only running a sprint. We have to use all our resources to complete all the way in front of us. Nevertheless, we have the necessary reserves to make it to the finish line."

Towards the end of the same press release, however, Strube's words are adopted by the reporter:

(49)   (BASF, Brussels: 17 March 1994)
        In het algemeen kunnen we de gang van zaken in 1993 als
        ontgoochelend bestempelen.

        In general we can call events in 1993 disappointing.

Note, finally, that it has been argued that the very choice of direct quotation - as opposed to more indirect modes - conveys authority on the quoted source and thus serves to contribute to percolation. This might help to explain why most self-quotes in my corpus are direct and why, for example, the following is an indirect quote:

(33)   (Exxon, Houston, Texas: 24 July 1989)
        The controversy began in July when a recently fired Exxon employee contacted the media, saying that he had accidentally erased duplicate computer tapes containing data regarding the spill.[32]

5.4 A balancing act

All the above data seem to confirm that the views expressed in the self-quotations in my corpus are shared by the writers of the press releases. Percolation is the standard. Rather frequently it seems to be more or less subtly promoted, for example by means of reference to the quoted source's impressive job title or to the elevated context of delivery. Occasionally, it is even strongly implied; think of the use of linking words.

The question remains, however, why in the end there are only very few explicit signals of percolation to be found in the corpus. Why, for example, is the use of linguistic action verbs so obsessively uncommitted?

I would now argue that the answer to this question lies in the peculiar audience-directedness of press releases. Surely, any explicit signal of percolation, as the linking word in (13), is in conflict with the objectivity requirements of preformulation$_{ii}$:

(13)   (Royal Life, Brussels: 20 April 1994)
        Starheid kenmerkt tot op vandaag heel wat verzekeringsproduk-
        ten. De markt daarentegen is continu onderhevig aan verande-
        ringen op fiscaal, sociaal en financieel vlak. Bijgevolg is de
        onzekerheid groot. (...) Wat bij ziekte of tijdelijke werkonge-
        schiktheid? Wat met het rendement van mijn pensioenvoorzie-
        ning? Neem ik genoegen met 4,75%?
        Zoals consumentenmiddens reeds aanhaalden: "de consument wil
        maatwerk, flexibiliteit en indien mogelijk actief deelnemen aan
        de besteding van zijn investeringen".

Until today rigidity is a feature of a lot of insurance companies. In contrast, the market is in constant change, fiscally, socially and financially. As a result, the uncertainty is big. (...) What in case of illness or temporary inability to work? What about the return of my pension provision? Am I satisfied with 4.75%?

As consumer organizations have already pointed out: "the consumer wants made-to-measure work, flexibility and if possible active participation in the expenditure of his investment".

Instead of being seen to distance themselves from the views expressed between quotation marks, journalists who copy (13) would actually serve as mouthpieces for Royal Life's public relations campaign.

On the other hand, it looks as if (20) can be safely retold by journalists in their own news reporting:

(20)   (Citibank, Brussels: April 1994)
De naam Famibank verdwijnt door deze integratie niet. "De naam Famibank is belangrijk", zegt J.-P. Votron, "Het is een merknaam met grote bekendheid die veel betekent voor de klanten."

The name Famibank does not disappear through this integration. "The name Famibank is important", says J.-P. Votron, "It is a brand name with great renown that means a lot to the customers".

It could be argued that the self-quote in (20) seems to perform a delicate balancing act: as I have argued, there can be no doubt that the writer of this Citibank press release and the quoted source, Citibank's J.-P. Votron, are in complete agreement and that, hence, the quoted words serve as an argument of authority to make the Citibank's case more convincing; at the same time, since there are no explicit signals of percolation, it looks as if they can be copied by journalists as part of their own news reporting: in that case, the reporter's attitude towards the quoted words will normally be seen to be one of careful reservation. Clearly, distancing is a double-edged sword since the degree of commitment with which the journalists can relay the quote to their readers appears to be very different from that with which Citibank originally issued it - in the form of a self-quote - to the journalists.[33] In other words, self-quotation in press releases turns out to be a negotiating device: as far as the attitude function is concerned, it walks the thin line between reservation and agreement and, in doing so, it goes some way to reconcile the persuasive efforts of news managers with the scepticism of newsmakers.

5.5 Beyond co-operation

5.5.1 Elite sources

All this is not to say that preformulation in press releases is always a fully co-operative undertaking. On the contrary, just as in the third chapter I indicated that journalists may turn out less than neutral after all if they copy some of the preformulated forms of third-person self-reference from press releases in their own news reporting, I would now argue that the same may happen with self-quotation. For example, I have shown that in (1) the reference to Harrison as 'general manager of Exxon's Valdez operations' serves to enhance the speaker's authority and, hence, if not to imply, then at least to subtly promote percolation. While this looks an inappropriate preformulation that journalists can be expected to resist, everyday newsmaking practice seems to point in the opposite direction: it is not just people in the news who tend to parade their own high status,[34] it has been shown that journalists too prefer elite sources (e.g. Van Dijk 1988, Bell 1991, Jucker 1996). As Fishman (1980) notes, "a newsworker will recognize an official's claim to knowledge not merely as a claim, but as a credible, competent piece of knowledge" (144-145). Cook (1989) even suggests that the authority of the quoted source is more important for newsworthiness than quotability (57): i.e. who says something is - to some extent at least - more important to journalists than what he or she says or how it is said.[35] It follows that the reference to Harrison as 'general manager of Exxon's Valdez operations' constitutes an appropriate preformulation after all, but there can be no doubt that for journalists to copy the self-quote in (1) in their own news reporting is not as innocent as it may seem.

In the next section I shall elaborate on another, more drastic way in which journalists who copy the self-quotes in press releases may fail the test of objective reporting. Take (20) once again. I have suggested that in the press release the use of 'say' is only *apparently* neutral, but that, when copied in news reporting, it can be taken to serve as the neutral introducer it really is. But that still leaves us with the puzzling question how - and indeed if at all - it is possible for a quote to serve as an argument of authority to make the writer's case more convincing in one context (viz. percolation in press releases) and to serve as a distancing device for the same text in another context (viz. no percolation in news reporting). To try and answer that question, I shall turn to the theory of presuppositions, in particular to Karttunen's research on the projection problem (1973).

5.5.2 ·Plugging

Take the following utterance:

John managed to stop in time.

In the terminology of pragmatics, it 'presupposes' that John tried to stop in time.[36] The relevance to news reporting and the issue of objectivity should be clear straight away: if a journalist writes that "John managed to stop in time", this means that the journalist believes that John indeed tried to do so.

Research on the so-called projection problem focuses on what happens to an utterance's presuppositions under embedding. Using a range of metaphors from the same source domain as Spooren and Jaspers's (1990) 'percolation', Karttunen (1973) suggests that some complement-taking verbs (or 'sentential operators') serve as 'holes', i.e. they allow the presuppositions of the embedded utterance to transcend and become presuppositions of the complex whole. For example, to say that

Bill knew that John managed to stop in time.

presupposes that John tried to stop in time,[37] just like

John managed to stop in time.

Vendler (1976) calls 'know', like 'be glad', 'regret', 'realize', 'mention', 'remind', 'factive' verbs; he says that they are 'transparent' (cf. also Kiparsky and Kiparsky 1971).

Alternatively, some complement-taking verbs serve as 'plugs', i.e. they prevent the presuppositions of the embedded utterance from transcending and becoming presuppositions of the complex whole; in other words, the presuppositions are cancelled, they do not survive. These include verbs of propositional attitude and verbs of saying. For example,

Bill said that John managed to stop in time.

does not presuppose that John tried to stop in time.[38] Vendler (1976) calls these verbs ('say', 'believe', 'assert', 'predict', 'assert', 'declare', 'affirm', 'contend', 'maintain', 'insist', etc.) 'non-factives'; he says that they are 'opaque'.

I would now argue that this is the basis of the assumption that verbs like 'say' express uncommittedness and serve as distancing devices. Here is Karttunen's example from news reporting. A headline like

Nixon will stop protecting his aides.

presupposes that Nixon has been protecting his aides or at least that the journalist who wrote the article thinks so. Compare with the following headline:

Ziegler announced that Nixon will stop protecting his aides.

Here 'announce', like 'say', serves as a plug. In the journalist's perspective, it is not presupposed that Nixon has been protecting his aides: in other words, it may or may not be true that Nixon has been protecting his aides. Levinson (1983: 208) too provides an example from media discourse.

Nato claims that the nuclear deterrent is vital.

does not presuppose that there exists a nuclear deterrent. Locher and Wortham (1994), in the introduction to their analysis of news broadcasts, compare

George lied.

where the speaker's evaluative judgment of George's utterance is clear (i.e. it casts George as speaking falsely), and

Joan said that George lied.

where it is just not possible to know with certainty what the speaker believes about George's utterance because 'said' deflects any such perspectival reading. Such 'sourcing' is a major feature of media discourse (Gans 1979: 130). "Ultimately", Gaye Tuchman (1978) argues, "the use of graded sources who may be quoted as offering truth-claims is converted into a technical device designed to distance the reporter from phenomena identified as facts" (27).

Let's apply this to press releases. Compare the following two utterances about the Exxon Valdez accident:

Exxon is disappointed that an officer would have jeopardized his ship, crew and the environment through such actions.

and

(50)   (Exxon, Houston, Texas: 30 March 1989)
        Iarossi said: "We are all disappointed that an officer would have jeopardized his ship, crew and the environment through such actions."

The first presupposes that the writer indeed thinks that the officer in question, Captain of the Exxon Valdez John Hazelwood, has jeopardized his ship, crew and the environment.[39] In writing these words, he or she actually lays the blame for the accident on the captain. Following Karttunen's theory of plugging, no such presuppositions would come out of the second; no matter who is to blame, the second can always be spoken felicitously. It follows that in a press release the second only could be an acceptable preformulation and it should therefore not be surprising that the second appears in my corpus and not the first. In other words, just as in

> Nixon is guilty too.

the use of 'too' brings in a presupposition (viz. that somebody else is guilty in addition to Nixon), self-quotation in press releases serves to *remove* a presupposition. It carries an offer of immunity, since it is an anticipation of the quoting practices in the media where any interpretive material must be attributable to a news source (Sigal 1973: 66).[40] Self-quotation in press releases "guarantees a hearing for [one's own] views regardless of reporters' personal judgment of their veracity or validity" (67).

5.5.3   Objectively-voiced text

Crucially, I would now argue that it is wrong to assume that verbs like 'say' invariably express uncommittedness and that they serve as unambiguous distancing devices. The reason is that, rather awkwardly in terms of the imagery, plugging does not mean that there can be no percolation. Plugging of presuppositions simply means that there does not *have to* be percolation but, contrary to what the term 'plugging' might evoke, there *may* always be percolation. When the Exxon press release says

> (50)   (Exxon, Houston, Texas: 30 March 1989)
>   Iarossi said: "We are all disappointed that an officer would have
>   jeopardized his ship, crew and the environment through such
>   actions."

then the presupposition that the captain is to blame is plugged; so, theoretically, (50) could well make sense even if the writer of the press release feels that the captain of the Exxon Valdez is innocent. In Spooren and Jaspers's terminology, there is no explicit textual indication of percolation. But there are no indications 'to the opposite' either and so, as I have argued, percolation *may* take place. Indeed, in this case there can be no doubt that the writer of the Exxon press release shares Iarossi's views. I would now suggest that, similarly, for journalists to copy (50) does not guarantee uncommittedness since it may leave the impression that they feel the captain is to blame.[41]

So we are now finally able to answer the question whether for journalists to copy the self-quotations of press releases in news reporting should be taken as distancing or agreement. The answer is: neither. As the notion of plugging confirms, it does not necessarily imply agreement, so I have to disagree with Spooren and Jaspers's claim that percolation occurs as soon as there are no indications 'to the opposite'. Still, as I suggested above, it does not guarantee uncommittedness either; at best, it offers a sense of uncommittedness, which is typically mistaken as real uncommittedness.

It should be clear by now that what I described above is not just true of copying the self-quotes in press releases. It is true of any quotation in the news and this helps to explain why self-quotations in press releases serve as appropriate preformulations after all. If they are not objective, then no quotation can ever be 100% objective. As Locher and Wortham (1994) stress, "[t]he opacity of the construction (for determining evaluative perspective) passes for real objectivity: because the audience cannot *definitively* assign a perspective to the reporter, they assume that there is no perspective" (531).

Real objectivity, apart from a verbatim rendering of the other's words, would require 'perspectivelessness'. I have shown that no verbatim rendering is possible or desirable. As far as perspectivelessness is concerned, even if it was possible, then it would just not be desirable in press releases. On the other hand, it is desirable, but not possible in news reporting. So instead, since the press produces "unavoidably non-objective text", we have "objectively-voiced text" (519, 531). In Gaye Tuchman's words, objectivity is a mere strategic ritual. I shall now briefly look at two cases that provide illustrations of how journalists' quoting practices, like the self-quoting practices in press releases, are part of a 'politics of reality' (1972: 666).[42]

5.5.4   Quoting in the news

In the first case, Tuchman (1978) shows how news reporters, just like writers of press releases, remove their own opinions from the story by getting others to say what they themselves, i.e. the news reporters, think. It is the story of a journalist who was covering a concerned group's visit to a federal attorney in order to request action on the killing of black students in Orangeburg, South Carolina. When the journalist asked a minister for his reaction to the lawyer's behaviour, the minister's reply was:

> We have a great deal of concern for what is going on. It's unfortunate that our concern was responded to in a way that really didn't recognize that when people have been killed, a great deal of emotion evolves, which is not taken care of by telling people to hurry along.

The journalist then asked:

> To put it briefly, are you dissatisfied?

To which the minister replied:

> I think there was unnecessary harshness.

After a pause, Tuchman reports, the minister concluded:

> Rudeness is the word.

Afterwards, the journalist explained that he had interviewed the minister "specifically to get those statements so as to avoid editorializing that the federal attorney was rude" (95-96). In other words, from the very beginning, the journalist had set out to charge the lawyer with 'rudeness', but he managed to elicit a quote, i.e. he got someone else to say those words for him, so that, strictly speaking, he could remain objective.

The second example goes one step further. Hardt-Mautner (1995) reports on an article in the British *Sun* daily newspaper in which a series of ordinary citizens are interviewed on European Union. Here again "[t]he basic principle is to introduce a persona into the discourse that authenticates the news coverage" (196). But, unlike in Tuchman's example, the quotes were not *elicited* by the journalist, they were almost certainly *invented*. Although the *Sun* journalist is taking great care to draw clear boundaries between the quoted words and the journalist's own language, through typography for example, in the end, Hardt-Mautner argues, it can be doubted "whether any proper interviewing ever took place at all, and if so, whether any serious attempt was made to faithfully reproduce the anterior discourse" (197). So it is a "fake interactivity": the *Sun* journalist is simply expressing his own and the paper's strongly anti-European feelings but at the same time he is giving the impression that he is representing the people's opinion. He is doing this to suggest that "what is going on is not so much top down indoctrination as enlightenment responding to grass-roots initiatives" (192). Hardt-Mautner concludes that a major

> consequence of (and possibly reason for) extensive 'verbatim' quoting is that it allows the editorial voice of the paper to step back behind the voice of the quoted persona. By yielding the floor completely to the man and woman in the street, the paper positions itself as a public forum of discussion rather than as a disseminator of editorial wisdom (197).[43]

5.6 Exposing the unavoidable non-objectiveness of press releases

Based on these two radical illustrations of the 'non-objectiveness' of quotation, I would conclude that any analysis of self-quotation in press releases should be integrated in a wider, necessarily also diachronic, view on the meaning of objectivity in news reporting as a whole.

Michael Schudson, for example, reports how the workings of military propaganda during the first World War convinced journalists "that the world they reported was one that interested parties had constructed for them to report" (1978: 6) and how, paradoxically, this acute awareness of "the impossibility of overcoming subjectivity in the news" (7) gave rise to the search for objectivity.[44] Crucially, it was not just news reporters who tried to be objective by identifying their sources; PR practitioners did same thing.

Ivy Lee, for example, who is generally regarded as one of the first public relations agents, is reported to have said that

> The effort to state an absolute fact is simply an attempt to achieve what is humanly impossible; all I can do is to give you my interpretation of the facts (135).

And Edward L. Bernays, a prominent publicist (and Sigmund Freud's nephew), claimed that the only test in the struggle among ideas is

> the power of thought to get itself accepted in the open competition of the market (136).

I would suggest that, what Schudson calls, this 'cynical epistemology' is also at work in press releases. Just take (25) again:

(25)   (Exxon, Valdez, Alaska: 23 August 1989)
The man who is heading Exxon's cleanup of the Exxon Valdez oil spill today called on Alaska Governor Steve Cowper to "stop playing politics and start working constructively to serve the best interest of Alaska."
In response to Governor Cowper's claim that Exxon failed to address concerns raised by the state, Otto Harrison, general manager of Exxon's Valdez operations, said: "This is truly amazing. I have to question the governor's motives because once again he has prepared his press statement before thoughtfully considering a very comprehensive plan which clearly addresses concerns previously raised by the state." (...)
Harrison said most of the activities which Governor Cowper claims were omitted from the Exxon plan "are there in black and white", and "raise the question of whether the governor had even taken the time to read it."
"The key suggestion from Governor Cowper which is not included in Exxon's plan," Harrison said, "could jeopardize the safety of workers on the shorelines. We have no intention of playing Russian roulette with work crews by following the governor's suggestion that we try to operate an additional six weeks after winter winds and waves make it unsafe to be there."

> Harrison said: "Following this morning's briefing, Commissioner Kelso asked a few clarifying questions. But despite the quote attributed to Kelso in the governor's press release, he made no reference to 'a blizzard of numbers' and, to the contrary, gave no indication that Exxon's winter program was not reasonable."
> Harrison said (...).

I have shown that the repeated reference to Harrison may well enhance the source's authority. At the same time, it serves to clearly separate the quoted words from the reporter's and to remind the audience that they are listening - in Hartley's (1982) terminology - to accessed voices, and not institutional ones.[45] Crudely, in Hardt-Mautner's story, the *Sun* newspaper, which could be expected to be neutral, uses quotation to hide its self-interest; in my data, press releases, which normally present the case of whatever organization they work for, use self-quotation to expose their own 'unavoidable non-objectiveness' (Locher and Wortham 1994).[46] This is another way in which self-quotation serves a purpose of preformulation$_{ii}$. Note that earlier on, in chapter 3, I made the same remark for third-person self-reference and I shall argue in the next chapter that explicit semi-performatives play a similar preformulating role.

Here again there is a clear danger, though. Since in press releases some utterances are attributed to accessed voices, others seem to be offered as the transparent, neutral discourse of the institutional voices; in other words, they get naturalized. The same thing happens of course, in news reporting. In order to analyse the preformulating role of self-quotation in press releases, it is therefore necessary to be aware that, as Hartley (1982) suggests,

> At [the level of the news-narrative as a whole], all the voices contribute to the production of the reality effect. (...) the credibility of the news story depends on 'knitting together' the apparently transparent, neutral discourse of the institutional voices and the contending mêlée of accessed voices. What the story means, then, depends on the successful integration of a known and trusted institutional discourse and an 'authentic' representation of the 'factual' world of phenomena 'out there' (114-115).

6.   Conclusions

In this chapter I have looked at the various functions of self-quotation in press releases and I have provided corpus-based evidence of the complex preformulating roles they play. In particular, as far as the issue of objectivity is concerned, it has been shown that self-quotation plays a negotiating role, reconciling the widely divergent ambitions of those who issue press releases and those who receive (and retell) them; on the other hand, I have argued that no real objectivity is possible in the news and, instead, I have proposed a notion of 'objectively-voiced' text.

In the next chapter I shall turn to a third and final interesting feature of the metapragmatics in my data, viz. explicit semi-performatives.

Chapter 6
Explicit Semi-Performatives in Press Releases

1. Explicit Semi-Performatives in Press Releases

1.1 Explicit performatives vs. self-quotation

Let's look at the following extract from a press release issued by the customs authorities of the Port of Antwerp:

(1) (Administratie der Douane en Accijnzen, Antwerp: 28 September 1994)

De Administratie der Douane en Accijnzen deelt mee dat haar Opsporingsinspectie te Antwerpen erin geslaagd is 32 kg zuivere cocaïne in beslag te nemen. De marktwaarde van de inbeslaggenomen drug kan worden geraamd op 112 miljoen F. (...)
De Administratie der Douane en Accijnzen merkt daarbij op dat bij deze actie opnieuw de effectiviteit blijkt van het gebruik van kleine en wendbare patrouilleboten in de strijd tegen de drugsmaffia.

The Customs and Excise Administration announces that its investigation inspectorate in Antwerp has succeeded in confiscating 32 kg of pure cocaine. The market value of the confiscated drug can be estimated at 122 million F. (...)
The Customs and Excise Administration remarks that with this action the effectiveness of the use of small and maneuverable patrol boats in the fight against the drugs maffia has been proved again.

This extract contains two examples of the typical metapragmatic pattern that I would like to focus on in this chapter, viz.

> *De Administratie der Douane en Accijnzen deelt mee dat ...*

> The Customs and Excise Administration announces that ...

and

> *De Administratie der Douane en Accijnzen merkt daarbij op dat ...*

> The Customs and Excise Administration remarks that ...

Although both are marked by a reflexive use of linguistic action verbs, I would like to argue that they should not be mixed up with the examples of self-quotation in press releases that I discussed in the previous two chapters. As it is, there are several reasons which together make strong evidence not to do so:

- To start with, there is no direct speech, there are no quotation marks. At best, the patterns in (1) could be considered forms of indirect speech.

- Next, the linguistic action verbs used are almost never 'say' or 'continue', which, I demonstrated in the previous chapter, are typical of self-quotation in press releases.

- Unlike for self-quotation, no use of the past tense can be found for this type of self-reference.

- Finally, the grammatical subject is almost never a person; instead, it is usually the organization that issued the press release.

It follows that the metapragmatics in (1) differ markedly from the self-quotations described in the previous two chapters. In particular, all these characteristics taken together seem to indicate that here the writer of the press release is making no effort whatsoever to create the impression that the embedded words provide an accurate report of what was said on a previous occasion. More so, in this case there can even be no doubt that there was no previous announcement of the administration's success altogether since further on in the same press release it is said that the press meeting is scheduled for later that day. In fact, the press release could be said to serve as an invitation for this press meeting:

(2)   (Administratie der Douane en Accijnzen, Antwerp: 28 September 1994)

Verdere details zullen aan de media worden verstrekt op een persontmoeting die deze namiddag plaats heeft om 14 uur in het directiegebouw van de Administratie der Douane en Accijnzen, 4e verdieping, Kattendijkdok, Oostkaai 22 te 2000 Antwerpen.

Further details will be supplied to the media at a press meeting which will take place this afternoon at 14 hours in the direction building of the Customs and Excise Administration, 4th floor, Kattendijkdok, 22 Oostkaai in 2000 Antwerp.

Therefore, instead of looking at the patterns in (1) as examples of self-quotation, I suggest that they should be taken as explicit performative utterances.[1] After all, in the very act of saying that they 'announce that they managed to confiscate 32 kg of pure cocaine', the customs authorities are indeed announcing that they did so. In other words, the press release *is* the announcement and this seems to be in line with Allan Bell's claim that press releases are performative documents (1991).

At the end of this chapter I shall come back to the relationship between explicit performatives and self-quotation and I shall argue that it is difficult to distinguish between the two. Indeed, it should be noted that some of the issues that were dealt with in chapter 5 will crop up again in this chapter but, crucially, they will be approached from a different angle. That is why, for the discussion in this chapter, I would like to focus exclusively on those utterances in my corpus that conform to the *ad hoc* performative characteristics spelled out above. I shall also have to leave out from my investigation any performative-like utterances that can be directly linked to quotations elsewhere in the same press release as in

> (3)   (Exxon, Washington, D.C.: 11 May 1989)
>   EXXON ANNOUNCES ADDITIONAL PERSONNEL AND EQUIPMENT WILL BE USED IN SHORELINE CLEAN-UP EFFORT

If we stick to the four characteristics, then indeed this looks like a performative, but later on in the same press release it becomes clear that the headline is a summary of words that were previously spoken - or, since this could well be a case of pseudo-direct speech, *supposedly* previously spoken - by Exxon's William D. Stevens:

> (4)   (Exxon, Washington, D.C.: 11 May 1989)
>   William D. Stevens, president of Exxon Company, U.S.A., announced that Exxon will use additional personnel and equipment in its shoreline clean-up effort in Alaska. (...)
>   "This means we will deploy a total of 50 landing craft and 20 barges in our clean-up effort", Stevens said.

My specific purpose in drawing attention to the patterns in (1) is to explore the peculiar audience-directedness of what is yet another interesting feature of the metapragmatics of press releases and to check if the concept of preformulation, which has proved so useful for my analysis of self-reference and self-quotation in press releases, could equally be applied to this special brand of performatives in my corpus. In doing so, I shall have to draw from - and indeed point out the misconceptions at the heart of - various speech act theoretic accounts of what explicit performatives really are.

1.2 Semi-performatives

It should be noted that the explicit performatives I am referring to here do not have the canonical form. The canonical form of an explicit performative, as spelled out by John Austin in *How To Do Things With Words* (1962), is

I (hereby) V [simple present, indicative, active] ...

as in

I (hereby) apologize (for stepping on your toes).

Apart from the absence of 'hereby', which, even in Austin's view, is optional, third-person self-reference instead of 'I' - along with a different form of the verb - is the major deviation in press releases.

As far as 'hereby' is concerned, it is clear that it could easily be added in (1). In (5) 'hereby' is actually included, so that apparently no doubt can be left about its performative nature:

(5)   (CBR, Brussels: 9 February 1995)
        Ter informatie van de aandeelhouders en het publiek maakt CBR Cementbedrijven N.V. hierbij het programma bekend van de bijeenkomsten van zijn maatschappelijke organen en van de berichten over de evolutie van zijn activiteiten en resultaten.

        For the information of the shareholders and the public CBR Cement companies N.V. hereby announces the programme of meetings of its social organs and of the messages on the evolution of its activities and results.

On closer scrutiny, however, since this press release is accompanied by a separate document, Dutch "hierbij" is ambiguous between the English equivalents 'hereby', which would point to a performative, and 'attached' or 'enclosed', which would lead the reader to interpret the utterance as descriptive.[2]

As for the grammatical subject of explicit performative patterns, it must be added that third-person self-reference is altogether not exceptional either. Austin is already aware of this possibility (1962: 57). Here is a nice example from Levinson (1983):

The company hereby undertakes to replace any can of Doggo-Meat that fails to please, with no questions asked (260).

Verschueren sees such performatives with a third-person subject as one category of a much larger group of 'non-central cases of performatives' or 'semi-performatives' (1995b: 301-302).

1.3 Research questions

The first question now is: why do press releases go for such an explicit semi-performative? Why

    (6)   (Administratie der Douane en Accijnzen, Antwerp: 28 September 1994)

        De Administratie der Douane en Accijnzen deelt mee dat haar Opsporingsinspectie te Antwerpen erin geslaagd is 32 kg zuivere cocaïne in beslag te nemen.

        The Customs and Excise Administration announces that its investigation inspectorate in Antwerp has succeeded in confiscating 32 kg of pure cocaine.

instead of simply

    De Opsporingsinspectie te Antwerpen van de Administratie der Douane en Accijnzen is erin geslaagd 32 kg zuivere cocaïne in beslag te nemen.

    The Antwerp investigation inspectorate of the Customs and Excise Administration has succeeded in confiscating 32 kg of pure cocaine.

Or why does the National Council of the WOW senior citizen party start its press release about a party meeting with

    (7)   (WOW, Brasschaat: 7 November 1994)

        De Nationale Raad van WOW in vergadering te Antwerpen deelt mede: WOW - Waardig Ouder Worden - wil bij gelegenheid van de komende feestdagen bijzondere aandacht verlenen aan enkele bijzondere items uit haar programma, namelijk betreft de veiligheid en het geweld in de samenleving.

The National Council of WOW meeting in Antwerp announces: on the occasion of the forthcoming festive season WOW - Waardig Ouder Worden - would like to pay special attention to some special items in its programme, viz. about the safety and violence in society.

and not with

WOW - Waardig Ouder Worden - wil bij gelegenheid van de komende feestdagen bijzondere aandacht verlenen aan enkele bijzondere items uit haar programma, namelijk betreft de veiligheid en het geweld in de samenleving.

On. the occasion of the forthcoming festive season WOW - Waardig Ouder Worden - would like to pay special attention to some special items in its programme, viz. about the safety and violence in society.

I shall now try to explore the difference between the two variants. In particular, still bearing in mind the research set-up described in the first chapter, I shall deal with the question how the distribution of explicit semi-performatives can be related to the peculiar audience-directedness of press releases.

2.   Preformulation$_i$

2.1 From performative to report

I would like to argue straight away that the explicit semi-performative utterances in extracts from press releases like (8) can easily be retold verbatim by journalists in their own news reporting and that therefore they serve a perfect preformulating$_i$ role:

(8)   (Central Hispano Benelux N.V.: 4 March 1994)
         Central Hispano Benelux N.V., het Belgisch filiaal van de grootste Spaanse privé bank, kondigt een winst na belastingen

> *aan van BEF 114 miljoen voor het boekjaar 1993, een stijging met 26% ten opzichte van 1992.*
>
> Central Hispano Benelux N.V., the Belgian affiliate of the biggest Spanish private bank, announces a profit after taxes of BEF 114 million for the financial year 1993, a rise of 26% compared with 1992.

Surely, it is not difficult to imagine (8) in its present form as part of a newspaper article. Note that no shift in tense is necessary here since I have shown that the simple present can easily be used with past time reference in media discourse. What would happen then is that, in the mouth of a journalist, the same utterance that had performative power in the press release is now turned into a report. Since such reports are a typical feature of any kind of news reporting, it may be argued that explicit semi-performatives, like self-quotation, help press releases meet this major stylistic requirement of media discourse and hence they serve as another preformulating$_i$ device.

This transformation from a performative to an assertive use of explicit semi-performatives should not be surprising since, as Verschueren (1995b) shows, performativity requires complete self-reference and this includes the possibility of making a linguistic action A coincide with a description D of that linguistic action.[3] In the act of retelling, A and D simply get disentangled and since we have third-person self-reference here, no further changes are necessary. In Austin's words, this seems to be one of those "clear cases where the very same formula seems sometimes to be an explicit performative and sometimes to be a descriptive, and may even trade on this ambivalence" (1962: 78).[4]

Interestingly, in my own corpus of press releases I found a number of similar cases where there is strong evidence that another organization's speech act is being continued as a report. (9), for example, is from the opening paragraph of a press release issued by the Kredietbank and includes a reference to the Flemish local government's announcement of a decision to expand one of its financial programmes.

(9)   (Kredietbank, Brussels: 15 May 1995)
De Vlaamse Gemeenschap kondigt de uitbreiding aan van het thesauriebewijzenprogramma waarover zij beschikt bij de Kredietbank.

The Flemish Community announces the expansion of the programme of treasury certificates that it has with the Kredietbank.

Since the performative use of such patterns is very popular in my own corpus of press releases, I would say that it is not unlikely that the very same utterance quoted in (9) previously served as an explicit semi-performative in a press release issued by the Flemish local government.

Here are some more examples:

(10)   (GB, Brussels: 4 March 1994)
De firma Honig in Koog aan de Zaan (NL) raadt aan om alle pakken Brinta uit de handel te nemen.

The company Honig in Koog aan de Zaan (NL) advises to take all Brinta packs out of the market.

(11)   (Domo, Gent: 17 March 1994)
De Treuhandanstalt verwelkomt het engagement van de DOMO GROUP in de 5 nieuwe bondsstaten.

The Treuhandanstalt welcomes the commitment of the DOMO GROUP in the 5 new federal states.

In each of these extracts, the writer of the press release is reporting on what another organization has said, using an utterance that may well have served as a performative in that other organization's original announcement. Actually, the performative reading is so strong in press releases that, if no name of a sender were mentioned on the press release, the average reader's - i.e. journalist's - interpretation would be that (9) was taken from a press release issued by the Flemish local government rather than the Kredietbank,

(10) by Honig rather than GB and (11) by the Treuhandanstalt rather than Domo.[5]

It is interesting to note in this respect what Jenny Thomas has to say about so-called 'metalinguistic' verbs like 'invite' and 'offer'. She argues that it would be "most odd" to use them in explicit performatives like 'I invite you' and 'I offer you' and she suggests that they would rather be used in reporting (1995: 47). At first sight, the fact that similar linguistic action verbs, be it with third-person subjects, do occur frequently as explicit performatives in my corpus seems to be in conflict with Thomas's observation. However, once again playing on the notion of preformulation in press releases, I would suggest that, far from taking the edge off Thomas's argument, this special performative use serves to anticipate the very kind of reporting that Thomas is thinking of.

2.2   Formulations as preformulations$_i$

2.2.1   Formulations

One specific reason why such explicit semi-performatives like in (12) serve as powerful preformulations$_i$ in my corpus is that most of them are 'formulations': i.e. they furnish the gist of what the press release as a whole is about.

(12)   (Westerlund, Antwerp: 29 March 1994)
        Westerlund bevestigt investeringen in ultra moderne infrastruc-
        tuur na bekendmaking gunstige resultaten voor 1993

        Westerlund confirms investments in ultra modern infrastructure
        after announcement of positive results for 1993

Let me briefly explain this.

Garfinkel and Sacks (1970) use the term 'formulation' to refer to those parts of a text that writers use "to describe [it], to explain it, or characterize it, or explicate, or translate, or summarize, or furnish the gist of it, or take note of its accordance with rules, or remark on its departure from rules"

(351). This is exactly what most of the explicit semi-performatives in my corpus are doing: they tell the reader what the press release is all about.

2.2.2   Formulations in the news

Various researchers have drawn attention to the specific role played by formulations in the news. In a classic paper, Heritage and Watson (1979), for example, point to the use of formulations in delivering and receiving news. In particular, they show that instances of 'saying-in-so-many-words-what-we-are-doing' are frequently used by news receivers to demonstrate understanding of what news deliverers are saying and to have that understanding confirmed by them. Significantly, in this case, most formulations can be shown to be strategic *re*formulations, with only some of the original information preserved and the rest - often consciously - deleted or even transformed, as with the journalist's intervention in this extract from a radio interview with the 'Slimmer of the Year':

> (S: Slimmer of the Year; J: journalist)
> S: You have a shell that for so long protects you but sometimes things creep through the shell and then you become really aware of how awful you feel. I never felt my age or looked my age I was older always older - people took me for older. And when I was at college I think I looked a matronly fifty. And I was completely alone one weekend and I got to this stage where I almost jumped in the river. I just felt life wasn't worth it any more - it hadn't anything to offer and if this was living I had had enough
> J: You really were prepared to commit suicide because you were a big fatty
> S: Yes, because (...). (132)

Interestingly for my purposes, Heritage (1985) adds that such reformulations may be a summing up of what the other said not just for the benefit of the news deliverer, in this case the Slimmer of the Year, but also for that of other news receivers, i.c. the overhearing radio audience.

Formulations may play a similar reformulating role in news deliveries. In news interviews and press conferences, for example, they help the interviewee to steer an awkward question into a more desirable direction (Clayman 1993), as with the following inquiry into Democratic candidate for the U.S. presidency Gary Hart's affair with Donna Rice:

> (GH: Gary Hart; J: journalist)
> J:　　I told you some days ago when we spoke, and I told our audience this evening that I would ask both questions. I will ask you the first now just before we take a break because I think I know what your answer's gonna be. Did you have an affair with Miss Rice?
> GH:　　Mister Koppel if the question is: in the twenty years of my marriage, including two public separations have I been absolutely and totally faithful to my wife I regret to say the answer is no (168).

2.2.3　Formulations in press releases

Let's now return to formulations in that other type of news delivering, viz. press releases. Since we are looking at performatives and not at reports, I would like to suggest that the formulations in my corpus cannot function as reformulations of what was previously said. Instead, just like pseudo-direct speech, they seem to be *pre*formulations of what the writer of the press release hopes will be said afterwards. In this sense formulations in press releases are close to what Walker (1995) calls optimistic formulations, in which, "[t]hrough cautious lexical and phrasal selection, the participants design their talk so that they will be heard to be saying what they want to be heard to be saying" (132).

It should be mentioned in this respect that most performatives in my corpus, including (12), appear in the headlines or first paragraph of press releases. This means that, apart from helping journalists instantly decide on the newsworthiness of the press release, they stand an even better chance of being selected for publication: the reason is that in newspaper reporting, the headline and first sentence(s) - or lead - usually express the major topic of the text (Van Dijk 1988: 53); as a result, press releases that start with formulations like (12) require a minimum of reworking on the part of journalists (cf. also Lebar 1985). Clearly, Brookes's account of what role headlines play in news reporting could equally be applied to press releases:

> Headlines, as part of the characteristic pattern of organization of news discourse, are a focusing act. They function as initial summaries of news texts and foreground what the producer regards as most relevant and of maximum interest or appeal to readers. By so doing, headlines provide preferred meaning for news texts and frameworks within which readers may interpret them (1995: 467).

In summary: performatives in press releases, since they are formulations, allow the news deliverers to provide a powerful 'candidate reading' of their own words, they "[offer] an adequate paraphrase" (Polanyi 1985: 16), and highlight those aspects that are especially reportable, thus controlling subsequent (re)formulation in the media.[6]

I have shown in this section that explicit semi-performatives may play a preformulating$_i$ role in press releases in that they allow journalists to simply copy them in their own news reporting: they help press releases meet some of the formal and stylistic requirements of media discourse. However, as Gandy (1982) puts it, not just form but also "content" should be "structured in such a way as to flow in sync with" the target genre (57) and both for self-reference and self-quotation I have demonstrated that they have such a further preformulating$_{ii}$ effect on the overall utterance: i.e. they were shown to play a major role in bringing news managers' and newsmakers' conflicting ambitions somewhat closer together. This is what I shall now turn to for explicit semi-performatives.

3.   Preformulation$_{ii}$

3.1 In newspaper articles

Let's start with the simplest question of the two: what happens, 'content-wise', to the explicit semi-performatives of press releases when they are retold in news reporting?

(1)   (Administratie der Douane en Accijnzen, Antwerp: 28 September 1994)

De Administratie der Douane en Accijnzen deelt mee dat haar Opsporingsinspectie te Antwerpen erin geslaagd is 32 kg zuivere cocaïne in beslag te nemen. De marktwaarde van de inbeslaggenomen drug kan worden geraamd op 112 miljoen F. (...)

De Administratie der Douane en Accijnzen merkt daarbij op dat bij deze actie opnieuw de effectiviteit blijkt van het gebruik van kleine en wendbare patrouilleboten in de strijd tegen de drugsmaffia.

The Customs and Excise Administration announces that its investigation inspectorate in Antwerp has succeeded in confiscating 32 kg of pure cocaine. The market value of the confiscated drug can be estimated at 122 million F. (...)

The Customs and Excise Administration remarks that with this action the effectiveness of the use of small and maneuverable patrol boats in the fight against the drugs maffia has been proved again.

I have argued that if a journalist simply copies (1) in his or her own news reporting, the result is a report, and so, as I showed in the previous chapter for self-quotation, in the embedded forms there is a dramatic as well as a distancing effect, which, in the journalists' view, for a wide range of reasons is preferable to the immediacy of the bare equivalents:

De Opsporingsinspectie te Antwerpen van de Administratie der Douane en Accijnzen is erin geslaagd 32 kg zuivere cocaïne in beslag te nemen.

The Antwerp investigation inspectorate of the Customs and Excise Administration has succeeded in confiscating 32 kg of pure cocaine.

and

Bij deze actie blijkt opnieuw de effectiviteit van het gebruik van kleine en wendbare patrouilleboten in de strijd tegen de drugsmaffia.

With this action the effectiveness of the use of small and maneuverable patrol boats in the fight against the drugs maffia has been proved again.

As far as the choice of verbs is concerned, it should be noted that, since performativity requires that the linguistic action (A) and its description (D) coincide, no verbs expressing any interpretive, evaluative or temporal distance whatsoever can be used (Verschueren 1995b). It follows that, just as for self-quotation, here again retelling press releases contributes to that 'rhetoric of objectivity' in which the typical news story is biased toward "broad, categoric vocabulary" - 'say', rather than 'shout' or 'insist' (Weaver 1974: 94-95): in this case journalists are encouraged to simply copy the neutral and perhaps somewhat tedious linguistic action verbs 'announce' and 'point out' rather than that they are left to come up with more cóloured as well as lively equivalents like 'boast' or 'claim'.[7]

3.2   In press releases

3.2.1   Suspending truth conditions?

But what about the explicit semi-performatives in the press releases themselves? What is the real difference between these explicit performatives and their implicit counterparts?

It is Austin who, in *How To Do Things With Words* (1962), first distinguished between 'constatives', i.e. utterances that merely describe some state of affairs, and 'performatives', i.e. utterances that accomplish, in their very enunciation, an act that generates effects. According to his original theory, constatives have truth conditions only (and no felicity conditions) and performatives have felicity conditions only (and no truth conditions). This is what Levinson (1983) calls the 'thesis'.

If performatives have no truth conditions - i.e. they cannot be true or false because they are not used to say something but to do something - the question arises if the use of explicit semi-performatives in press releases could serve to suspend the bothersome truth conditions that would have to be reckoned with if the embedded part was taken on its own? As in:

(13)   (Noblesse, Londerzeel: 30 March 1994)

Noblesse Benelux, gespecialiseerd in machines en gereedschap-
pen, deelt mede dat zij het handelsfonds van de failliete firma
Taecke heeft overgenomen.

Noblesse Benelux, specialized in machines and tools, announces
that it has taken over the funds of the bankrupt Taecke firm.

(14)   (Kredietbank, Brussels: 16 January 1995)

De Kredietbank en haar dochterbank Crédit Général delen mee
dat de IBOS-associatie, waarvan zij de vertegenwoordigende
leden in België zijn, haar expansie in Europa voortzet met de
toetreding van een Deense partner: UNIBANK.

The Kredietbank and its subsidiary Crédit Général announce that
the IBOS association, whose representing members they are in
Belgium, continues its expansion in Europe with the entry of a
Danish partner: UNIBANK.

Could it be that in each of these extracts the explicit performative helps
remove the suggestion that Noblesse really took over Taecke and that the
IBOS association is really continuing its expansion with the entry of
Unibank? According to Austin's original theory, that is exactly what
happens. But clearly this is against any common-sense interpretation of what
press releases are all about: they are normally meant to provide more or
less unambiguous information; alternatively, if you want to keep people in
doubt, you might as well not issue a press release at all.

    In a subsequent version of speech act theory, this radical distinction
between performatives and constatives is slightly adjusted. It is acknowledged that performatives do have truth conditions: they are true by virtue of
being felicitously uttered, they are considered to involve declarations which
are true by virtue of creating the state of affairs they represent. In
particular, it is uptake by the reader that makes a performative true. This is
how the French philosopher François Recanati articulates the modified
thesis of performatives as self-verifying utterances:

a speech act is performed by means of the hearer's recognition of the speaker's communicative intention. Because I can bring about this recognition by saying what speech act I am performing, it is, in a sense sufficient to have said this in order to guarantee that I have said something true. In saying what act I am performing, I effectively perform that act, and my utterance is true merely by virtue of being uttered (1987: 89; cf. also Searle 1989).

Note that this emphasis on the hearer or reader is not altogether absent from Austin's work either. Levinson even deplores that the interactional emphasis in Austin has been neglected in most later work in speech act theory (1983: 237).

This point that uptake is necessary to make a performative true sheds light on what is happening in the following telephone conversation between the Israeli Colonel Bar-Lev and President Idi Amin of Uganda shortly after Israeli commandos had rescued the Jewish passengers of a French plane, who were kept hostage by Palestinian terrorists at the Ugandan airport at Entebbe. At the time of the phone call, Amin, who had supposedly collaborated with the terrorists, did not yet know what had happened at the airport:

BL: Sir, I want to thank you for your cooperation and I want to thank you very much.
A: You know I did not succeed.
BL: Thank you very much for your cooperation. What? The cooperation did not succeed? Why?
A: Have I done anything at all?
BL: I just want to thank you, sir, for the cooperation?
A: Have I done anything at all?
BL: I did exactly what you wanted.
A: Wh-- Wh-- What happened?
BL: What happened?
A: Yes?
BL: I don't know.
A: Can't you tell me?
BL: No. I don't know. I have been requested to thank you for your cooperation.

A: Can you tell me about the suggestion you mentioned?

BL: I have been requested by a friend with good connections in the government to thank you for your cooperation. I don't know what was meant by it, but I think you do know.

A: I don't know because I've only now returned hurriedly from Mauritius.

BL: Ah...

A: ... In order to solve the problem before the ultimatum expires tomorrow morning.

BL: I understand very well, sir... Thank you for the cooperation. Perhaps I'll call you tomorrow morning? Do you want me to call you again tomorrow morning?

A: Yes.

BL: Very well, thank you sir. Goodbye. (Verschueren 1980: 65-66)

If Amin does not know what the other is thanking him for (and indeed, if Bar-Lev is only thanking him because he has been requested to do so by a friend with good connections in the government), the question arises: did Bar-Lev thank Amin at all?

Let's return to press releases once again. Far from disqualifying my initial claim about the role of performatives in press releases, this revised version of the thesis would actually confirm that the explicit performatives in (13) and (14) could serve to deflect any questions about whether Noblesse really took over Taecke or the IBOS association is really continuing its expansion with the entry of Unibank: the press release, in view of its performative nature, would simply be true by being uttered and recognized.

That such rather sophisticated considerations are no simple theoretical exercise is also illustrated by the following anecdote quoted by Thomas (1995: 36). Norman Tebbit, at that time Britain's Conservative Secretary of State for Employment, is reported to have declared to the media:

I predict that unemployment figures will fall by one million, within a year.

Later Roy Hattersley, deputy leader of the Labour party, in true Austinian fashion, declared on the radio about Tebbit's statement:

> Notice he said "I predict they will fall" and not "They will fall". That means when next year comes and they haven't fallen he will have a let out.

Apparently, the problem of the truth conditions of explicit performatives is a reality in nation-wide politics.

Former White House spokesman Marlin Fitzwater seems to point in the same direction when, in his autobiography, he tells a childhood story of how he managed to buy a nudic magazine in a country store. When the old man behind the counter asks 'Do you think you're old enough for this?", young Marlin simply replies 'Yes' and walks quickly out the door:

> I instinctively knew that he had asked the right question, the one that allowed me to tell the truth, be confident, and still accomplish the task. He didn't ask if I *was* old enough, only if I *thought* I was. In later years I would often search frantically for the more narrow press question that I could seize upon to answer (1995: 23).

3.2.2   Antithesis

Of course, Roy Hattersley's suspicion, young Fitzwater's confidence and my own initial suggestion about the role played by performatives in press releases are largely unfounded. It is important in this respect to recognize that the distinction between constatives and performatives cannot be maintained in the language. After all, any apparent constative like

> The world is flat

can be shown to merely hide a performative

> I state to you that the world is flat.

Similarly, even if Tebbit had said

Unemployment figures will fall by one million, within a year.

in the end this would have been equal to

I predict that unemployment figures will fall by one million, within a year.

Here is an example from my corpus that seems to prove this point:

> (15)   (Kredietbank, Brussels: 28 July 1995)
> *Als gevolg van de renteontwikkeling op de financiële markten, verlaagt de Kredietbank haar rentetarieven voor woningkredieten. (...)*
> *Belangrijk is dat deze tariefverlaging eveneens van toepassing is op (...).*
> *De Kredietbank wijst er bovendien op dat (...).*
>
> As a result of the interest development on the financial markets, the Kredietbank lowers its interest rates for mortgages. (...)
> It is important that this lowering of the rate is also applicable to (...).
> The Kredietbank also points out that (...).

The use of "bovendien" [also] in the final sentence of the extract implies that this explicit performative is preceded by a hidden performative earlier on in the same press release, like

> *De Kredietbank stelt dat het belangrijk is dat deze tariefverlaging eveneens van toepassing is op (...).*

The Kredietbank states that it is important that this lowering of the rate is also applicable to (...).

This is the 'performative hypothesis' or what Levinson (1983) calls the 'antithesis'. Levinson warns readers of *How To Do Things With Words* that Austin is "playing cunning" and that "there is an internal evolution to the argument, so that what is proposed at the beginning is rejected by the end" (231). From a focus on extralinguistic, institutional acts like baptizing, bequeathing, etc. only, Austin leads to a much more general theory of what he calls 'illocutionary acts' including both performatives and constatives. It is suggested that performatives have truth conditions and constatives have felicity conditions. As a result, he brings about a shift from the view that performatives are a special class of utterances to the view that there is a general class of performatives that includes both explicit performatives (the old class of "relatively specialized ways of being unambiguous or specific about what act you are performing in speaking") and implicit ones ("the latter including lots of other kinds of utterances, if not all" - Levinson 1983: 231).

For my purposes, it is important to remember, as Recanati (1987: 24) notes, that if

The world is flat

equals

I state to you that the world is flat.

then the latter, explicit performative utterance cannot be simply true by being uttered. Similarly, George Lakoff (1977) suggests that "in sentences where there is an overt performative verb of saying or stating or asserting, the propositional content, which is true or false, is not given by the sentence as a whole, but rather by the object of the performative verb" (110). From a systemic-functional point of view, Eggins (1994), quoting an example from Halliday, makes the same point by matching an explicit performative and its appropriate question-tag:

I reckon Henry James wrote "The Bostonians", didn't he?

vs.

*I reckon Henry James wrote "The Bostonians", do I?

This means that Tebbitt could have said

> I predict that unemployment figures will fall by one million, within a year, won't they?

but not, as Hattersley seems to imply:

> *I predict that unemployment figures will fall by one million, within a year, don't I?

Finally, Vandenbergen (1996) argues that what is negotiated in the following exchange is not if the interviewer heard that the school would be closed down, but if what he or she heard is correct.

> - I heard today that they're going to close down the school. Is that so?
> - That's right.[8]

This then would mean that the explicit semi-performatives in the above extracts from press releases have no different truth conditions than their simple non-embedded equivalents would have had and that therefore they cannot serve to deflect questions about the embedded proposition.

So the question remains: apart from the preformulating$_i$ role specified above, in the press releases themselves is there no difference whatsoever between

> (13)   (Noblesse, Londerzeel: 30 March 1994)
> *Noblesse Benelux, gespecialiseerd in machines en gereedschappen, deelt mede dat zij het handelsfonds van de failliete firma Taecke heeft overgenomen.*
>
> Noblesse Benelux, specialized in machines and tools, announces that it has taken over the funds of the bankrupt Taecke firm.

and

Noblesse Benelux, gespecialiseerd in machines en gereedschappen, heeft het handelsfonds van de failliete firma Taecke overgenomen.

Noblesse Benelux, specialized in machines and tools, has taken over the funds of the bankrupt Taecke firm.

3.2.3   Announcements as communicated acts?

Goffman (1974) thinks that there is a difference. This is the way he gives voice to his doubts about the performative hypothesis:

> It might, of course, be claimed that every statement uttered by an individual carries at least an implied or tacit connective, such as 'I aver that', and that every utterance can therefore be construed as a reporting on of sorts. Presumably a query as to who made any last statement could then recover the connective, as in the answer, 'I said that'. However, even were this doubtful claim granted, there would remain the task of accounting for why individuals use an explicit connective at certain points in their talk, obtruding an 'I think that', or an 'I feel that', even though an implied reporting (along with an implied distance from what is reported) might be claimed to be already present (532).

Similarly, Robin Lakoff compares the explicit performative

I (hereby) say to you that prices slumped

and the implicit

Prices slumped.

and concludes that even if there is a "similarity of truth values" (there is, after all, no circumstance in which one can be truthfully said but not the other), they are certainly not functionally or pragmatically equivalent (1980: 41; cf. also 1977: 84).

I would now like to suggest that a clue to the difference between the two is in the idea of uptake after all. I mentioned above that it was suggested quite early in a revised version of the thesis, even by Austin, that the truth of a performative depends on the uptake. Surely, no understanding can be reached without reader recognition and explicit performatives may therefore be said to serve to make unambiguous what act you are performing in speaking. Money can only be collected if you say

I bet £ 100 that Lucy will leave the room

and not for

Lucy will leave the room.

These are what Blakemore (1991) calls communicated acts (200). Here is a similar example from my corpus of press releases:

(16)   (GB, Brussels: 3 May 1994)
GB betreurt dat de wet op de Ecotaksen niet voorafgegaan werd door een wetenschappelijke studie.

GB deplores that the law on Eco taxes was not preceded by a scientific study.

(16), with the explicit performative, is very different from the simple

De wet op de Ecotaksen werd niet voorafgegaan door een wetenschappelijke studie.

The law on Eco taxes was not preceded by a scientific study.

Blakemore says that these are institutional acts, which can only be described with reference to a particular social framework.[9]
But let's look at (14) again:

(14)   (Kredietbank, Brussels: 16 January 1995)
De Kredietbank en haar dochterbank Crédit Général delen mee dat de IBOS-associatie, waarvan zij de vertegenwoordigende

leden in België zijn, haar expansie in Europa voortzet met de toetreding van een Deense partner: UNIBANK.

The Kredietbank and its subsidiary Crédit Général announce that the IBOS association, whose representing members they are in Belgium, continues its expansion in Europe with the entry of a Danish partner: UNIBANK.

Here the explicit performative is not really necessary to make the reader of the press release aware that Kredietbank is making an announcement, certainly not in the same way as in (16) the performative is necessary to show that GB is expressing regret. Of course, uptake is necessary in (14) too. As Thomas (1995) puts it, in a question that seems to be formulated to apply to press releases: "Can an announcement be made if there is no one to hear it?" (42) However, announcing is a non-communicated act and it looks as if the following would be an equally effective announcement:

De IBOS-associatie, waarvan de Kredietbank en haar dochterbank Crédit Général de vertegenwoordigende leden in België zijn, zet haar expansie in Europa voort met de toetreding van een Deense partner: UNIBANK.

The IBOS association, whose representing members in Belgium are the Kredietbank and its subsidiary Crédit Général, continues its expansion in Europe with the entry of a Danish partner: UNIBANK.

Or would it?

3.2.4   Strong communicators

Blakemore is aware of the problem. She notes that

The path is slippery here

can be an effective warning. It is not necessary to say

I warn you that the path is slippery here

"I warn you that" can therefore be left out. Still, she argues, "I warn you that" can be and very often is included. Similarly, announcements in my corpus of press releases are almost invariably of the type

    (14)   (Kredietbank, Brussels: 16 January 1995)
           De Kredietbank en haar dochterbank Crédit Général delen mee dat de IBOS-associatie, waarvan zij de vertegenwoordigende leden in België zijn, haar expansie in Europa voortzet met de toetreding van een Deense partner: UNIBANK.

           The Kredietbank and its subsidiary Crédit Général announce that the IBOS association, whose representing members they are in Belgium, continues its expansion in Europe with the entry of a Danish partner: UNIBANK.

and not

De IBOS-associatie, waarvan de Kredietbank en haar dochterbank Crédit Général de vertegenwoordigende leden in België zijn, zet haar expansie in Europa voort met de toetreding van een Deense partner: UNIBANK.

The IBOS association, whose representing members in Belgium are the Kredietbank and its subsidiary Crédit Général, continues its expansion in Europe with the entry of a Danish partner: UNIBANK.

What's its purpose?
    I would now like to argue that, in order to accurately identify the role played by explicit performatives in my corpus of press releases, it is crucial to appreciate that reader recognition of the speech act is a necessary, but not a sufficient condition for a performative to be true. Long before Austin, Gardiner (1932) was already aware that we cannot communicate without communicating that we are communicating because communication will succeed *only if* - but not necessarily *as soon as* - the hearer identifies the type of communication at hand. Austin's thesis, however, has obscured that

with explicit performatives, next to promoting reader recognition of the speech act, what George Lakoff (1977) calls 'the object of the performative' counts too. I would now argue that to identify the role of explicit performatives it is crucial to find out how the 'performative' can be related to its 'object'. As Recanati puts it, "[i]t is not because I make explicit the nature of my act while I am performing it that I make no statement on this subject" (1987: 88).

Let's return to the data. Blakemore argues that in

I warn you that the path is slippery.

there are two speech acts, two distinct acts of communication going on:

(i)   the speaker communicates the information that the path is slippery
(ii) the speaker communicates that (i) is made as a warning

Crucially, the second act serves to help understand the first:[10] in particular, the point of (ii) is to spell out the utterance's force (i.e. the speaker's or writer's commitment to it: in this case the information that the path is slippery is treated as important and urgent) as well as its ratification (i.e. the hearer's or reader's consequent action: in this case to do something to avoid slipping). In this view, the function of "I warn you that" seems to be close to that of what Urmson calls parentheticals like "I think", which

> function as signals guiding the hearer to a proper appreciation of the statement in its context, social, logical, or evidential. They are not part of the statement made, nor additional statements, but function with regard to a statement made rather as 'READ WITH CARE' functions in relation to a subjoined notice, or as the foot stamping and saluting can function in the Army to make clear that one is making an official report. Perhaps they can be compared to such stage-directions as 'said in a mournful (confident) tone' with reference to the lines of the play. They help the understanding and assessment of what is said rather than being part of what is said (1963: 239-240).

However, the crucial difference between "I warn you that" or "The Kredietbank announces", on the one hand, and Urmson's account of parentheticals, on the other hand, - and indeed what distinguishes the present view from Austin's thesis - is that it should be clear by now that the former are not just signals or indicators. Instead, they are part of the utterance as a whole. They play a fully descriptive role. They are what Levinson calls 'illocutionary force indicating devices', which serve to demonstrate "how [the description is] to be taken or what the [hearer or reader] is meant to do with [it]" (1983: 246). In Herb Clark's (1995) terminology, "I warn you that" is not a type 1 action (specifying what the speaker is actually doing) but a type 2 action (co-ordinating what the speaker or writer thinks about what he or she is doing as well as instructing the other how to take it). It is these two features, viz. force and ratification, and how they operate in explicit semi-performatives in press releases that I shall turn to now.

Before that, however, it should be noted that all this seems to suggest that Roy Hattersley may have been right after all when he was drawing attention to the fact that Tebbit said

I predict unemployment figures will fall

and not

Unemployment figures will fall.

It is now clear that the explicit performative serves to indicate that Tebbit holds less than conclusive evidence about the fall of unemployment figures (force), hence offering him, as Hattersley suggested, a 'let out' in that, at least, he should not be charged with lying if the economy fails to recover (ratification).

3.2.5   Force

From some of the comments made above it may look as if the use of explicit performatives in press releases, like that of self-quotation, constitutes a diversion from that highly rational, maximally efficient mode of communication we have come to associate with Grice. Crucially, as Brown and Levinson (1987) suggest, "one powerful and pervasive motive for not talking Maxim-wise is the desire to give some attention to face. (...)

Politeness is then a major source of deviation from such rational efficiency, and is communicated precisely by that deviation" (95). While I disagree with the view of performatives as indirect speech acts whose meaning is derivable through implicature (e.g. Bach and Harnish 1979, Recanati 1987, Fraser 1996), I shall now try to find out how the explicit performatives in my corpus of press releases serve to modify the force of what is said in them.

Brown and Levinson only address the problem of explicit performatives indirectly when they say that usually impersonal

It is so.

is preferred to

I tell you that it is so.

and simply add that "[o]f course, in formal speeches explicit performatives are often retained as a rhetorical device" (190). Elsewhere, they seem to deal with the same problem more thoroughly when they talk about strategies to hedge, i.e. strengthen, illocutionary force, like the Tzeltal modifiers "solel" [I declare emphatically] and "skal" [I say] (151). The question arises if some of the explicit performatives in my corpus of press releases could serve a similar purpose. This would mean that, far from expressing doubt about whether Noblesse really purchased Taecke, the explicit performative would actually make the announcement more confident:

(13)   (Noblesse, Londerzeel: 30 March 1994)
        Noblesse Benelux, gespecialiseerd in machines en gereedschap-
        pen, deelt mede dat zij het handelsfonds van de failliete firma
        Taecke heeft overgenomen.

        Noblesse Benelux, specialized in machines and tools, announces
        that it has taken over the funds of the bankrupt Taecke firm.

Robin Lakoff (1980) discusses the same question, viz. the difference between

Prices slumped.

and

I (hereby) say (to you) that prices slumped.

She confirms the interactional function spelled out above, viz. that the latter suggests that the speaker is concerned that the addressee should recognize the speech act type correctly and respond appropriately to it. At first sight, Lakoff also seems to agree with what Brown and Levinson said, viz. that the explicit performative serves to strengthen the speaker's or writer's commitment, to underline that he or she has the right to say so. Crucially, however, she then adds that, in doing so, the speaker or writer is actually calling that very right into question. That would mean that what she calls 'speech act qualification' through 'intensives' is actually strengthening and tentative at the same time.

In an earlier paper, Robin Lakoff had already made a similar suggestion:

> Although sentences with explicit performatives may seem the antithesis of sentences with hedged performatives, actually they're not that far apart pragmatically: both occur where the speaker lacks self-confidence, both are opposed to the simple, unembellished speech act, and both represent excrescences added to the simple logical structure in the interest of making it clear how you feel about what you're saying, rather than being merely concerned with the transmission of information (1977: 85).

In the later, 1980 paper she is much more determined on this point: just as 'I think' in

I think that Carter is a Democrat

weakens the speaker's authority, explicit performatives, like

I say that …

"are used when [the speaker's] authority must for some reason be explicitly invoked, precisely because it has been (or he believes it may be) called into question" (45), she argues. It is concluded that "mitigated and intensified performatives have about the same conversational force: they state their claims more weakly than do simple direct performative utterances" (46).[11]

In the language of systemic-functionalism, explicit performatives belong to the domain of modality, that complex area of grammar which has to do with the different ways in which language users can intrude on their messages, expressing attitudes and judgments of various kinds (Eggins 1994). In particular, they seem to play a 'modalizing role', i.e. they allow the writer to take an intermediate position between the propositions that something *is* and something *is not* (181-2).[12] Modalization may play one of two roles: to express tentativity towards either the embedded proposition or the other interactants (cf. also Holmes 1984).

About the first role, Lee (1992) suggests that speaker intrusion and reference to the process of perception have the effect of "modalising the associated statement. That is [they express] a lower degree of commitment on the part of the speaker to the truth of the associated proposition". They allow the 'speaker' to "[identify] a particular position" but at the same time "[establish] the possibility of some sort of distance from that perspective" (138). This would mean that in (13), through the explicit performative, Noblesse expresses some doubt about its own purchase of Taecke after all. As I suggested above, this is against any common-sense interpretation of what press releases are all about. I would argue that, on the contrary, explicit performatives in press releases serve to enhance the writer's commitment to the truth of his or her words.

Alternatively, as Eggins points out, modalization may have "little to do with the speaker's judgements about probability, but is instead functioning to signal interactants' recognition of the unequal power or infrequent contact between them" (195). I suggest that this is at work in press releases too: viz. that in addition to making the press release more confident, explicit performatives at the same time serve to anticipate the reader's scepticism about it, i.c. the journalists' suspicions about public relations propaganda.

3.2.6   *Ratification*

That brings us to ratification.

I have shown that writers of press releases hope that the journalists will recover a very specific, well-described proposition and retell it. Therefore I would now argue that the explicit semi-performative clauses in press releases should serve to narrow down, to constrain the journalists' interpretation. In this sense press releases are supposed to be 'strong communicators'.

It has been suggested that such strong communication is a typical feature of institutional discourse:

> clearly, some speakers invest more effort in the communication process than others. Speakers and writers who are presenting arguments in favour of a particular theoretical position, or teachers who are teaching students about a phenomenon or theory, have a particular interest in the hearer's and reader's ability to understand their utterances, a particular interest in the ability to derive the right (intended) contextual effects. Failure to communicate successfully will have far-reaching consequences - bad reviews, the need to repeat a class (Blakemore 1993: 109).

Or, using Habermas's distinction between 'strategic discourse', oriented to success, and 'communicative discourse', oriented to understanding, it could be argued that institutional discourse should be more strategic than ordinary, everyday discourse. However, various research has shown that most discourse, even that prototypically oriented to understanding, contains some strategic elements (Harris 1995); Blakemore's own analysis of the performative prefix "I warn you that" is a case in point.

As far as the explicit semi-performatives in my data are concerned, I have shown that they have a double edge. Like the other features of the metapragmatics of press releases analysed in this study, they seem to play a negotiating role, striking a balance between news managers' and news-makers' conflicting ambitions. Explicit performatives allow writers of press releases to make a strong point. At the same, though, just like for self-quotation, "[w]hat follows the self-referential connective is to be placed in parentheses, a voice slightly different from the one the speaker had been using, one which presumably allows the speaker and his listeners to align themselves over against the figure to whom the remarks are to be attributed" (Goffman 1974: 531).

Clearly, press releases provide a nice illustration of Austin's suggestion, quoted earlier, that there "seem to be clear cases where the very same formula seems sometimes to be an explicit performative and sometimes to be a descriptive, and may even trade on this ambivalence" (1962: 78). In particular, just as, in Myers's (1992) view, explicit performatives like "In this paper we report" allow authors of scientific papers to be both convincing (make interpretations that follow definitely from observations of external facts) and tentative (retain a caution that acknowledges that it is the community that must evaluate the claim and attribute any discovery), explicit performatives seem to do the same thing for authors of press releases. While Myers shows how science is made, I hope that my analysis of explicit semi-performatives in press releases - and, more generally, of the metapragmatics of press releases - has contributed to a better understanding of news managing and newsmaking practices.

4. Self-Quotes and Performatives

Let's come back to the question raised at the beginning of this chapter, viz. how to distinguish between the explicit semi-performatives in my corpus of press releases and that special brand of self-quoting called pseudo-direct speech. I would now suggest that it is difficult to keep the two apart since pseudo-direct speech is of a performative nature and performativity requires self-quoting. Indeed, in hindsight, - since self-quotation and explicit semi-performatives have been shown to play very similar negotiating roles in my data - it is now clear that such a distinction is not even necessary. At various points in this chapter I have drawn attention to the fact that performativity requires self-quoting. I would now like to briefly demonstrate that pseudo-direct speech is of a performative nature.

In the previous chapters I looked at quotations in press releases, in particular at pseudo-direct speech, which, I argued, included words that were not verbalized by the named source, but written by a press officer. This of course appears to be in conflict with the traditional view that quotation involves two distinct discourse situations, one embedded in the other.[13] However, it could be argued that, with pseudo-direct speech, there are after all two discourse situations, but that they coincide. For the pseudo-direct speech in (17), for example, getting quoted in a press release actually is the quoted source Votron's way of making the very statement; the copy and the original are one.

(17)　(Citibank, Brussels: April 1994)

De naam Famibank verdwijnt door deze integratie niet. "De naam Famibank is belangrijk", zegt J.-P. Votron. "Het is een merknaam met grote bekendheid die veel betekent voor de klanten. Beide concepten zijn complementair. Citibank heeft een uitgesproken stedelijk karakter, terwijl Famibank in meer landelijke gebieden een belangrijke taak te vervullen heeft."

The name Famibank does not disappear as a result of this integration. "The name Famibank is important", says J.-P. Votron. "It is a widely known brandname that means a lot to the customers. Both concepts are complementary. Citibank has a clear urban character, while Famibank has an important role to play in more rural areas."

In analogy with Mick Short (1988), who introduces the term 'hypothetical reporting' for quotes that anticipate future utterances, I would like to call this performative reporting. Let me briefly explain why.

Short notes that some quotes serve to anticipate future utterances rather than look back at the past, as in the *Daily Mail* headline

Your job is safe, soccer boss told

Later on in the article, it is announced that

[Manchester] United chairman, Martin Edwards, *was planning to* tell 45-year-old [Manchester United manager Ron] Atkinson: "Your job is safe" (quoted in Short 1988: 72-73; my italics).[14]

In (17) then, I propose, we are looking at 'performative reporting' since in the quotation, the words actually get 'spoken'.[15] This can be represented as follows:

Fig. 1 Pseudo-direct speech as performative reporting

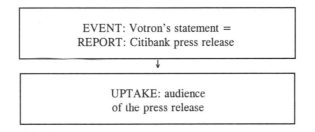

Levinson (1983) associates explicit performatives with reporting when he criticizes the performative hypothesis and says that in an explicit performative

I bet you six pence I will win the race

"there is something over and above a mere concurrent report" (259). I hope to have shown in the previous chapters that the same goes for pseudo-direct speech like in (17).

Chapter 7
A Case Study of the Valdez Corpus

1. Introduction

In this chapter I shall resume some of the major points in my analysis of preformulation in press releases by focusing on the Valdez corpus. As I explained before, it is a collection of some 60 press releases that were issued by the multinational Exxon in the first eight months following the accident with the Exxon Valdez mammoth tanker and the oil spill in Prince William Sound, South Alaska, on 24 March 1989. 240,000 barrels containing over 10 million gallons of crude oil were released into what was known as one of the last few areas of outstanding natural beauty. 'America's Chernobyl', the accident was called (*Newsweek*, 10 April 1989), killing sea otters, walruses and eagles as well as threatening the livelihoods of the local fishing communities. In no time 40,000 Americans cut up their Exxon credit cards and over the next few weeks the multinational would spend 2 billion dollars to clean up.

I now set out to document how Exxon tried to manage the news about the accident over an extended period. Crucially, I am not presenting this case in order to tell the history of the Exxon Valdez crisis; instead, paying special attention to the metapragmatics in the Valdez press releases, it is my central purpose to confirm that what I have so far discussed in a number of separate chapters of in-depth language analysis blends together into a holistic study addressing a narrowly defined research question: viz. how press releases are preformulated for news reporting. I have dealt with third-person self-reference, self-quotation and explicit semi-performatives separately, each time drawing from a wide range of individual press releases that were issued by many different organizations to address many different issues; by concentrating on how Exxon handled the Valdez crisis, I shall now try to demonstrate how all these metapragmatics are part of a single preformulating effort.

For these purposes, I shall start from Exxon's first press release in the Valdez corpus (fig. 1). This is, perhaps symbolically, the one which was quoted in the introduction to this study and which, I have argued, helped awaken my interest in press releases. I shall also integrate the other press releases in the Valdez corpus into my analysis in order to be able to present a balanced picture of the communication effort supporting Exxon's emergency response and of how it developed over time.

In focusing on the Valdez corpus, we will of course need to learn more about the facts of the oil spill in Alaska. That is why, throughout this chapter, I shall make use of a selection of media reports on the accident and its aftermath as well as of other relevant materials both from Exxon and third parties. In addition, in order to get a better view of the press releases that we shall deal with in this chapter and of what they are all about, I shall first cast a cursory glance at some of the major themes in the Valdez corpus as a whole.

Before that, however, I would like to draw attention to at least two important limitations of this case study. To begin with, since this chapter is meant to take a broader perspective and, in doing so, to make a number of connections that may so far have remained unclear, some of the detailed language inquiry of the previous chapters will have to make way for a more general discussion here. Apart from that, it should be noted that just a mere fraction of the points covered above can come up within the limited scope of this case study; evidently, completeness will have to be sacrificed for the sake of transparency.

2. Exxon's Valdez News

In this section I shall provide a quick overview of the spread of news items in the Valdez corpus of press releases. For one thing, the question could be raised what it is that Exxon has to offer to the media months after the accident occurred.

Clearly, only a handful of press releases in the Valdez corpus have 'hard' news to announce. One of the real stories is that of the widely disputed dismissal of Captain of the Exxon Valdez John Hazelwood, who, on the night of the accident, retired to his cabin, leaving the Third Mate to steer the mammoth tanker onto submerged rocks three miles outside the designated channel and who was tested legally drunk ten and a half hours after the wreck (*Newsweek*, 10 April 1989). Another story-line has to do with developments in the lawsuit that was started following allegations by a former employee that Exxon had destroyed computer tapes about the oil spill.

Most of the other press releases deal with the details of the operations in Alaska and they seem simply meant to restore Exxon's reputation by demonstrating the organization's unconditional commitment to clean up the spilt oil; they are public relations efforts to make sure that, as Exxon spokesman Fred Davis put it at an Environmental Issues Conference (7 September 1989), "[Exxon's] side of the story will be told while the story is still news". Indeed, more precisely, they serve to keep the story in the news and, by telling Exxon's side, to try and undo some of the damage that has been done.

Most noticeably, the press releases centre on the extent of Exxon's shoreline "mobilization" (2 May).[1] The corpus presents a scrupulously accurate count of the rising number of Exxon employees and contract personnel at work in Prince William Sound (250 on 6 April; 5,916 on 11 May; 10,405 on 14 July), of how many millions of pounds of material and equipment have been airlifted to the area and of how many miles of boom have been put in place. Exxon's focus on its efforts rather than the success of its efforts has actually been compared to that of 'a student who argues that he deserves a better grade because he spent six hours studying' (Tyler 1992: 157). Another concern is with the astronomical cost of the emergency response (\$ 115 million on 18 May, \$ 200 million on 30 June), including - very prominently - the damages awarded to local fishermen.[2] In addition, press releases are issued to inform the media, and the public, about the development of a cultural resources centre (27 April), the construction of otter rehabilitation facilities (27 April) and the establishment of an eagle capture programme (9 June). One of them tells the story of an otter - later named Lazarus - that was rescued after two hours of cardiopulmonary resuscitation (20 April).[3]

On top of that, Exxon keeps an accurate score of the number of miles of impacted shoreline that have been treated (64 on 29 May, 478 on 14 July, 915 on 22 August), offering minute details of the South Alaska maritime topography from Snug Harbour and Nelly Juan Narrows to Point Eleanor and Kodiak Archipelago.[4] It is repeatedly stated that the clean-up is ahead of the schedule proposed by Exxon and approved by the State authorities. On 30 August a press release is issued to announce that "Exxon [has surpassed] 1,000 miles of shoreline treated". A couple of weeks later, it is dramatically headlined that "WITH LESS THAN A MILE TO GO VALDEZ CLEANUP WINDS DOWN" for the winter (18 September): 1088 miles of shoreline have been treated and less than one mile remains to be done.[5]

Apart from highlighting Exxon's commitment to the clean-up through hard numbers, the press releases also serve to show Exxon's top managers in action, testifying before specially appointed committees, inspecting emergency operations, meeting Alaska state officials and speaking at international conferences. On 13 September it is reported that Exxon chairman Larry Rawl has flown over the area and walked on some of the shorelines "to have first-hand knowledge" of the clean-up. The impact of such announcements had been confirmed earlier after the same Larry Rawl was publicly criticized for not having rushed to Alaska as soon as the news of the spill became known and for making his first public comments only on 30 March, six days after the spill.[6]

A final point of interest in the Valdez corpus that I would like to single out - one that I shall come back to later on - is the debate about the use of a chemical dispersant called Corexit to help fight the oil spill. In a number of press releases Exxon blames State of Alaska Governor Steve Cowper for waiting too long in granting permission to use it. As early as 1 April it is suggested in a headline that "EXXON WAS READY FOR FULL-SCALE DISPERSANT APPLICATION MARCH 25", but that they "did not get unconditional authority" to start the clean-up until 6.45 pm the next day when gale force winds kept aircraft grounded until the opportunity for large-scale containment on the initial, concentrated spill had gone. The row with the Alaskan government over the delayed use of the chemical dispersant culminates in Exxon's decision to seek damages from the State for "[negligent interference] with efforts to contain and treat the spill" (26 October):

Exxon demands reimbursement for a part of the clean-up cost on the grounds that the immediate use of chemical dispersants was a central feature of the oil business's state-approved contingency plan and that therefore the State of Alaska should not have delayed authorization. Even worse, it is pointed out that on 20 March 1989, only four days before the spill, the State of Alaska had executed an amendment to this agreement, designating as prime target area for chemical dispersants that very portion of Prince William Sound where the accident occurred and where most of the spilt oil remained for two days after the tanker grounding (26 October). I shall demonstrate later in this chapter that the frustration underlying Exxon's desperate legal initiative against the State of Alaska[7] can be accurately traced in the language of some of the press releases in the Valdez corpus.

3. General Structure

Let's now turn to the data.

A quick look at the first press release in the Valdez corpus shows that it is nicely preformulated. Surely, Exxon's handout satisfies most of the formal requirements of news reporting and it looks as if it can be simply copied as a newspaper article. Whatever hidden agendas may be revealed by a more detailed inspection of the data later on, it could be argued that this in itself should count as evidence of the negotiated character of the interaction between news managers and newsmakers: after all, in prefabricating press releases, news managers seem to go quite a long way to meet the demands of newsmakers.

Take the structure of Exxon's press release. It starts with a bold and block-lettered headline whose syntax conforms to that of most newspaper headlines, including the suppression of the definite article and of 'and' (Vandenbergen 1981), but no superheadline or subheadline. Next, there is an indication of the place and time of the announcement, just like in a newspaper report. The body of the press release has an opening paragraph with all the content features of a lead (Van Dijk 1988), though not marked off by special printing type; the other paragraphs present gradually less important information so that, at any point, the journalists can decide to

Fig. 1 Press release March 27, 1989

LIGHTERING, OIL SPILL CLEANUP EFFORTS CONTINUE IN ALASKA

HOUSTON, TEXAS -- March 27, 1989 -- The Exxon Valdez, a 987-foot tanker carrying 1.3 million barrels of crude oil, ran aground on Bligh Reef about 25 miles south of the Trans Alaska Pipeline Terminal at Valdez about 12:30 a.m. Alaska time on Friday, March 24, while maneuvering to avoid ice. There were no personnel injuries. However, the vessel ruptured a number of cargo tanks, and an oil spill estimated at 240,000 barrels occurred in Prince William Sound.

Only five hours after word was received of the grounding, Exxon Shipping Company President Frank Iarossi and five specially qualified advisors were en route by air to Alaska. Another 25 members of Exxon's casualty response team also arrived in Alaska on Friday. In addition, arrangements had been made to augment equipment available in Alaska by chartering five aircraft to move oil spill skimming, booming and dispersant equipment from Texas, Arizona, California and the United Kingdom.

The Valdez remains aground on the reef. The Exxon Baton Rouge is alongside her, transferring the damaged vessel's oil cargo. Exxon Shipping Company estimates that lightering operations involving the Baton Rouge and other Exxon vessels will require about one week to complete. Repair and salvage operations for the Valdez are being evaluated.

Oil spill clean-up operations have been under way through the Easter weekend. The size of the oil slick is estimated at about 2 miles by six miles. Much of the oil is still in the middle of the Sound; hence, to date shore effects appear to be minimal. Facilities have been set up to treat oiled birds, and operations to treat oiled mammals are being arranged. Some 200 people have been employed for clean-up operations. Exxon is working with local fishing interests to identify and protect the most environmentally sensitive areas.

In Houston, Exxon USA senior management is closely monitoring the situation and providing all necessary support. "The full resources of the company, including people with special expertise and additional equipment, have been brought to bear," according to W.D. Stevens, president of Exxon Company, U.S.A. "In addition, we have received outstanding cooperation from oil spill cooperatives in the lower 48 states. And we are working closely with involved agencies of the State of Alaska as well as Federal authorities".

stop copying the press release and, if indeed the press release gets copied as
- say - a newspaper article, the general public can decide to stop reading.

Much the same can be said about the rest of the Valdez corpus. As far
as headlines are concerned, one press release has no headline (19 April) and
another received the rather uninformative headline 'Exxon Valdez' (13
April); all others, however, have headlines that look as if they were taken
from newspapers. (1) is a typical example:

(1)   (Exxon, Valdez, Alaska: 4 May 1989)
        EXXON SUBMITS REVISED SHORELINE CLEANUP PLAN
        Exxon submitted a revised plan to the Coast Guard on May 2.

Here, in true newspaper style the simple present is used to refer to an event
that, as the first sentence of the press release makes clear, happened in the
past.

Surely, not all headlines from the Valdez corpus are perfectly
preformulated. In spite of the use of ellipsis, a couple of them are probably
too long to have a chance of being copied by journalists, such as

(2)   (Exxon, Washington D.C.: 28 July 1989)
        EXXON EMPHASIZES COMMITMENT TO ALASKA
        CLEANUP, WILL NOT ABANDON THE JOB UNTIL IT'S
        PUT RIGHT

Even if most headlines in the Valdez corpus meet the formal requirements
of newspaper reporting, it should be noted that, content-wise, they represent
Exxon's views on the oil spill. For one thing, like the press releases they
are part of, most headlines have invariably good news to announce about the
clean-up effort and, perhaps not surprisingly, as in (1) and (2) Exxon often
features prominently in front position and can be seen to resolutely take the
initiative in fighting the oil spill. I shall come back to this issue of who is
shown to be in charge later on in this chapter when we look at the
metapragmatics of the Valdez corpus.

As for the indications of place and time, it is interesting to see how, even
half a year after the accident, Exxon continues to try and manage the news

about the oil spill by issuing press releases with an almost undiminished frequency. It was not appreciated by U.S. and other media that the vast majority of them were sent from South Alaska, with far-away Valdez serving as the location for Exxon's regular briefings. Even the *Oil & Gas Journal* complained about this: "it was Valdez or nothing" (*International Herald Tribune*, 22-23 April 1989). In an address delivered to the New York University Club (24 October 1989), Exxon President L. R. Raymond later reported that such a decentralized 'real-time' communications policy was not effective since "public perceptions on the East Coast were hardly influenced by our answers to reporters' questions four time zones away in Alaska. We should have provided an electronic linkage to the Lower-48, with two-way Q&A capability" (cf. also Tyler 1992).

Finally, like the first press release, most others in the Valdez corpus have a structure that resembles that of newspaper articles. They are short texts of one or two pages, with the most important information in front and background further on.[8] As Hess argues, press releases "almost substitute for objective wire service copy" (1984: 77); they are "written as ersatz news stories" (79). One regular feature of the press releases in the Valdez corpus that is perhaps not really meant as a preformulation is the status reports, including separate tables with statistics about the scale and progress of Exxon's clean-up effort (see fig. 4 for an example).

4. Presupposition Manipulations

I would now like to return to the first press release.

As I pointed out in chapter 3 in the section on presupposition manipulations, in the headline of this press release it looks as if the news of the oil spill in Alaska and even of the start of the clean-up operations is taken for granted. In this headline there is no announcement that 'one of Exxon's tankers ran aground on a reef and caused a major oil spill in Alaska' or that 'Exxon has started to clean up the oil'. Instead, it is reported in a positive mood that the clean-up of the oil spill '*continues*'. Since the accident took place on Good Friday 24 March and the press release was only issued at the end of the Easter weekend on 27 March, this looks like a reasonable choice. Most - if not all - journalists who read this press release would already have heard about the events in Alaska anyway. In addition, the choice to take the news of the accident for granted in the headline may even serve a preformulating role. After all, most news reports too tend to presuppose a certain amount of background knowledge that readers may have gained from previous issues or broadcasts, or through alternative mass media (cf. Jucker 1995: 4). So this may be considered another way in which Exxon's press release meets the requirements of news reporting.[9]

On the other hand, from the information in the first paragraph there can be no doubt that, contrary to what a close reading of the headline suggests, the news of the oil spill is not presupposed after all and that the very purpose of the press release is actually for Exxon to officially announce that one of its tankers was involved in an accident off the coast of Alaska.[10] If this is true, it could be argued that the headline, which allows Exxon to focus on the good news, is a less than perfectly innocent preformulation.

The opposite strategy seems to be at work in a couple of later press releases where, as I have shown, four or five days after the accident, Exxon does not take the news of the accident in Alaska for granted, but rather seems to refuse to accept that everybody knows about the tragic oil spill:

(3)   (Exxon, Darien, Conn.: 29 March 1989)
        An Exxon Chemical Company oil dispersant called Corexit is being used to help clean up crude oil spilled last Friday morning in a shipping accident in Alaska's Prince William Sound.

Here, I would argue, the references to "crude oil" (rather than '*the* crude oil') and to "a shipping accident" (rather than '*the* shipping accident') imply that this is a new information and hence serve to downplay the impact of the Exxon Valdez crisis on the public opinion. Alternatively, the use of the indefinite article in (3) could be explained not just in terms of 'given' and 'new', but in terms of degrees of saliency: it is not that Exxon refuses to accept that everybody knows about the news of the Alaskan oil spill; instead, - and this is in line with what happens in the headline of Exxon's first press release - what the use of the indefinite article here does is to move the accident to the back of the readers' consciousness and foreground the clean-up operations.

All this is in clear contrast with the start of chairman Larry Rawl's 'open letter to the public', which Exxon ran as an advertisement in US newspapers on 3 April:

> By now you all know that our tanker, the Exxon Valdez, hit a submerged reef and lost 240,000 barrels of oil in the waters of the Sound.

Here, still another mechanism seems to be at work: even if in these words Rawl may be seen to blame himself and his company for not facing the country until a full ten days after the accident, the fact that the news has become common ground by then certainly makes this opening a lot easier.

5. Self-Reference

That brings us to the metapragmatics. In the first press release from the Valdez corpus, self-reference is invariably realized through the third person, in particular by means of the organization's proper name, except in the final paragraph, where Exxon's own president, Mr W. D. Stevens, is quoted: here, between quotation marks, there is a definite description ('the company') as well as two occurrences of the first-person plural pronoun 'we'. In the other press releases, the picture is hardly any different; self-reference is to 'Exxon' or, quite frequently, to 'the company', as in:

(4)   (Exxon, Valdez, Alaska: 30 August 1989)
        Exxon has treated over 1,000 miles of affected shoreline in the Gulf of Alaska and Prince William Sound. With just over 70 miles remaining the company is confident that shoreline treatment work will be completed by mid-September.

I would argue that, apart from anticipating the typical reference forms of news reporting (what I have referred to as preformulation$_i$), third-person self-reference makes the press releases look more neutral and disinterested along the lines I suggested earlier in chapter 3: through it, Exxon's version of the events appears somewhat more objective (preformulation$_{ii}$).

Even more so, talking about objective reporting, what is interesting about the first press release in the Valdez corpus is that both in the headline and in the account of the accident in the first, 'lead' paragraph, reference to Exxon is not in the third person; it is carefully avoided, except, inevitably, in the name of the wrecked ship.[11] Instead, it is said that the ship 'ran aground', that 'there were no personnel injuries' and that 'an oil spill estimated at 240,000 barrels occurred'. I would argue that the result here is that whoever carries the responsibility for the events is kept notably absent from this impersonalized syntax of a tragedy of fate.[12]

Another example is when Exxon has to report delays in the clean-up:

(5)   BAD WEATHER INCREASINGLY AFFECTS CLEANUP OF VALDEZ OIL SPILL IN ALASKA
Weather conditions in the Gulf of Alaska and Prince William Sound are affecting shoreline cleanup operations with greater frequency. Since early August Gulf of Alaska crews have been weathered in six times.

This dominant use of third-person self-reference, combined with the avoidance of self-reference altogether, puts the press releases in sharp contrast with some of Exxon's other communications about the accident, including the 'open letter to the public'. In it Rawl repeatedly refers to himself as 'I' and to Exxon as 'we':

I hope that you know we have already committed several hundred people to work on the cleanup.

Note also that the reader is referred to as 'you', which - combined with first-person self-reference - allows for the organization and its top manager to be seen as remorseful and compassionate, as in

I want to tell you how sorry I am that this accident took place.

and as determined and responsible

I can assure you that, since March 24, the accident has been receiving our full attention and will continue to do so.[13]

In the first press release of the Valdez corpus no such direct address and no apologies or promises can be found. Indeed, throughout the sixty or so press releases issued by Exxon there is not a single case of frame break to be found. As I shall argue in the next section; whenever the multinational wanted to show a human face in press releases, requirements of preformulation forced any personalized expressions to be embedded between quotation marks (cf. below).[14]

This is certainly not to say that Exxon is absent from its own press releases. On the contrary, I have pointed out that the company's name takes a special place in a lot of headlines. Even in the first press release it is striking to see that, starting with the second paragraph, self-reference is no longer avoided and the sister organizations Exxon Company, U.S.A., and Exxon Shipping Company are mentioned at least seven more times, not including the self-quotation in the final paragraph. Clearly, as soon as it is time for the good news of the clean-up, self-reference is far more explicit: it is confidently announced that Exxon is en route to Alaska, that Exxon is co-operating with other interested parties and that Exxon is monitoring the situation. Here, the use of the proper name plays another preformulating$_{ii}$ role: perhaps even more than that of 'I' or 'we' quoted above, it puts Exxon in the limelight as a responsible organization, demonstrating that the multinational takes the lead in dealing with the emergency.

Clearly, the various forms of self-reference described above play a strategic role. Apart from serving a simple preformulating$_i$ purpose, they also allow Exxon to shift into the centre of attention when there is good news to announce and to shift out of it again when a lower profile seems more appropriate.

A final remark about time and place. While self-reference seems to be strictly determined by the requirements of preformulation, reference to the time and place of the oil spill and clean-up show a different pattern. Not in the first press release, though, where time and place seem to be nicely preformulated: writing from Houston, Texas, the author - naturally - refers to the location of the oil spill as 'Alaska' and not as 'here'; hardly more conspicuously, the day is identified to be 'Friday, March 24' and not, for example, 'last Friday'. In contrast, the second, third and fourth press releases do refer to 'last Friday' (28 March, 29 March and 30 March)[15] and in a lot of others - about the progress of the clean-up - we find 'today'. As for place, there seems to be more preformulation, also in those press releases issued in Valdez, except for one or two, in which the clean-up operations are rather awkwardly situated 'here' (e.g. 13 April).

6. Self-Quotation

I have argued, among other points, that third-person self-reference, apart from anticipating the typical reference forms of news reporting (preformulation$_i$), also makes the press releases in the Valdez corpus look more objective and gives prominence to Exxon's commitment to clean up the oil spill (preformulation$_{ii}$). I would now like to suggest that the repeated use of self-quotation plays a similar preformulating role in the data.

Let's start with the first press release (fig. 1) again. First, president W. D. Stevens's words in the final paragraph demonstrate that Exxon is taking the oil spill seriously, with no less than a top manager handling the crisis and informing the press about the latest developments. In addition, they allow Exxon to keep control over the flow of information by offering a single streamlined company view.[16] For the journalists, the quote (from an elite source!) provides a unique opportunity to touch up their reports at a time when most probably no one at Exxon is available for comments anyway (cf. *International Herald Tribune*, 22-23 April 1989). Significantly, the self-quotation is at the very end of the press release since it contains a background statement only.

It should be mentioned here that self-quotations play an important role not just in this first press release, but in the Valdez corpus as a whole. Since they are to be found in over two-thirds of the press releases, they can be considered a major feature of the rhetoric of Exxon's emergency response. Indeed, unlike in the first press release, in several others nearly all the words are between quotation marks, as in the press release shown in fig. 2 reporting on one of Exxon's top managers' testimony before a Senate

Fig. 2 Press release July 25, 1989

EXXON POSITION ON ALASKA SPILL CLEAN-UP IS UNCHANGED

HOUSTON, TEXAS -- July 25, 1989 -- Exxon's schedule for oil spill related activities in Alaska is unchanged from the plans discussed by Exxon Company, U.S.A. President W. D. Stevens on July 20 before a Senate Subcommittee, the company said.

Stevens said in testimony to the National Ocean Policy Study Subcommittee of the Senate Commerce, Science and Transportation Committee, "With regard to the close-down date for the winter, we do not intend to work on the shoreline clean-up past mid-September. Most importantly, we are concerned about weather impacts on operations, but we also continue to believe all significantly impacted shorelines will have been treated".

"General weather data analyses, as well as the advice of knowledgeable people in the area, indicate the need to plan for a mid-September shutdown. The ability to work safely in an offshore environment and on exposed shorelines dictates this conclusion. Also, the effectiveness of clean-up activities will decrease significantly as wind, wave, daylight and temperature conditions deteriorate rapidly. Detailed analysis of weather data, as well as the time required for efficient and safe demobilization, is currently under study to establish specific plans".

"Looking ahead, we plan to inspect the shoreline after the winter. Whether any work should be done next year and the magnitude, location and type of work will, of course, depend on the assessment made at that time. Over the winter, a program of scientific investigation and field monitoring will be continued. This will provide good bases for next spring's assessment of the present shoreline treatment efforts, as well as the ongoing evaluation of environmental impacts of the spill".

Subcommittee. Here the self-quotation is not part of the background. Rather, it is the very purpose of this press release to supply the official record of what was said on that occasion.

Similarly, in a press release issued on 7 July Exxon makes abundant use of quotation to disclose the contents of the letter that its associate general counsel wrote to the attorney general of Alaska in the court case of the computer tapes that Exxon was accused of having destroyed. It is interesting to note that, unlike most of the others, these quotes are no 'pseudo-direct speech', written up by Exxon's press officers and approved by the 'source'; instead, they can be considered more or less accurate reproductions of what was 'really' said or written.

But, surely, the self-quotations - and especially the pseudo-direct speech - in the Valdez corpus play a more complex role. To start with, the self-quotation in the first press release includes a number of, what I have called, 'extreme case formulations': the president of Exxon Company, U.S.A., is reported to have said that the organization is using its '*full* resources', that there is '*outstanding* co-operation' and that Exxon is 'working *closely*' with the state authorities (my italics). By putting these hidden superlatives between quotation marks, the writer of the press release seems to be disclaiming personal responsibility for them. Typically, Stevens's words are introduced with the neutral 'according to'. As a result, it could be argued that the quotation plays a preformulating role: it looks as if journalists can simply copy the words between quotation marks in their own news reporting without being seen to express agreement with them.

The same strategy seems to be at work in a lot of other press releases from the Valdez corpus. On 24 April - to give just one example - one of Exxon USA's senior vice-presidents, K. T. Koonce, is quoted as having said that the company has been 'quite successful' in oil recovery, that they are making 'an enormous effort' and that they remain 'absolutely committed to the clean-up'. Here again the strong words are between quotation marks and they are introduced by neutral *verba dicendi*, which apparently create a distance between the reporter and the quoted source and thus seem to anticipate the requirements of objective news reporting. Even more convincingly, in a number of press releases Exxon is praised not by the senior executives on its own payroll, but by 'outside', presumably independent experts. In the following extract, Dr. Randall Davis of the Seaworld Research Institute, and appointed as director of the mammal center that Exxon constructed in Valdez, offers high marks for the multinational's emergency response:

(6)   (Exxon, Valdez, Alaska: 13 April 1989)
        "Although we were faced with significant problems in mounting

a successful rescue effort, we were fortunate to have the complete backing of Exxon in mobilizing our forces (...). Exxon has given us total commitment and complete co-operation. We appreciate Exxon's fast response in meeting our needs for a new mammal center. They have been terrific in their support".

In the same press release, Alice Berkner, director of the International Bird Rescue and Research Center in Berkeley, California, and manager of Exxon's bird rescue operations, calls the company's support no less than "absolutely tremendous". In a later press release, one of Exxon's spokespersons, operations co-ordinator Jim Nalls, is happy to return the compliment:

(7)   (Exxon, New York: 30 June 1989)
        "The credit goes not to Exxon but to the communities and citizens - volunteers and paid workers alike - who are cleaning the shorelines and beaches."

In chapter 5 of this study, I provided a lot more illustrations from my data - including from the Valdez corpus - to demonstrate this preformulating$_{ii}$ role of various kinds of self-quotation. One final point that I would like to make here, from a great many, is that the words of Exxon's spokespersons, when they were really spoken, are usually shown to be part of an authoritative context of delivery. On 24 July, for example, Exxon's view on the case of the lost computer tapes is presented as 'evidence from sworn affidavits' that have 'conclusively disproved misleading allegations' from a 'disgruntled former employee' and his attorney.

So far I have argued that self-quotation in press releases has a distancing effect and that, through embedding, it looks as if some of the extreme case formulations referred to above can be simply copied by journalists. I would now claim that, on closer scrutiny, there can be no doubt that, at least, whoever wrote the press release is in complete agreement with the information between quotation marks. Indeed, Stevens's words quoted in the first press release of the Valdez corpus are actually anticipated by the first sentence of the last paragraph, in which more or less the same information is provided, but this time without any quotation marks: it is said that Exxon is 'closely monitoring the situation and providing all necessary support'. Surely, any journalists who copy Stevens's words in their own news reporting should realize that the quotation offers no guarantee of uncommittedness; as I demonstrated in chapter 5, since what the president is reported to have said 'percolates' to the overall perspective of the press release, journalists who simply retell the press release in their own reporting may well be seen to express agreement with Exxon's views on the crisis. The following example from a press release issued on 1 April is perhaps even clearer, with the words quoted in the first sentence actually adopted by the writer of the press release as his or her own in the preceding headline:

> (8)   (Exxon, Valdez, Alaska: 1 April 1989)
> EXXON WAS READY FOR FULL-SCALE DISPERSANT APPLICATION MARCH 25
> Exxon Shipping Company President Frank Iarossi today said that Exxon was ready to begin full-scale application of aerial dispersants to the Exxon Valdez oil spill on Saturday, March 25.

There is more. Quotations may not only lead to a false sense of objectivity by appearing to create a distance between the perspective of the quoted source and that of the reporter; they can also do so by 'naturalizing' the information that is not between quotation marks. Take the first press release once more: in contrast with the words of Exxon President Stevens, whose blatant subjectivity is clearly signalled by the use quotation marks, the other paragraphs contain no quotations and hence could be seen to provide purely factual information.

Here the rhetoric of precise numbers as a persuasive content feature (cf. Van Dijk 1988) in the first paragraph should be mentioned again: the fatal ship is described with accuracy as a '987-foot' tanker carrying '1.3 million barrels' and the accident is reported to have happened 'about 25 miles south of the Trans Alaska Pipeline Terminal at Valdez about 12:30 a.m. Alaska time on Friday, March 24'. The other paragraphs too contain lots of detailed information, which, because it is so detailed, makes the press release look more objective.[17]

Still, in the end there can be no doubt that these paragraphs, just like the final one, merely represent Exxon's version of events. Indeed, there are several subtle indications to that extent: it is said that Exxon's emergency response was started '*only* five hours after word was received of the grounding' and that Exxon Shipping Company President Frank Iarossi was accompanied by five 'specially qualified' advisors. Later it is emphasized that the clean-up was continued 'through the *Easter* weekend' (my italics), almost as if to work on a day off counts as penance for spilling the oil.[18]

On the whole, then, the quote in the final paragraph does not only serve to secure media attention for Stevens's words and, in doing so, to give a public platform of credibility to what are, after all, Exxon's private views on the oil spill; as I have argued, indirectly it also renders the rest of the press release more authoritative: if the writer, just like a journalist, cares to expose some parts of the press release as quotes, it follows that the truth of other parts will be seen to be far less debatable.

One final remark about self-quotation in the Valdez corpus. I have shown how the simple use of quotation marks enables Exxon to sound more neutral in what, we can safely assume, even for the weathered multinational must have been a time of unprecedented drama. I have already referred to the fierce disagreement with the State authorities over the use of chemical dispersants in fighting the oil spill. Another issue is that of the so-called 'winter program': on 22 August Exxon announces that it will suspend all major shoreline activities by mid-September because, from then on, the unpredictable Alaskan weather conditions could jeopardize the safety of workers; the State of Alaska, represented by Governor Steve Cowper, feels that this is unacceptable and demands that Exxon should continue to operate for another six weeks. I shall now elaborate on how, starting with a press release issued on the next day (23 August; fig. 3), Exxon has reacted to Cowper's suggestions. I shall do so because it sheds further light on the preformulating$_{ii}$ role of self-quotation in press releases.

Fig. 3 Press release August 23, 1989

EXXON CHALLENGES ALASKA GOVERNOR TO STOP POLITICS, WORK TOGETHER

Valdez, Alaska (23 August 1989) -- The man who is heading Exxon's clean-up of the EXXON VALDEZ oil spill today called on Alaska Governor Steve Cowper to "stop playing politics and start working constructively to serve the best interest of Alaska".

In response to Governor Cowper's claim that Exxon failed to address concerns raised by the state, Otto Harrison, general manager of Exxon's Valdez operations, said:

"This is truly amazing. I have to question the governor's motives because once again he has prepared his press statement before thoughtfully considering a very comprehensive plan which clearly addresses concerns previously raised by the state".

The Exxon 1989-90 Alaska winter program was discussed in detail during a series of briefings Friday with the federal on-scene coordinator, Rear Admiral D. E. Ciancaglini, Commissioner Dennis Kelso of the Alaska Department of Environmental Conservation and representatives of other state and federal agencies.

Harrison said most of the activities which Governor Cowper claims were omitted from the Exxon plan "are there in black and white", and "raise the question whether the governor had even taken the time to read it".

"The key suggestion from Governor Cowper which is not included in Exxon's plan", Harrison said, "could jeopardize the safety of workers on the shorelines. We have no intention of playing Russian roulette with work crews by following the governor's suggestion that we try to operate an additional six weeks after winter winds and waves make it unsafe to be there".

Harrison said: " Following this morning's briefing, Commissioner Kelso asked a few clarifying questions. But despite the quote attributed to Kelso in the governor's press release, he made no reference to 'a blizzard of numbers', and, to the contrary, gave no indication that Exxon's winter program was not reasonable".

Harrison said Exxon has been waiting since August 3 for Commissioner Kelso to fulfill his promise at the Alaska Oil Spill Commission hearing to provide Exxon a checklist of activities the state would like to see in the work plan.

"However, his list was only released today - after Exxon had presented the plan", Harrison said.

Exxon has tried repeatedly to work cooperatively with the state, Harrison said, but the latest statements form Governor Cowper and Commissioner Kelso are "misleading and without basis".

"Equally disturbing", Harrison said, "is the fact that the never-ending and politically-motivated criticism of the clean-up effort detracts from the outstanding work being done by thousands of Alaskans in this challenging task".

In its first reaction, Exxon calls the Alaska Governor's attitude 'truly amazing'. Cowper's statements are said to be 'misleading', 'without basis' and 'politically motivated'. In addition, looking at one of the State's press releases about a meeting of Alaska Commissioner Kelso with representatives from Exxon, it is suggested that Kelso's words were seriously misquoted by Cowper: while, in the State's press release, Commissioner Kelso is reported to have criticized Exxon's winter programme at that meeting, Exxon claims that, 'to the contrary, he gave no indication that it was not reasonable'. Crucially, in Exxon's press release all these accusations are placed between quotation marks; they have been scrupulously attributed to Otto Harrison, the general manager of Exxon's Valdez operations. Hence, strictly speaking, none of these extreme case formulations should keep journalists from simply copying the press release in their own reporting.

Still, from the force of the accusations, it is clear that Exxon's row with the State of Alaska is gradually coming to a head. As Exxon Public Affairs spokesman Fred Davis reports at an Environmental Issues Conference shortly afterwards (7 September 1989) with reference to the same press release (and featuring a striking example of referential switch):

Was Exxon frustrated? You bet we were! So frustrated, in fact, that we even issued a news release calling on the Governor to quit playing politics with the clean-up and suggesting that he had not even read the plan before publicly reacting to it.

A couple of weeks later, on 18 September (fig. 4), Exxon's increasing frustration with the Alaskan authorities is abruptly unleashed when it is reported that the clean-up is 'closing in on the finish line': with 1,088 miles done, less than one mile remains and task forces are said to be 'mounting all-out efforts'. Still, Exxon reaffirms its resolve not to extend the operations past mid-September. This time, there are no preformulating quotation marks to be found; Exxon finally goes on record in a determined defence of its clean-up policy.

In the final paragraph all previous efforts at preformulation are abandoned when Exxon directly blames the State of Alaska's 'bureaucratic run-around' for the poor results of the waste disposal at Valdez: more than $ 5 million was spent and still 'not a single bag' was burned, because the

Fig. 4   Press release September 18, 1989

WITH LESS THAN A MILE TO GO VALDEZ CLEAN-UP WINDS DOWN

VALDEZ, Alaska (18 September 1989) -- Exxon's 1989 shoreline clean-up operations personnel in Prince William Sound and the Gulf of Alaska are closing in on the finish line. Over 1,088 miles have been treated, and less than one mile remains.

   Three task forces are mounting all-out efforts on Latouche, Elrington and Knight Islands in Prince William Sound, and Gulf of Alaska shoreline teams are targeting remaining areas for final treatment and touch-up.

   Teams are nearing the goal of bioremediating 72 miles of shoreline. Sixty-six miles have been treated, and the initial results from bioremediation are even better than expected.

   After intensive review of data compiled by the National Weather Service, Exxon operations personnel remain firm in their resolve not to endanger the lives of workers by extending major shoreline operations past mid-September.

   According to data analyzed, as mid-September approaches, the frequency and abruptness of storms rises dramatically. The average period between wind storms of 25 knots or higher drops to 1 to 1.5 days in Prince William Sound, and daily average wind speed rarely drops below 18 knots.

   These observed weather patterns increase the safety risk to people tarveling from base locations to work sites, and elevate the probability of having a team marooned in the sound.

   After enduring nearly four months of bureaucratic run-around that resulted in not a single bag of waste being burned, Exxon is releasing the incinerator barge at Kodiak Island. More than $ 5 million was spent to have it sit idle while the state of Alaska stalled the permitting process for the waste disposal system they once called the "preferred method".

Statistical Update

Vessels deployed:	860
Boom deployed:	56,000 ft.
Skimmers deployed:	35
Personnel:	7,260
Aircraft:	55

State failed to promptly authorize the use of a system that they once called their 'preferred method'. Here, at the very end, it is not Exxon's, but the State of Alaska's words that are quoted; the effect - unlike with self-quotation - is not one of mild (and ultimately false) distancing, but rather of crude, unmistakable irony.[19]

Here, in this last press release, where self-quotation is notably absent, the preformulating role played by the metapragmatics is perhaps at its clearest.

7.   Explicit Semi-Performatives

The third and final feature of the metapragmatics of press releases that I have investigated in this study is the frequent use of so-called 'explicit semi-performatives'.

It should be pointed out straight away that, in contrast with the abundance of self-quotation, there are only very few explicit semi-performatives in the Valdez corpus. Here are two typical examples:

(9)   (Exxon, Houston, Texas: 12 July 1989)
        Exxon welcomes the opportunity to present its position to the
        court (...).

and

(10)   (Exxon, Anchorage, Alaska: 3 October 1989)
        (...) Exxon regrets, deeply, what happened (...).

In the previous chapter I suggested that such explicit semi-performative utterances can easily be retold verbatim by journalists in their own news reporting: what happens is that, in the mouths of the journalists, the same utterance that had performative power is turned into a report. Hence, explicit semi-performatives play a perfect preformulating[i] role.

It should be noted that, in both examples, we are looking at what I have called 'communicated acts': unlike the typical prefix "The Kredietbank announces" discussed in the previous chapter, "Exxon welcomes" and

"Exxon regrets" cannot be left out. Hence, where "The Kredietbank announces" has been shown to play a negotiating role, making the press release more convincing and more tentative at the same time, the explicit semi-performatives in (9) and (10) seem to have the exclusive effect of making unambiguous what act is being performed and, in doing so, of enhancing the writer's - i.e., in this case, Exxon's - commitment to it.

On closer scrutiny, it becomes clear that the explicit semi-performatives shown above - like the others in the Valdez corpus - are embedded: they are part of a report.

(11)   (Exxon, Houston, Texas: 12 July 1989)
        Exxon welcomes the opportunity to present its position to the court, the company said.

(12)   (Exxon, Anchorage, Alaska: 3 October 1989)
        [W. D. Stevens, president of Exxon USA,] stated that "Exxon regrets, deeply, what happened".

I would suggest that this plays a further preformulating$_{ii}$ role in that it serves to background some of the confidence of the explicit performatives that I have hinted at.

8.   Conclusions

In summary, it can be concluded that the press releases in the Valdez corpus clearly anticipate a number of the journalists' crucial concerns about how to present the story of the Alaskan oil spill. Indeed, from an analysis of the metapragmatics it can be concluded that Exxon's version of the accident and of its aftermath is framed as a series of newspaper articles. In particular, I have shown that the metapragmatics play a prominent preformulating role in the data.

Crucially, I have also shown that - in spite of this undeniable preformulating effort - the press releases in the Valdez corpus are bound to reflect Exxon's perspective, from the simple focus on good news in headlines right to the complex functioning of quotes and self-quotes. As I have repeatedly argued in this study, preformulation is a type of negotiation: press releases are determined by news reporting, but at the same time they are meant to actively determine news reporting.

In an article published in the *International Herald Tribune* (16 May 1989), TV producer Jack Hilton, who had been hired by Exxon to document the scene of the accident at Valdez, reports that, even if a massive amount of oil was spilt into the ocean, the area remained essentially unharmed: after all, 240,000 barrels in the vast Prince William Sound is the equivalent of a teaspoon in an Olympic-sized swimming pool.[20] It should be borne in mind, he argues, that 'no lens is wide enough to capture the vastness of Prince William Sound'. 'The key word', Hilton the cameraman says, 'is perspective'. In the Valdez corpus that I have investigated here - just like, no doubt, in Hilton's analysis - the perspective is ultimately but at times so subtly Exxon's.

Chapter 8
Conclusions and Perspective

1. Introduction

As the title indicates, this final chapter has a double purpose: on the one hand, looking back, spelling out the major findings from the study of preformulation in press releases presented here; on the other hand, looking ahead, pointing to fruitful areas of further research that have been beyond the scope of my own work. In particular, I shall draw attention to the question of the balance of power in the news and I shall argue that my analysis of the preformulating role played by the metapragmatics in press releases could be the starting-point for a renewed look at the concept of hegemony in the media. Finally, in what can be seen as a *coda*, I shall briefly reflect on my own analytical practice.

2. Overview

To start with, I have unravelled some of the intricate participation framework that makes press releases so special. In particular, drawing from corpus-based evidence, I have shown that there can be no doubt that press releases are not just aimed at journalists *per se*, but that they are meant to be retold by them as accurately as possible, preferably even verbatim, in their own news reporting. This seems to confirm and, indeed, supplement the view of the news as a 'history of discourse', a diachronic phenomenon, which consists of a chain of 'textualizations', right from 'news management' over 'newsmaking' to 'news consumption'. Elaborating on this peculiar audience-directedness of my data, in chapter 2 I argued that the journalists who receive press releases should be seen as intermediaries (or mediators) and the journalists' own audiences of newspaper readers etc. as absent ultimate destinations. Press releases can therefore be characterized as a type of indirectly targeted, projected discourse.

The main goal of my study has been to trace all this in the language. From an analysis of a number of closely related features of the metapragmatics in my data - third-person self-reference, self-quotation and explicit semi-performatives -, it was argued that press releases are, what I have called, preformulated: through 'point of view operations', press releases can simply be copied by journalists. Crucially, I have shown that it is not just the 'form' but also the 'content' of press releases that is structured to meet the requirements of news reporting. As far as 'content' is concerned, I have made it clear at various points in my analysis that preformulation involves negotiation: that those who issue press releases walk a thin line between what, ideally, they would like to get the journalists to say and what, realistically, they know the journalists will want to say.

I first looked at self-reference. In particular, it was shown that most press releases use the third person to refer to the organizations that issue them: both proper names and definite descriptions prove popular for such purposes of self-reference. Similarly, most reflexive time and place deixis is neutral. I have argued that all this is part of a point of view operation which allows journalists to simply copy press releases in their own news reporting. In addition, I have drawn attention to so-called 'empathetic discourse' in press releases, where the writer does not just switch out of his or her own perspective, but goes some way to actively encode that of the journalists. At the end of chapter 3 I argued that this data seems to support a social-interactional view of the deictic field, but that it may equally serve less harmonious purposes.

Next self-quotation. In a lot of press releases, I showed in chapter 4, so-called 'pseudo-direct speech' helps anticipate the requirements of news reporting: the quoted words were never spoken by the named source, who is usually one of the organization's own top figures, but simply written up by a press officer. In general terms, such self-quotes seem to make press releases more lively and more reliable. At the same time, from an analysis of how they are typically introduced in the corpus (including the predominant use of neutral *verba dicendi*), it looks as if the self-quotes also make press releases more objective. On closer scrutiny, however, it becomes clear that no objectivity is possible in the news and that, instead, press releases propose 'objectively-voiced', yet 'unavoidably non-objective' text.

The final feature of the metapragmatics of press releases that I have investigated is the interesting distribution of explicit semi-performatives. Drawing from corpus-based data once again, I have argued that such explicit semi-performatives combine commitment with tentativity and that, in doing so, just like third-person self-reference and self-quotation, they allow writers of press releases to strike a balance between news managers' and newsmakers' conflicting ambitions.

In chapter 7 most of the points referred to above were brought together in a case study of the Valdez corpus, documenting how Exxon managed the news on the oil spill in Alaska.

As I have suggested, the remaining question now is how this analysis of preformulation in press releases sheds light on the distribution of power in the news. In this chapter I hope to contribute to an emerging answer to it. The discussion can best be seen not as a set of conclusions, but as a start for further research in the field of media discourse and in related fields, taking press releases as a suitable point of departure for more elaborately exploring the balance of power in the news. As it is, right now I shall simply spell out, within a broader view of the news, the interactional asymmetries that arise from the differential distribution of knowledge and rights to participation that, I have shown, are at work in press releases and some of the linguistic traces of which have been documented in my analysis of the metapragmatics in my data. In doing so, I shall resume the discussion of newsmaking and news management practices started at the end of the first chapter.

3.   Perspective: Asymmetries in the News

3.1   A hybrid genre

What with the metapragmatics of third-person self-reference, self-quotation and explicit semi-performatives analysed in this study, I have argued that press releases can be situated somewhere in between what writers of press releases, ideally, would want journalists to retell and what, realistically, they know journalists would be willing to retell. In other words, the 'unpaid publicity' that press releases are said to be geared at seems to keep the middle ground between advertising and news reporting. Press releases are what Norman Fairclough would call a 'hybrid' genre (1994, 1995, 1996), one that serves to reconcile the languages of newsmaking and news management into a complex new form of merged, or what in the introduction to this study I called 'entextualized', discourse. In particular, I have shown in this study that press releases are both 'histoire' and 'discours' (Benveniste 1966), 'displaced' as well as 'situated' (Auer 1988). In John B. Thompson's terminology, they are at once 'depersonalized' and 'repersonalized', presenting an experience that is 'mediated' as well as 'lived' (1995: 196-197, 227-228).

Fairclough suggests that such a redrawing or weakening of the boundaries between, what he calls, 'orders of discourse' can be related to patterns of commodification and that it reflects divisions of 'hegemonic' power. Among other features, he points to conversationalization in this respect and shows how, for example, the discourses of politics and education are being colonized by market discourses. Opening up a wide area for debate that deserves a much more thorough treatment than the cursory remarks below, I shall now try to indicate how the findings of my research on press releases may be related to this concept of commodification and, as an agenda for future work on the genre, I shall indicate that they seem to support a view of hegemony that allows for "the complex social process through which people construct meanings, values and their own subjectivities" (Brantlinger 1990: 101).

3.2   Commodification of sources

In chapter 1 I argued that, in pointing to news management practices and denouncing the complicity of the press, critical linguistics did well to draw attention to another crucial influence in the social conditioning of the news: viz. it is not only determined by what (some) people want to hear but also by what (some) people have to say. In the subsequent chapters, by focusing on the metapragmatics of press releases, I showed how press releases are preformulated to meet the requirements of news reporting. It follows that news is not simply what (some) people have to say; conversely, what those people have to say is also - to some extent at least - determined by the news.[1]

Based on the so-called 'political economic' view of the news as "largely an outcome of the workings of market forces" (Herman and Chomsky 1988: xii), a mutual asymmetrical relationship of exchange can be identified between newsmakers and news managers: while the media offer PR officers key opportunities of news coverage, it should be noted that PR officers offer first-hand information to the media, who need stories. This is in some ways similar to the relationship between a doctor and his or her patient: the doctor has to rely on the patient for receiving crucial information, just as much as the patient depends on the doctor for obtaining advice about the remedy (Mey 1993: 147-148). Peltu (1988) talks about a 'symbiotic relationship'.

In true market discourse, press releases have even been considered 'information subsidies', i.e. "efforts to reduce the prices faced by others [i.e. journalists] for certain information, in order to increase its consumption" (Gandy 1982: 8). This view can be related to Fairclough's comments on commodification as the progressive enlargement of the capitalist economic domain to take in aspects of life which used to be separate from production: educational courses, holidays, health insurance, and funerals, he says, are now bought and sold like soap powders (1989). My research seems to indicate that not just the news itself has been commodified, but the sources of the news have been commodified too: it has been shown that journalists cannot simply write what they want since, for one thing, they have to rely on what sources supply them with; my analysis of the metapragmatics of press releases suggests that sources are constrained too, viz. by what journalists want to hear from them.[2]

Note that this profound ambiguity is already present in applying the concept of gatekeeping to journalism: while the freedom of gatekeepers is restricted by the stories made available to them, no stories that are not made available to them have a chance of passing the gate. In Berger's words, this would mean that "the news we get is, in the final analysis, someone's view of what is important news or news that will attract and keep the attention of readers or audiences - not necessarily what is important news" (1995: 65). Here 'someone' is not (just) the sources who manage the news, it is (also) the journalists who make it.[3] This is in line with John B. Thompson's (1990) claim that "[w]ith the commodification of symbolic forms, the channels of selective diffusion acquire a key role in the process of economic valorization, as they become the mechanism through which symbolic goods are exchanged in the market" (168).

Clearly, there seems to be a delicate balance of power in the news and I would suggest that it is in this light that we will have to further look at press releases. To illustrate this balance, here is an embarrassingly explicit expression of the relation between news managers and newsmakers in an extract from a cover letter accompanying one of the press releases in my corpus:

(1)   (ASQ, Houthalen: 23 February 1994)
       Wij zijn er van overtuigd, geachte heer, dat deze tekst de basis vormt voor een krachtig artikel, zodat wij beiden er de vruchten van mogen plukken.

       We are convinced, dear sir, that this text is the basis for a powerful article, so that we can both reap the fruits from it.[4]

3.3   Hegemony

All this seems to serve as preliminary evidence that, as Lull (1995) argues, the orthodox critical stress on determinacy is "not wrong but incomplete" (166). Surely there are patterns of power and domination in the news, but these appear to be open-ended. Gramsci's use of the term 'hegemony' is useful here: it is not just a state of control, but also a process of consensus formation or, as Gramsci himself put it, of "compromise equilibrium" (Brantlinger 1990: 98).

For one thing, ideology is often contested, resisted and transformed: in particular, just as those who, in the end, consume the news are suspicious about the "promotional designs upon [them]" (Fairclough 1994: 258) and therefore do not always take the news for granted, journalists do not simply swallow what sources have to tell them either. In addition, - and this is what my analysis of the metapragmatics in press releases has focused on -

counter-tendencies are already built into the very vehicles of ideology. In this view, preformulation in press releases can be considered a form of 'self-transformation' (Thompson 1995; cf. Giddens 1991 on 'reflexivity'). As Lull says, resistance "is not initiated solely by media consumers. Texts themselves are implicated. Ideology can never be stated purely and simply. Ways of thinking are always reflexive and embedded in a complex, sometimes contradictory, ideological regress" (40-41). I have shown, through my analysis of the metapragmatics in press releases, that the news managers' ways of writing are *literally* reflexive and embedded.[5]

Of course, it may - and indeed should - be questioned if the self-transformation in press releases is real resistance, if there is genuine two-way interaction and not what Thompson calls 'quasi-interaction'. After all, in my own analysis I have shown that third-person self-reference, self-quotation and explicit semi-performatives may be less than innocent negotiating devices: journalists who copy press releases in their own news reporting may well turn out less than fully objective. In Bauman and Briggs's (1992) and Silverstein and Urban's (1996) terminology, the metapragmatics in my data serve as entextualization devices: they spell out to journalists how they are expected to take press releases. Through them, direct address to newsmakers is turned into an indirect one, as when the live audience for a TV chat show counters the interlocutors' uncertainty by providing immediate feedback as well as furnishing the viewers at home with a set of model responses (Thompson 1995: 97). In sharp contrast with - for example - real interviewing, the interaction in press releases "is administered" and the journalists' inquiry through question and answer "has been replaced by the privatized appropriation of a conversation carried out in their name" (Thompson 1995: 131-132).

The best illustration of such 'quasi-interaction' in my corpus is perhaps in a press release issued by the software distributors AB Computers. In this press release, the metapragmatics play an undeniable preformulating role: it is announced that 'AB Computers have been appointed official Lotus Notes distributors for Belgium and Luxembourg' and Director Doubi Ajoumi is quoted as having said that 'this appointment is of vital importance for the distribution of new Lotus Notes server versions on UNIX and Novell'. Exceptionally, there is a wide margin on the left of the text with handwritten notes that offer a summary of the press release and that look as if they were hastily jotted down by a journalist on a press conference. On closer scrutiny, however, there can be no doubt that these notes were made by AB Computers themselves on each copy of the press release, probably even computer-printed. To the hasty journalists, however, it might appear that the press release has already been meticulously processed for them, editorialized even. Clearly, this press release offers a perfect example of how the interaction between newsmakers and news managers can be 'administered', with the newsmakers' critical inquiry replaced by a set of pseudo-notes made by the news managers in their name.

Still, even if no press releases - by their very nature - offer true interaction, the corpus-based analysis of metapragmatics presented here has elaborately demonstrated a process of preformulation through which press releases do not just determine news reporting, but are also determined by it. Myers (1996) argues that, in divided discourse, vagueness is often "used strategically to allow a written text to take on a range of meanings for different audiences with different interests" (4), for example by avoiding proper names and by leaving illocutionary force uncertain. In my data, however, the opposite seems to be true: I have shown that, through third-person self-reference, self-quotation and explicit semi-performatives, writers of press releases apparently do not leave any doubt about what it is that they are saying (or doing) and who is saying (or doing) it. I have argued that such metapragmatics actually even expose the non-avoidable objectiveness of press releases.[6]

Then again, I have shown that preformulation in press releases serves to constrain subsequent reformulation by journalists, often in less than innocent ways, and I would therefore suggest that the truly ambivalent role played by the metapragmatics of press releases is perhaps best captured in Goffman's frame theoretical notion of 'boundary markers' or 'conventionalized brackets' (cf. also chapter 2). "[L]ike the wooden frame of a picture, [they] are presumably neither part of the content of the activity proper nor part of the world outside the activity but rather both inside and outside" (1974: 252). Similarly, it is on the borderline between news management and newsmaking that my own investigation of the metapragmatics of press releases should be situated.

4.   Interpretation and Pre-Interpretation

So far, in this final chapter, I have presented an overview of the main issues in my study of preformulation in press releases and I have tried to make a provisional round-up of what this study implies for the distribution of power in the news. At the very end, it is perhaps time to briefly reflect on my own analytical practice.

From my initial discussion of the research method, in general, and of the notion of context, in particular, it should be clear that my analytical practice has not been unhampered by *a priori* perspective-taking. First of all, I pointed out in the first chapter that, for this kind of project, substantial amounts of background information will always be taken for granted. For one thing, to approach the question of power in the news by looking at press releases is a form of perspective-taking in itself. In addition, far from excluding 'pretext', in concentrating on news management practices it has been my central research target to integrate this study of the metapragmatics of press releases in a wider view of the news, demonstrating how the media constitute an intertextual crossroads. Thirdly, and finally, with reference to Verschueren's notion of 'the salience of adaptation processes' (1995c) that I referred to in the first chapter, it is important to keep in mind that I have investigated preformulation as a process of 'self-transformation', i.e. writers of press releases actively anticipate the journalists' requirements. It has been argued that such self-transformation points to the 'pre-interpreted character' of the socio-historical world (Thompson 1990: 21), in general, and of our data, in particular: apparently, throughout this study, we have been seeking to understand a range of phenomena which are in some way already understood by the individuals who are part of them. As Thompson puts it, "the critical questioning and revision of everyday understanding is not an activity undertaken by the analyst alone (...): rather it is an activity which may be undertaken by the very individuals whose everyday understanding is called into question by the process of interpretation" (323).

Returning to the debate about context earlier on, this means that to stick to the text only, even if it had been possible and desirable, could have been no guarantee of a perspectiveless analysis. On the contrary, it now appears that if we had really tried to do so we would probably have got caught in the very ideology that we were trying to deconstruct in the first place; rather than calling into question the social order in which discourse functions, we would have adopted the basic structure of this social order and we would have integrated it in our way of viewing the object (cf. Blommaert 1997). Instead, I argued in the first chapter that to look at the data only cannot keep us from pre-interpreting the data. One reason, it should now be clear, is that the data may have been pre-interpreted for us.[7]

Here is Sacks:

> In so far as you have dealt with a society that was aware of a history, that was oriented to a history, then you damn well have to consider that the things you found were put there for you, or for someone such as you, and could have been put there with various attitudes. For example, these things could have been put there as a way of suggesting the society was a social structure other than it really was.[8]

Sacks is talking about social history here, but there can be no doubt that the same goes for discursive histories like the one that, I have argued, press releases are a part of.

And Goffman:

> If an individual can claim unseriousness in order to avoid penalty for an act he has committed, the claim being made after the fact, then certainly at times the individual may from the beginning arrange his actions so that if he is called to account he can argue for its unseriousness. In brief, action can be styled to carry its own excuse in advance of an actual call for it (332).

Clearly, it would be wrong to conclude on the basis of a data-driven analysis that the individual in Goffman's example was unserious. Similarly, in concluding that writers of press releases are in some way 'giving in to' journalists, we have to be aware that such self-transformation may have 'been styled to carry an excuse' for press releases in the first place.

What then may have been the use of this research? Hardly, as Thompson ambitiously points out about his own books, to become "a potential intervention in the very circumstances about which it is formulated" (323). Still, there is no need for too much pessimism either. If we are aware of the unavoidable bias of background information and of the pre-interpreted nature of our object itself, then our analysis may contribute to a clearer perception of the field among the various parties involved in the news as well as to a better understanding of our own analytical practice. In my work, I have tried to demonstrate that press releases are an interesting object of pragmatic analysis and deserve further research in various fields. The effort may have been worthwhile if only, as I pointed out at the outset of this study, by raising a dozen or so new questions for every problem that I have begun to provide a solution for.

Appendix: corpus

In order to obtain a wide variety of press releases, I contacted representatives of the media that receive press releases as well as a number of organizations that issue them. More specifically, the corpus includes the following subcorpora:

- press releases issued by Exxon in the wake of the oil spill at Valdez, Alaska (March - November 1989)

- press releases received by the economy editors of the Belgian Dutch-language quality newspaper *De Standaard* (between 23 February and 9 May 1994)

- press releases received by press agency Belga (Antwerp) (between 7 September and 15 November 1994

- press releases issued by the BEL 20 companies, i.e. Belgium's top 20 companies that are quoted on the stock exchange (from 1 December 1994)[1]

A quick look at the press releases in this corpus shows that there is no agreement on what press releases really are. While most of the documents have the word 'press release' or any of its synonyms on top of them, some look more like formal invitations, direct mail letters or sales brochures. Apparently, labelling and announcing a piece of writing as a press release does not *ipso facto* make it one.[2]

Or does it? I have not wanted to make any selection from the corpus based on these intuitions, in any case. I started from the idea that press releases are a functionally specialized category of writing that is restricted by certain institutionalized conventions. The temptation to specify just what those conventions are must be resisted, because it would undoubtedly lead us to make pretheoretical claims about the linguistic structure of press releases. To find out how they deviate from more 'ordinary' discourse - and, incidentally, how they agree with it - is the very purpose of this research.

As for sources, the majority of the press releases in the corpus comes from business and industry (over 70%); other sources include government (10%) and special interest groups (10%). This division is, to some extent, predictable from the way I collected the press releases (cf. above). At the same time business seems to be the biggest source of press releases, anyway; Morton & Ramsey (1994), for example, report similar figures for a U.S. news wire's one day's transmission.[3]

Finally, it should be noted that the varied, highly asymmetrical make-up of the corpus reflects the organic development of the empirical research that lies at the basis of this study. In addition, it ensures that different types of press releases and categories of subject matter are represented. Among other things, the press releases in the corpus serve to communicate the sponsor's activities, announce coming events, report on past events, provide consumer information or profile people.[4] At the same time, they deal with financial information, personnel affairs, economics, social issues, politics, etc.[5] As for languages, most press releases are in Dutch, a minority are in English. The English translations of the extracts from press releases in Dutch are my own, unless indicated differently. No contrastive perspective is aimed at in this study. Though I have no evidence whatsoever to claim that the metapragmatic features analysed above are in any way universal, at least the combination of Dutch and English data has posed no problems in this study.

Valdez corpus

Exxon	Houston, Texas	LIGHTERING, OIL SPILL CLEANUP EFFORTS CONTINUE IN ALASKA	27 03 1989
Exxon	Houston, Texas	EXXON SHIPPING COMPANY PLACES TOP PRIORITY ON ALASKA CLEAN-UP	28 03 1989
Exxon	Darien, Conn.	Exxon Chemical's Corexit 9527 used against Valdez oil spill	29 03 1989
Exxon	Houston, Texas	EXXON SHIPPING TERMINATES CAPTAIN OF EXXON VALDEZ	30 03 1989
Exxon	Valdez, Alaska	EXXON WAS READY FOR FULL-SCALE DISPERSANT APPLICATION MARCH 25	01 04 1989
Exxon	Juneau, Alaska	EXXON USA PRESIDENT MEETS WITH ALASKA GOVERNOR, LEGISLATORS	03 04 1989
Exxon	Valdez, Alaska	EXXON MOUNTS MASSIVE EFFORT TO CONTAIN, CLEAN UP OIL SPILL	06 04 1989
Exxon	Washington, D.C.	Rawl makes statement about Valdez to U.S. Congressional Committees	06 04 1989
Exxon	Valdez, Alaska	EXXON AND OTHERS PUSH AHEAD WITH CLEANUP OF PRINCE WILLIAM SOUND	12 04 1989
Exxon	Houston, Texas	Exxon Valdez	13 04 1989
Exxon	Valdez, Alaska	EXXON CONSTRUCTS EXPANDED SEA MAMMAL RESCUE CENTER	13 04 1989
Exxon	Valdez, Alaska	EXXON EXPANDS OIL RECOVERY OPERATIONS	15 04 1989

Date	Headline	Location	Source
17 04 1989	Valdez oil spill is not the reason for gasoline price hikes, says Exxon	Washington, D.C.	Exxon
19 04 1989	ALASKA RESIDENTS EXPECTED TO FILL VALDEZ CLEANUP HIRING NEEDS	Houston, Texas	Exxon
19 04 1989	*NO TITLE*	Washington, D.C.	Exxon
20 04 1989	EXXON-SUPPORTED OTTER CENTER HIGHLY SUCCESSFUL	Valdez, Alaska	Exxon
24 04 1989	EXXON AHEAD OF SCHEDULE ON ALASKA SHORELINE CLEANUP	Valdez, Alaska	Exxon
27 04 1989	EXXON BOARD CREATES INDEPENDENT LITIGATION COMMITTEE	New York	Exxon
27 04 1989	EXXON BUILDING OTTER CENTER IN SEWARD	Valdez, Alaska	Exxon
27 04 1989	EXXON CONDUCTS CULTURAL RESOURCE STUDIES IN ALASKA'S PRINCE WILLIAM SOUND	Valdez, Alaska	Exxon
02 05 1989	VALDEZ RESCUE CENTERS BURIED BY TOWELS	Valdez, Alaska	Exxon
02 05 1989	ALASKA SHORELINE CLEANUP MOBILIZATION NEARING PEAK	Houston, Texas	Exxon
04 05 1989	EXXON SUBMITS REVISED SHORELINE CLEANUP PLAN	Valdez, Alaska	Exxon
11 05 1989	EXXON ANNOUNCES ADDITIONAL PERSONNEL AND EQUIPMENT WILL BE USED IN SHORELINE CLEAN-UP EFFORT	Washington, D.C.	Exxon
11 05 1989	OVER 5,000 PERSONNEL AT WORK IN ALASKA; EXPANDED STAFF SUPPORT IN HOUSTON	Valdez, Alaska	Exxon
13 05 1989	COAST GUARD APPROVES EXXON BEACH-CLEANING TEST	Valdez, Alaska	Exxon

Exxon	Parsippany, New Jersey	L.G. RAWL, EXXON CHAIRMAN, DETAILS ALASKA CLEANUP AT SHAREHOLDERS MEETING	18 05 1989
Exxon	Valdez, Alaska	VALDEZ CLEANUP COSTS REACH $115 MILLION AS 7,000 WORK TO MOP UP SPILLED OIL	24 05 1989
Exxon	Valdez, Alaska	8,373 AT WORK IN VALDEZ CLEANUP	29 05 1989
Exxon	Valdez, Alaska	9,200 AT WORK ON VALDEZ OPERATIONS, ABOUT 115 MILES OF SHORELINE TREATED	07 06 1989
Exxon	Valdez, Alaska	EXXON FUNDS EAGLE RESCUE TEAMS	09 06 1989
Exxon	San Diego, California	AGREEMENT REACHED TO REPAIR EXXON VALDEZ IN SAN DIEGO	12 06 1989
Exxon	Valdez, Alaska	SKIMMED OIL FROM VALDEZ TO BE TRANSPORTED TO SEATTLE FOR TREATMENT AND CLEANING	16 06 1989
Exxon	New York	EXXON NOW HAS 10,000 WORKERS AT OIL SPILL AS CLEANUP COSTS EXCEED $ 200 MILLION	30 06 1989
Exxon	Houston, Texas	EXXON RESPONDS TO ALASKA ATTORNEY GENERAL: VALDEZ RECORDS INTACT	07 07 1989
Exxon	Houston, Texas	EXXON SEEKS COURT HEARING IN COMPUTER BACK-UP TAPE CASE	12 07 1989
Exxon	Valdez, Alaska	VALDEZ CLEANUP REPORT	14 07 1989
Exxon	Houston, Texas	EXXON VALDEZ STRUCTURALLY SOUND	14 07 1989
Exxon	Houston, Texas	U.S. COAST GUARD FINDS NO OIL IN SLICK LINKED TO THE VALDEZ	17 07 1989
Exxon	Washington, D.C.	OIL SPILL RESPONSE EFFORT TREATS 500 MILES OF ALASKA SHORELINE	20 07 1989

	Headline	Location	Date
Exxon	OIL SPILL DOCUMENTS INTACT, EXXON PROVES IN COURT FILING	Houston, Texas	24 07 1989
Exxon	EXXON POSITION ON ALASKAN SPILL CLEANUP IS UNCHANGED	Houston, Texas	25 07 1989
Exxon	EXXON EMPHASIZES COMMITMENT TO ALASKA CLEANUP, WILL NOT ABANDON THE JOB UNTIL IT'S PUT RIGHT	Washington, D.C.	28 07 1989
Exxon	COMMITMENT TO OIL SPILL CLEANUP CLEARLY DEMONSTRATED, SAYS EXXON	Anchorage, Alaska	03 08 1989
Exxon	EXPANDED TESTING OF COREXIT BEGINS AT VALDEZ	Valdez, Alaska	08 08 1989
Exxon	EXXON PAYMENTS TO FISHERMEN TOP $38 MILLION MARK	Valdez, Alaska	16 08 1989
Exxon	BAD WEATHER INCREASINGLY AFFECTS CLEANUP OF VALDEZ OIL IN ALASKA	Valdez, Alaska	18 08 1989
Exxon	EXXON RESPONDS TO LAWSUIT FILED BY STATE OF ALASKA	Juneau, Alaska	18 08 1989
Exxon	EXXON UPDATES SPILL CLEANUP, ANNOUNCES WINTER PROGRAMME	Valdez, Alaska	22 08 1989
Exxon	EXXON CHALLENGES ALASKA GOVERNOR TO STOP POLITICS, WORK TOGETHER	Valdez, Alaska	23 08 1989
Exxon	EXXON SURPASSES 1,000 MILES OF SHORELINE TREATED	Valdez, Alaska	30 08 1989
Exxon	FEDERAL COURT UPHOLDS EXXON POSITION REGARDING ERASED COMPUTER TAPE	Houston, Texas	11 09 1989
Exxon	RAWL VISITS VALDEZ SHORELINES, REVIEWS PLANS FOR THE WINTER	Juneau, Alaska	13 09 1989

Exxon	Valdez, Alaska	EXXON BEGINS BUILDUP FOR WINTER PROGRAM IN VALDEZ	15 09 1989
Exxon	Valdez, Alaska	WITH LESS THAN A MILE TO GO VALDEZ CLEANUP WINDS DOWN	18 09 1989
Exxon	Irving, Texas	EXXON FILES AGREEMENTS TO SETTLE VALDEZ CRIMINAL AND CIVIL CASES WITH FEDERAL AND ALASKAN GOVERNMENTS	30 09 1989
Exxon	Anchorage, Alaska	EXXON USA PRESIDENT ADDRESSES ALASKA CHAMBER GROUP	03 10 1989
Exxon		FEDERAL COURT APPROVES AGREEMENTS TO SETTLE VALDEZ CRIMINAL AND CIVIL CASES WITH FEDERAL AND ALASKAN GOVERNMENTS	09 10 1989
Exxon	Anchorage, Alaska	EXXON SUIT SEEKS DAMAGES AGAINST ALASKA FOR DELAYING USE OF DISPERSANTS IN CLEANUP	26 10 1989
Exxon	New York City	EXXON USA PRESIDENT SAYS TIMELY DECISIONS CRITICAL TO EFFECTIVE OIL SPILL RESPONSE	07 11 1989

De Standaard corpus

		NO TITLE	
AB Computers	Brussels	NO TITLE	18 04 1994
AEG	Brussels	AEG Transportation Systems neemt de activiteiten van Von-Roll-Monorail-Systems over	19 04 1994
Alcatel Bell	Antwerp	ALCATEL BELL LEVERT INTELLIGENTE NETWERKEN AAN ZUID-KOREA	28 02 1994
Allshare	Brussels	COMSHARE lanceert: COMMANDER FDC 2.1 - De Windows-oplossing voor Management en Statutaire Rapportering	15 04 1994
Allshare	Brussels	ALLSHARE KONDIGT AAN: Jaarlijkse gebruikersconferentie PERSONNEL/VIEW.	11 05 1994
Alvey Europe	Willebroek	Nieuw Europees CE-keurmerk voor Alvey Europe Palletizers	s.d.
Artisoft	Amsterdam	Omzet en winst Artisoft stijgt in 3e kwartaal	26 04 1994
ASQ	Houthalen	ASQ: Maatgesneden efficiëntie - wil hoogste kwaliteit in informatiseringsprojekten	23 02 1994
AST	Irvine/Kontich	AST BRAVO LC desktops: Nieuwe generatie energiezuinige 486 computers met CD-ROMS	19 04 1994
ATAB	Antwerp	Driemaal ISO 9002 voor ATAB	30 03 1994
Barenbrug		Tuinieren: gazonzaden - Barenbrug, kunst van het gazon	04 1994
BASF	Brussels	Dividend 1993: 8 DEM	08 03 1994
BASF	Brussels	BASF: geen voorjaarsmoeheid - De onderneming zet haar structurele aanpassingen onverminderd voort	17 03 1994

Name	City	Title	Date
Bayer	Antwerp	Bayer versterkt engagement in fijnchemikaliën - Miles Inc. neemt Chemdesign Corp. over	20 04 1994
Bekaert	Kortrijk	N.V. BEKAERT BEEINDIGT ZIJN SAMENWERKINGSAKKOORD MET BRIDGESTONE'CORPORATION	25 03 1994
Belgospace	Brussels	*NO TITLE*	24 02 1994
Boelwerf Vlaanderen	Temse	BOELWERF VLAANDEREN DOOPT 2 KOELSCHEPEN	24 02 1994
Bonduelle	Mechelen	*NO TITLE*	04 03 1994
Bose	Ternat	BELGISCHE LUCHTMACHT KIEST VOOR DE ACTIVE NOISE REDUCTION (ANR) HEADSETS VAN BOSE	05 1994
Buchmann	Kapellen	ACTIE "SCHATTEN OP ZOLDER" 1994 - BUCHMANN OPTICAL INDUSTRIES SCHENKT BRILLEN AAN BELGISCHE EN NEDERLANDSE HULPORGANISATIES VOOR DE DERDE WERELD	16 04 1994
Bulo	Mechelen	Nike kiest Vlaams, voor Bulo	29 03 1994
CBR	Brussels	ACTIVITEIT EN RESULTATEN VAN CBR IN 1993	17 03 1994
Central Hispano		Central Hispano blijft op koers	04 03 1994
Christelijke Vakbond van Communicatiemiddelen en Cultuur/ACOD	Brussels	*NO TITLE*	08 03 1994
Citibank	Brussels	FAMIBANK-AGENTEN WORDEN GEINTEGREERD IN CITIBANK-NETWERK CITIBANK BELGIUM: van 58 tot 316 verkooppunten	04 1994
Desimpel	Kortemark	DESIMPEL KORTEMARK: GECONSOLIDEERDE RESULTATEN OVER 1993	25 03 1994

Domo	Gent	DOMO GROUP NEEMT CAPROLACTAM-ACTIVITEITEN LEUNE WERKE AG OVER	17 03 1994
EMC	Brussels	HOGERE WINST EN OMZET VOOR EMC IN EERSTE KWARTAAL - Winst per aandeel stijgt met 175% t.o.v. het eerste kwartaal '93 - Verdere groei van klantenbestand in alle regio's	20 04 1994
Ericsson	Brussels	ERICSSON INTRODUCEERT DE KLEINSTE DIGITALE MOBIELE TELEFOON TER WERELD VOOR HET GSM-NETWERK	16 03 1994
Ericsson	Brussels	De kleinste en de lichtste GSM telefoon ter wereld heeft nu "Full Type Approval"	22 04 1994
Ericsson	Brussels	De oorlog van de mobiele telefoon laait op: De spreektijden worden langer en langer en de telefoons worden lichter en kleiner	16 05 1994
Esselte	Saina, Sweden	REPORT ON 1993 OPERATIONS	08 03 1994
Europay	Waterloo	EUROPAY DOET HET GOED IN TURKIJE - Grootste geldautomatennet van Turkije wordt voor het toeristische zomerseizoen uitgebreid	05 05 1994
General Motors	Antwerp	General Motors versterkt de merknaam Opel - Alle Europese dochterondernemingen en fabrieken werken voortaan onder de naam Opel	08 03 1994
Generale Bank	Brussels	Generale bank opent in Utrecht	24 02 1994
Gils & Gils	Lommel	NIEUWE DESIGN OPPERVLAKKEN VOOR KRANEN	s.d.
Group Van Hecke	St-Genesius-Rode	NO TITLE	s.d.

Helpelec	Brussels	Als de batterij niet louter toebehoren is	11 04 1994
Hilaire Van de Haeghe	Harsewinkel	Helmut Claas stelt Claas-jaarrekening 1992/93 voor: Nieuwe produkten en een continu verbeteringsproces	s.d.
ibens	Antwerp	Oprichting dochterbedrijven in Hongarije en Polen - JUBILE-RENDE AANNEMINGEN J & E iBENS OP DE OOSTEURO-PESE MARKT	21 03 1994
Immodef	Brussels	Het huidige kapitaal van Immodef bedraagt BEF 539 MIO na het intreden van twee nieuwe belangrijke aandeelhouders	05 1994
ITT Sheraton	Liège	ITT SHERATON CORPORATION - INTERNATIONALE PROFIEL - SITUATIE VAN DE AFDELING EUROPA, AFRIKA EN MIDDEN-OOSTEN	03 1994
Jadrimex	Elewijt	Overname van de divisie geldverwerking van GENERAL COMMUNICATIONS n.v. door JADRIMEX Belgium	30 03 1994
Kredietbank	Brussels	Kredietbank binnenkort vertegenwoordigd in Boedapest	08 03 1994
Madge	Hoofddorp	Madge introduceert Smart 100 AT Ringnode-adapterkaarten voor glasvezel- en koperdraadkabels - Nieuwe ISA Bus FDDI-kaarten gerekend tot de beste in hun klasse	26 04 1994
Metalim	Overpelt	"Groep Metalim behaalt derde en vierde ISO-9002 certifikaat"	s.d.
Milltronics	Deurne	Ultrasore niveaumeting voor voeding- en drankenindustrie	s.d.
Motorola	Vilvoorde	MOTOROLA LEVERT GSM NETWERK AAN ANDORRA	06 05 1994
Nestor	Tielen	FA. NESTOR KOOPT VOORRADEN CONCORDIA MAIL	18 04 1994
Noblesse	Londerzeel	NOBLESSE BENELUX NEEMT TAECKE OVER	30 03 1994
Océ	Brussels	G9020-S: Direct thermische plotkwaliteit voor de prijs van een penplotter	27 04 1994

Company	City	Title	Date
Ogilvy & Mather	Brussels	NIEUW TELEMARKETING-BUREAU VAN START: OGILVY & MATHER TELE-SERVICES	s.d.
Pasteur Sanofi Diagnostics/ Centocor		PASTEUR SANOFI DIAGNOSTICS EN CENTOCOR SLUITEN EEN BELANGRIJK AKKOORD OP HET TERREIN VAN DE KANKER	s.d.
Petrofina		*NO TITLE*	30 03 1994
Pfizer	Brussels	PFIZER INC. MELDT STIJGING VAN OMZET EN WINST OVER HET EERSTE KWARTAAL	26 04 1994
Puma	Herzogenaurach	"Fit for profit" - PUMA bereikt voortijdig gestelde doelstellingen - Reeds in 1994 winst verwacht	25 04 1994
R.J. Reynolds	Brussels	BUNDELING VAN NEDERLANDSE EN BELGISCH-LUXEMBURGSE ACTIVITEITEN - R.J. REYNOLDS TOBACCO INTERNATIONAL RICHT BENELUX-ORGANISATIE OP	23 02 1994
Recticel	Brussels	MILIEUPRIJS VOOR DE INDUSTRIE 1993-1994 - CATEGORIE: ECOPRODUKT	s.d.
Recticel	Brussels	RESULTAAT VAN DE GROEP RECTICEL VOOR HET JAAR 1993 EN PERSPECTIEVEN - TERUGKEER NAAR WINST IN EEN MOEILIJKE ECONOMISCHE CONTEXT	11 03 1994
Royal Belge	Brussels	OMZET: DE GRENS DER 100 MILJARD DOORBROKEN	15 03 1994
Royal Life	Brussels	FLEXIBEL VERZEKEREN EN BELEGGEN: EEN UNIEKE COMBINATIE VOOR DE BELGISCHE MARKT	20 04 1994
Sagem-B	Leuven	*NO TITLE*	28 03 1994
SAS Institute	Leuven	SAS INSTITUTE: GLOBALE OMZETSTIJGING VAN 15%	s.d.
Service Station	Kortrijk	SCHITTERENDE START VOOR 2DE EDITIE VAN SERVICE STATION	24 04 1994

Slough Estates	Sint-Stevens-Woluwe	OFFICIELE INHULDIGING VAN DE NIEUWE HOOFDZE-TEL VAN RANK XEROX BELGIE DOOR DE HEER JEAN-LUC DEHAENE, EERSTE-MINISTER OP WOENSDAG 1 JUNI 1994 OM 18 UUR	29 04 1994
Solvay	Brussels	SOLVAY-GROEP: BOEKJAAR 1993 - GEKONSOLIDEERD VERLIES VAN 6,9 MILJARD BEF - WINST VAN 3,5 MILJARD BEF VOOR SOLVAY N.V. - NETTODIVIDEND GEHANDHAAFD OP 500 BEF PER AANDEEL	14 04 1994
Sterling	Diegem	Sterling Software ondersteunt IBM's System/390 parallelle processing-technologie	10 05 1994
Stork	Sint-Niklaas	STORK-CONCERN - RESULTATEN 1993 OVERSTIJGEN DE VERWACHTINGEN	28 03 1994
Sun	Brussels	Sun lanceert twee nieuwe desktops - Dubbele prestaties voor lagere prijs	29 03 1994
Ter Beke	Waarschoot	ISO 9002 kwaliteitscertifikaat toegekend aan Ter Beke Kook-warenproduktie N.V.	28 03 1994
Tessenderlo Chemie	Tessenderlo	ALTERNATIEF VOOR VERWERKING GECHLOREERDE KOOLWATERSTOFFEN VAN TESSENDERLO CHEMIE	24 02 1994
Timmers	Houthalen	NV TIMMERS OPENT EEN NIEUWE PRODUKTIEHAL IN HET VOORMALIGE OOST-DUITSLAND	24 02 1994
Timmers	Houthalen	TIMMERS: HET VERHAAL VAN EEN GESTAGE GROEI	24 02 1994
Tritec	Perwez	TRITEC ADHESIVES: nu al ISO 9002	28 03 1994
Tulip	's-Hertogenbosch	*NO TITLE*	24 03 1994
Union Minière	Brussels	*NO TITLE*	25 03 1994

Varta	Groot-Bijgaarden	De kleinste mijlpaal in de batterijgeschiedenis - Industriële innovatieprijs voor milieuvriendelijke mini-batterij van Varta	17 03 1994
Varta	Groot-Bijgaarden	Industriële innovatieprijs voor cadmiumvrije mini-batterij van Varta	17 03 1994
Vertongen	Puurs	VERTONGEN N.V. TERUG FAMILIEBEDRIJF	s.d.
Vlaamse Lucht-transportmaatschappij	Deurne	NO TITLE	19 05 1994
Wagons-Lits	Brussels	Wagons-Lits renoveert vier restauratierijtuigen voor de NMBS	24 02 1994
Wagons-Lits	Brussels	Wagons-Lits: Vermindering van 97,5 arbeidsplaatsen ingevolge het verlies van de spoorrestauratie	25 03 1994
Westerlund	Antwerp	Westerlund bevestigt investeringen in ultra moderne infrastructuur na bekendmaking gunstige resultaten voor 1993	29 03 1994

Belga corpus

ABVV	Antwerp	*NO TITLE*	06 10 1994
ABVV	Antwerp	*NO TITLE*	13 10 1994
ACV/ABVV/ ACLVB	Temse	*NO TITLE*	06 10 1994
Administratie der Douane en Accijnzen	Antwerp	*NO TITLE*	28 09 1994
AFF	Antwerp	NAAR EEN ANDER BELEID?	10 10 1994
Agalev	Antwerp	Hoezo geen aanplakborden?	15 09 1994
Agfa-Gevaert	Mortsel	Otto-Bayer-medaille	14 10 1994
Aktiegroep rol- stoelen en hulp- middelen	Grimbergen	AANKONDIGING AKTIE	26 09 1994
Aktiegroep rol- stoelen en hulp- middelen	Grimbergen	*NO TITLE*	28 09 1994
Alcatel Bell	Antwerp	Multimedia-contract van Alcatel Bell in de UK is van strategisch belang	15 11 1994

Antwerpse Kamer van Koophandel en Nijverheid	Antwerp	ACTIEPROGRAMMA VOOR DE GEMEENTERAADS-VERKIEZINGEN IN ANTWERPEN	21 09 1994
Antwerpse Waterwerken	Antwerp	TENTOONSTELLING - Arthur Bernard Festraets: Orchestratie van ritme en gevoel	06 10 1994
APEC	Antwerp	Antwerpen als gaststad voor het 14de APEC/UNCTAD internationaal seminarie "Container Terminal Management"	26 09 1994
Argenta	Antwerp	Rentewijzigingen	08 09 1994
Argenta	Antwerp	Drie nieuwe onderhandse leningen van Argentabank Luxembourg	08 09 1994
Argenta	Antwerp	Rentewijzigingen	09 09 1994
Argenta	Antwerp	Aanpassing hypotheektarieven	22 09 1994
Argenta	Antwerp	Rentewijzigingen	22 09 1994
Argenta	Antwerp	Halfjaarlijks resultaat per 30.06.'94 van de Groep Argenta	22 09 1994
Argenta	Antwerp	Nieuwe onderhandse lening van Argenta Nederland N.V., achtergesteld	07 10 1994
Argenta	Antwerp	Hypotheken	19 10 1994
Argenta	Antwerp	Drie nieuwe onderhandse leningen van Argentabank Luxembourg	28 10 1994
Asia Westbound Rate Agreement	Singapore	AWRA-INTERIM CAF	29 09 1994

BASF	Brussels	BASF en GE Plastics: Gemeenschappelijke kunststofproduktie te Schwarzheide	13 10 1994
BASF	Antwerp	Nieuwe verantwoordelijke afdeling Leefmilieu en Energie	14 10 1994
BASF	Antwerp	Meetstrategie BASF-Milieudienst goedgekeurd door externe experten	14 10 1994
BASF	Antwerp	BASF Antwerpen publiceert eerste milieurapport	14 10 1994
BASF	Brussels	De oprichting van BASF Magnetics Benelux	18 10 1994
BASF/Knoll	Brussels	IVAX en Knoll AG ondertekenen een intentieverklaring; Joint-venture voor generische geneesmiddelen	21 10 1994
Bayer	Antwerp	Acquisitie versterkt de produktdivisie "consumer care" - BAYER NEEMT NIET-RECEPTPLICHTIGE GENEESMIDDELEN VAN STERLING OVER IN NOORD-AMERIKA - Naamrechten na 75 jaar terug naar Leverkusen	13 09 1994
Bayer	Antwerp	2K-polyurethaan-waterlak voor Zwitserse locomotief in de "Agfa-look"	16 09 1994
Bayer	Antwerp	Zuivere lucht in de auto: "Fogging"-arme zachte polyurethaan-schuimstoffen	16 09 1994
Bayer	Antwerp	Elektror=ologische vloeistoffen van Bayer: een nieuwe generatie "intelligente oliën"	16 09 1994
Bayer	Antwerp	Lakharsbedrijf Bitterfeld - Veiligheid en langdurige bescherming met PUR-vloerbekleding	19 09 1994
Bayer	Antwerp	Nieuwe =opolyamiden voor de verpakkingssector	19 09 1994

Bayer	Antwerp	Bescherming tegen corrosie in het waterzuiveringsstation - Sanering van gastank	29 09 1994
Bayer	Antwerp	AEG "Teleport 9020": Nieuwe mobiele telefoon met behuizing uit Bayblend	29 09 1994
Bayer	Leverkusen	Reinforcing presence in generic drugs market - Bayer and Schein create an international management company for generic drugs - First co-promotion agreement for the US market	04 10 1994
Bayer	Antwerp	BRAND IN GLASVEZELPRODUKTIE-INSTALLATIE BIJ BAYER ANTWERPEN TE KALLO-BEVEREN	10 10 1994
Bayer	Antwerp	Bayer versterkt rubberactiviteiten in Japan	08 11 1994
Bayer	Antwerp	Nieuw expocentrum in Leipzig: Duurzame corrosiebescherming met PUR-lakken	08 11 1994
Bayer	Antwerp	Een nieuwe verpakking voor een nieuw melkprodukt: Lichte kunststof-retourflessen uit Makrolon	08 11 1994
Bayer	Antwerp	Bayer bouwt rubberdivisie uit - BUNA Kautschuk GmbH opgericht	10 11 1994
Bayer	Antwerp	Nieuw bedrijf produceert zoetstof voor Europese markt - Bayer concentreert Natrena-produktie in Mijdrecht, Nederland	10 11 1994
Bedevaart naar de Graven aan de IJzer	Diksmuide	*NO TITLE*	30 09 1994
Belgische Boerenbond	Leuven	*NO TITLE*	27 10 1994

Boekenbeurs voor Vlaanderen	Antwerp	*NO TITLE*	06 11 1994
Boris	Antwerp	*NO TITLE*	07 09 1994
Boris	Antwerp	*NO TITLE*	09 09 1994
Boris	Antwerp	*NO TITLE*	19 09 1994
Brook Hansen	Vilvoorde	BROOK HANSEN PRODUKTEN AANGEWEND VOOR HET BEHOUD VAN VLAANDERENS BOUWKUNDIG ERFGOED	26 09 1994
BSV	Antwerp	*NO TITLE*	09 09 1994
BTR	Antwerp	Paul Buysse benoemd tot Executive Director BTR plc	08 09 1994
CBS	Voorburg	GOEDE VOORUITZICHTEN VOOR DE BOUW TOT MEDIO 1995	05 10 1994
Charta 91	Berchem	ANTWERPEN: NOG EEN NIEUW POLITIEK INITIATIEF	12 09 1994
Charta 91	Antwerp	*NO TITLE*	07 11 1994
Compas	Brussels	Beweging in internationale verhuiswereld	02 11 1994
CVB	Antwerp	*NO TITLE*	07 10 1994
CVB	Antwerp	*NO TITLE*	13 10 1994
Dialoog in het Straatbeeld	Antwerp	*NO TITLE*	30 09 1994
Electrabel	Antwerp	Kerstconcert 'Op weg naar morgen' voor Cliniclowns	03 11 1994
Ericsson	Brussels	Système de téléphone sans fil Freeset "Mains-libre" - Idéal pour l'utilisation en milieu industriel	30 09 1994

Europa Nostra	The Hague	EUROPA NOSTRA MEDAL OF HONOR AWARDED TO KENNETH V. PRICHARD JONES (UK)	s.d.
European Shippers' Councils	Brussels	COMMISSION DECISION WILL AID EXPORTS ON US MARKET	20 10 1994
First Alert	Brussels	FIRST ALERT LANCEERT DE EERSTE KOOLMONOXY-DEDETECTOR OP BATTERIJEN VOOR HUISHOUDELIJK GEBRUIK	04 10 1994
First Alert	Brussels	DE KOOLMONOXYDE DETECTOR VAN FIRST ALERT REDDE REEDS 600 LEVENS IN DE VERENIGDE STATEN - VANDAAG OOK TER BESCHIKKING VAN DE BELGEN	07 10 1994
Forum der Joodse Organisaties	Antwerp	NO TITLE	14 10 1994
Groepering der Havenbelangen van Antwerpen	Antwerp	Antwerpse Havendag in Lyon - De haven van Antwerpen verstevigt zijn banden met het cliënteel uit de streek Rhône-Alpes	04 10 1994
Groepering der Havenbelangen van Antwerpen	Antwerp	Antwerpen bezoekt klanten in Londen en Bristol	24 10 1994
Grote Routepaden	Antwerp	DE EUROPESE WANDELVERENIGING KOOS EEN NIEUWE PRESIDENT	s.d.
Hand in Hand	Puurs	Perskonferentie over de resultaten van de kampagne "Cordon Sanitaire" in de regio Klein-Brabant-Willebroek	28 09 1994

Handelshoge-school Antwerpen	Antwerp	ACADEMISCHE OPENING HANDELSHOGESCHOOL ANTWERPEN	27 09 1994
HBK	Antwerp	Studie over werknemersparticipatie	s.d.
HBK	Antwerp	Contrapunto Europeo - Vlaanderen/Castilië	23 09 1994
IGAO	Antwerp	Aardgas in de lift in Essen	09 11 1994
Immobiliën Hugo Ceusters	Gent	NIEUW GEBOUW VOOR BELGACOM DIENST KIJK- EN LUISTERGELD TE AALST	03 11 1994
Info Jeugd	Antwerp	Wegwijzer Rechtbank	s.d.
Integan	Hoboken	WORLD RADIO NETWORK - MONDIALE NIEUWSRADIO IN HET ANTWERPSE	04 10 1994
IVEG	Hoboken	IVEG HELPT ENERGIE BESPAREN EN ZORGT VOOR HET MILIEU	s.d.
IVEKA	Antwerp	ER ZIT ELEKTRICITEIT IN UW AFVAL - IGEAN EN IVEKA BOUWEN ELEKTRICITEITSCENTRALE OP STORTPLAATS	05 10 1994
Kamer van Koophandel en Nijverheid van Antwerpen	Antwerp	PLATO-MANAGER VERSTERKT STRATEGISCH PLAN REGIO ANTWERPEN	09 09 1994
Kamer van Koophandel en Nijverheid van Antwerpen	Antwerp	Kamers van Koophandel van Antwerpen en Rotterdam vragen de dringende herneming van het Vlaams-Nederlands overleg over de verdieping van de Schelde aan de nieuwe Nederlandse regering en de Vlaamse Minister-President L. Van den Brande	16 09 1994

Kamer van Koophandel en Nijverheid van Antwerpen	Antwerp	Kamer houdt opendeur Euro Info Centrum	14 10 1994
Kamer van Koophandel en Nijverheid van Antwerpen	Antwerp	Kamer reikt prijs voor eindverhandeling economie uit	03 11 1994
KIHA	Antwerp	Dirk Frimout op mozaïekkanaal	13 10 1994
Koen Mortelmans	Wommelgem	NO TITLE	07 10 1994
Koninklijk Ballet van Vlaanderen	Antwerp	KONINKLIJK BALLET VAN VLAANDEREN ENTHOUSIAST ONTHAALD IN BELFAST	10 11 1994
Koninlijk Ballet van Vlaanderen	Antwerp	KONINKLIJK BALLET VAN VLAANDEREN ENTHOUSIAST ONTHAALD IN CAIRO	10 10 1994
LBC-NVK	Antwerp	GEMEENSCHAPPELIJK FRONT GEHANDIKAPTENZORG STEUNT AKTIES GEBRUIKERSORGANISATIES	03 10 1994
Marc Van Peel	Antwerp	Oproepers eenheidslijst tevreden met Antwerpen 94	20 09 1994
MECC	Maastricht	MECC DESIGN AWARD VOOR BESTE ONTWERP VAN DE EUREGIO	08 09 1994
Monsanto	Antwerp	VEILIGHEIDS- EN GEZONDHEIDSBEHEER VAN MONSANTO ANTWERPEN BEHAALT KWALITEITSCERTIFICAAT	09 11 1994

NCMV	Mechelen	Boze NCMV-brief aan minister van Sociale Zaken De Galan - "De Galan verhoogt kosten arbeidsintensieve KMO"	16 09 1994
Patsy Sörensen	Antwerp	Reactie op advertentie van de VLD in de Gazet van Antwerpen van Zaterdag 17 september 1994	18 09 1994
PIDPA	Antwerp	PIDPA TEKENT VOOR NATUURBEHEER	10 10 1994
Pre-Text	Borgerhout	DUTSE "PROMS" PRIMA ONTHAALD - OVERROMPELING VOOR ANTWERPSE EDITIE 1995	27 10 1994
Provinciebestuur Antwerpen	Antwerp	Provinciebestuur van Antwerpen in de kijker	s.d.
Provinciebestuur Antwerpen	Antwerp	1.000 MOUNTAINBIKERS BEZETTEN PROVINCIAAL RECREATIECENTRUM DE SCHORRE TE BOOM - RUMST	09 09 1994
Provinciebestuur Antwerpen	Antwerp	De provincie Antwerpen verwelkomt haar bezoekers!	27 09 1994
Provinciebestuur Antwerpen	Antwerp	Provinciebestuur van Antwerpen is herfstanimator in de Provinciale dorreinen van Ranst, Retie, Mechelen, Deurne, Schoten en Heist-op-den-Berg	05 10 1994
Provinciebestuur Antwerpen	Antwerp	NO TITLE	21 10 1994
Provu	Antwerp	NO TITLE	16 09 1994
PVDA	Antwerp	Kalmthouts gemeentebestuur verwijdert PVDA-affiches van gemeenteli·ke borden!	29 09 1994
Recht op waardig sterven	Antwerp	Kiezer est recht op vrijwillige milde dood	21 10 1994

RUCA	Antwerp	STUDENTENKOOR UIT ROSTOCK TREEDT OP AAN RUCA	22 09 1994
RUCA	Antwerp	Samenwerkingsakkoord RUCA - GDANSK	19 10 1994
Solvay	Antwerp	CERTIFICATIE	07 09 1994
Stad Antwerpen	Antwerp	BLOEMENVANDALISME OP DE EIERMARKT	19 10 1994
Stad Antwerpen	Antwerp	BEZOEK BOEDHISTISCHE PRIESTER UIT JAPAN	15 11 1994
Stichting "Camille Huysmans"	Antwerp	Sociaal-Ekonomische Prijs "Stichting Camille Huysmans"	18 10 1994
Symantec	Leiden	SYMANTEC informeert en ondersteunt wereldwijd via Internet - Nieuwe Worldwide Web- en FTP-server biedt veelzijdige informatie gateway	09 11 1994
TNT/City-bike		TNT EXPRESS WORLDWIDE EN CITY-BIKE, EEN NIEU-WE TANDEM ONDER DE KOERIERSDIENSTEN - EEN MILIEUVRIENDELIJKE EXPRESS DISTRIBUTIEDIENST	23 09 1994
UFSIA	Antwerp	Samenwerking UFSIA en Universiteit Namen	s.d.
UIA	Antwerp	*NO TITLE*	10 10 1994
VBVB	Antwerp	*NO TITLE*	07 10 1994
Vlaams Blok	Antwerp	GEMEENTERAADSVERKIEZINGEN: VLAAMS BLOK NA BEDREIGINGEN TOEGANG TOT ZAAL ONTZEGD	14 09 1994
Vlaams Blok	Antwerp	Vlaams Blok laakt beslissing stadsbestuur om geen aanplakborden te plaatsen	16 09 1994

Vlaams Blok	Antwerp	*NO TITLE*	28 09 1994
Vlaams Blok	Antwerp	*NO TITLE*	04 10 1994
Vlaamse Esperantobond	Antwerp	JULES VERSTRAETEN GEHULDIGD IN ESPERANTO-CLUB	04 10 1994
Vlaamse Jeugdraad	Brussels	WECKX SCHAFT VLAAMSE JEUGDRAAD AF	06 10 1994
Vlaamse regering	Brussels	Incubatie- en innovatiecentrum Antwerpen wordt erkend en gesubsidieerd	09 11 1994
Voorpost	Antwerp	VOORPOST-ACTIE TEGEN AJOKAR	09 11 1994
Ward Beysen	Wilrijk	*NO TITLE*	24 10 1994
WOW	Antwerp	Koffie en gebak voor Seniorenstemmen - Met alle sinjoren, maar niet met de Senioren!	08 09 1994
WOW	Brasschaat	*NO TITLE*	07 11 1994
Zoo Antwerpen	Antwerp	NUBISCHE NETGIRAF GEBOREN	04 10 1994

BEL 20 corpus

BBL	Brussels	BBL zet AFV-aandelen om in aandelen met verlaagde roerende voorheffing	08 11 1994
BBL	Brussels	Prijsaanpassing Bancontact/Mister Cash - en Eurochequeservices	22 11 1994
BBL	Brussels	BBL Renta Fund opent 2 nieuwe compartimenten - BBL Renta Fund Obli-Fix 2003 - BBL Renta Fund Obli-Fix 2005	03 02 1995
BBL	Brussels	BANK BRUSSEL LAMBERT (ZWITSERLAND) N.V. - Netto-winst stijgt met 14 %	06 02 1995
BBL	Brussels	BBL-Prijs 1994	07 02 1995
BBL	Brussels	Batibouw: BBL verlaagt haar tarieven	17 02 1995
BBL	Brussels	Het bod van Konings op Lilac wordt onvoorwaardelijk	17 02 1995
BBL	Brussels	BBL lanceert BBL Top Lux	17 02 1995
BBL	Brussels	BBL Renta Fund opent twee nieuwe compartimenten - BBL Renta Fund Obli-fix 2000 - BBL Renta Fund Obli-fix 2000 Gulden	24 02 1995
BBL	Brussels	BBL lanceert achtergestelde certificaten op 6 en 8 jaar	24 02 1995
BBL	Brussels	Nieuwe stijging van de resultaten	03 03 1995
BBL	Brussels	BBL biedt een reserverekening voor zelfstandigen en KMO's aan: BBL Business Account	24 03 1995
BBL	Brussels	Overval BBL-Kantoor Londerzeel	30 03 1995
BBL	Brussels	Crédit Européen S.A. Luxembourg - Sterke stijging van de netto resultaat (+19,5%)	06 04 1995

BBL	Brussels	Daling van de rentevoeten	06 04 1995
BBL	Brussels	Nieuwe daling van de rentevoeten	07 04 1995
BBL	Brussels	JERRY VAN WATERSCHOOT NAAR STUDIEDIENST VAN BBL	14 04 1995
BBL	Brussels	GEWONE EN BUITENGEWONE ALGEMENE VERGADE-RINGEN	26 04 1995
BBL	Brussels	BBL TRAVEL: 1995 kondigt zich veelbelovend aan	27 04 1995
BBL	Brussels	BBL lanceert EVAL - een nieuw evaluatiesysteem voor beleg-gingsprodukten	11 05 1995
BBL	Brussels	BBL Invest: NIEUWE COMPARTIMENTEN ASIAN GROWTH EN HONG KONG & CHINA	31 05 1995
BBL - Generale Bank - Kre-dietbank	Brussels	*NO TITLE*	16 11 1994
Bekaert	Kortrijk	*NO TITLE*	20 10 1994
Bekaert	Kortrijk	*NO TITLE*	28 10 1994
Bekaert	Kortrijk	UITREIKING VAN DE TWEEJAARLIJKSE PRIJS N.V. BEKAERT S.A.	10 11 1994
Bekaert	Kortrijk	BEKAERT KENT DE VINCENT GAEREMYNCK AWARD TOE AAN FAGERSTA STAINLESS	18 11 1994
Bekaert	Kortrijk	*NO TITLE*	23 11 1994
Bekaert	Kortrijk	*NO TITLE*	26 01 1995
Bekaert	Kortrijk	RECORDWINST IN 1994 VOOR BEKAERT	16 03 1995
Bekaert	Kortrijk	SAMENWERKING TUSSEN BEKAERT EN SPALECK	13 07 1995

Bekaert	Kortrijk	BEKAERT VERHOOGT GECONSOLIDEERDE WINST EERSTE HELFT 1995 VOOR DE COURANTE OPERATIES MET MEER DAN 25 %	11 09 1995
Bekaert	Kortrijk	"BEKAERT-ZDB BOHUMIN S.R.O." - BELANGRIJKE SAMENWERKING TUSSEN BEKAERT EN ZDB IN DE TSJECHISCHE REPUBLIEK	18 09 1995
Bekaert	Kortrijk	BEKAERT IS VAN PLAN OM DE ACTIVITEIT "HANDELS-PRODUKTEN" VAN TREFILEUROPE OVER TE NEMEN	18 09 1995
Bekaert	Kortrijk	DELAWARE COMPUTING EN PKS ELECTRONICS GAAN SAMENWERKEN	26 09 1995
Bekaert	Kortrijk	BEKAERT-STANWICK N.V. NEEMT STORCK MANAGE-MENT CONSULTING N.V. OVER	18 10 1995
Bekaert	Kortrijk	BEKAERT KENT DE VINCENT GAEREMYNCK AWARD TOE AAN UGINE-SAVOIE	20 11 1995
Bekaert	Kortrijk	BEKAERTS NIEUWE ACTIVITEITEN GAAN INTERNATIO-NAAL	30 01 1996
Bekaert	Kortrijk	Bekaert increases profit from current operations for 1995 by 10%	21 03 1996
Bekaert	Kortrijk	Announcement	15 05 1996
Bekaert	Kortrijk	Bekaert-Stanwick obtains a major contract in Tunisia	14 06 1996
Bekaert	Kortrijk	Management buy-out at N.V. Werkhuizen Huwaert	28 06 1996
Bekaert	Kortrijk	Bekaert expands in South East Asia	03 07 1996
Bekaert	Kortrijk	First half year 1996 reporting Bekaert Group	11 09 1996
Bekaert	Kortrijk	Announcement	13 09 1996

Company	City	Title	Date
Bekaert	Kortrijk	Awarding of the Biennial N.V. Bekaert S.A. Prize	20 11 1996
Bekaert	Kortrijk	Structural profit improvement programme underway at Bekaert	16 12 1996
Bekaert	Kortrijk	Bekaert grants the Vincent Gaeremynck Award to Georgetown Steel Corporation	17 12 1996
CBR	Brussels	TOESTAND VAN DE GROEP CBR OP 30 JUNI 1994 EN VOORUITZICHTEN	15 09 1994
CBR	Brussels	*NO TITLE*	30 11 1994
CBR	Brussels	*NO TITLE*	09 02 1995
CMB	Brussels	RESULTATEN 1994	06 02 1995
Delhaize	Brussels	GECONSOLIDEERDE OMZET 1994: BEF 381 MILJARD	06 01 1995
Delhaize	Brussels	BOEKJAAR 1994: GECONSOLIDEERDE COURANTE RESULTATEN: + 65 % - NETTODIVIDEND: BEF 23, EEN STIJGING MET 15 %	31 03 1995
Delhaize	Brussels	Eerste semester 1995: omzet en geconsolideerde resultaten in stijging bij constante wisselkoersen	01 09 1995
Delhaize	Brussels	Groep Delhaize "De Leeuw" in 1995: Nieuwe groei in zijn 5 markten. Delhaize "De Leeuw" overschrijdt de kaap van BEF 100 miljard omzet in België.	05 01 1995
Delhaize	Brussels	1995: nieuwe stijging van de groep op haar 5 markten	29 03 1996
Delhaize	Brussels	FOOD LION, INC. SLUIT EEN AKKOORD AF BETREFFENDE DE OVERNAME VAN KASH N' KARRY FOOD STORES, INC. VOOR EEN BEDRAG VAN USD 341 MILJOEN	03 11 1996
Electrabel	Brussels	Werking van de kerncentrales over de maand september 1994	17 10 1994

Electrabel	Brussels	VLIEGENDE ONDERHOUDSPLOEG ELEKTRICITEITS-CENTRALES ELECTRABEL HOUDT OPENDEURDAG OP ZONDAG 27 NOVEMBER, VAN 14 TOT 18 h	21 11 1994
Electrabel	Brussels	AANKONDIGING NOODPLANOEFENING DOEL 1994	07 12 1994
Electrabel	Brussels	Werking van de kerncentrales over de maand november 1994	15 12 1994
Electrabel	Brussels	KNP LEYKAM EN ELECTRABEL ONDERTEKENEN INTENTIEVERKLARING VOOR INVESTERING IN WARM-TEKRACHTKOPPELING	13 02 1995
Electrabel	Brussels	Werking van de kerncentrales over de maand januari 1995	23 02 1995
Electrabel	Brussels	SLUITING OUDE ELEKTRICITEITSCENTRALE WATER-SCHEI	18 11 1995
Electrabel	Brussels	Werking van de kerncentrales over de maand oktober 1994	22 11 1995
Electrabel	Brussels	Werking van de kerncentrales over de maand december 1994	13 12 1995
Electrabel	Brussels	Noodplanoefening in Kerncentrale Doel is gestart	15 12 1995
Electrabel	Brussels	Noodplanoefening in Kerncentrale Doel is ten einde	15 12 1995
GB	Evere	*NO TITLE*	19 01 1994
GB	Brussels	*NO TITLE*	27 01 1994
GB	Brussels	*NO TITLE*	04 03 1994
GB	Brussels	*NO TITLE*	21 04 1994
GB	Brussels	PIERRE CARDIN PARFUMS TE KOOP BIJ GB	21 04 1994
GB	Brussels	GB BIEDT ZIJN KLANTEN DE KEUZE TUSSEN DE HER-BRUIKBARE PLASTIC FLES OF DE RECYCLEERBARE FLES	03 05 1994
GB	Brussels	*NO TITLE*	10 06 1994

Company	City	Title	Date
GB	Brussels	*NO TITLE*	10 06 1994
GB	Evere	GB OPENT EEN NIEUWE MAXI IN KORTRIJK	20 09 1994
GB	Brussels	Blokkering Distributiecentrum Kontich door staking Vleesfabriek	22 09 1994
GB	Brussels	Verklaring Direktie GB na bijeenroeping Verzoeningsbureau	23 09 1994
GB	Evere	*NO TITLE*	26 09 1994
GB	Brussels	Blokkade Distributiecentrum opgeheven - Direktie GB heeft persoonlijk onderhoud met werknemers - Vleeswarenfabriek opnieuw aan het werk	06 10 1994
GB	Brussels	GB verlaagt definitief 2400 prijzen	11 10 1994
GB	Brussels	GB en andere supermarkten moeten gelijk zijn voor de wet	02 12 1994
GB	Brussels	Oplossing conflict GB Oudergem	25 01 1995
GB	Brussels	EEN NIEUW CONCEPT VAN MAXI GB IN BELLE-ILE TE LUIK	22 03 1995
GB	Brussels	GB start samenwerking met QUELLE - Postorderverkoop	13 04 1995
GB	Brussels	GB RAADPLEEGT VERSCHILLENDE AGENTSCHAPPEN VOOR DE COMMUNICATIE VAN DE GB PRODUKTEN	26 04 1995
GB	Brussels	GB LANCEERT REVOLUTIONAIR VLOEIBAAR WASMIDDEL GB MICRO	08 05 1995
GB	Brussels	MET GB BIO VLEES WAARBORGT GB NOG BETER VOLKOMEN GEZOND RUNDVLEES	17 05 1995
Generale Bank	Brussels	De Generale bank lanceert een nieuw "G-Certificaat Achtergesteld" op 10 jaar	s.d.
Generale Bank	Brussels	Behoud van groei	06 09 1994
Generale Bank	Brussels	Stijging rentetarieven van kasbons bij de Generale Bank	13 09 1994

Generale Bank	Brussels	STIJGING RENTETARIEVEN VAN HYPOTHECAIRE LENINGEN BIJ DE GENERALE BANK	20 09 1994
Generale Bank	Brussels	G-RENTINFIX STELT TWEE NIEUWE COMPARTIMENTEN OPEN	14 10 1994
Generale Bank	Brussels	Omzetting van AFV1- en AFV2-aandelen in aandelen met verlaagde voorheffing	18 10 1994
Generale Bank	Brussels	Daling % kas, disconto & accept	18 10 1994
Generale Bank	Brussels	Stijging rentetarieven van kasbons bij de Generale Bank	27 10 1994
Generale Bank	Brussels	G-RENTINFIX STELT TWEE NIEUWE COMPARTIMENTEN OPEN	09 11 1994
Generale Bank	Brussels	De Generale Bank in China	25 11 1994
Generale Bank	Brussels	Daling rentetarieven van kasbons bij de Generale Bank	25 11 1994
Generale Bank	Brussels	Nieuwe tarieven voor Mister Cash/Bancontact en Eurochèque	30 11 1994
Generale Bank	Brussels	Generale Bank opent een nieuw vertegenwoordigingskantoor in Ho Chi Minh City	01 12 1994
Generale Bank	Brussels	G-RENTINFIX STELT EEN NIEUW COMPARTIMENT OPEN	07 12 1994
Generale Bank	Brussels	PRIJS GENERALE BANK 1994	16 12 1994
Generale Bank	Brussels	De Post kiest Generale Bank als bancaire partner	19 12 1994
Generale Bank	Brussels	G-RENTINFIX STELT DRIE NIEUWE COMPARTIMENTEN OPEN	27 01 1995
Generale Bank	Brussels	Een oplossing bij onverwachte kosten: de "SKIP"	17 02 1995
Generale Bank	Brussels	Hanoi: De Generale Bank ondertekent twee nieuwe kredietovereenkomsten	21 02 1995

Company	City	Title	Date
Generale Bank	Brussels	NIEUWE HYPOTHECAIRE RENTETARIEVEN BIJ DE GENERALE BANK	28 02 1995
Generale Bank - De Post	Brussels	ONDERTEKENING VAN HET AKKOORD TOT PARTNERSCHAP INZAKE DISTRIBUTIE TUSSEN DE POST EN DE GENERALE BANK	01 03 1995
Generale Bank	Brussels	Regelmatige groei van de nettowinst	07 03 1995
Generale Bank	Brussels	WIJZIGING BASISRENTEVOET KAS- & DISCONTOKREDIETEN	08 03 1995
Generale Maatschappij	Brussels	*NO TITLE*	19 12 1994
Kredietbank	Brussels	KB Renta uitgebreid met Lirarenta	27 10 1994
Kredietbank	Brussels	Kredietbank introduceert "kasbon op maat"	02 11 1994
Kredietbank	Brussels	KB opent in Taiwan "Kredietbank Taipei Branch"	15 11 1994
Kredietbank	Brussels	Kredietbank ondertekent kaderakkoord met Kazakstan	22 11 1994
Kredietbank	Brussels	Benoemingen aan de top van de Kredietbank	28 11 1994
Kredietbank	Brussels	KB brengt "ABC van de Verkeersveiligheid" uit, het eerste naslagwerk voor àlle weggebruikers	29 11 1994
Kredietbank	Brussels	Kredietbark start met nieuwe versie van haar imagocampagne	02 12 1994
Kredietbank	Brussels	Kredietbank verhoogt participatie in HSA Spaarbank	23 12 1994
Kredietbank	Brussels	Kredietbank biedt haar cliënten met een autoverzekering een gratis toemaatje	05 01 1995
Kredietbank	Brussels	Deense Unibank treedt toe tot IBOS-Associatie	16 01 1995
Kredietbank	Brussels	Wim Van Goethem laureaat van de Persfotowedstrijd Vlaanderen 1994	18 01 1995

Kredietbank	Brussels	Kredietbank neemt Spaarkrediet over	25 01 1995
Kredietbank	Brussels	Kredietbank sluit kaderakkoord met Zuidafrikaanse ABSA Bank Limited	31 01 1995
Kredietbank	Brussels	First Fidelity heeft als eerste VS-bank een samenwerkingsak-koord met de IBOS-Associatie ondertekend	15 02 1995
Kredietbank	Brussels	Kredietbank brent vastgoedbevek op de markt	01 03 1995
Kredietbank	Brussels	Kredietbank toont haar nieuwe Havenlaan-gebouw aan de pers	01 03 1995
Kredietbank	Brussels	Kredietbank introduceert risicoloze wereldbelegging 'World Best Invest 1' en 'Belgian Invest 1'	03 03 1995
Kredietbank	Brussels	Ammonieten - Speuren naar het ammonietdier	10 03 1995
Kredietbank	Brussels	WINST VAN KREDIETBANK STIJGT MET 7,4 %	16 03 1995
Kredietbank	Brussels	Zweedse bank treedt toe tot Inter-Alpha Bankengroep	28 03 1995
Kredietbank	Brussels	Kredietbank: een van de eerste Belgische banken op Internet	31 03 1995
Kredietbank	Brussels	Nieuwe benoemingen in de Kredietbank	18 04 1995
Kredietbank	Brussels	Van Dyck op bezoek in het Rockoxhuis	21 04 1995
Kredietbank	Brussels	De Kredietbank investeert in de Tsjechische Republiek	24 04 1995
Kredietbank	Brussels	De Kredietbank nu ook in Warschau aanwezig	26 04 1995
Kredietbank	Brussels	Marc Santens, voorzitter Raad van Bestuur Kredietbank: "Desin-termediatie neemt alsmaar toe in de Belgische financiële sector, maar onze kredietinstellingen vervullen daarin een sleutelfunc-tie."	27 04 1995
Kredietbank	Brussels	De Kredietbank participeert in Zuidamerikaanse bank voor han-delsfinanciering	11 05 1995

Kredietbank	Brussels	Uitbreiding van het thesaurieprogramma voor de Vlaamse Gemeenschap	15 05 1995
Kredietbank	Brussels	Kredietbank lanceert KB Fixobli, een fixfonds met een gegaran-deerd rendement	30 05 1995
Kredietbank	Brussels	Kredietbank opent twee nieuwe compartimenten in KB Equisafe: Belgium Invest 2 en Belgium Flexinvest 1	12 06 1995
Kredietbank	Brussels	Istituto Bancario San Paolo di Torino treedt toe tot IBOS-Associatie	27 06 1995
Kredietbank	Brussels	Linnig hertoren - Het restauratieproject "Linnig-aquarellen" van het Museum Vleeshuis	29 06 1995
Kredietbank	Brussels	KB-woningkrediet wordt goedkoper	28 07 1995
Kredietbank	Brussels	Benoeming aan de top van de Kredietbank	31 07 1995
Kredietbank	Brussels	Kredietbank opent vestiging in Hulst "Het mooie effect"	09 08 1995
Kredietbank	Brussels		24 08 1995
Kredietbank	Brussels	Europese richtlijn voor grensoverschrijdend betalingsverkeer	29 08 1995
Kredietbank	Brussels	Antwerpen is poort tot Europa - Kamer van Koophandel en Nij-verheid van Antwerpen geeft unieke brochure uit	30 08 1995
Kredietbank	Brussels	Kredietbank breidt KB Multi Cash uit met drie compartimenten: ECU, ITL en Short Medium CAD	01 09 1995
Kredietbank	Brussels	Kredietbank vertoont continue groei	21 09 1995
Kredietbank	Brussels	ING Bank treedt toe tot IBOS-Associatie	25 09 1995
Kredietbank	Brussels	Kredietbank sluit kaderakkoord met Turkmenistan	26 09 1995
Kredietbank	Brussels	Kredietbank-Bankverein opent vestiging in Hamburg	27 09 1995
Kredietbank	Brussels	Kredietbank groepeert éénmuntsobligatiesicavs in KB RENTA	28 09 1995

Kredietbank	Brussels	Kredietbank International Finance NV kondigt Euro Medium Term Note-programma aan van 1.000.000.000 ECU	29 09 1995
Kredietbank	Brussels	Kredietbank krijgt hoge rating van Thomson BankWatch	02 10 1995
Kredietbank	Brussels	"KB Internationaal, handel drijven op de internationale snelweg"	05 10 1995
Kredietbank	Brussels	De Kredietbank en Omniver brengen een innovatie op de Belgische verzekeringsmarkt	09 10 1995
Kredietbank	Brussels	Kredietbank brent Maxibon Plus uit	11 10 1995
Kredietbank	Brussels	Kredietbank (Nederland) zet expansie voort met nieuw kantoor in Oostburg	13 10 1995
Kredietbank	Brussels	"Liever bij de Bank van hier"? - De Kredietbank houdt tevredenheidsonderzoek onder haar cliënten	16 10 1995
Kredietbank	Brussels	Kredietbank brengt vastgoedcertificaat "Antares" op de markt	26 10 1995
Kredietbank	Brussels	Kredietbank heeft hoogste rating van de Belgische grootbanken bij Standard & Poor's	31 10 1995
Kredietbank	Brussels	De Kredietbank verstevigt haar positie op de Chinese markt	02 11 1995
Kredietbank	Brussels	Kredietbank kan via EIB voor 2 miljard BEF krediet toestaan aan KMO's	03 11 1995
Kredietbank	Brussels	Retrospectieve Albert Poels - "Van eigenzinnige kubisme tot geronnen sierlijkheid"	03 11 1995
Kredietbank	Brussels	Chase wordt aandeelhouder van IBOS Ltd	07 11 1995
Kredietbank	Brussels	De Kredietbank nu ook vertegenwoordigd in Tunesië	21 11 1995
Kredietbank	Brussels	Kredietbank (Nederland) zet expansie voort met nieuw bedrijvenkantoor in Utrecht	24 11 1995
Kredietbank	Brussels	Kredietbank heeft goed nieuws voor de beleggers in KBP Security Click USA 1!	30 11 1995

Kredietbank	Brussels	De Kredietbank breidt haar bevek KB Horizon uit met nieuw compartiment	01 12 1995
Kredietbank	Brussels	Kredietbank kan van EIB voor 2 miljard BEF krediet geven aan KMO's	14 12 1995
Kredietbank	Brussels	De Kredietbank verstevigt haar positie op de Braziliaanse markt	15 12 1995
Kredietbank	Brussels	Asia-Pacific: belangrijke groeimarkt voor de Kredietbank	19 12 1995
Kredietbank	Brussels	De Kredietbank breidt haar bevek KBP Security Click uit met twee nieuwe compartimenten	03 01 1996
Kredietbank	Brussels	Persfotowedstrijd Vlaanderen 1995: 70 jaar Antwerpse fotopers	12 01 1996
Kredietbank	Brussels	Kredietbank verwerft definitief meerderheid in Bank van Roese-lare	17 02 1996
Kredietbank	Brussels	Kredietbank-vertegenwoordiging in Tunis officieel geopend	31 01 1996
Kredietbank	Brussels	Benoeming bij de Kredietbank	02 02 1996
Kredietbank	Brussels	Kredietbank (Nederland) NV vestigt een bedrijvenkantoor in Arnhem	05 02 1996
Kredietbank	Brussels	First Union treedt toe tot IBOS-Associatie	12 02 1996
Kredietbank	Brussels	De Kredietbank investeert in Polen	14 02 1996
Kredietbank	Brussels	Beleidsstructuur van de Kredietbank aangepast: accent op dienst-verlening aan cliënteel	14 02 1996
Kredietbank	Brussels	Kredietbank biedt kandidaat-bouwers/kopers voortaan maximale rentezekerheid met "KB-Woningkrediet met eenrichtingstarief"	15 02 1996
Kredietbank	Brussels	Benoemingen bij de Kredietbank	16 02 1996
Kredietbank	Brussels	Benoemingen bij de Kredietbank	23 02 1996

Kredietbank	Brussels	Bod van de Kredietbank op de Bank van Roeselare succesvol afgesloten	26 02 1996
Kredietbank	Brussels	Tentoonstelling "Mysterieuze Horlogerie" - Uit de verzameling van het Horlogerie-museum in Mechelen	08 03 1996
Kredietbank	Brussels	Spaarkrediet en HSA fusioneren	11 03 1996
Kredietbank	Brussels	Winst van de Kredietbank stijgt met 10% - aansprakelijk vermogen overschrijdt BEF 200 miljard	14 03 1996
Kredietbank	Brussels	Kredietbank bekroont origineelste Leuvens studentenkot	28 03 1996
Kredietbank	Brussels	Kredietbank breidt uit aan de Havenlaan	02 04 1996
Kredietbank	Brussels	Kredietbank opent eerste volwaardige "Kantoor van de toekomst" in Lummen	03 04 1996
Kredietbank	Brussels	Kredietbank verder actief in Indiase groeimarkt	17 04 1996
Kredietbank	Brussels	Nieuwe benoemingen bij HSA	23 04 1996
Kredietbank	Brussels	Proton-kaart opladen kan nu ook via KB-Matic	07 06 1996
Kredietbank	Brussels	Tentoonstelling John Michaux	10 06 1996
Kredietbank	Brussels	De Kredietbank breidt verder uit in Centraal-Europa	02 07 1996
Kredietbank	Brussels	Kredietbank vertoont verdere groei van activiteiten en resultaten	12 09 1996
Kredietbank	Brussels	Tentoonstelling "Antwerpen, Antwerpenaren in het beeldverhaal"	12 09 1996
Kredietbank	Brussels	Europese Ondernemingsraad opgericht in de Kredietbank	19 09 1996
Kredietbank	Brussels	Kredietbank opent "Offshore Banking Unit" op de Filipijnen en vertegenwoordigingskantoor in Indonesië	04 10 1996
Kredietbank	Brussels	Kredietbank maakt evaluatie van vijf jaar assurantiebedrijf	09 10 1996

Kredietbank	Brussels	Kredietbank biedt kandidaat-bouwers/kopers nieuwe formules woningkrediet	16 10 1996
Kredietbank	Brussels	Kredietbank krijgt vergunning tot openen van een branch in Sjanghai, Volksrepubliek China	04 12 1996
Kredietbank	Brussels	Kredietbank maakt grensoverschrijdend betalingsverkeer transparanter en goedkoper	04 12 1996
Kredietbank - Almanij	Antwerp	GOEDE RESULTAATSONTWIKKELING BIJ ALMANIJ	10 05 1995
Kredietbank - Almanij	Antwerp	ALMANIJ NV: GUNSTIGE VOORUITZICHTEN VOOR BOEKJAAR 1995	12 09 1995
Kredietbank - Almanij	Antwerp	Goede resultaatsontwikkeling bij Almanij	30 04 1996
Kredietbank - Almanij	Antwerp	Almanij N.V.: gunstige vooruitzichten voor boekjaar 1996	17 09 1996
Kredietbank - Almanij-Fidelitas	Antwerp	Prof. Theo Peeters volgt de Heer Guy-J. Kreutsch op aan het hoofd van Fidelitas	04 10 1995
Kredietbank - Fidisco	Brussels	Fidisco verhoogt winst, eigen vermogen en solvabiliteit	12 04 1995
Kredietbank - Fidisco	Diegem	Fidisco voert productie spectaculair op	10 04 1996
Kredietbank - Fidisco	Diegem	Benoeming aan de top van Fidisco	11 06 1996
Kredietbank - Immolease	Brussels	Immolease verhoogt nettowinst met 12,7 % in 1994	20 04 1995
Kredietbank - Immolease	Brussels	Immolease vertoont ononderbroken groei	19 04 1996

Kredietbank - Krefima	Antwerp	Krefima boekt mooie winststijging	27 03 1995
Kredietbank - Krefima	Antwerp	Krefima: exploitatieresultaat 1995 stijgt met 45% ondanks moeilijke marktomstandigheden	28 03 1996
NESA	Louvain-la-Neuve	NESA RIJFT BELANGRIJK CONTRACT IN NEDERLAND BINNEN	09 12 1994
Petrofina		NO TITLE	29 03 1995
Petrofina - Montedison		NO TITLE	24 02 1995
Sogem	Brussels	NO TITLE	20 10 1995
Sogem	Brussels	NO TITLE	20 10 1995
Sogem	Brussels	SOGEM WORDT EXCLUSIEF AGENT VAN THAI COPPER INDUSTRIES VOOR DE BEVOORRADING VAN HAAR NIEUWE RAFFINADERIJ	25 10 1995
Sogem	Brussels	SOGEM, EXCLUSIVE AGENT FOR THE SUPPLY OF COPPER CONCENTRATES TO THAI COPPER INDUSTRIES	25 10 1995
Sogem	Brussels	CAWSE NICKEL PROJECT	19 12 1996
Sogem	Brussels	CAWSE NIKKELPROJECT	19 12 1996
UCB	Brussels	UCB: stijging van de courante resultaten met 21 %	28 07 1994
UCB	Brussels	UCB: aankoop van een farmaceutisch bedrijf in de Verenigde Staten	16 09 1994
UCB	Brussels	UCB: inhuldiging van Rodleben Pharma	05 10 1994
UCB	Brussels	UCB: ontwikkelingen in de Verenigde Staten	11 10 1994

Company	Title	City	Date
UCB	UCB: VOORSCHOT OP DIVIDEND - BELANGRIJKE INVESTERINGS- EN RESEARCHPROGRAMMA'S VOOR 1995	Brussels	15 12 1994
UCB	UCB laat dochtermaatschappij UCB Ftal over aan de groep Sisas	Brussels	13 01 1995
UCB	UCB in 1994: belangrijke verhoging van de courante winst	Brussels	16 02 1995
UCB	UCB: cetirizine (Zyrtec) kreeg vanwege de Verenigde Staten een "approvable letter"	Brussels	22 02 1995
UCB	UCB-Groep: sterke stijging van de courante resultaten	Brussels	10 04 1995
UM Engineering	UM Engineering werkt mee aan de uitbreiding van een zinkfabriek	Louvain-la-Neuve	05 10 1995
UM Engineering	UM Engineering, partner in the expansion of a zinc plant	Louvain-la-Neuve	05 10 1995
Union Minière	NO TITLE	Brussels	09 11 1994
Union Minière	AMMEBERG MINING CORPORATION - OPENBAAR BOD TOT HET VERWERVEN VAN AANDELEN	Brussels	22 11 1994
Union Minière	NO TITLE	Brussels	13 12 1994
Union Minière	NO TITLE	Brussels	14 02 1995
Union Minière	Winst uit de gewone bedrijfsuitoefening in 1994 geraamd op 1 miljard Belgische frank - Naar een licht positief geconsolideerd nettoresultaat	Brussels	23 02 1995
Union Minière	NO TITLE	Brussels	23 03 1995
Union Minière	NO TITLE	Brussels	23 03 1995
Union Minière	NO TITLE	Brussels	05 07 1995
Union Minière	NO TITLE	Brussels	05 07 1995

Union Minière	Brussels	UNION MINIERE SELLS ITS SWEDISH MINE TO NORTH (AUSTRALIA)	24 08 1995
Union Minière	Brussels	UNION MINIERE VERKOOPT HAAR ZWEEDSE MIJN AAN NORTH (AUSTRALIE)	24 08 1995
Union Minière	Brussels	NO TITLE	08 09 1995
Union Minière	Brussels	NO TITLE	08 09 1995
Union Minière	Brussels	RESULTS OF THE UNION MINIERE GROUP AT JUNE 30, 1995, AND FUTURE PROSPECTS - THE CURRENT RESULT HAS MORE THAN DOUBLED	18 09 1995
Union Minière	Brussels	RESULTATEN VAN DE UNION MINIERE GROEP OP 30 JUNI 1995 EN VOORUITZICHTEN - RESULTAAT UIT DE GEWONE BEDRIJFSUITOEFENING MEER DAN VERDUBBELD	18 09 1995
Union Minière	Brussels	NIEUW INDUSTRIEEL PLAN VOOR UNION MINIERE - 22 MILJARD INVESTERINGEN OM EEN LEIDERSPOSITIE UIT TE BOUWEN	27 10 1995
Union Minière	Brussels	UNION MINIERE'S NEW INDUSTRIAL PLAN 22 BILLION IN INVESTMENTS TO BECOME THE LEADER IN ITS FIELD	27 10 1995
Union Minière	Brussels	NO TITLE	31 10 1995
Union Minière	Brussels	NO TITLE	31 10 1995
Union Minière, Centrale der metaalbewerkers in België, ACV-Metaal, ACLVB	Brussels	SOCIALE BEGELEIDINGSMAATREGELEN VAN HET INDUSTRIEEL PLAN UNION MINIERE 1996-1998	27 11 1995

Union Minière, Centrale der metaalbewerkers van België, ACV-Metaal, ACLVB	Brussels	UNION MINIERE 1996-1998 INDUSTRIAL PLAN - SOCIAL MEASURES FOR STAFF	27 11 1995
Union Minière, Non Ferrous International	Brussels	Union Minière neemt een deelneming van 19,9% in het kapitaal van Non Ferrous International	12 01 1996
Union Minière, Non Ferrous International	Brussels	Union Minière has acquired a 19.9% stake in Non Ferrous International	12 01 1996
Union Minière	Brussels	UNION MINIERE VERWERFT 10% VAN DE AANDELEN IN EEN NIEUWE KOPERSMELTER EN -RAFFINADERIJ IN THAILAND	30 01 1996
Union Minière	Brussels	UNION MINIERE ACQUIRES A 10% STAKE IN A NEW COPPER SMELTER AND REFINERY IN THAILAND	01 02 1996
Union Minière	Brussels	UM establishes Cobalt Joint venture in China	09 02 1996
Union Minière	Brussels	UM richt kobaltpartnerschap op in China	09 02 1996
Union Minière	Brussels	UM incorporates additional activities in newly renamed Business Unit Cobalt & Energy Products	09 02 1996
Union Minière	Brussels	UM hergroepeert aantal activiteiten in haar nieuwe Business Unit Cobalt & Energy Products	09 02 1996
Union Minière	Brussels	Message of the Chief Executive Officer of Union Minière - Significant improvement of the current profit	01 03 1996
Union Minière	Brussels	Boodschap van de gedelegeerd bestuurder van Union Minière -	01 03 1996

Union Minière	Brussels	Gevoelige verbetering van de winst uit de gewone bedrijfsuit-oefening voor boekjaar 1995	21 03 1996
Union Minière	Brussels	Significant improvement in current profit	21 03 1996
Union Minière	Brussels	Gevoelige verbetering van de winst uit de gewone bedrijfsuit-oefening voor boekjaar 1995	17 09 1996
Union Minière	Brussels	Resultaten van de Union Minière Groep op 30 juni 1996 en vooruitzichten	17 09 1996
Union Minière	Brussels	Union Minière Group results at 30 June 1996, and future prospects	17 09 1996
Union Minière	Brussels	UM Groep: akkoord over Europese ondernemingsraad	17 09 1996
Union Minière	Brussels	UM Group agreement on setting up a European works council	19 09 1996

Notes

Notes to the Preface

1. At the outset of her research on the Valdez oil spill, Tyler reports, she tried to get hold of Exxon's press releases and she requested interviews with Exxon's top executives. After that failed, she read Art Davidson's *In the Wake of the Exxon Valdez*, a book that she was sent by Exxon, and reviewed hundreds of U.S. newspaper and magazine articles as well as a number of documentary TV programmes. "Granted the lack of access to original sources, an exploration of the plethora of secondary materials available seemed warranted", Tyler concludes (1992: 150).

2. In a letter to the editor of the *New York Times* on 21 February 1990, almost one year after the tragic oil spill in Alaska, Exxon's fiercely criticized chairman Larry Rawl admitted that
   Yes, there are things we could have done differently - including the job of communicating our efforts to the media and explaining ourselves to the public.

3. Cf. Schegloff (1988/89: 216) on Dan Rather's famous interview with George Bush.

4. Moore compares transcripts of tape-recorded conversations between the shuttle programme managers with testimonies to the Presidential Commission on the accident and suggests that the shuttle programme managers should have been more direct in telling NASA officials that the Challenger was unsafe to launch.

5. Based on the black-box recording of cockpit conversations, it is concluded that the co-pilot repeatedly tried to call the captain's attention to the dangerous weather conditions, but did not directly say that they should abort the take off, "with unspeakably tragic results" (93). Cf. also Linde (1988) on discourse failure in this and seven more aviation accidents and Cushing's (1994) *Fatal Words*.

6. On the other hand, it should be borne in mind that, as I have suggested, the series of Exxon press releases about the Valdez oil spill provides interesting data of how, over a longer period of time, a single organization was trying to manage the news on a single issue. That is why, even if they are not the central focus of my analysis, the Valdez press releases are concentrated on in the case study at the end, in chapter 7: viz. to try and see if in the Valdez press releases I can bring out more clearly what is at work in the much larger, more varied overall corpus that I have assembled and, also, to point out some of the patterns in the development of Exxon's communicative efforts.

7.   For a full description of the corpus see the appendix.

8.   Although I am aware that 'retelling' in English may have the implication of using one's own, different words, I shall use the term throughout this book to refer to the ideal of verbatim transmission.

9.   For some of the difficulties in comparing press releases and news reports, see Bernaers (1995) and Riksen (1996) as well as my own analysis (reported in Bernaers, Jacobs and Van Waes 1996) juxtaposing the headlines of 120 press releases issued by major Belgian business organizations with those of newspaper reports based on those press releases in two of the country's leading Dutch-language business newspapers *De Financieel-Ekonomische Tijd* and *De Standaard*.

10. See chapter 1 for a closer inspection of this terminology.

11. Note that Briggs and Bauman (1992) seem to allow for this latter possibility when they talk about the "transferability of genres from their primary situational contexts of use to other speech events" as well as "the differential mobilization of particular genres in a range of events" (142).

     Also, in listing a number of procedures for social control, Foucault (1984) says that there are discourses "which give rise to (...) new speech acts" , "which, over and above their formulation, (...) are to be said again" (115).

12. See chapter 1 for more details on method.

13. See, for example, Scollon (1998) for a recent social-interactionist perspective on the news as mediation.

Notes to Chapter 1

1.   Following Renkema's view that most institutional discourse is meant to enlarge its own domain (1993: 46-7), press releases could be considered an inroad into the news domain from various other domains, including business and politics.

2.   Apart from Drew and Heritage (1992), recent CA studies in this domain include readers edited by Boden and Zimmerman (1991), Ten Have and Psathas (1995) and Firth (1995) as well as Boden's (1994) full-length study of business talk and Drew and Sorjonen's (1997) survey article.

3.   My own work on press releases deals of course with the news. Later on in this chapter I shall provide a summary of some of the major developments in this field.

4.   For related research in French see, among others, Catherine Kerbrat-Orecchioni and Jean-Baptiste Marcellesi.

5.   It should now be clear from this selected survey that CA's share in opening up this field, though by no means unimportant, is relatively limited. Significantly, even a lot of the interactional work in this area, in particular on classroom conversation, is

to be situated outside of the research perspective of Conversation Analysis (Hymes, Bernstein, Mehan).

6. Cf. Wittgenstein's view of 'language games' and the notion of 'activity type' developed by Levinson (1979), Gumperz (1982, 1992) and Goodwin and Goodwin (1992).

7. Cf. Atkinson and Heritage (1984: 6).

8. Cf. Cicourel 1992.

9. Note that Levinson (1979) seems to take the Co-operative Principle for granted when he argues that "there could be some quite interesting relations between Grice's maxims and different kinds of activities, of a sort where some of the maxims are selectively relaxed to varying degrees in activities of specific types" (375). Similarly, in Sperber and Wilson's view, questions of style are simply about to what extent the speaker thinks he or she has to help the hearer in recovering contextual assumptions (1986). From a systemic-functionalist perspective, finally, Thompson and Thetela look at whether the language of advertising is organized to help readers or, alternatively, to manage them (1995).

10. The difference between the two variants is dealt with in chapter 6.

11. Cf. also so-called 'dress rehearsals' at the opening of job interviews, where the identity details of the candidate are established orally, despite the fact that all members of the panel have the candidate's CV in front of them and are supposed to be familiar with what is in it.

12. I am aware that my use of the term explicitness is by no means unproblematic. As it is, explicitness on one point invariably serves to obscure implicitness on another. In (2), for example, Union Minière's long corporate profile says hardly anything about its colonial roots.

13. John Gumperz, for example, stresses that context is not the same as the 'outside world' or the 'social episode'. In his view, 'activities' should be distinguished from 'events': they are no simple "stretches of interaction bounded in time and space"; instead, they are "members', and for that matter also analysts', constructs with respect to which the interaction is managed and interpreted" (1992: 44).

14. Cf. also Moerman (1988), who, from within Conversation Analysis, asserts the necessity of using transcript-extrinsic information and calls for the combination of ethnographic data about contexts and ethnomethodological data in what he labels "Culturally Contexted Conversation Analysis":

> But our events are human events, events of meaning. Their description, explication, and analysis requires a synthesis of ethnography - with its concern for context, meaning, history, and intention - with the sometimes arid and always exacting techniques that conversation analysis offers for locating culture *in situ* (xi).

In a recent paper Tom Koole (1997) tries to reconcile the CA notion of participants' own accomplishment with that of institutional knowledge prestructuring discourse and concludes that an inductive analysis should be supplemented by ethnographic information.

15. Note that a similar starting-point is characteristic of systemic-functionalism (Eggins 1994).

16. Clearly, no unidirectional view of adaptation is intended here, with text determined by context and not the other way round.

17. Cf. also the new genre of video releases.

18. Cf. recent studies by Bernaers, Jacobs and Van Waes (1996) and Riksen (1996).

19. Such signalling devices may seem superfluous. It has been brought to my attention, however, that in one - surely rather exceptional - case, a local newspaper retold a press release verbatim, including the labels "press release" and "end of press release", as well as the full notes for journalists at the end.

20. But see Auer (1992) who claims that such explicit statements of intent as in the cover letters from my corpus do not qualify as real contextualization cues.

21. That a lot of press releases have no cover letters to instruct the journalists what to do with them even seems to confirm Sacks's (1992b) claim that "[t]he sheer telling of a story is something in which one makes a claim for its tellability" (12).

22. In using this term I do not want to suggest that press releases' complex 'communicative ends' described above are simply a function of different audiences. As I have argued, getting media coverage is only a means to serving business, political, etc. interests.

23. M.M. Bakhtin, V.N. Voloshinov, P.M. Medvedev and others gathered in Leningrad in the 1920s. It has been argued that Bakhtin is the author of some of the texts attributed to the others. In this study I shall draw especially from Bakhtin's "Discourse in the novel" (in *The Dialogic Imagination*, 1935/1981) "Discourse in Dostoevsky" (in *Problems of Dostoevsky's Poetics*, 1929/1984) and "Speech Genres" (in *Speech genres and other late essays*, 1953/1986) and from Voloshinov's *Marxism and the Philosophy of Language* (1929/1973). I do not enter into the dispute of the authorship of the texts, though.

24. Kerbrat-Orecchioni (1997) argues that the mistaken association of dialogue with interaction between two participants - and not more than two - is owing to the confusion between the Greek prefixes 'dia-' (through) and 'di-' (two).

25. Apart from drawing attention to the concept of 'dialogue' in writing, Bakhtin's reference to Dostoevsky's novels - some of which are notoriously long-winded - shows that his so-called 'utterances' are not restricted in size. Note also that a related use of Bakhtin's dialogism can be found in performance theory in anthropology, which looks at how a "given performance is tied to a number of speech events that precede and succeed it (past performances, readings of texts, negotiations, rehearsals, gossip, reports, critiques, subsequent performances, and the like)" (Bauman and Briggs 1990: 60). From still another perspective, Lynch and Bogen

provide a complex example of dialogue when they stress that Oliver North's and John Pointdexter's testimonies at the Iran-Contra hearings were

recorded, transcribed, summarized, quoted, and recycled again and again in news reports, on video clips, and in various official or unofficial histories of these events (...). Moreover, the interrogators and witnesses were surrounded by a desktop archive comprising several loose-leaf binders of committee exhibits and other writings prepared for the occasion (...). The questions and answers were undoubtedly rehearsed many times over before the hearings, both by the committee staff and by the witness's legal team (1996: 203-204).

26. That not everybody has yet been convinced of this should be clear from a recent paper by Schegloff in which he distinguishes between naturally occurring conversation, on the one hand, and all "other sorts of material than talk-in-interaction - written texts, monologues, talk or writing produced under experimental or quasi-experimental conditions, and the like", on the other hand. Although he admits that the latter need not be "unworthy of study", Schegloff seems to imply that they are bound to be much less interesting since, he claims, such interactional practices as recipient design, relevance to the interactional project at hand and parsing of just prior ·and projected sequence are "largely or totally absent" (1996: 468). For a critique see Jacobs (1997).

27. Cf. Lucy's (1993) *Reflexive Language* for a recent influential collection of articles on the subject.

28. I adopted a radically empirical technique of investigation, browsing through the corpus to try and find repeated occurrences of 'candidate phenomena'. As Sacks (1992a. 471) put it, "[t]he first rule is to learn to be interested in what it is you've got" (also Psathas 1990 on 'unmotivated looking', but see Edwards 1997 for a critique of unmotivated looking as implausibly naive).

29. Cf. also Paul Knippenberg's words quoted in (20) above.

30. Note that, as I suggested in the introduction to this book, Briggs and Bauman (1992: 156) mention metapragmatic framing in their list of strategies for manipulating intertextual gaps. In my analysis, I shall demonstrate how metapragmatics can bring press releases and news reports closer together.

31. Similarly, Scollon (1998) aims at extending the scope of interactional sociolinguistic analysis from conversation to mass communication: his central argument is that the social practices through which everyday interactions are constructed are also at work in the news.

32. That is why 'newsgathering' is a misleading term.

33. But see also, more recently, Ronald N. Jacobs (1996) for an ethnographic study of a local television news station, "Producing the news".

34. Note, however, that this availability through the media is fundamentally different from that in contexts of co-presence. In Thompson's words, mass communication is seen as a form of 'quasi-interaction'.

35. The term 'keying' is derived from Gregory Bateson's analysis of otters' play at fighting (1978).

36. To give just one example, in a classic study Lang and Lang (1971) point out that people who saw the 1951 MacArthur Day parade in Chicago on TV thought it was far more exciting than did observers along the parade route: while the cameras followed the action, the eyewitnesses in the street got only a brief glimpse of MacArthur as he passed by.

37. The term 'agenda-setting' was first used by McCombs and Shaw (1972), who asked undecided voters to identify key issues in the election campaign and subsequently correlated their answers to a hierarchy of media topics. Today's agenda-setting is, of course, a very complex, multi-layered process; Gandy (1982), for example, indicates that wire services like Associated Press or United Press International set the front page agendas of the national papers, while influential papers like the *Times* set the agenda for the networks.

38. The term 'news management' was first used by James Reston in 1955 in his testimony before a US congressional committee on government information. Schudson (1978) - with awkward precision - situates the start of news management at the Paris 1919 peace conference. As far as press releases are concerned, Cook (1989) says that while in the 1880s US presidents still thought granting interviews improper, members of Congress were "willing subjects. Many dropped by Newspaper Row, that section of 14th Street between Pennsylvania Avenue and F Street where most bureaus were located, and others went so far as to interview themselves, the first appearance of what are now known as press releases". In Cook's view, Representative Benjamin Butler was the first to send in such "lengthy self-prepared opinions" (20).

      Note that Cook (1989) and Bell (1991), among others, use the term 'newsmakers' for what I call 'news managers'.

39. Cf. Goffman on 'getting the first word in' (1974: 257).

40. Cf. Gans on the use of 'peer sources' (1979: 126) and Shoemaker and Reese on 'intermedia influences', i.e. the institutionalized practice of relying on other newspapers' reporting (1991: 101-104).

41. About the MacArthur Day parade mentioned above, Lang and Lang (1971) add that people in the street cheered, not because they were seeing MacArthur but because they were about to be on TV for the first time in their lives.

      Rather exceptionally, the media themselves may actively try to change the nature of events as when, during the ghetto disturbances, journalists were said to be urging people to throw stones for the benefit of the cameras (reported by Gans 1979: 124).

42. Cf. Baudrillard's apocalyptic vision of information blizzards: "Everything is destined to reappear as simulation. Landscapes as photography, women as the sexual scenario, thoughts as writing, terrorism as fashion and the media, events as television. *Things seem only to exist by virtue of this strange destiny.* You wonder

whether the world itself isn't just here to serve as advertising copy in some other world" (quoted in Keane 1991: 182; my italics).

43. This observation lies at the basis of the concept of 'preformulation', which will be introduced in chapter 2.

44. The term 'gatekeeping' was first applied to journalism by White (1950), who looked at how a wire editor on a small-city newspaper made use of the stories available to him.

45. Peltu coined the term when he denounced the media for not alerting the audience to public hazards (1988: 16).

46. The term was first used by Walter Lippmann in *Public Opinion* (1921). Similarly, Fairclough talks about the news as "control by consent" (1989: 37).

47. Tuchman (1978) sees the newsmaking business as an ally of various legitimated news managing institutions (e.g. because ministers have more access to the media).

48. That there has not been enough empirical research to address this question is clear from the disagreement about the simple question whether or not press releases get copied verbatim. Cook (1989), in a span of a couple of pages, mentions one source that "hundreds of press releases are sent to the media by members of Congress, and hundreds are run verbatim or with insignificant changes" (103) and another source that "[a] very small percentage of press releases ever gets reprinted, and relatively few form the basis for stories. In fact so few releases are used, one might ask whether their production is a waste of time" (108). Romano (1986) says that the practice of reprinting press releases was rather common in the past, but that current journalistic practice demands otherwise, except in matters of culture and entertainment. Bell (1991) points out that it is not unusual for press releases to get 'published' (largely) untouched. No empirical evidence is presented, though. Working on a small corpus of press releases issued by major Belgian business organizations, Bernaers (1995), finally, reports that no press releases got quoted verbatim.

49. For one thing, it should be borne in mind that the term news management is typical of liberal democratic countries and that even there some sources have more news managing power than others (Van Ginneken 1996).

Notes to Chapter 2

1. This chapter appears, in a slightly different form, as Jacobs (1999b).

2. I am aware, of course, that press releases may not just be meant to be retold in the papers but also in a wide range of other written as well as audio-visual modes of news reporting (cf. also chapter 1). Still, there is perhaps a sense in which press releases are the ideal vehicles for newspaper reporting since they involve the same medium. In the case of television, for example, the pressure on journalists to

complement press releases with other materials - in particular with recorded interviews - is much stronger.

3. See Clark and Carlson (1980) for an even more extensive list.

4. While some of the ideas presented in this research tradition are very far removed from what we find in the analysis of ordinary speech or functionally specialized writing, Ong's (1975) claim that writers often 'create within the message a context that the reader agrees to enter' is in some ways related to the concept of preformulation elaborated later in this chapter.

5. No doubt this is overstating the issue. Clark (1996), for example, demonstrates the complexity of communication in general, including everyday interaction.

6. Note that the term 'participation framework' is somewhat misleading since in Goffman's terminology it only refers to receiver and not producer roles. In contrast with Goffman's use of the term, I shall take 'participation' to include both producer and receiver roles.

7. I shall use the term 'participancy' - which is Levinson's (1988) - to refer to such ratified participation. In addition, from now on, I shall reserve the term 'participant' for ratified receivers (and producers).

8. In his textbook *Pragmatics* Levinson uses 'bystander' still differently, viz. as a cover term for what he calls, rather awkwardly, 'participants in audience role', i.e. presumably unaddressed participants (1.b), and for overhearers (2.a) (1983: 90).

9. Note that Levinson's componential approach has been criticized by Jenny Thomas, who proposes a prototype approach, which, unlike Levinson's scheme, allows for degrees of category membership, so that discourse roles are not hermetically sealed categories, but represent points on a continuum. In her view, this should provide an explanation for why interactants often imperceptibly slip role boundaries (1989).

10. It is, incidentally, the same notion of 'embedding' that Bell uses to define the special producer roles in news language and that accounts for the impact of press releases on today's journalism (cf. chapter 3).

11. There may be exceptions, though. On 6 January 1995 the Belgian Dutch-language newspaper *Het Nieuwsblad* published a full-size photograph of a press release issued by Flemish prime minister Van den Brande on its front page.

12. I shall argue later on that the handout quoted in (4) is no conventional press release in the sense that, unlike most others, it was not meant to be retold. This then would confirm absence of second-person reference to journalists as a typical feature of press releases.

13. Note, however, that not all newspaper readers need to be Heineken consumers (just as in extract (2) above not all newspaper readers will be interested in NIKON's latest model).

14. Note that the concepts of address and recipientship are closely related since, in Levinson's words, address may be marked by 'sheer singularity of possible *recipients*' (1988: 174; my italics).

15. Surely, it could be argued that, in the end, the information in this press release is also meant for h_2, just like that in all others, but that it is embargoed, thus safe-guarding the element of surprise in the wheelchair users' demonstration. The point I would like to make, however, is that, in its present form, the press release in (4), unlike - for example - the embargoed press release from Bekaert that I shall deal with in chapter 5, is not meant to be simply copied by journalists in their own news reporting.

16. I am aware that this representation may be too categorical. As I have pointed out, it serves to obscure that at least some interest from journalists is indispensable as well as glossing over those press releases that are meant for the journalists and not for the general public, as in (4).

17. In a study of the news the term 'mediator' is perhaps more appropriate.

18. Cf. for example Drew (1994) on silence in interaction.

19. See De Rycker (1987) on so-called 'turns at writing' for an interesting application of the principle of turn-taking to the organization of correspondence.

20. Note that Levinson (1988) makes a similar point about news interviews as well as about cross-examinations in court; alternatively, Lynch and Bogen (1996) show how, in the Iran-Contra hearings, Oliver North had been prohibited from delivering a speech to the mass TV audiences at home, but still, at various points, managed to do so, without being interrupted, because he packaged it as a reply to the attorney's question (118).

21. Note that Clark and Schaefer (1992) talk about 'overhearers' and I also used the term in the title of this section. In general I prefer to talk about 'non participants' because 'overhearers' implies co-presence or, at least - in Levinson's terminology (1988) - some form of channel-linkage. As I suggested above and as I shall demonstrate later in this chapter, no channel-linkage can be taken for granted here.

22. Goffman (1981) is aware of this possibility and talks about 'collusion' and 'innuendo' in this respect (134).

23. I shall argue later in this chapter that, since h_2 is not normally supposed to realize that the news is a retelling of a press release, there may also be an element of disguisement in press releases.

24. Alternatively, in case of concealment or disguisement, a speaker or writer might want to *exploit* such discrepancies.

25. This observation shows that categories like 'given' and 'new' cannot be safely conceived of without a prior analysis of receiver roles (cf. Ford and Fox 1996: 162).

26. Again a similar use has been observed in cross-examinations before a jury in court (cf. Levinson's extract from a rape trial quoted in the first chapter).

27. Cf. Scmino (1997) on the definite article as a signal of identifiability.

28. See chapter 3 for the related strategy of presupposition manipulation in the same press release.

29. Note that it is of course not the journalist only, but the complete complex newspaper hierarchy that plays a role here. However, such considerations, for example of editing routines, though by no means unimportant, fall outside the scope of this study.

    Also, retelling press releases is not a matter of all or nothing: journalists can decide to copy some parts of a press release while leaving out others, they may radically rewrite it or make further inquiries with the organization that issued it or with other parties involved, etc.

30. Note that such a special type of intermediary is not limited to press releases. Except for live TV or radio broadcasting, for example, all interviews have an element of power in them since it is the journalists who decide if and what parts of the interview will be further transmitted to their own audiences. I would like to suggest that most accounts of talk for overhearers have ignored this power of the intermediary so far.

31. Compare Keane (1991) who says that press conferences "are used to *project* the opinions" of whoever organizes them (102, my italics).

32. The terms 'speech event' and 'utterance event' are Levinson's (1988).

33. For example, in case a journalist fails to take up his or her producer role and decides not to 'publish' the press release, there is simply no second utterance event.

34. It is interesting to note in this respect that in Dutch the term 'persbericht' has the two meanings: a message issued by business organizations, political parties, etc., to the press (i.e. a press release) as well as a newspaper article, an item on the TV news, etc.

35. For a view of newspaper style as audience design, see Jucker (1992). The idea appears as early as Crystal and Davy (1969).

    Interestingly, Grunig (1984) sees accommodation as a central feature of public relations activities.

36. Shelby (1994), among others, argues that the market-oriented notions of effectiveness and efficiency should be supplemented by other, for example moral or aesthetic, criteria.

37. Once again I would like to stress that no unidirectional view of the impact of context on language use is intended here.

38. Note that since the secretary, in calling in Johnny, can use the same utterance as the doctor used to instruct the secretary, the doctor's utterance could be considered preformulated projected discourse.

39. Case studies of the role of self-reference in divided discourse cover a wide range of topics, including the reception of the German politician Jenninger's controversial parliamentary speech commemorating the *Reichskristallnacht* (Ensink 1992) and Austrian president and presidential candidate Waldheim's TV performance after he

had been accused of national-socialist sympathies (Gruber 1993a, b) as well as the rap singer Sister Souljah's alleged racist interview with the *Washington Post* (debate on the *Linguist List* described in Sanders 1994) and the CIA's internet pages (Connell and Galasinski 1996).

40. Bernaers (1995), in 82 newspaper articles based on press releases, found 8 references to the press release, like:

> *De G-Bank maakte dit gisteren via een persbericht bekend.*
> The G Bank announced this in a press release yesterday.

41. This is in contrast with another, very much related type of indirectly targeted discourse, viz. 'letters to the editor', where the horizons of the writer and the intermediary are not supposed to melt. Significantly, the difference with press releases is reflected in the fact that in letters to the editor the intermediary, viz. the newspaper editor, is referred to as 'you' (cf. Clark and Carlson 1982: 339, Morrison and Love 1996).

As for the difference between press releases and (direct) advertising it has been argued that communication is most effective when it looks unprepared, undesignated, not targeted. Walster and Festinger, for example, have shown that - in Goffman's terminology - bystanders are more easily persuaded by what they heard as eavesdroppers than as overhearers (referred to in Clark and Schaefer 1992: 271). In a somewhat different context, Lynch and Bogen (1996) report that at the Iran-Contra hearings electronic messages on the White House computer network were considered especially significant evidence because Oliver North and his colleagues had not realized that even when they 'deleted' the messages, they could not erase them permanently and backup copies were stored in - and later recovered from - the computer memory banks (210). James Lull, finally, argues that when media content is sponsored indirectly by elites, its 'ideological impact is magnified' if it is not easily recognized who it comes from (1995: 15). Note that this kind of benign deception through the use of press releases could be seen as disguisement. Then again, it should be borne in mind that here it is not the essence of the message that is hidden, just the communicative trajectory.

Notes to Chapter 3

1. This chapter appears, in a slightly different form, as Jacobs (1999a).

2. The term is derived from Panis's (1995) analysis of that other type of corporate disclosure discourse, viz. business organizations' annual reports (cf. also Lebar 1985).

3. Cf. Ducrot (1984) on 'producteur', 'locuteur' and 'énonciateur'.

4. Jucker (1995) says that in media discourse

> the concept of animator does not have a clear counterpart. (...) The final newspaper text may have started as a set of scribbled notes taken by a jour-

nalist during a press conference. After having been keyed into a computer it will have been worked on by the journalist, sub-editors, perhaps even the editor and the proofreaders (3; cf. also Bell (1991) - discussed below - on the role of the editor in newspaper reporting).

5. See Borstlap (1995) for a study of the collaborative writing process for press releases contracted to outside agencies. For my own purposes, the question whether press releases were produced in-house or not falls outside the scope of this study.

6. I take definite description to include all noun phrases with the definite article.

7. Note that in Dutch this use of third-person pro-forms for reference to the proper names of organizations may lead to inconsistency in terms of number and gender:

    (i)   (BSV, Antwerp: 9 September 1994)

De B[eweging voor] S[ociale] V[ernieuwing] is alleszins van plan haar kampagne naar de wijken verder te zetten en zal zijn vergadering met de buurt houden in (...).

The Movement for Social Innovation certainly intends to continue her campaign to the districts and will hold its meeting with the neighbourhood in (...).

    (ii) (WOW, Antwerp: 8 September 1994)

WOW rekent er echter op dat, nu ze voldoende bekend zijn bij de bevolking, zij ook hun stemmenaantal gevoelig zullen verhogen (...). WOW blijft erbij dat ze geen anti-politieke campagne zal voeren tegen de traditionele partijen (...).

WOW counts on it that, now they have grown sufficiently well-known with the population, they will also substantially increase their number of votes (...). WOW maintains that she will not hold an anti-political campaign against the traditional parties (...).

    (iii) (Bayer, Antwerp: 13 September 1994)

Bayer AG neemt via haar Amerikaanse dochtermaatschappij Miles Inc. de Noordamerikaanse activiteiten in niet-receptplichtige geneesmiddelen (OTC-Business) over van de firma Sterling Winthrop. (...)
Met deze acquisitie verruimt Bayer zijn pallet van receptvrije genees-middelen in de USA en Canada met een aantal bekende merken.

Via her American subsidiary Miles Inc. Bayer AG takes over the North American activities in medicines for which no recipes are obligatory (OTC-Business) from the Sterling Winthrop company. (...)
With this acquisition Bayer expands its range of recipe-free medicines in the USA and Canada with a number of well-known brands.

The confusion about pro-forms can be avoided through the use of the definite article, as in extract (7) above and in:

    (iv) (Vertongen, Puurs: s.d.)

VERTONGEN N.V. TERUG FAMILIEBEDRIJF
(...) Het bedrijf stelt zich de verdere ontwikkeling van de eigen produkten alsook de organisatie van een dealernet binnen Europa als één van de prioriteiten.

[VERTONGEN N.V. AGAIN A FAMILY BUSINESS
(...) The company considers the further development of (the) own
products as well as the organization of a dealer network within Europe as
one of the priorities.]

8. In English the use of 'one' for self-reference has been said to be sociolinguistically
    marked as royal or upper-class (Wales 1996: 82-83).

9. Quotations excepted (cf. chapter 5).

10. One way in which such referential switches seem to be accountable for in my corpus
    is that they frequently occur towards the end of press releases. Hence, they could
    point at an issue of 'finishing'. Alternatively, it looks as if in (31) the use of 'we'
    may serve to express trade union solidarity. For either suggestion, further research
    is necessary.

11. Surely, what may be a preferred way of handling self-reference in one commu-
    nicative genre may turn out to be dispreferred in another. As   I already pointed
    out in the introduction, however, any consideration of the genre concept falls
    outside the scope of this study. For a survey of relevant categories in the analysis of
    'culturally patterned speaking (or writing) practices' see, for example, Günthner and
    Knoblauch (1995).

12. Also think of the reference to journalists (h1) as 'you', discussed in chapter 1:
    (v)   (Aktiegroep rolstoelen en hulpmiddelen, Grimbergen, 26 September
          1994)
          *Deze aktie werd niet aangekondigd op de kabinetten. Wij vragen u te
          mogen rekenen op uw diskretie.*
          This action has not been announced at the ministers' offices. We ask you
          if we can count on your discretion.
    (vi) (Slough Estates, Sint-Stevens-Woluwe: 29 April 1994)
          Uw aanwezigheid op deze plechtigheid wordt zeer op prijsgesteld.
          Your presence at this ceremony is very much appreciated.

13. One explanation is that in film commentaries the basis of shared visual experience
    establishes a link between speaker (commentator) and hearer (viewer). I showed in
    chapter 2 that no such common ground can be assumed with press releases.

14. Interestingly, another feature of 'discours', according to Benveniste, is the use of
    quotation. I would argue that, strictly speaking, quotation is not in contrast with the
    definition of 'histoire' as objective reporting, though. On the contrary, Adamson
    (1995) says that embedding is one way of actually translating contextually anchored
    discourse
          When will Columbus accept that the earth is flat?
    into co-textually anchored discourse
          The king wondered when Columbus would accept that the earth was flat.
    Significantly, I shall argue in the next chapter that press releases, which - I have
    suggested - look like 'histoire', are also characterized by a high degree of such
    embedding.

Note that the connection between third-person self-reference and quotation is further suggested by Schegloff's claim that self-reference by proper name "can be understood as marking the utterance as a putative quote of what others might be saying among themselves" (1996: 444).

15. Auer (1988) addresses the same issue when he notes that, curiously, it is only lay interpreters who avoid first person pronouns in their translations and replace them by 'he said' or 'she said'. Here once again it is suggested that there is a link between the issue of self-reference and quotation.

16. This is not to say that proper names are always semantically neutral. Business organizations in particular have been known to change their names during merger operations or in the wake of public crises (cf. chapter 7 about the oil spill at Valdez, Alaska).

17. Cf. Wilson (1990) on the somewhat related notion of 'blocks', i.e. the repetition of the same reference form three or more times in the same syntactic position in consecutive sentences to stress key points, mark issues of contrast or add flavour (63, 73) and Clayman (1995) on the "formulaic nature of such formats, which endow an assertion with heightened emphasis and prominence" (132).

18. Cf., in contrast, Heritage and Watson (1979) on the use of pro-forms: "While the large range of pro-terms have a particular value in eliminating word repetition as a central tying device in conversation and hence generate large-scale interactional economies, the achievement of these economies necessitates considerable collaborative close-order inspectional work on the sequential placement of pro-terms so as to redress their indexicalities" (147).

19. Note that Lyons's term fits in nicely with Te Molder's (1995) claim that "improving communication is primarily a matter of improving empathetic capacities" (71). Cf. also Adamson (1994).

20. I am grateful to Stef Slembrouck for drawing my attention to this press release.

21. Jucker (1992) calls this a noun phrase name apposition.

22. The same goes for most pre-recorded TV and radio programmes.

23. Note, however, that, as Schudson (1986) points out, in the *New York Times* stories are written from the temporal viewpoint of the reporter, not the reader: "When the story says 'today', it means January 11, even though the story appears in the January 12 edition of the paper and readers read it on January 12". He adds that this use "signals [the Times's] professional and antipopulist stance" (97).

24. Note that in Dutch, unlike in English, the simple present tense can be used with a future reference.

25. Cf. also Maes (1991) who believes that writers and speakers employ "totally different" identification strategies (63).

26. Note that the typical forms of time deixis ("Thursday 23 February" instead of "today") and place deixis ("in Herzogenaurach" instead of "here") indicated above seem to play similar preformulating$_{ii}$ roles.

27. Note that, in Auer's view, the typical speech activities of displaced discourse include reporting. Significantly, this is one more hint at the relationship between third-person self-reference and quotation. Also, Auer notes that displacedness is a "matter of degree" (1988: 269), which allows for the fact that some occurrences of 'we', 'today', 'here', etc. can be found in my corpus of press releases after all.

One difference between displaced discourse and press releases is that displaced discourse is 'empractic', i.e. it has no purpose other than the discourse itself and it is responded to by more discourse only. As for press releases, since they are meant to be retold, it could be argued that it is their very purpose to be responded to by more (of the same) discourse.

28. Cf. Van Leeuwen (1996b) on framing as decontextualization. Interestingly, Schegloff uses Auer's terminology when he says that while the 'absolutism' of proper names might seem to set them in contrast with deictics whose usability depends on the context, in the end they are equally "situated" (1996: 478).

29. This seems to echo Allerton's (1996) remarks referred to earlier in this chapter. Note also that Jones refers to Bakhtin's and Voloshinov's stress on genre and on the impact of the other.

30. Cf. John B. Thompson (1995: 92-93) introduces the term 'space-time interpolation' to describe how film audiences temporarily forget about their own lives and go on a mental journey to meet the people they see on the screen.

31. This translation is taken from the corresponding English press release issued by Union Minière.

32. Note that such patterns of agency have of course been elaborately investigated in the research tradition of critical linguistics and critical discourse analysis.

33. In this context the choice for 'Vlaams Blok' as the name of the organization may seem rather unfortunate, except of course that there is also a sense in which they want to radically distinguish themselves from the "traditionele partijen" [the traditional parties] (16 September 1994).

34. It could be argued that even in the relatively innocent example quoted above

> Mother saying to father, in the presence of little Billie: Can Billie have an ice-cream, Daddy? (Levinson 1983: 82)

Billie's father is presented as the one who controls the money for icecreams. In my data, a more drastic, but equally inconspicuous non-identificational effect is to be found in the simple reference to 'Exxon' carrying all the connotations of big business power.

35. Dealing with the same phenomenon, Lambrecht (1994) distinguishes between logical (or semantic) presuppositions and pragmatic presuppositions. In Karttunen's example, then, that parents should not bring their kids along is logically - but not pragmatically - presupposed.

36. Another source of less-than-helpful preformulation is simply in the wording. The following title of a press release introduces a rise in the prices of the bank's services as a 'price adjustment':

(vii) (BBL, Brussels, 22 November 1994)

Prijsaanpassing Bancontact/Mister Cash - en Eurochequeservices

Price adjustment Bancontact/Mister Cash - and Eurocheque services

Such patterns of 'overlexicalization' (popular in critical linguistics, cf. Fowler and Kress 1979) are of course beyond the scope of my research.

Notes to Chapter 4

1. Note that such contempt for what the source really said is by no means restricted to self-quotation in press releases and can, perhaps somewhat surprisingly, also be found in the quoting practices of newspaper language. Caldas-Coulthard (1994), for example, looks at the crime pages of a local newspaper and compares two "almost exactly the same" quotations attributed to different policemen at different occasions. She cautiously suggests that "the reporter (...) may have created (...) sayings that the two policemen did not actually produce" (301).

2. Cf. Molotch and Lester's (1974) definition of 'routine events'.

3. The Kredietbank's quotation of what chairman of the IBOS banking association Charles de Croisset said in (6), (7) and (8) can also be mentioned here.

4. Voloshinov (1973: 128) already fiercely criticized this "mechanical, purely grammatical mode of translating reported speech from one pattern into another, without the appropriate stylistic reshaping" and said that it was "nothing but a bogus and highly objectionable way of manufacturing classroom exercises in grammar".

5. Note that I am using the term 'accessibility' here with a somewhat different meaning from that in chapter 2 on managing the accessibility of press releases.

6. More indirect forms of representing the words of others ('oratio obliqua'), on the other hand, adopt the frame of orientation of the reporting speech event, invite a 'de re' interpretation and are assumed to rather foreground content.

7. This is not to say that the reproductionist view of quotation has been taken for granted in literary studies. On the contrary, the concept of 'mimesis', drawn from Aristotelean poetics, centrally takes into account the fictional and therefore necessarily non-reproductionist nature of dialogue in literary texts; it is actually linguists who have been responsible for reducing mimesis to 'a verbatim rendering of what was said'.

8. Payne talks about 'apocryphal' quotes (i.e. quotes which possibly could, would, may or might happen) (quoted in Buttny 1995).

9. In contrast, former White House spokesman Marlin Fitzwater claims that Helen Thomas, who was a long-standing reporter for UPI, never scrawled more than five

or six words on every page of her notepad, but that she somehow managed to turn them

> into full quotes, accurate to the smallest pronoun and transcribed with every verb and adjective in place, the product of decades of note taking and mental discipline. Anyone finding her notebook with every page filled could never put together a complete sentence. She has her own secret code of note taking that even she cannot explain. "I just remember", she says (1995: 91).

10. Think also of the continuing debate about the accuracy of transcription methods in Conversation Analysis.

11. It should be noted that this is a rather straightforward example and that it is usually more difficult to check if, for example, a definite description or proper name in the quotation is a literal rendering of the original or, alternatively, the result of what Slembrouck (1992a) calls co-designative referential substitution, in which the proper name or definite description is used by the reporter to replace, say, a pro-form that was used to designate the same object in the original.

    A related point, also mentioned by Slembrouck, is that items between quotation marks can enter into a wide range of anaphoric or cataphoric relations with items in the reporter's text before or after, as in

    (i)   (Ogilvy & Mather Direct, Brussels: s.d.)

    [Ogilvy & Mather Tele-Services] biedt de gebruikers van telemarketing nieuwe mogelijkheden en beantwoordt daarbij aan de groeiende vraag naar interactieve communicatie.

    "Maar wij willen zeker geen telemarketing-fabriek zijn", aldus Bart Bastien. (my emphasis)

    [Ogilvy & Mather Tele-Services] offers the users of telemarketing new opportunities and, in doing so, meets the growing demand for interactive communication.

    "*But* we certainly do not want to be a telemarketing factory", according to Bart Bastien.

    Here again, the degree of reporter intervention is hard to determine.

12. These are clear cases of pseudo-direct speech. I disagree with Waugh's (1995) suggestion that with plural subjects often only one person is quoted "more or less verbatim" and that he or she is understood as speaking for a larger group. In the following extract from *Le Monde*, for example, Waugh claims that the speaker's identity is not given for political reasons:

    "All types of bombs were tried on us, except the one which could have destroyed us: the atomic bomb", say the inhabitants (165).

13. I have to disagree with Waugh (1995) again, who says that this is always a metonymic identification of the speaker and thus presupposes that there was an original.

    There may be such metonymic identification in the following example of non-reflexive quotation, though, where the Kredietbank refers to a statement by the IBOS banking association:

    (ii)   (Kredietbank, Brussels: 12 February 1996)

> *"De toetreding van First Union Corporation zal de commerciële slag-*
> *kracht en de mogelijkheden van onze bedrijven cliënten nog vergroten",*
> *aldus de IBOS-associatie.*
> "The entry of First Union Corporation will further increase the commer-
> cial power and possibilities of our client companies", according to the
> IBOS association.

14. It should be noted that the brackets in this extract are not mine.

15. Note that all this is certainly not to let reproduction back in by the back door. As I have said, it is the very act of quoting, no matter how accurate, that changes the original words (cf. Tannen below).

16. Also note that, in the case of reports of speeches and press conferences as in (20), (21) and (25), the use of quotation can be considered the default representation mode, as the original words were part of spoken language (cf. Sanders 1994 on quotation as a 'natural' feature of biblical narrative). This is of course in strong contrast with pseudo-direct speech.

17. I am indebted to Kristin Davidse for suggesting this term to me.

18. As I pointed out earlier in this chapter, quotation foregrounds form. Hence, I would suggest that pseudo-direct speech in press releases may well serve to draw the journalists' attention away from what is really said to how it is said. In addition, I have suggested that quoted words are traditionally considered referentially impenetrable, with the slightest interference of the reporter affecting their truth status. This means that the kind of self-quotation we are looking at here might also play a role in convincing journalists to retell press releases verbatim in their own news reporting.

19. Compare Bauman and Briggs (1990) on 'entextualization' (73, cf. my introduction).

20. Obviously, no in-depth discussion of Bakhtin's concept of double-voiced discourse and of Voloshinov's linear and pictorial styles is aimed at here.

21. Note that Thomas and Hawes (1994) confirm Bakhtin's claim about the institution-ality of quotation when they say that reference to other researchers' work "seems to have a central role in creating the generic identity and communicative purpose of research articles" (16).

22. It should come as no surprise that, once more, I cannot share the views of Waugh (1995), who maintains that there is a "categorical separation" between direct speech as non compressive, verbatim and replicative and indirect speech as compression, paraphrasing and inferencing (163, 165).

Notes to Chapter 5

1. I am aware that there are no clear-cut distinctions between the various functions of quotation mentioned above.

2. Cf. Li (1986) on a theatrical element; Holt (1996). Clark and Gerrig (1990) talk about 'engrossment' through direct experience.

3. Note that in (3) not just the reporting ("zegt" [says]) but the action reported between quotation marks too ("tonen" [show]) is referred to in the simple present. I would argue that this again may be related to the use of self-quotation, i.e. if the words were not between quotation marks, a present perfect could be expected:

    Madge's tests of several frequently used 100 Megabit network adaptors have shown that (...).

    For a further preformulating$_{ii}$ role of the choice of the simple present with self-quotation in press releases see the section on the attitude function below.

4. Note that this use of the present in headlines is not restricted to reporting verbs and that, as I pointed out before in chapter 3, it seems to be a regular feature of the syntax of headlines in general, as in:

    (i) (Nestor, Tielen: 18 April 1994)
        FA. NESTOR KOOPT VOORRADEN CONCORDIA MAIL.
        De firma NESTOR, gevestigd te Tielen, heeft vandaag de voorraden van Concordia Mail gekocht.
        NESTOR BUYS CONCORDIA MAIL STOCKS.
        The company NESTOR, based in Tielen, has bought the stocks of Concordia Mail today.

    (ii) (Kamer van Koophandel en Nijverheid van Antwerpen, Antwerp: 14 October 1994)
        Kamer houdt opendeur Euro Info Centrum
        Op 13 en 14 oktober 1994 zette de Kamer van Koophandel en Nijverheid van Antwerpen de deuren van haar Euro Info Centrum (EIC) open.
        Chamber holds open house Euro Info Centre
        On 13 and 14 October 1994 the Chamber of Commerce and Industry has opened the doors of its Euro Info Centre (EIC).

    Schudson (1986) calls this the "continuous present". He says that "[n]ewspaper headlines are almost always in the present tense, but newspaper stories are almost invariably written in the past tense" (88-89).

5. Hoyle (1993) shows how in sporting boys frequently report their own actions and sayings to an imaginary audience as if they were the actions and sayings of third parties (so-called 'sportscasting'). Barnes and Vangelisti (1995) point to children's use of double-voiced discourse to construct consensus and to address a multiplicity of goals, including to advance their personal agendas.

6. Another concern is for journalists to provide a balanced view by quoting several, opposing sources. It should be noted that no such balance can be expected from press releases, which, by definition, present the case of whatever organization issued them. Surely, this is one way in which press releases *a priori* fail to meet the objectivity requirements of journalism.

7. Hoeken and Van Wijk (1997) report experimental research that the use of persons in written advertisements enhances credibility.

8.　Cf. Hallin (1986) on reference to place as serving to establish the authority of news reports, showing that the reporter was really there (112).

9.　After all, in the previous chapter I pointed out that the journalists' own quoting practices are not always reliable either (cf. also, later in this chapter, Tuchman 1978, Cook 1989 and Hardt-Mautner 1995). It follows that they should not be expected to be too scrupulous to retell the suspicious quotes in press releases.

10.　Since the general public - as I pointed out above - is in no position to find out the quote's origin, it remains to be seen whether, ethically speaking, journalists are free to preserve - or even to promote - the impression that they worked hard to get their information straight from the horse's mouth or, alternatively, whether they should explicitly acknowledge that the quote was nicely preformulated for them in a press release.

11.　Voloshinov talks about 'auctoriality', Benveniste about 'subjectivity' (Auer 1988: 265, 288).

12.　For an analysis of the news managing potential of "high government officials, major corporate figures, and to a lesser extent, certain glamour personalities", see Molotch and Lester's (1974: 107) views on President Nixon's inspection of a 1969 California oil spill as a 'routine event'.

13.　Note that my own reference to Thomas and Hawes (1994) is an illustration of this use.

14.　Note that the fact that, in most cases, it proved impossible to show from the data that quotations were invented does not imply that it would be impossible to demonstrate agreement between the quoted source and the reporter. This is altogether a different question.

15.　The first four points in the list below are among what Voloshinov, in his analysis of the relation between reported speech and reporting context, calls "the more primitive devices for authorial retort and commentary" (1973: 134); Fairclough (1988) talks about 'setting devices'.

16.　Note that he also mentions the use of so-called 'epitheta ornantia' in this respect. These too occur in my corpus, not for reference to the quoted source, but for reference to the organization that issued the press release.
　　　　(iii) (Bekaert, Kortrijk:)
　　　　　　Bekaert, wereldwijd leider in de productie en verkoop van staaldraad, staaldraadprodukten en staalkoord, met directiekantoren te Kortrijk in België, (...).
　　　　　　Bekaert, worldwide leader in the manufacturing and sales of steel wire, steel wire products and steel cord, with direction offices at Kortrijk in Belgium, (...).

17.　Cf. Maes (1991) on violations of the so-called 'precede-condition', viz. that the proper name must normally precede the definite description (cf. also 1987: 136; Wales 1996: 41-42).

18. Cf. Bauman and Briggs's (1990) notion of 'entextualization', referred to in the introduction to this study.

19. But see Cerf and Navasky (1984) for a hilarious catalogue of experts' incompetence.

20. I suggested above that reference to the context of delivery confirms that the quotations report on a real past speech event (chapter 4) and that it may also make the report more reliable (chapter 5).

21. This count is based on self-quotes in a random subcorpus of 100 press releases that all contain self-quotes. In the table, Dutch verbs have been listed under their English equivalents.

22. An example of 'no verb' or what Yule, Mathis and Hopkins (1992) call the zero-quotative:

> (iv) (ASQ, Houthalen: 23 February 1994)
> *Paul Knippenberg: "De ISO 9000-certificering die SIAC in de wacht sleepte, was voor ons een belangrijk pluspunt."*
> Paul Knippenberg: "The ISO 9000 certification thet SIAC carried off, was an important advantage for us."

23. Note that there has been some interest in the use of reporting verbs in newspaper articles from the field of experimental research: Merrill (1965) looks at "attribution bias" by asking a panel to evaluate the synonyms of 'say' that *Time* used to attribute speech to US presidents Truman, Eisenhower and Kennedy; Cole and Shaw (1974) show that 'strong' attributive verbs have an impact on the reader and that 'say' is judged most objective as well as dullest, confirming, in their view, that those who advocate its use appear to be correct.

24. The table seems to confirm that 'according to' is neutral and this is in conflict with Waugh's (1995: 145) claim that it often shows scepticism on the part of the reporter. An example of 'according to' in a self-quote, where it cannot be meant to show scepticism:

> (v) (Exxon, Anchorage, Alaska: 26 October 1989)
> "The state's decision of March 1989 established a state policy approving the use of dispersants in an oil spill emergency as well as a policy that state agencies were not to interfere in the approval for use or use of dispersants," according to the Exxon suit.

25. Note that Kress (1983) argues that 'state' is not so neutral after all and that it conveys authority and validity because it belongs to a more formal register than, for example, 'say' (53). Incidentally, in his view, absence of a report verb conveys even greater authority and actually constitutes the highest ranking.

26. The practice of adding such qualification invalidates, to some extent at least, the type of counts shown in fig. 1 above.

27. Cf. Tannen (1986) on the dominance of so-called 'graphic' introducers in everyday conversations.

28. Focusing on so-called metapragmatic metaphors in international news reporting, Verschueren (1985) finds systematic differences in the same newspaper's characterization of different speakers (cf. also Geis 1987).

29. This seems to be confirmed by Johnstone (1987) who shows that shifts from past to present tense are meant to capture speakers' heightened status.

30. Such pseudo-direct speech is, as I have argued, of a performative nature and the simple present tense can therefore even be considered a natural choice (cf. next chapter).

31. Vandenbergen (1981), in her analysis of newspaper headlines, suggests that this is the so-called 'aorist', denoting that both writer and reader are detached from the actual process. She says that it contributes to a more factual and impersonal reporting style. While this may seem to be in conflict with the notion of percolation, I would argue that it is not. On the contrary, this use of the simple present contributes to the authority of the quoted information, which can then be used to further strengthen the reporter's overall case.

32. Cf. Fairclough (1988: 127) who raises the question whether direct quoting really conveys authority on the quoted source or, alternatively, whether direct quoting is typically used for sources that are authoritative anyway.

33. It is interesting to add in this respect that Levinson (1988) criticized his own scheme of participant roles by suggesting that an additional component was needed at the production end to distinguish between what he calls the source of the information and the source of illocutionary force.

34. Trognon and Larrue have a nice example of authority through role taken from a political debate in France between representatives of the left and right. Fabius, who speaks for the left, also happened to be prime minister at the time:

    | Fabius: | écoutez je vous rappelle que vous parlez au Premier ministre de la France |
    | Chirac: | non (…) je m'adresse à Monsieur Fabius, représentant du Parti socialiste (…) |
    | Fabius: | qu'est-ce que ce comportement, c'est scandaleux |
    | Journaliste: | reprenons le débat |
    | (1994: 63-64) | |

    Also remember Norman Tebbit's defence of his attack on the BBC's coverage of the 1986 US bombing of Libya (chapter 3).

35. In this respect Kress (1983) even proposes to rank speakers' utterances along an institutional-personal axis (52): from what is said by someone who serves as a representative of an organization to what is said by someone who is 'merely' a private person. Van Leeuwen (1996a) agrees that "[a]t present the category of 'belonging to a company or organisation' begins to play a more important role in identification" (55).

36. The utterance 'entails' that John stopped in time. Presuppositions, in contrast with entailments, survive under negation, though: since both

John managed to stop in time.

and its negative counterpart

John didn't manage to stop in time.

can only make sense if indeed John tried to stop in time (Levinson 1983: 178), the utterance presupposes that John tried to stop in time.

37. Note that the negative counterpart

Bill didn't know that John managed to stop in time.

also presupposes that John tried to stop in time.

38. Even if John didn't try to stop in time, it is possible to say

Bill didn't say that John managed to stop in time.

39. Note that the use of 'would' here cannot be taken to express doubt since the very purpose of this press release is for Exxon to justify why it has just terminated Captain Hazelwood's contract. Instead, a notion of volition appears to be involved, with 'would' further criticizing Hazelwood's actions.

40. Note that this is at the basis of the distinction between hard news (stories based on eye witness reports, etc) and soft news or news analysis.

41. Note that even this slimmed-down notion of plugging has been criticized, for example, by Levinson, who suggests that it works only because of the background knowledge we have (1983: 215). Look at the following:

The student said that he hadn't realized that Wales was a republic.

Here, the presupposition of the embedded utterance

The student hadn't realized that Wales was a republic.

viz. that Wales is a republic, is plugged, not because it falls under a verb of saying, but rather because we happen to know that Wales is not a republic.

42. Weaver (1974) criticizes this false 'rhetoric of objectivity' in which, he argues, form constitutes content, and the typical news story is biased, but not toward right, left or center. Rather the bias is toward statements of fact which are observable and unambiguous, toward "broad, categorical vocabulary" - 'say', rather than 'shout' or 'insist' (94-95; cf. Schudson 1978 on 'new journalism' and, more recently, Taels and Vanheeswijck's 1995 case for abandoning the fiction of neutrality).

43. Cf. Shuman (1990) reports that political junk mailings to raise money often start with a typical story of a named victim of some global problem:

Reported speech can be an effective means for establishing, for countering, "Who says?" In appropriating personal narratives, the authors of (...) junk mail attempt to close off discussion concerning interpretation and instead to give the appearance of "raw" facts (178).

44. Schudson says that the term 'objectivity' was unknown in the news before World War 1.

45. This paradox is also noticed by Sanders (1994) when she argues that quotation is "most subjective as the embedded space is strictly bound to a certain character in the text" (65) and "at the same time very objective" because the reporter appears not to exert any influence (77).

46. This would mean that, unlike 'journalized' advertising copy (Schudson 1978: 78), press releases are no exploitive fabrications (Goffman 1974: 103).

Notes to Chapter 6

1. Vincent and Perrin (1996) too are aware that it may be difficult to distinguish between explicit performatives and quotations and confirm that, to draw a clear-cut line between the two, the utterance can only be considered a quotation if it refers to an utterance - past, hypothetical or future - that is independent of the current interaction situation.

2. In addition, even with the first, performative 'hereby' reading, it should be borne in mind that not this single utterance itself serves as an announcement of CBR's programme, but rather the press release as a whole (compare with Myers 1992 who shows that in scientific writing a performative opening like 'In this paper we report ...' merely *leads up to* the report, with the actual report realized by the complete paper).

3. Fraser (1996) even argues that performatives are descriptions in origin.

4. It should now be clear why the performative 'hereby' is absent from my corpus of press releases.

5. Note that here, like - for example - in the Bayer press releases discussed in chapter 3, the organizations that issued the press releases are backgrounded and that this serves to hide their self-interests.

6. Cf. Heritage, Clayman and Zimmerman (1988) on news announcement as agenda projecting in news interviews; Clayman (1991) on news interview openings; Fairclough (1992) on formulations as a means of interactional control.

7. Cf. chapter 5 for a more extensive analysis of the choice of linguistic action verbs in self-quotation.

8. Note that here, strictly speaking, we have no performative, but a report that somewhat functions like a performative. This example once again illustrates the close link between performativity and reporting.

9. Interestingly, she then quotes Sperber and Wilson's claim that the need for such background information is "no more and no less interesting to pragmatics than the fact that in order to discover by looking out of the window that there is rain on the way some meteorological knowledge is required" (1986: 12).

10. Again confirming the link between quotation and performatives, Lucy (1993) says exactly the same thing about reporting: reporting and reported events are indistinguishable, and the utterance cannot be subject to the usual judgments of truth value; in a sense, he argues, the first part of the utterance makes explicit the way the second part is to be read.

11. Lakoff refers to the Gricean maxim that anything that requires explicit statement is *ipso facto* open to doubt. As Brown and Levinson suggest, it seems to be typical of institutional contexts: "The purpose of the ceremony is precisely to insist on the powers of those performing ceremonial functions, and to remind observers of these powers" (1987: 45).

12. Note that embedding under explicit performatives is a case of external modalization: the message is modalized by the addition of a pseudo-clause (Eggins 1994: 183). Moreover, since the pseudo-clause functions metaphorically as an adjunct, it can be looked at as a 'grammatical metaphor'. It is interesting to note in this respect that Blakemore (1995) compares embedding under explicit performatives with reformulating adjuncts.

13. For a recent defence of this view see Waugh (1995: 134-135).

14. Roch and Nir (1990) suggest that direct quotation is rare for such hypothetical reporting and that narrative reports of speech acts are normally preferred because the words have not yet been spoken, as in:
    Foreign Minister Shamir will ask the Market leaders to improve trade conditions between Israel and the Market countries.

15. I would argue that, via Vendler's (1976) notion of illocutionary suicide, it is this performative nature of pseudo-direct speech that explains why there are almost no negative linguistic action verbs to be found in my corpus of press releases.

Notes to Chapter 7

1. There are a great many military metaphors in the Valdez corpus: 'task forces' are said to 'attack' the oil spill 'utilizing four different types of operations' (28 March), dispersants are sprayed on "target areas" (29 March), skimmers and booms are 'deployed' in 'strategic locations' (12 April, 15 April), etc.

2. In a letter to the Editor of the *New York Times* on 21 February 1990 Exxon chairman Larry Rawl mentions the provisional figure of $ 2 billion. Significantly, while - throughout the crisis - Exxon's readiness to spend huge amounts was widely advertised in an attempt to please the general public, shareholders were reassured as early as 30 March that the total cost of the clean-up "[would] not be burdensome for the company" (*Reuter Newswire*).

3. It has been suggested that Exxon spent $ 80,000 per animal saved (*Columbus Ledger-Enquirer*, 15 December 1989).

4. Clearly, all these facts and figures serve a purpose of persuasion. Speaking at the same conference referred to above, Davis seems to confirm this 'rhetoric of precise numbers' (Van Dijk 1988) when he - rather cynically - claims that the spill response was the number one growth industry in Alaska that summer, but adds that 'admittedly' he has no 'hard numbers to back this up'.

5. Note that in the original plan only 364 miles were scheduled to be treated (4 May); also a peak employment of 3,400 persons was provided for (compare with the record workforce of over 10,000 announced three months later).

6. "The biggest mistake was that Exxon's chairman, Lawrence G. Rawl, sent a succession of lower-ranking executives to Alaska to deal with the spill instead of going there himself and taking control in a highly visible way" (*International Herald Tribune*, 22-23 April 1989; cf. also Tyler 1992).

7. Only two years later, in September 1991, did the story come to a close when Exxon filed agreements to settle all Valdez criminal and civil cases with the authorities, providing for the release of Exxon's claims against the state as well as for over 1 billion dollars in fines to be paid by Exxon.

8. The same gradual decline in newsworthiness can be observed in the Valdez corpus as a whole, with the first few press releases issued shortly after the spill carrying what was undeniably 'world news' and later ones calling attention to the far less spectacular details of the clean-up, except for the close-down of the operations in September, which led to a late flare-up of international media interest.

9. In more general terms, it could be argued, perhaps rather crudely, that, in the middle of misfortune, one good thing about the accident with the Exxon Valdez was that it took place at the beginning of the Easter weekend, a time when media activity is traditionally low.

10. Compare with a similar headline "EXXON AND OTHERS PUSH AHEAD WITH CLEANUP OF PRINCE WILLIAM SOUND" (12 April) for a press release that, unlike the one on 27 March, serves as a real update on Exxon's emergency response, almost three weeks after the accident.

11. In the wake of the Valdez oil spill, Exxon seems to have regretted this practice of including the company name in the name of its tankers. In defence against sharply negative reactions from the public, for example, Exxon has contended that most other oil companies have had similar, often even much bigger, accidents, but that on most occasions the name of the company failed to be associated with the oil spill simply because, unlike the Exxon Valdez, the ship's name did not include the name of the organization.

12. This question of agency has been a popular object of study in critical linguistics and critical discourse analysis.

13. The same goes for speeches
    > (...) let me say once again - to you in this audience and to all Alaskans - that Exxon regrets, deeply, what happened. However much we have sought to mitigate the impact and deal responsibly with the cleanup, we know that in the eyes of some our efforts have been lacking. But we have been here and done our best. We did not run and hide.
    > (Exxon U.S.A. President W. D. Stevens to the Alaska State and Anchorage Chambers of Commerce at Anchorage, Alaska, on 2 October 1989)

    and for letters to the editor

(...) you and the public should know that our most important objective is to restore our reputation (...).
(Letter to the editor of the *New York Times*, 21 February 1990).

14. It is interesting to note in this respect that Exxon has been charged with arrogantly failing to take the blame for the oil spill:
    The best antidote to crisis management is, of course, to prevent a crisis from happening (...). The next-best thing, when a crisis occurs, is to confess error, demonstrate concern and move quickly to restore public trust. (...) Exxon hasn't [done that] (*New York Times*, 14 February 1990).
    Top managers repeatedly said that they felt sorry, but not - probably out of legal considerations - that they were responsible. Instead, the blame was first cast on Captain of the Exxon Valdez John Hazelwood, later on the State of Alaska for refusing to permit the use of chemical dispersants (cf. below). Significantly, looking back on the accident that badly affected a region of rare natural beauty, company spokespersons have said that their biggest mistake was that they did not get their message across to the general public. This preoccupation with image was bitterly denounced in a cartoon showing a tanker that has just hit a reef and has started to leak huge amounts of oil, with the captain running to the phone, shouting "Mayday! Mayday! Give me Public Relations".

15. Of course this is not to say that the reference to 'last Friday' could not be copied by journalists. Instead, while not deictically neutral, it may even turn out to be a better preformulation than 'on 24 March'.

16. But see Exxon Public Affairs spokesman Fred Davis on the company's "seeming inability to communicate effectively in the news media":
    On every issue, you have numerous spokesmen, each trying to slant the issue and subsequent stories a certain way.
    (Environmental Issues Conference, 7 September 1989)

17. Note that Exxon's rhetoric of precise numbers reaches its high on 1 April. In a press release about the much disputed delay in using chemical dispersants to fight the oil spill, it is announced that one of the company's C-130s spray planes carrying the chemical dispersant Corexit arrived in Valdez at "6.12 a.m. Saturday", but that it was not authorized by the State to take off for tests until "4.18 p.m." on the same day. It is added that Exxon only received full authority to use the dispersant at "6.45 p.m. Sunday".

18. The same conclusion can be drawn from a press release issued on 13 April. Reporting on the transformation of the gymnasium at Growden Harrison Elementary School into a sea mammal rescue center, the writer adds that construction crews have been "working around the clock for several days".

19. Earlier, on 8 August, when reporting on new tests with chemical dispersants, Exxon had already represented the State of Alaska's views on the issue, but at that stage the company's attitude towards the words quoted from a press release issued by the Alaska Department of Environmental Conservation still appeared pretty much neutral.

20. The same rhetoric is at work in the 4-million-dollar advertising campaign for Alaskan tourism that Exxon sponsored, showing a picture of Marilyn Monroe without her beauty mark and suggesting that, similarly, no one will notice any changes in Prince William Sound (Tyler 1992).

Notes to Chapter 8

1. I am aware that this is a highly simplified formulation. For one thing, I argued before that the internal complexity of newsmaking, including the effect of the hierarchy in a news organization (cf. Gans 1979, Bell 1991), is completely denied. In addition, I have suggested that not all people have equal news managing potential, of course.

2. Using the same economic metaphor, Leudar and Antaki (1996) compare such a process of joint "message production" to the way in which "managers, shareholders, supervisors and workers are in different relationship to industrial products" (13).

3. Note that this is why I prefer to use the term newsmakers for journalists and not for sources: while there can be no doubt that journalists are highly restricted in making the news, I would argue that sources usually face a number of constraints too. Ultimately, sources - or events, for that matter - can only make the news in the figurative (and passive) sense of 'being covered by the media', as in

    The president made the news three times this week.

4. Another example of the balance between newsmaking and news management is offered by Clayman's (1995) analysis of Democratic vice presidential candidate Lloyd Bentsen's assertion that his opponent Dan Quayle is "no Jack Kennedy", which was then preserved as a sound bite in the media. Pointing at the interaction between newsmaking and news management, Clayman concludes that news coverage of debates "tends to focus on memorable one-liners rather than substantive issues" (newsmaking) and that this in turn "encourages candidates to frame their remarks in such terms" (news management) (134).

5. Cf. Similarly, Clayman (1990) looks at newspaper accounts of reporter-source interactions and concludes from an analysis of embedding practices that "a media-centred theory of hegemony is difficult to sustain" (99).

6. Dealing with the notion of hegemony as power through consent in organizational discourse, Mumby and Clair (1997) argue that "[t]he most effective use of power occurs when those with power are able to get those who have less power to interpret the world from the former's point of view" (184). With reference to the 'point of view operations' in my data, I would argue that this seems to confirm that, to some extent at least, newsmakers (and news consumers) have control over news managers.

7. Hak (1995) argues that a text-intrinsic view of context is not sensitive to participants' hidden agendas.

8. Quoted in Lynch and Bogen (1996), who characterize the CIA's proscribed policy of prestructuring historical evidence through the technique of 'plausible deniability' as "applied deconstructionism" (62, 88).

Notes to the Appendix

1. Note that this is an open-ended corpus. Some organizations have continued sending me press releases, which were subsequently added to the corpus; the list below includes all press releases issued before 1 January 1997. In addition, others have sent me press releases that were issued before 1 December 1994.

    In addition, the four subcorpora specified above have been supplemented by individual press releases for purposes of illustration. They are not listed below, but I identified those that are used in the study itself.

2. Schegloff (1988/89) makes a similar comment on the nature of news interviews.

3. These are the sources they distinguish: business/industry (82% of their corpus), civic/service organizations, international organizations, lobbies/special interest groups, state/local governments, education, unions/professional organizations, religious groups, federal government.

4. Alcalay and Taplin (1989) distinguish only three reasons for issuing a press release: to announce an upcoming event this is called a press advisory -, to take a stand on an issue, and to provide background information. Morton and Ramsey distinguish 7 types of releases: institutional releases (reporting on the activities, services, accomplishments of the sponsor), coming events, past events, consumer information, timely topics, features and research.

5. Morton and Ramsey distinguish the following mutually exclusive categories of subject matter: finance, personnel, economics, health & fitness, home & garden, social issues, fashion & beauty, government & politics, education, research, new products & services, joint ventures & mergers and other.

References

Adamson, S.
    1994   "From empathetic deixis to empathetic narrative: stylisation and (de-)subjectivisation as processes of language change". *Transactions of the Philological Society* 92(1): 55-88.
    1995   "Text, co-text and context: context as co-text". Paper presented at the 3rd International Summer School in English and Applied Linguistics, University of Cambridge, UK.

Alcalay, R. and Taplin, S.
    1989   "Community health campaigns: from theory to action". In R. Rice and C. Atkin (eds), *Public Communication Campaigns*. London: Sage, 105-129.

Allerton, D.
    1996   "Proper names and definite descriptions with the same reference: a pragmatic choice for language users". *Journal of Pragmatics* 25: 621-633.

Astroff, R.J. and Nyberg, A.K.
    1992   "Discursive hierarchies and the construction of crisis in the news: a case study". *Discourse & Society* 3(1): 5-23.

Atkinson, J.M. and Heritage, J.C. (eds)
    1984   *Structures of Social Action: Studies in conversation analysis.* Cambridge: Cambridge University Press.

Auer, P.
    1988   "On deixis and displacement". *Folia Linguistica* 23(3-4): 263-292.
    1991   Review of P. Drew and A. Wootton (eds), *Erving Goffman: Exploring the interaction order. Linguistics* 29(1): 177-189.
    1992   "John Gumperz' approach to contextualization". In P. Auer and A. di Luzio (eds), *The Contextualization of Language*. Amsterdam and Philadelphia: Benjamins, 1-37.

1995   "Context and contextualization". In J. Verschueren, J. Östman and J. Blommaert (eds), *Handbook of Pragmatics 1995*. Amsterdam and Philadelphia: Benjamins, 1-19.

Auer, P. and Di Luzio, A. (eds)
    1992   *The Contextualization of Language*. Amsterdam and Philadelphia: Benjamins.

Austin, J.
    1962   *How To Do Things With Words*. Oxford: Oxford University Press.

Bach, K. and Harnish, R.
    1979   *Linguistic Communication and Speech Acts*. Cambridge, MA: MIT Press.

Bakhtin, M.M.
    1935/81 *The Dialogic Imagination*. Austin, TX: Texas University Press.
    1929/84 *Problems of Dostoevsky's Poetics*. Minneapolis.
    1953/86 "The problem of speech genres". In E. Emerson and M. Holquist (eds), *Speech Genres and Other Late Essays*. Austin, TX: Texas University Press, 60-102.

Banfield, A.
    1982   *Unspeakable Sentences: Narration and representation in the language of fiction*. Boston, MA: Routledge & Kegan Paul.

Barnes, M.K. and Vangelisti, A.L.
    1995   "Speaking in a double-voice: role-making as influence in preschoolers' fantasy play situations". *Research on Language and Social Interaction* 28(4): 351-389.

Bateson, G.
    1955/78 "A theory of play and fantasy". In *Steps to an Ecology of the Mind*. London: Granada, 150-166.

Bauman, R. and Briggs, C.L.
    1990   "Poetics and performance as critical perspectives on language and social life". *Annual Review of Anthropology* 19: 59-88.

Baynham, M.
    1996   "Direct speech: what's it doing in non-native discourse?" *Journal of Pragmatics* 25: 61-81.

Bazerman, C. and Paradis, J. (eds)
  1991   *Textual Dynamics of the Professions: Historical and contemporary studies of writing in professional communities.* Madison, WI: University of Wisconsin Press.

Bell, A.
  1984   "Language style as audience design". *Language in Society* 13: 145-204.
  1991   *The Language of News Media.* Oxford: Blackwell.

Benveniste, E.
  1966   *Problèmes de Linguistique Générale, I.* Paris: Gallimard.

Berger, A.A.
  1995   *Essentials of Mass Communication Theory.* London: Sage.

Bernaers, B.
  1995   *Van Persbericht tot Kranteartikel.* Thesis, University of Antwerp.

Bernaers, B., Jacobs, G. and Van Waes, L.
  1996   "Van persbericht tot kranteartikel: wat gebeurt er met titels?" *Tekstblad* 2(2): 16-22.

Blakemore, D.
  1991.   "Performatives and parentheticals". *Proceedings of the Aristotelian Society* 91: 197-214.
  1993   "The relevance of reformulations". *Language and Literature* 2(2): 101-120.
  1995   "Relevance theory and context construction". Paper presented at the 3rd International Summer School in English and Applied Linguistics, University of Cambridge, UK.

Blommaert, J.
  1997   "Whose background? Comments on a discourse-analytic reconstruction of the Warsaw Uprising". *Pragmatics* 7(1): 69-81.

Boden, D.
  1994   *The Business of Talk: Organizations in action.* Cambridge: Polity Press.

Boden, D. and Zimmerman, D. (eds)
  1991   *Talk and Social Structure: Studies in ethnomethodology and conversation analysis.* Cambridge: Polity Press.

Boorstin, D.
1961   *The Image: A guide to pseudo-events in America*. New York: Atheneum.

Booth, W.C.
1961   *The Rhetoric of Fiction*. Chicago: Chicago University Press.

Borstlap, A.
1995   *Het Schrijven van Persberichten: Onderzoek in externe communicatie-bureaus*. Thesis, University of Antwerp.

Brantlinger, P.
1990   *Crusoe's Footprints*. New York: Routledge.

Briggs, C.L. and Bauman, R.
1992   "Genre, intertextuality, and social power". *Journal of Linguistic Anthropology* 2(2): 131-172.

Brookes, H.J.
1995   "'Suit, tie and a touch of juju' - the ideological construction of Africa: a critical discourse analysis of news on Africa in the British press". *Discourse & Society* 6(4): 461-494.

Brown, G. and Yule, G.
1983   *Discourse Analysis*. Cambridge: Cambridge University Press.

Brown, P. and Levinson, S.C.
1987   *Politeness: Some universals*. Cambridge: Cambridge University Press.

Brown, R. and Gilman, A.
1960   "The pronouns of power and solidarity". In T. A. Sebeok (ed), *Style in Language*. Cambridge, MA: MIT Press, 253-276.

Bruck, P.A.
1989   "Strategies for peace, strategies for news research". *Journal of Communication* 39(1): 108-129.

Buttny, R.
1995   "Talking race on campus: reported speech sequences of racism and interracial contact on a university campus". Paper presented at the conference on "Advances in Discourse Analysis", Georgetown University, USA.

Caldas-Coulthard, C.R.
1994   "On reporting reporting: the representation of speech in factual and factional narratives". In M. Coulthard (ed),

Advances in Written Text Analysis. London: Routledge, 295-320.

Caldas-Coulthard, C.R. and Coulthard, M. (eds)
1996   *Texts and Practices*. London: Routledge.

Cameron, D.
1985   *Feminism and Linguistic Theory*. London: Macmillan.

Cerf, C. and Navasky, V.
1984   *The Experts Speak: The definitive compendium of authoritative misinformation*. New York: Pantheon Books.

Chafe, W. (ed)
1986   *Evidentiality: The linguistic coding of epistemology*. Norwood, N.J.: Ablex.

Cicourel, A.
1992   "The interpenetration of communicative contexts: examples from medical encounters". In A. Duranti and C. Goodwin (eds), *Rethinking Context: Language as an interactive phenomenon*. Cambridge: Cambridge University Press, 219-310.

Clark, H.H.
1995   "Context, mutual knowledge, beliefs". Paper presented at the 3rd International Summer School in English and Applied Linguistics, University of Cambridge, UK.
1996   *Using Language*. Cambridge: Cambridge University Press.

Clark, H.H. and Carlson, T.B.
1982   "Hearers and speech acts". *Language* 58: 332-373.

Clark, H.H. and Gerrig, R.J.
1990   "Quotations as demonstrations". *Language* 66(4): 764-805.

Clark, H.H. and Schaefer, E.F.
1992   "Dealing with overhearers". In H.H. Clark (ed), *Arenas of Language Use*. Chicago: University of Chicago Press, 248-274.

Clark, H.H. and Wilkes-Gibbs, D.
1986   "Referring as a collaborative process". *Cognition* 22: 1-39.

Clayman, S.E.
1990   "From talk to text: newspaper accounts of reporter-source interactions". *Media, Culture and Society* 12: 79-103.

1991   "News interview openings: aspects of sequential organization". In P. Scannell (ed), *Broadcast Talk*. London: Sage, 48-75.

1992   "Footing in the achievement of neutrality: the case of news-interview discourse". In P. Drew and J. Heritage (eds), *Talk at Work: Interaction in institutional settings*. Cambridge: Cambridge University Press, 163-198.

1993   "Reformulating the question: a device for answering/not answering questions in news interviews and press conferences". *Text* 13: 159-188.

1995   "Defining moments, presidential debates, and the dynamics of quotability". *Journal of Communication* 45(3): 118-146.

Cole, R.R. and Shaw, D.L.
1974   "'Powerful' verbs and 'body language': does the reader notice?" *Journalism Quarterly* 51: 62-66.

Connell, I. and Galasinski, D.
1996   "Cleaning up its act: the CIA on the Internet". *Discourse & Society* 7(2): 165-186.

Cook, T.E.
1989   *Making Laws and Making News: Media strategies in the U.S. House of Representatives*. Washington, D.C.: The Brookings Institute.

Cornelis, L.
1995   "Passief en polyphonie". *Tijdschrift voor Taalbeheersing* 17: 44-54.

1997   *Passive and Perspective*. Amsterdam and Atlanta, GA: Rodopi.

Coulthard, M.
1994   "On the use of corpora in the analysis of forensic texts". *Forensic Linguistics* 1: 27-44.

Crystal, D. and Davy, D.
1969   *Investigating English Style*. London: Longman.

Cushing, S.
1994   *Fatal Words: Communication clashes and aircraft crashes*. Chicago: University of Chicago Press.

De Fina, A.
1995   "Pronominal choice, identity, and solidarity in political discourse". *Text* 15(3): 379-410.

De Fornel, M.
  1987   "Reference to persons in conversation". In J. Verschueren and M. Bertuccelli-Papi (eds), *The Pragmatic Perspective*. Amsterdam and Philadelphia: Benjamins, 131-140.

De Rycker, T.
  1987   "Turns at writing: the organization of correspondence". In J. Verschueren and M. Bertuccelli-Papi (eds), *The Pragmatic Perspective*. Amsterdam and Philadelphia: Benjamins, 613-648.

Declerck, R.
  1993   "On so-called tense simplification". In C. Vet and C. Vetters (eds), *Tense and Aspect in Discourse*. Berlin: Mouton de Gruyter, 77-98.

Donnellan, K.
  1971   "Reference and definite descriptions". In D.D. Steinberg and L.A. Jakobovits (eds), *Semantics*. Cambridge: Cambridge University Press, 100-114.

Downing, P.A.
  1996   "Proper names as a referential option in English conversation". In B. Fox (ed), *Studies in Anaphora*. Amsterdam and Philadelphia: Benjamins, 95-143.

Drew, P.
  1994   "Analysing institutional discourse: some methodological objectives". Paper presented at the 6th International Systemic-Functional Workshop, University of Antwerp, Belgium.

Drew, P. and Heritage, J.
  1992   "Analyzing talk at work: an introduction". In P. Drew and J. Heritage (eds), *Talk at Work: Interaction in institutional settings*. Cambridge: Cambridge University Press, 2-65.

Drew, P. and Sorjonen, M.
  1997   "Institutional dialogue". In T.A. Van Dijk (ed), *Discourse as Social Interaction*. London: Sage, 92-118.

Ducrot, O.
  1984   *Le Dire et le Dit*. Paris: Les Editions de Minuit.

Duranti, A. and Goodwin, C.
  1992   *Rethinking Context: Language as an interactive phenomenon*. Cambridge: Cambridge University Press.

Dyer, S.C., Jr., Miller, M.M. and Boone, J.
1991 "Wire service coverage of the Exxon Valdez crisis". *Public Relations Review* 17(1): 27-36.

Ede, L. and Lunsford, A.
1984 "Audience addressed/audience invoked: the role of audience in composition theory and pedagogy". *College Composition and Communication* 35: 155-171.

Edwards, D.
1997 *Discourse and Cognition*. London: Sage.

Eggins, S.
1994 *An Introduction to Systemic Functional Linguistics*. London: Pinter.

Ensink, T.
1992 *Jenninger: De ontvangst van een Duitse rede in Nederland*. Amsterdam: Thesis.

Fairclough, N.
1988 "Discourse representation in media discourse". *Sociolinguistics* 17(2): 125-139.
1989 *Language and Power*. Harlow: Longman.
1991 "What might we mean by 'enterprise discourse'?" In R. Keat and N. Abercrombie (eds), *Enterprise Culture*. London: Routledge, 38-57.
1992 *Discourse and Social Change*. Cambridge: Polity Press.
1994 "Conversationalization of public discourse and the authority of the consumer". In R. Keat, N. Whiteley, and N. Abercrombie (eds), *The Authority of the Consumer*. London: Routledge, 253-268.
1995 *Media Discourse*. London: Edward Arnold.
1996 "Technologisation of Discourse". In C.R. Caldas-Coulthard and M. Coulthard (eds), *Texts and Practices*. London and New York: Routledge, 71-83.

Ferrara, K., Brunner, H. and Whittemore, G.
1991 "Interactive written discourse as an emergent register". *Written Communication* 8(1): 8-34.

Fill, A.F.
  1986   "'Divided illocution' in conversational and other situations and
           some of its implications". *International Review of Applied
           Linguistics* 24: 27-34.

Fillmore, C.
  1971/75 *Santa Cruz Lectures on Deixis*. Mimeo, Indiana University
           Linguistics Club.

Firth, A. (ed)
  1995   *The Discourse of Negotiation: Studies of language in the
           workplace*. Oxford: Pergamon.

Fishman, M.
  1980   *Manufacturing the News*. Austin: Texas University Press.

Fitch, K.L. and Philipsen, G.
  1995   "Ethnography of speaking". In J. Verschueren, J. Östman and
           J. Blommaert (eds), *Handbook of Pragmatics: Manual*.
           Amsterdam and Philadelphia: Benjamins, 263-269.

Fitzwater, M.
  1995   *Call the Briefing*. New York: Times Books.

Fludernik, M.
  1993   *The Fictions of Language and the Languages of Fiction: The
           linguistic representation of speech and consciousness*. London:
           Routledge.

Ford, C.E. and Fox, B.A.
  1996   "Interactional motivations for reference: He had. This guy
           had, a beautiful, thirty-two O:lds". In B. Fox (ed), *Studies in
           Anaphora*. Amsterdam and Philadelphia: Benjamins, 145-168.

Foucault, M.
  1970/84 "The order of discourse". In M.J. Shapiro (ed), *Language and
           Politics*. London: Blackwell, 108-138.

Fowler, R., Hodge, B., Kress, G. and Trew, T. (eds)
  1979   *Language and Control*. London: Routledge & Kegan Paul.

Fowler, R. and Kress, G.
  1979   "Critical linguistics". In R. Fowler, B. Hodge, G. Kress and
           T. Trew (eds), *Language and Control*. London: Routledge &
           Kegan Paul, 185-213.

Fraser, B.
  1996   "Pragmatic markers". *Pragmatics* 6: 167-190.

Galtung, J. and Ruge, M.
1973   "Structuring and selecting news". In S. Cohen and J. Young (eds), *The Manufacture of News: Social problems, deviance and the mass media*. London: Constable, 62-72.

Gandy, O.H., Jr.
1982   *Beyond Agenda Setting: Information subsidies and public policy*. Norwood, NJ: Ablex.

Gans, H.J.
1979   *Deciding What's News*. New York: Pantheon Books.

Gardiner, A.H.
1932   *The Theory of Speech and Language*. Oxford: Clarendon Press.

Gardiner, M.
1992   *The Dialogics of Critique: M.M. Bakhtin and the theory of ideology*. London: Routledge.

Garfinkel, H. and Sacks, H.
1970   "On formal structures of practical actions". In J. McKinney and E. Tiryakian (eds), *Theoretical Sociology*. Appleton-Century-Crofts, 337-366.

Geis, M.L.
1987   *The Language of Politics*. New York: Springer-Verlag.

Giddens, A.
1991   *Modernity and Self-Identity: Self and society in the late modern age*. Cambridge: Polity Press.

Goffman, E.
1959   *The Presentation of Self in Everyday Life*. New York: Anchor Books.
1974   *Frame Analysis: An essay on the organization of experience*. New York: Harper and Row.
1981   *Forms of Talk*. Oxford: Blackwell.

Goodwin, C.
1986   "Audience diversity, participation and interpretation". *Text* 6(3): 283-316.

Goodwin, C. and Goodwin, M.H.
1992   "Context, activity and participation". In P. Auer and A. di Luzio (eds), *The Contextualization of Language*. Amsterdam and Philadelphia: Benjamins, 77-99.

Goodwin, M.H.
  1990   *He-said-she-said: Talk as social organization among black children*. Bloomington and Indianapolis: Indiana University Press.
  1990-91 "Retellings, pretellings and hypothetical stories". *Research on Language and Social Interaction* 24: 263-276.

Gruber, H.
  1993a   "Political language and textual vagueness". *Pragmatics* 3: 1-28.
  1993b   "Evaluation devices in newspaper reports". *Journal of Pragmatics* 19: 469-486.

Grunig, J.
  1984   *Managing Public Relations*. Fort Worth, TX: Harcourt Brace Jovanovitch.

Gumperz, J.
  1982   *Discourse Strategies*. Cambridge: Cambridge University Press.
  1992   "Contextualization revisited". In P. Auer and A. di Luzio (eds), *The Contextualization of Language*. Amsterdam and Philadelphia: Benjamins, 39-53.

Gunnarsson, B.-L., Linell, P. and Nordberg, B. (eds)
  1997   *The Construction of Professional Discourse*. London: Longman.

Günthner, S. and Knoblauch, H.
  1995   "Culturally patterned speaking practices: the analysis of communicative genres". *Pragmatics* 5: 1-32.

Hak, T.
  1995   "Ethnomethodology and the institutional context". *Human Studies* 18: 109-137.

Hall, S., Critcher, C. and Jefferson, T. (eds)
  1978   *Policing the Crisis: Mugging, the state, and law and order*. London: MacMillan.

Hallin, D.C.
  1986   "Cartography, Community and the Cold War". In R.K. Manoff and M. Schudson (eds), *Reading the News*. New York: Pantheon Books, 109-145.

Hardt-Mautner, G.
1995   "'How does one become a good European?': the British press and European integration". *Discourse & Society* 6(2): 177-205.

Harris, S.
1995   "Pragmatics and power". *Journal of Pragmatics* 23: 117-135.

Hartley, J.
1982   *Understanding News*. London: Methuen.

Heller, M.
1994   *Crossroads: Language, education and ethnicity in French Ontario*. Berlin: Mouton de Gruyter.

Heritage, J.
1984   *Garfinkel and Ethnomethodology*. Cambridge: Polity Press.
1985   "Analyzing news interviews: aspects of the production of talk for an overhearing audience". In T.A. van Dijk (ed), *Handbook of Discourse Analysis, Vol. 3: Discourse and dialogue*. London: Academic Press, 95-117.

Heritage, J., Clayman, S.E. and Zimmerman, D.H.
1988   "Discourse and message analysis: the micro structure of mass media messages". In *Advancing Communication Science*. London: Sage, 77-109.

Heritage, J. and Greatbatch, D.
1991   "On the institutional character of institutional talk". In D. Boden and D. Zimmerman (eds), *Talk and Social Structure*. Cambridge: Polity Press, 93-137.

Heritage, J. and Roth, A.L.
1995   "Grammar and institution: questions and questioning in the broadcast news interview". *Research on Language and Social Interaction* 28(1): 1-60.

Heritage, J. and Watson, D.
1979   "Formulations as conversational objects". In G. Psathas (ed), *Everyday Language: Studies in ethnomethodology*. New York: Irvington, 123-162.

Herman, E.S. and Chomsky, N.
1988   *Manufacturing Consent: The political economy of the mass media*. New York: Pantheon Books.

Hess, S.
>   1984   *The Government/Press Connection.* Washington, D.C.: The
>   Brookings Institute.
>   1989   *Live from Capitol Hill: Studies of Congress and the media.*
>   Washington, D.C.: The Brookings Institute.

Hill, J. and Irvine, J. (eds)
>   1993   *Responsibility and Evidence in Oral Discourse.* Cambridge:
>   Cambridge University Press.

Hinnenkamp, V.
>   1992   "Comments on Christian Heath, 'Gesture's Discreet Tasks'".
>   In P. Auer and A. di Luzio (eds), *The Contextualization of
>   Language.* Amsterdam and Philadelphia: Benjamins, 129-133.

Hoeken, H. and Van Wijk, C.
>   1997   "Het effect van het opvoeren van een personage op de
>   geloofwaardigheid en overtuigingskracht van een advertentie".
>   *Taalbeheersing* 19(1): 15-31.

Hoey, M.
>   1994   "Signalling in discourse: a functional analysis of a common
>   discourse pattern in written and spoken English". In M.
>   Coulthard (ed), *Advances in Written Text Analysis.* London:
>   Routledge, 26-45.

Holmes, J.
>   1984   "Modifying illocutionary force". *Journal of Pragmatics* 8:
>   345-365.

Holquist, M.
>   1990   *Dialogism: Bakhtin and his world.* London: Routledge.

Holt, E.
>   1996   "Reporting on talk: the use of direct reported speech in
>   conversation". *Research on Language and Social Interaction*
>   29(3): 219-245.

Hoyle, S.M.
>   1993   "Participation frameworks in sportscasting play: imaginary and
>   literal footings". In D. Tannen (ed), *Framing in Discourse.*
>   Oxford: Oxford University Press, 114-145.

Hymes, D.
>   1974   *Foundations in Sociolinguistics: An ethnographic approach.*
>   Philadelphia: University of Pennsylvania Press.

Iser, W.
1974 *The Implied Reader*. London and Baltimore: John Hopkins University Press.

Jacobs, G.
1994a "Performative reporting: speech presentation in press releases". In *Belgian Essays on Language and Literature*, 63-71.

1994b "Reporting a crisis: the 'unavoidable contextedness of press releases'". In L. Van Waes, E. Woudstra and P. Van den Hoven (eds), *Functional Communication Quality*. Amsterdam and Atlanta, GA: Rodopi, 128-136.

1995 "Organization in institutional discourse: putting press releases on a proper footing". In B. Wärvik, S. Tanskanen and R. Hiltunen (eds), *Organization in Discourse*. Turku, 301-307.

1996 "Nu hoort u het ook 's van een ander: percolatie en plugging in persberichten". In H. van den Bergh, D. Janssen, N. Bertens and M. Damen (eds), *Taalgebruik Ontrafeld*. Dordrecht: Foris, 487-494.

1997 "'Not unworthy of study': interactivity in press releases". Paper presented at the 4th ESSE conference, University of Debrecen, Hungary.

1999a "Self-reference in press releases". *Journal of Pragmatics* 31(2): 219-242.

1999b "Projected discourse: an analysis of receiver roles in press releases". *Text*.

Jacobs, R.N.
1996 "Producing the news, producing the crisis: narrativity, television and news work". *Media, Culture & Society* 18: 373-397.

Jakobson, R.
1971 "Shifters, verbal categories, and the Russian verb". In *Selected Writings II*. The Hague: Mouton, 130-147.

Johnstone, B.
1987 "'He says.. so I said': verb tense alternation and narrative depictions of authority in American English". *Linguistics* 25: 33-52.

Jones, P.
1995 "Philosophical and theoretical issues in the study of deixis: a critique of the standard account". In K. Green (ed), *New Essays on Deixis: Discourse, narrative, literature*. Amsterdam and Atlanta, GA: Rodopi, 27-48.

Jucker, A.H.
1986 *News Interviews: A pragmalinguistic analysis*. Amsterdam and Philadelphia: Benjamins.

1992 *Social Stylistics: Syntactic variation in British newspapers*. Berlin and New York: Mouton de Gruyter.

1995 "Mass Media". In J. Verschueren, J. Östman and J. Blommaert (eds), *Handbook of Pragmatics 1995*. Amsterdam and Philadelphia: Benjamins, 1-14.

1996 "News Actor Labelling in British Newspapers". *Text* 16: 373-390.

Karttunen, L.
1973 "Presuppositions of compound sentences". *Linguistic Inquiry* 4: 169-193.

1974 "Presupposition and linguistic context". *Theoretical Linguistics* 1: 181-194.

Keane, J.
1991 *The Media and Democracy*. Cambridge: Polity Press.

Kerbrat-Orecchioni, C.
1997 "A multilevel approach in the study of talk-in-interaction". *Pragmatics* 7(1): 1-20.

Kiparsky, P. and Kiparsky, C.
1971 "Fact". In D.D. Steinberg and L.A. Jakobovits (eds), *Semantics: An interdisciplinary reader in philosophy, linguistics and psychology*. Cambridge: Cambridge University Press, 345-369.

Kline, S.L. and Kuper, G.
1994 "Self-presentation practices in government discourse: the case of US Lt. Col. Oliver North". *Text* 14(1): 23-43.

Koole, T.
1997 "The role of ethnography in the analysis of institutional discourse". In L. Lentz and H. Pander Maat (eds), *Discourse*

Analysis and Evaluation: Functional approaches. Amsterdam and Atlanta, GA: Rodopi, 59-86.

Kress, G.
1983   "Linguistic processes and the mediation of 'reality': the politics of newspaper language". *International Journal of the Sociology of Language* 40: 43-57.

Lakoff, G.
1977   "Pragmatics in natural logic". In A. Rogers, B. Wall and J.P. Murphy (eds), *Proceedings of the Texas Conference on Performatives, Presuppositions, and Implicatures*. Arlington, Virginia: Centre for applied linguistics, 107-134.

Lakoff, R. T.
1970   "Tense and its relation to participants". *Language* 46(4): 838-849.
1977   "What you can do with words: politeness, pragmatics and performatives". In A. Rogers, B. Wall and J.P. Murphy (eds), *Proceedings of the Texas Conference on Performatives, Presuppositions and Implicatures*. Arlington, Virginia: Center for applied linguistics, 79-105.
1980   "How to look as if you aren't doing anything with words: speech act qualification". *Versus,* 29-47.
1982   "Some of my favorite writers arc literate: the mingling of oral and literate strategies in written communication". In D. Tannen (ed), *Spoken and Written Language: Exploring orality and literacy*. Norwood, NJ: Ablex, 239-260.

Lambrecht, K.
1994   *Information Structure and Sentence Form*. Cambridge: Cambridge University Press.

Lang, K. and Lang, G.
1971   "The unique perspective of television and its effects: a pilot study". In W. Schramm and D. Roberts (eds), *The Process and Effects of Mass Communication*. Urbana: University of Illinois Press, 169-188.

Lebar, M.T.
1985   *A General Semantics Analysis of Corporate Disclosure Documents: Form 10-K, the annual report to shareholders, and the corporate financial press release*. Michigan: Ann Arbor.

Lee, D.
  1992   *Competing Discourses: Perspective and ideology in language.*
          London: Longman.

Leech, G.N. and Short, M.H.
  1981   *Style in Fiction: A linguistic introduction to English fictional
          prose.* London: Longman.

Lehrer, A.
  1989   "Remembering and representing prose: quoted speech as a
          data source". *Discourse Processes* 12: 105-125.

Lerman, C.
  1983   "Dominant discourse: the institutional voice and control of
          topic". In H. Davis and P. Walton (eds), *Language, Image,
          Media.* London: Blackwell, 75-103.

  1985   "Media analysis of a presidential speech: impersonal identity
          forms in discourse". In T.A. van Dijk (ed), *Discourse and
          Communication: New approaches to the analysis of mass
          media discourse and communication.* Berlin: Mouton de
          Gruyter, 185-215.

Lerner, G.H.
  1993   "Collectivities in action". *Text* 13: 213-245.

Leudar, I. and Antaki, C.
  1996   "Discourse participation, reported speech and research
          practices in social psychology". *Theory and Psychology* 6(1):
          5-29.

Levinson, S.C.
  1979   "Activity types and language". *Linguistics* 17: 365-399.
  1983   *Pragmatics.* Cambridge: Cambridge University Press.
  1988   "Putting linguistics on a proper footing: explorations in
          Goffman's concepts of participation". In P. Drew and A.
          Wootton (eds), *Erving Goffman: Exploring the interaction
          order.* Cambridge: Polity Press, 161-227.

Li, C.
  1986   "Direct and indirect speech: a functional study". In F.
          Coulmas (ed), *Direct and Indirect Speech.* New York: Mouton
          de Gruyter, 29-45.

Linde, C.
   1988   "The quantitative study of communicative success: politeness
             and accidents in aviation discourse". *Language in Society* 17:
             375-399.

Linell, P.
   1995   "Dialogical analysis". In J. Verschueren, J. Östman and J.
             Blommaert (eds), *Handbook of Pragmatics: Manual.*
             Amsterdam and Philadelphia: Benjamins, 575-577.

Locher, M.A. and Wortham, S.E.
   1994   "The cast of the news". *Pragmatics* 4: 517-534.

Lucy, J.A.
   1993   "Reflexive language and the human disciplines". In J.A. Lucy
             (ed), *Reflexive Language: Reported speech and
             metapragmatics*. Cambridge: Cambridge University Press, 9-
             32.

Lull, J.
   1995   *Media, Communication, Culture: A global approach*. Cam-
             bridge: Polity Press.

Lynch, M. and Bogen, D.
   1996   *The Spectacle of History: Speech, text and memory at the Iran-
             Contra hearings*. Durham and London: Duke University
             Press.

Lyons, J.
   1977   *Semantics*. Cambridge: Cambridge University Press.

Maes, F.
   1987   "The pragmatic value of cataphoric relations". In J. Nuyts and
             G. De Schutter (eds), *Getting one's Word into Line: On word
             order and functional grammar*. Dordrecht: Foris, 131-146.
   1991   *Nominal Anaphors and the Coherence of Discourse*. University
             of Tilburg.

Malone, M. J.
   1995   "How to do things with friends: altercasting and recipient
             design". *Research on Language and Social Interaction* 28(2):
             147-170.

Mayes, P.
   1990   "Quotation in spoken English". *Studies in Language* 14: 325-
             363.

Maynard, S.K.
 1996 "Multivoicedness in speech and thought representation: the case of self-quotation in Japanese". *Journal of Pragmatics* 25: 207-226.

McCombs, M. and Shaw, D.
 1972 "The agenda-setting function of mass media". *Public Opinion Quarterly* 36: 176-187.

McHale, B.
 1978 "Free indirect discourse: a survey of recent accounts". *Poetics and Theory of Literature* 3: 235-287.

Meeuwis, M.
 1994 "Leniency and testiness in intercultural communication: remarks on ideology and context in interactional sociolinguistics". *Pragmatics* 4: 391-408.

Merrill, J.C.
 1965 "How *Time* stereotyped three U.S. Presidents". *Journalism Quarterly* 42: 563-570.

Mey, J.
 1993 *Pragmatics*. Oxford: Blackwell.

Moerman, M.
 1988 *Talking Culture*. Philadelphia: University of Pennsylvania Press.

Molotch, H. and Lester, M.
 1974 "News as purposive behavior: on the strategic use of routine events, accidents and scandals". *American Sociological Review* 39(Feb.): 101-112.

Moore, P.
 1992 "When politeness is fatal: technical communication and the *Challenger* accident". *Journal of Business and Technical Communication* 6(3): 269-292.

Morrison, A. and Love, A.
 1996 "A discourse of disillusionment: letters to the editor in two Zimbabwean magazines 10 years after independence". *Discourse and Society* 7(1): 39-75.

Morton, L.P. and Ramsey, S.
 1994 "A benchmark study of the PR news wire". *Public Relations Review* 20: 171-182.

Mumby, D.K. and Clair, R.P.
1997   "Organizational discourse". In T.A. van Dijk (ed), *Discourse as Social Interaction*. London: Sage, 181-205.

Myers, G.
1989   "The pragmatics of politeness in scientific articles". *Applied Linguistics* 10(1): 1-35.
1992   "'In this paper we report...': speech acts and scientific facts". *Journal of Pragmatics* 17, 295-313.
1996   "Strategic vagueness in academic writing". In E. Ventola and A. Mauranen (eds), *Academic Writing: Intercultural and textual issues*. Amsterdam and Phildelphia: Benjamins, 3-17.

Nelson, C.K.
1994   "Ethnomethodological positions on the use of ethnographic data in conversation analytic research". *Journal of Contemporary Ethnography* 23(3): 307-329.

Ong, W.
1975   "The writer's audience is always a fiction". *PMLA* 90: 247-257.

Östman, J.
1986   *Pragmatics as Implicitness*. Berkeley: University of California.

Panis, A.
1995   "IIct jaarverslag als communicatie-instrument: opinies en strategieën van de zender". University of Ghent.

Partee, B.
1971   "The syntax and semantics of quotation". In P. Kiparsky and S. Anderson (eds), *Festschrift for Morris Halle*. New York: Holt Rinehart and Winston.

Peltu, M.
1988   "Media reporting of risk information: uncertainties and the future". In H. Jungermann, R. Kasperson and P. Wiedemann (eds), *Themes and tasks of risk communication*. Jülich: KFA.

Philips, S.U.
1986   "Reported speech as evidence in an American trial". In D. Tannen and J.E. Alatis (eds), *Languages and Linguistics: The interdependence of theory, data and application*. Washington, D.C.: Georgetown University Press, 154-170.

Polanyi, L.
1985 *Telling the American Story: A structural and cultural analysis of conversational storytelling.* Norwood, N.J.: Ablex.

Pomerantz, A.
1984 "Giving a source or basis: the practice in conversation of telling 'how I know'". *Journal of Pragmatics* 8: 607-625.
1986 "Extreme case formulations: a way of legitimizing claims". *Human Studies* 9: 219-229.

Psathas, G.
1990 *Interaction Competence.* Washington, D.C: University Press of America.

Quine, W.V.O.
1960 *Word and Object.* Cambridge, MA: MIT Press.

Recanati, F.
1987 *Meaning and Force: The pragmatics of performative utterances.* Cambridge: Cambridge University Press.

Renkema, J.
1993 *Discourse Studies.* Amsterdam and Philadelphia: Benjamins.

Riksen, L.
1996 "Het persbericht als bron van nieuwsberichten". Thesis, University of Groningen.

Roeh, I. and Nir, R.
1990 "Speech presentation in the Israel radio news: ideological constraints and rhetorical strategies". *Text* 10(3): 225-244.

Rogers, P. and Swales, J.
1990 "We the People? An analysis of the Dana Corporation Policies Document". *Journal of Business Communication* 27: 293-313.

Romano, C.
1986 "The grisly truth about bare facts". In R.K. Manoff and M. Schudson (eds), *Reading the News.* New York: Pantheon Books, 38-78.

Rounds, P.L.
1987 "Multifunctional personal pronoun use in an educational setting". *English for Specific Purposes* 6(1): 13-29.

Rubin, D.
1987 "How the news media reported on Three Mile Island and Chernobyl". *Journal of Communication* 37(3): 42-57.

Sacks, H.
    1992a   *Lectures on Conversation, volume 1*. Oxford: Blackwell.
    1992b   *Lectures on Conversation, volume 2*. Oxford: Blackwell.
Sacks, H., Schegloff, E.A. and Jefferson, G.
    1974   "A simplest systematics for the organization of turn-taking for conversation". *Language* 50(4): 696-735.
Sanders, J.
    1994   *Perspective in Narrative Discourse*. University of Tilburg.
Sanford, A., Moar, K. and Garrod, S.
    1988   "Proper names as controllers of discourse focus". *Language and Speech* 31(1): 43-56.
Sarangi, S. and Slembrouck, S.
    1992   "Non-cooperation in communication: a reassessment of Gricean pragmatics". *Journal of Pragmatics* 17: 117-154.
    1996   *Language, Bureaucracy and Social Control*. London: Longman.
Schegloff, E.A.
    1988-89 "From interview to confrontation: observations on the Bush/Rather encounter". *Research on Language and Social Interaction* 22: 215-240.
    1992   "On talk and its institutional occasions". In P. Drew and J. Heritage (eds), *Talk at Work: Interaction in institutional settings*. Cambridge: Cambridge University Press, 101-134.
    1993   "Reflections on quantification in the study of conversation". *Research on Language and Social Interaction* 26(1): 99-128.
    1995   "Discourse as an interactional achievement III: the omnirelevance of action". *Research on Language and Social Interaction* 28(3): 185-211.
    1996   "Some practices for referring to persons in talk-in-interaction". In B. Fox (ed), *Studies in Anaphora*. Amsterdam and Philadelphia: Benjamins, 437-485.
    1997   "Whose text? Whose context?" *Discourse and Society* 8(2): 165-187.
Schiffrin, D.
    1981   "Tense variation in narrative". *Language* 57(1): 45-62.

Schriver, K.A.
　1997　*Dynamics in Document Design: Creating text for readers*. New York: John Wiley and Sons.

Schudson, M.
　1978　*Discovering the News: A social history of American newspapers*. New York: Basic Books.
　1986　"Deadlines, datelines, and history". In R.K. Manoff and M. Schudson (eds), *Reading the News*. New York: Pantheon Books, 79-108.
　1989　"The sociology of news production". *Media, Culture and Society* 11: 263-282.

Scollon, R.
　1998　*Mediated Discourse as Social Interaction: A study of news discourse*. London: Longman.

Scollon, R. and Wong Scollon, S.
　1995　*Intercultural Communication: A discourse approach*. Oxford: Blackwell.

Searle, J.R.
　1969　*Speech Acts: An essay in the philosophy of language*. Cambridge: Cambridge University Press.
　1989　"How performatives work". *Linguistics and Philosophy* 12: 535-558.

Semino, E.
　1997　*Language and World Creation in Poems and Texts*. London and New York: Longman.

Shannon, C. and Weaver, W.
　1949　*The Mathematical Theory of Communication*. Urbana, IL: University of Illinois Press.

Shelby, A.N.
　1994　"Communication quality as metacommunication: a conceptual analysis". In L. Van Waes, E. Woudstra and P. Van den Hoven (eds), *Functional Communication Quality*. Amsterdam and Atlanta: Rodopi, 5-16.

Shoemaker, P.J.
　1991　*Gatekeeping*. Newbury Park: Sage.

Shoemaker, P.J. and Reese, S.D.
  1991   *Mediating the Message: Theories of influences on mass media research*. New York: Longman.

Short, M.
  1988   "Speech presentation, the novel and the press". In W. van Peer (ed), *The Taming of the Text: Explorations in language, literature and culture*. London: Routledge, 61-81.

Shuman, A.
  1990   "Appropriated personal experiences: the case of abortion junk mail". *Critical Studies* 2(1/2): 165-187.

Sigal, L.V.
  1973   *Reporters and Officials: The organization and politics of newsmaking*. Lexington, MA: D.C. Heath.
  1986   "Sources make the news". In R.K. Manoff and M. Schudson (eds), *Reading the News*. New York: Pantheon Books, 9-37.

Silverstein, M.
  1976   "Shifters, linguistic categories, and cultural description". In K. Basso and H. Selby (eds), *Meaning in Anthropology*. Albuquerque: University of New Mexico Press, 11-55.

Silverstein, M. and Urban, G.
  1996   "The natural history of discourse". In M. Silverstein and G. Urban (eds), *Natural Histories of Discourse*. Chicago: Chicago University Press, 1-17.

Sinclair, J.
  1986   "Fictional Worlds". In M. Coulthard (ed), *Talking about Text*. University of Birmingham, 43-60.

Slembrouck, S.
  1992a   *The Study of Language Use in its Societal Context: Pragmatics and the representation of parliamentary debates in newspaper discourse*. University of Lancaster.
  1992b   "The parliamentary Hansard 'verbatim' report: the written construction of spoken discourse". *Language and Literature* 1(2): 101-119.

Sperber, D. and Wilson, D.
  1986   *Relevance: Communication and cognition*. Oxford: Blackwell.

Spooren, W. and Jaspers, J.
  1990   "Tekstoperaties en tekstperspectieven". *Gramma, tijdschrift voor taalkunde* 14(3): 195-219.
Stalnaker, R.C.
  1974   "Pragmatic presuppositions". In M.K. Munitz and P.K. Unger (eds), *Semantics and Philosophy*. New York: New York University Press, 197-214.
Sternberg, M.
  1982a   "Point of view and the indirections of direct speech". *Language and Style*, 66-117.
  1982b   "Proteus in quotation-land: mimesis and the forms of reported discourse". *Poetics Today* 3: 107-156.
Stevenson, N.
  1995   *Understanding Media Cultures: Social theory and mass communication*. London: Sage.
Swales, J.
  1990   *Genre Analysis: English in an academic and research setting*. Cambridge: Cambridge University Press.
Swales, J.M. and Rogers, P.S.
  1995   "Discourse and the projection of corporate culture: the mission statement". *Discourse and Society* 6(2): 223-242.
Taels, J. and Vanheeswijck, G.
  1995   "De Golfoorlog en het televisiejournaal". University of Antwerp.
Tannen, D.
  1986   "Introducing constructed dialogue in Greek and American conversational and literary narrative". In F. Coulmas (ed), *Direct and Indirect Speech*. Berlin: Mouton de Gruyter, 311-332.
  1989   *Talking Voices: Repetition, dialogue and imagery in conversational discourse*. Cambridge: Cambridge University Press.
  1995   *Talking from 9 to 5*. London: Virago.
Te Molder, H.
  1995   *Discourse of Dilemmas: An analysis of government communicators' talk*. University of Wageningen.

en Have, P. and Psathas, G. (eds)
   1995   *Situated Order: Studies in the social organization of talk and embodied activities*. Washington, D.C.: International Institute for Ethnomethodology and Conversation Analysis.

homas, J.
   1989   *The Dynamics of Discourse: A pragmatic analysis of confrontational interaction*. University of Lancaster.
   1995   *Meaning in Interaction: An introduction to pragmatics*. London: Longman.

homas, S. and Hawes, T.
   1994   "Theme and the rhetorical function of citation in research articles". *Interface: Journal of applied linguistics* 9(1): 15-27.

hompson, G. and Thetela, P.
   1995   "The sound of one hand clapping: the management of interaction in written discourse". *Text* 15(1): 103-127.

hompson, G. and Yiyun, Y.
   1991   "Evaluation in the reporting verbs used in academic papers". *Applied Linguistics* 12(4): 365-382.

hompson, J.B.
   1990   *Ideology and Modern Culture: Critical social theory in the era of mass communication*. Cambridge: Polity Press.
   1995   *The Media and Modernity: A social theory of the media*. Cambridge: Polity Press.

Toolan, M.
   1988   *Narrative: A critical linguistic introduction*. London: Routledge.

Toole, J.
   1996   "The effect of genre on referential choice". In T. Fretheim and J.K. Gundel (eds), *Reference and Referent Accessibility*. Amsterdam and Phildelphia: Benjamins, 263-290.

Triandafyllidou, A.
   1995   "The Chernobyl accident in the Italian press: a 'media story-line'". *Discourse and Society* 6(4): 517-536.

Trognon, A. and Larrue, J.
   1994   "Les débats politiques télévisés". In A. Trognon and J. Larrue (eds), *Pragmatique du Discours Politique*. Paris: Armand Colin, 55-126.

Tuchman, G.
1972 "Objectivity as strategic ritual: an examination of newsmen's notions of objectivity". *American Journal of Sociology* 77: 660-679.
1978 *Making News: A study in the construction of reality.* New York: The Free Press.

Tyler, L.
1992 "Ecological disaster and rhetorical response: Exxon's communications in the wake of the Valdez spill". *Journal of Business and Technical Communication* 6(2): 149-171.

Urmson, J.
1963/70 "Parenthetical verbs". In C.E. Caton (ed), *Philosophy and Ordinary Language.* Urbana: University of Illinois Press, 220-246.

Van Dijk, T.A..
1988 *News as Discourse.* Hillsdale, N.J.: Lawrence Erlbaum.

Van Ginneken, J.
1996 *De Schepping van de Wereld in het Nieuws: De 101 vertekeningen die elk 1 procent verschil maken.* Houten: Bohn Stafleu Van Loghum.

Van Leeuwen, T.
1996a "The representation of social actors". In C.R. Caldas-Coulthard and M. Coulthard (eds), *Texts and Practices.* London: Routledge, 32-70.
1996b "Frame and perspective as multimodal concepts". Paper presented at the conference on frame and perspective in discourse, University of Groningen, the Netherlands.

Vandenbergen, A.
1981 *The Grammar of Headlines in* The Times *1870-1970.* Brussels: Koninklijke academie voor wetenschappen, letteren en schone kunsten van België.
1996 "Image-building through modality: the case of political interviews". *Discourse and Society* 7(3): 389-415.

VanSlyke Turk, J.
1986 "Information subsidies and media content: a case study of public relations influence on the news". *Journalism Monographs* 100: 1-29.

Vendler, Z.
1976   "Illocutionary suicide". In A.F. MacKay and D.D. Merrill (eds), *Issues in the Philosophy of Language*. New Haven and London: Yale University Press, 135-145.

Verschueren, J.
1980   *On Speech Act Verbs*. Amsterdam and Philadelphia: Benjamins.

1985a   *International News Reporting: Metapragmatic metaphors and the U-2*. Amsterdam and Philadelphia: Benjamins.

1985b   *What People Say They Do With Words*. Norwood, N.J.: Ablex.

1987   "Metapragmatics and universals of linguistic action". In J. Verschueren (ed), *Linguistic Action: Some empirical-conceptual studies*. Norwood, N.J.: Ablex, 125-140.

1995a   "The pragmatic return to meaning: notes on the dynamics of communication, degrees of salience, and communicative transparency". *Journal of Linguistic Anthropology* 5(2): 127-156.

1995b   "The conceptual basis of performativity". In M. Shibatani and S. Thompson (eds), *Essays in Semantics and Pragmatics*. Amsterdam and Philadelphia: Benjamins, 299-321.

1995c   "The pragmatic perspective". In J. Verschueren, J. Östman and J. Blommaert (eds), *Handbook of Pragmatics: Manual*. Amsterdam and Philadelphia: Benjamins, 1-19.

1995d   "Metapragmatics". In J. Verschueren, J. Östman and J. Blommaert (eds), *Handbook of Pragmatics: Manual*. Amsterdam and Philadelphia: Benjamins, 367-371.

Vincent, D. and Perrin, L.
1996   "Performative utterances and reported speech in the first person, present indicative". Paper presented at the 5th International Pragmatics Conference, Mexico City, Mexico.

Voloshinov, V.
1929/73 *Marxism and the Philosophy of Language*. New York: Seminar Press.

Wales, K.
1996   *Personal Pronouns in Present-Day English*. Cambridge: Cambridge University Press.

Walker, E.
  1995   "Making a bid for change: formulations in union/management negotiations". In A. Firth (ed), *The Discourse of Negotiation: Studies of language in the workplace*. Oxford: Pergamon, 101-140.

Waugh, L.R.
  1995   "Reported speech in journalistic discourse: the relation of function and text". *Text* 15(1): 129-173.

Weaver, P.
  1974   "The politics of a news story". In H.M. Clor (ed), *The Mass Media and Modern Democracy*. Chicago: Rand McNally, 85-111.

Weinstein, E.A. and Deutschberger, P.
  1963   "Some dimensions of altercasting". *Sociometry* 26(4): 454-466.

Weizman, E.
  1984   "Some register characteristics of journalistic language: are they universals?" *Applied Linguistics* 5(1): 39-50.

White, D.M.
  1950   "The gatekeeper: a case study in the selection of news". *Journalism Quarterly* 27: 383-390.

Wilson, J.
  1990   *Politically Speaking: The pragmatic analysis of political language*. Oxford: Blackwell.

Wortham, S.E.
  1996   "Mapping participant deixis: a technique for discovering speakers' footing". *Journal of Pragmatics* 25: 331-348.

Wortham, S.E. and Locher, M.
  1996   "Voicing on the news: an analytic technique for studying media bias". *Text* 16: 557-585.

Yule, G., Mathis, T. and Hopkins, M.F.
  1992   "On reporting what was said". *ELT Journal* 46: 238-245.

Zelizer, B.
  1989   "'Saying' as collective practice: quoting and differential address in the news". *Text* 9(4): 369-388.

Zupnik, Y.
   1994   "A pragmatic analysis of the use of person deixis in political discourse". *Journal of Pragmatics* 21: 339-383.

Author Index

Subject Index

In the PRAGMATICS AND BEYOND NEW SERIES the following titles have been published thus far or are scheduled for publication:

1. WALTER, Bettyruth: *The Jury Summation as Speech Genre: An Ethnographic Study of What it Means to Those who Use it.* Amsterdam/Philadelphia, 1988.
2. BARTON, Ellen: *Nonsentential Constituents: A Theory of Grammatical Structure and Pragmatic Interpretation.* Amsterdam/Philadelphia, 1990.
3. OLEKSY, Wieslaw (ed.): *Contrastive Pragmatics.* Amsterdam/Philadelphia, 1989.
4. RAFFLER-ENGEL, Walburga von (ed.): *Doctor-Patient Interaction.* Amsterdam/Philadelphia, 1989.
5. THELIN, Nils B. (ed.): *Verbal Aspect in Discourse.* Amsterdam/Philadelphia, 1990.
6. VERSCHUEREN, Jef (ed.): *Selected Papers from the 1987 International Pragmatics Conference. Vol. I: Pragmatics at Issue. Vol. II: Levels of Linguistic Adaptation. Vol. III: The Pragmatics of Intercultural and International Communication* (ed. with Jan Blommaert). Amsterdam/Philadelphia, 1991.
7. LINDENFELD, Jacqueline: *Speech and Sociability at French Urban Market Places.* Amsterdam/Philadelphia, 1990.
8. YOUNG, Lynne: *Language as Behaviour, Language as Code: A Study of Academic English.* Amsterdam/Philadelphia, 1990.
9. LUKE, Kang-Kwong: *Utterance Particles in Cantonese Conversation.* Amsterdam/Philadelphia, 1990.
10. MURRAY, Denise E.: *Conversation for Action. The computer terminal as medium of communication.* Amsterdam/Philadelphia, 1991.
11. LUONG, Hy V.: *Discursive Practices and Linguistic Meanings. The Vietnamese system of person reference.* Amsterdam/Philadelphia, 1990.
12. ABRAHAM, Werner (ed.): *Discourse Particles. Descriptive and theoretical investigations on the logical, syntactic and pragmatic properties of discourse particles in German.* Amsterdam/Philadelphia, 1991.
13. NUYTS, Jan, A. Machtelt BOLKESTEIN and Co VET (eds): *Layers and Levels of Representation in Language Theory: a functional view.* Amsterdam/Philadelphia, 1990.
14. SCHWARTZ, Ursula: *Young Children's Dyadic Pretend Play.* Amsterdam/Philadelphia, 1991.
15. KOMTER, Martha: *Conflict and Cooperation in Job Interviews.* Amsterdam/Philadelphia, 1991.
16. MANN, William C. and Sandra A. THOMPSON (eds): *Discourse Description: Diverse Linguistic Analyses of a Fund-Raising Text.* Amsterdam/Philadelphia, 1992.
17. PIÉRAUT-LE BONNIEC, Gilberte and Marlene DOLITSKY (eds): *Language Bases ... Discourse Bases.* Amsterdam/Philadelphia, 1991.
18. JOHNSTONE, Barbara: *Repetition in Arabic Discourse. Paradigms, syntagms and the ecology of language.* Amsterdam/Philadelphia, 1991.
19. BAKER, Carolyn D. and Allan LUKE (eds): *Towards a Critical Sociology of Reading Pedagogy. Papers of the XII World Congress on Reading.* Amsterdam/Philadelphia, 1991.
20. NUYTS, Jan: *Aspects of a Cognitive-Pragmatic Theory of Language. On cognition, functionalism, and grammar.* Amsterdam/Philadelphia, 1992.

21. SEARLE, John R. et al.: *(On) Searle on Conversation.* Compiled and introduced by Herman Parret and Jef Verschueren. Amsterdam/Philadelphia, 1992.
22. AUER, Peter and Aldo Di LUZIO (eds): *The Contextualization of Language.* Amsterdam/Philadelphia, 1992.
23. FORTESCUE, Michael, Peter HARDER and Lars KRISTOFFERSEN (eds): *Layered Structure and Reference in a Functional Perspective. Papers from the Functional Grammar Conference, Copenhagen, 1990.* Amsterdam/Philadelphia, 1992.
24. MAYNARD, Senko K.: *Discourse Modality: Subjectivity, Emotion and Voice in the Japanese Language.* Amsterdam/Philadelphia, 1993.
25. COUPER-KUHLEN, Elizabeth: *English Speech Rhythm. Form and function in everyday verbal interaction.* Amsterdam/Philadelphia, 1993.
26. STYGALL, Gail: Trial Language. *A study in differential discourse processing.* Amsterdam/Philadelphia, 1994.
27. SUTER, Hans Jürg: *The Wedding Report: A Prototypical Approach to the Study of Traditional Text Types.* Amsterdam/Philadelphia, 1993.
28. VAN DE WALLE, Lieve: *Pragmatics and Classical Sanskrit.* Amsterdam/Philadelphia, 1993.
29. BARSKY, Robert F.: *Constructing a Productive Other: Discourse theory and the convention refugee hearing.* Amsterdam/Philadelphia, 1994.
30. WORTHAM, Stanton E.F.: *Acting Out Participant Examples in the Classroom.* Amsterdam/Philadelphia, 1994.
31. WILDGEN, Wolfgang: *Process, Image and Meaning. A realistic model of the meanings of sentences and narrative texts.* Amsterdam/Philadelphia, 1994.
32. SHIBATANI, Masayoshi and Sandra A. THOMPSON (eds): *Essays in Semantics and Pragmatics.* Amsterdam/Philadelphia, 1995.
33. GOOSSENS, Louis, Paul PAUWELS, Brygida RUDZKA-OSTYN, Anne-Marie SIMON-VANDENBERGEN and Johan VANPARYS: *By Word of Mouth. Metaphor, metonymy and linguistic action in a cognitive perspective.* Amsterdam/Philadelphia, 1995.
34. BARBE, Katharina: Irony in Context. Amsterdam/Philadelphia, 1995.
35. JUCKER, Andreas H. (ed.): *Historical Pragmatics. Pragmatic developments in the history of English.* Amsterdam/Philadelphia, 1995.
36. CHILTON, Paul, Mikhail V. ILYIN and Jacob MEY: *Political Discourse in Transition in Eastern and Western Europe (1989-1991).* Amsterdam/Philadelphia, 1998.
37. CARSTON, Robyn and Seiji UCHIDA (eds): *Relevance Theory. Applications and implications.* Amsterdam/Philadelphia, 1998.
38. FRETHEIM, Thorstein and Jeanette K. GUNDEL (eds): *Reference and Referent Accessibility.* Amsterdam/Philadelphia, 1996.
39. HERRING, Susan (ed.): *Computer-Mediated Communication. Linguistic, social, and cross-cultural perspectives.* Amsterdam/Philadelphia, 1996.
40. DIAMOND, Julie: *Status and Power in Verbal Interaction. A study of discourse in a close-knit social network.* Amsterdam/Philadelphia, 1996.
41. VENTOLA, Eija and Anna MAURANEN, (eds): *Academic Writing. Intercultural and textual issues.* Amsterdam/Philadelphia, 1996.
42. WODAK, Ruth and Helga KOTTHOFF (eds): *Communicating Gender in Context.* Amsterdam/Philadelphia, 1997.

43. JANSSEN, Theo A.J.M. and Wim van der WURFF (eds): *Reported Speech. Forms and functions of the verb.* Amsterdam/Philadelphia, 1996.
44. BARGIELA-CHIAPPINI, Francesca and Sandra J. HARRIS: *Managing Language. The discourse of corporate meetings.* Amsterdam/Philadelphia, 1997.
45. PALTRIDGE, Brian: *Genre, Frames and Writing in Research Settings.* Amsterdam/Philadelphia, 1997.
46. GEORGAKOPOULOU, Alexandra: *Narrative Performances. A study of Modern Greek storytelling.* Amsterdam/Philadelphia, 1997.
47. CHESTERMAN, Andrew: *Contrastive Functional Analysis.* Amsterdam/Philadelphia, 1998.
48. KAMIO, Akio: *Territory of Information.* Amsterdam/Philadelphia, 1997.
49. KURZON, Dennis: *Discourse of Silence.* Amsterdam/Philadelphia, 1998.
50. GRENOBLE, Lenore: *Deixis and Information Packaging in Russian Discourse.* Amsterdam/Philadelphia, 1998.
51. BOULIMA, Jamila: *Negotiated Interaction in Target Language Classroom Discourse.* Amsterdam/Philadelphia, n.y.p.
52. GILLIS, Steven and Annick DE HOUWER (eds): *The Acquisition of Dutch.* Amsterdam/Philadelphia, 1998.
53. MOSEGAARD HANSEN, Maj-Britt: *The Function of Discourse Particles. A study with special reference to spoken standard French.* Amsterdam/Philadelphia, 1998.
54. HYLAND, Ken: *Hedging in Scientific Research Articles.* Amsterdam/Philadelphia, 1998.
55. ALLWOOD, Jens and Peter Gärdenfors (eds): *Cognitive Semantics. Meaning and cognition.* Amsterdam/Philadelphia, 1999.
56. TANAKA, Hiroko: *Language, Culture and Social Interaction. Turn-taking in Japanese and Anglo-American English.* Amsterdam/Philadelphia, n.y.p.
57 JUCKER, Andreas H. and Yael ZIV (eds): *Discourse Markers. Descriptions and theory.* Amsterdam/Philadelphia, 1998.
58. ROUCHOTA, Villy and Andreas H. JUCKER (eds): *Current Issues in Relevance Theory.* Amsterdam/Philadelphia, 1998.
59. KAMIO, Akio and Ken-ichi TAKAMI (eds): *Function and Structure. In honor of Susumu Kuno.* 1999.
60. JACOBS, Geert: *Preformulating the News. An analysis of the metapragmatics of press releases.* 1999.
61. MILLS, Margaret H. (ed.): *Slavic Gender Linguistics.* n.y.p.
62. TZANNE, Angeliki: *Talking at Cross-Purposes. The dynamics of miscommunication.* n.y.p.
63. BUBLITZ, Wolfram, Uta LENK and Eija VENTOLA (eds.): *Coherence in Spoken and Written Discourse. How to create it and how to describe it.Selected papers from the International Workshop on Coherence, Augsburg, 24-27 April 1997.* n.y.p.
64. SVENNEVIG, Jan: *Getting Acquainted in Conversation. A study of initial interactions.* n.y.p.
65. COOREN, François: *The Organizing Dimension of Communication.* n.y.p.

AEK 3568